Microsoft Office Word Complete 2013

2013

A SKILLS APPROACH

Cheri Manning

Catherine Manning Swinson
Triad Interactive, Inc

Mc
Graw
Hill
Education

MICROSOFT OFFICE WORD 2013: A SKILLS APPROACH
Published by McGraw-Hill Education, 2 Penn Plaza, New York, NY 10121. Copyright © 2014 by
McGraw-Hill Education. All rights reserved. Printed in the United States of America. No part of this publication
may be reproduced or distributed in any form or by any means, or stored in a database or retrieval system, without the
prior written consent of McGraw-Hill Education, including, but not limited to, in any network or other electronic
storage or transmission, or broadcast for distance learning.

Some ancillaries, including electronic and print components, may not be available to customers outside the
United States.

This book is printed on acid-free paper.

1 2 3 4 5 6 7 8 9 0 RMN/RMN 1 0 9 8 7 6 5 4

ISBN 978-0-07-739421-9
MHID 0-07-739421-6

Senior Vice President, Products & Markets: *Kurt L. Strand*
Vice President, Content Production & Technology Services: *Kimberly Meriwether David*
Director: *Scott Davidson*
Senior Brand Manager: *Wyatt Morris*
Executive Director of Development: *Ann Torbert*
Development Editor: *Alan Palmer*
Development Editor: *Allison McCabe*
Digital Development Editor: *Kevin White*
Marketing Manager: *Tiffany Russell*
Lead Project Manager: *Rick Hecker*
Buyer: *Michael McCormick*
Design: *Srdj Savanovic*
Cover Image: *© Burazin/Photographer's Choice/Getty Images*
Content Licensing Specialist: *Keri Johnson*
Media Project Manager: *Brent dela Cruz*
Typeface: *10.5/13 Garamond Premier Pro Regular*
Compositor: *Laserwords Private Limited*
Printer: *R. R. Donnelley*

All credits appearing on page or at the end of the book are considered to be an extension of the copyright page.

Library of Congress Cataloging-in-Publication Data
Manning, Cheryl.
    Microsoft Office Word complete 2013 : a skills approach / Cheri Manning, Catherine Manning Swinson.
        pages cm
    Includes index.
    ISBN 978-0-07-739421-9 (acid-free paper) 1. Microsoft Word. 2. Word processing. I. Swinson, Catherine
        Manning. II. Title.
    Z52.5.M52M3545 2014
005.52—dc23   2014018978

The Internet addresses listed in the text were accurate at the time of publication. The inclusion of a website does not
indicate an endorsement by the authors or McGraw-Hill Education, and McGraw-Hill Education does not guarantee
the accuracy of the information presented at these sites.

www.mhhe.com

brief contents

contents

Contents

preface

How well do you know Microsoft Office? Many students can follow specific step-by-step directions to re-create a document, spreadsheet, presentation, or database, but do they truly understand the skills it takes to create these on their own? Just as simply following a recipe does not make you a professional chef, re-creating a project step by step does not make you an Office expert.

The purpose of this book is to teach you the skills to master Microsoft Office 2013 in a straightforward and easy-to-follow manner. But *Microsoft® Office 2013: A Skills Approach* goes beyond the ***how*** and equips you with a deeper understanding of the ***what*** and the ***why.*** Too many times books have little value beyond the classroom. The *Skills Approach* series has been designed to be not only a complete textbook but also a reference tool for you to use as you move beyond academics and into the workplace.

WHAT'S NEW IN THIS EDITION

This edition of the *Skills Approach* text includes a Let Me Try exercise and student data file for each skill. These exercises are the same as the simulated Let Me Try exercises in SIMnet 2013. We included the student data files to give students the opportunity to explore the skill in the live application in addition to practicing it in a simulated environment (SIMnet).

The Let Me Try exercises are not intended as a running project or case study. Each Let Me Try data file is independent of the others, so the skills may be taught in any order.

ABOUT TRIAD INTERACTIVE

Triad Interactive specializes in online education and training products. Our flagship program is SIMnet—a simulated Microsoft Office learning and assessment application developed for the McGraw-Hill Companies. Triad has been writing, programming, and managing the SIMnet system since 1999.

Triad is also actively involved in online health education and in research projects to assess the usefulness of technology for helping high-risk populations make decisions about managing their cancer risk and treatment.

about the authors

CHERI MANNING

Cheri Manning is the president and co-owner of Triad Interactive. She is the author of the Microsoft Excel and Access content for the *Skills Approach* series and SIMnet. She has been authoring instructional content for these applications for more than 12 years.

Cheri began her career as an Aerospace Education Specialist with the Education Division of the National Aeronautics and Space Administration (NASA), where she produced materials for K–12 instructors and students. Prior to founding Triad, Cheri was a project manager with Compact Publishing, where she managed the development of McGraw-Hill's Multimedia MBA CD-ROM series.

CATHERINE MANNING SWINSON

Catherine Manning Swinson is the vice president and co-owner of Triad Interactive. She is the author of the Microsoft Word and PowerPoint content for the *Skills Approach* series and SIMnet. She also authors SIMnet content for Microsoft Outlook, Windows, and Internet Explorer. She has been authoring instructional content for these applications for more than 12 years.

Catherine began her career at Compact Publishing, one of the pioneers in educational CD-ROM-based software. She was the lead designer at Compact and designed every edition of the *TIME Magazine Compact Almanac* from 1992 through 1996. In addition, she designed a number of other products with Compact, including the *TIME Man of the Year* program and the *TIME 20th Century Almanac*.

acknowledgments

CONTRIBUTORS

Kelly Morber, *Saints Philip and James School, English teacher and Malone University, master's degree candidate*
Timothy T. Morber, MEd, LPCC-S, *Malone University*

TECHNICAL EDITORS

Menka Brown
Piedmont Technical College

Sylvia Brown
Midland College

Mary Locke
Greenville Technical College

Daniela Marghitu
Auburn University

Judy Settle
Central Georgia Technical College

Pamela Silvers
Asheville-Buncombe Technical College

Candace Spangler
Columbus State Community College

Debbie Zaidi
Seneca College

REVIEWERS

Our thanks go to all who participated in the development of *Microsoft Office 2013: A Skills Approach.*

Sven Aelterman
Troy University

Nick Agrawal
Calhoun Community College

Laura Anderson
Weber State University

Viola Bain
Scott Community College

Greg Ballinger
Miami Dade College

Bill Barzen
Saint Petersburg College

Julia Bell
Walters State Community College

Don Belle
Central Piedmont Community College

Judy Boozer
Lane Community College

Ben Brah
Auburn University

Sheryl Starkey Bulloch
Columbia Southern University

Kate Burkes
Northwest Arkansas Community College

Michael Callahan
Lone Star College

Patricia Casey
Trident Technical College

Wally Cates
Central New Mexico Community College

Jimmy Chen
Salt Lake Community College

Sharon Cotman
Thomas Nelson Community College

Susan Cully
Long Beach City College

Jennifer Day
Sinclair Community College

Ralph De Arazoza
Miami Dade College

Bruce Elliot
Tarrant County College

Bernice Eng
Brookdale Community College

Penny Fanzone
Community College of Baltimore County

Valerie Farmer
Community College of Baltimore County

Jean Finley
Asheville-Buncombe Technical Community College

George Fiori
Tri-County Technical College

Deborah Godwin
Lake-Sumter Community College

Cathy Grant-Churchwell
Lane Community College

Diana Green
Weber State University

Joseph Greer
Midlands Technical College

Debra Gross
Ohio State University

Rachelle Hall
Glendale Community College

Dexter Harlee
York Technical College

Marilyn Hibbert
Salt Lake Community College

Judy Irvine
Seneca College

Sherry E. Jacob
Jefferson Community & Technical College

Linda Johnsonius
Murray State University

Rich Klein
Clemson University

Kevin Lee
Guilford Technical Community College

Mohamed Lotfy
Regis University

Carol Martin
Central Pennsylvania Community College

Sue McCrory
Missouri State University

Ken Moak
Tarrant County College

Cecil Morris
American Intercontinental University

Kathleen Morris
University of Alabama

Patrick J. Nedry
Monroe County Community College

Mitchell Ober
Tulsa Community College

Ashlee Pieris
Raritan Valley Community College

Pamela Silvers
Asheville–Buncombe Technical Community College

W. Randy Somsen
Brigham Young University–Idaho

Bonnie Smith
Fresno City College

Randy Smith
Monterey Peninsula College

Nathan Stout
University of Oklahoma

Carl Struck
Suffolk Community College

Song Su
East Los Angeles College

Kathleen Tamerlano
Cuyahoga Community College

Margaret Taylor
College of Southern Nevada

Debby Telfer
Colorado Technical University

David Trimble
Park University

Georgia Vanderark
Stark State College

Philip Vavalides
Guilford Technical Community College

Dennis Walpole
University of South Florida

Michael Walton
Miami Dade College

Paul Weaver
Bossier Parish Community College

Nima Zahadat
Northern Virginia Community College

Debbie Zaidi
Seneca College

Matthew Zullo
Wake Tech Community College

Instructor Walkthrough

Microsoft Office Word Complete
2013: A Skills Approach

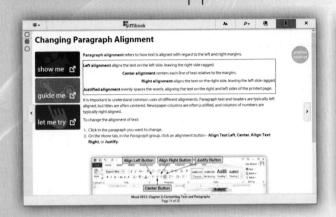

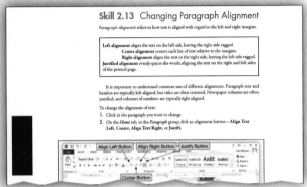

> ## 1-1 Content in SIMnet for Office 2013

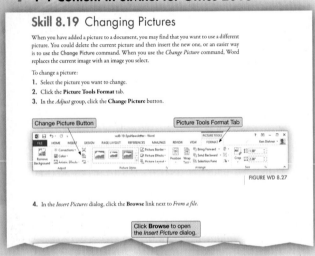

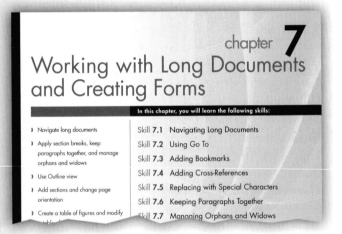

Skill 8.19 Changing Pictures

When you have added a picture to a document, you may find that you want to use a different picture. You could delete the current picture and then insert the new one, or an easier way is to use the Change Picture command. When you use the *Change Picture* command, Word replaces the current image with an image you select.

To change a picture:

1. Select the picture you want to change.
2. Click the **Picture Tools Format** tab.
3. In the *Adjust* group, click the **Change Picture** button.

4. In the *Insert Pictures* dialog, click the **Browse** link next to *From a file*.

chapter 7
Working with Long Documents and Creating Forms

In this chapter, you will learn the following skills:

> Navigate long documents

> Apply section breaks, keep paragraphs together, and manage orphans and widows

> Use Outline view

> Add sections and change page orientation

> Create a table of figures and modify table of contents

Skill **7.1**	Navigating Long Documents
Skill **7.2**	Using Go To
Skill **7.3**	Adding Bookmarks
Skill **7.4**	Adding Cross-References
Skill **7.5**	Replacing with Special Characters
Skill **7.6**	Keeping Paragraphs Together
Skill **7.7**	Managing Orphans and Widows

> ## At-a-glance Office 2013 skills

Quick, easy-to-scan pages, for efficient learning

> ## Introduction—Learning Outcomes are clearly listed.

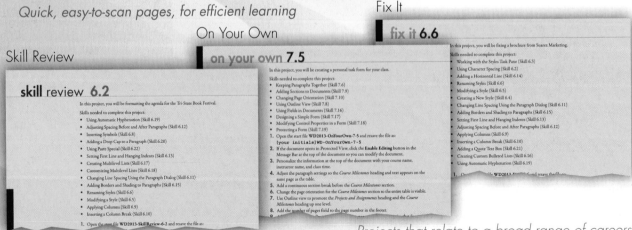

> ## Diverse end-of-chapter projects

Projects that relate to a broad range of careers and perspectives, from nursing, education, business, and everyday personal uses.

Features

From the Perspective of…

Tips and Tricks

from the perspective of . . .

MARKETING MANAGER
When creating marketing materials to send out to customers and potential customers, I always try to create a cohesive visual identity for our brand. In the past, I applied formatting to a part of a document and then used *Format Painter* to copy that formatting to other parts of the document. But I found that if I changed the formatting, I would have to go in and copy the formatting again. This was too much work! Now I use styles to apply formatting to my documents. I create my styles and then apply them to all the other parts of the document. The best part is that if I decide to change that style, all I have to do is modify the style one time and all the other text is updated automatically for me.

tips & tricks

Clicking the *Reset Picture* button does not revert the image to the original size. If you want to remove the formatting and change the picture back to the size it was when you first added it to the document, click the arrow next to *Reset Picture* and select **Reset Picture & Size**.

another **method**

To reset a picture, removing any formatting you added, you can also click the **Reset Picture** button arrow and select **Reset Picture**.

Tell Me More

tell me **more**

There are variety of SmartArt styles from which to choose. These styles include a combination of outlines and effects (such as gradients and bevels) that you can apply with a single command.

another **method**

To change the color and style of SmartArt, you can also right-click the diagram and click a button on the Mini toolbar.

let me **try**

Open the student data file **wd8-08-SpaNewsletter** and try this skill on your own:

Another Method

another **method**

» To change the Quick Style of a shape, you can also right-click the shape and click the **Styles** button on the Mini toolbar.

» To change the fill of a shape, you can also right-click the shape and click the **Fill** button on the Mini toolbar.

» To change the outline of a shape, you can also right-click the shape and click the **Outline** button on the Mini toolbar.

let me **try**

If you do not have the data file from the previous skill open, open the student data file **wd8-17-SpaNewsletter** and try this skill on your own:

1. Select the blue shape next to the *Four New Services* article on page 1.
2. Apply the **Color Fill–Orange, Accent 2** Quick Style to the shape.

Let Me Try

let me **try**

If you do not have the data file from the previous skill open, open the student data file **wd7-08-SpaProductReport** and try this skill on your own:

1. Navigate to page 3 of the document. Switch to **Outline** view.
2. Place the cursor in **The Basic Mani** heading and promote the heading one level.
3. Place the cursor on the next line (**What Customers Say**) and move the item down so it is under the paragraph beginning with *The Basic Mani is our most popular*.
4. Place the cursor back in **The Basic Mani** heading and hide the subtopics.
5. Close Outline view.
6. If you will be moving on to the next skill in this chapter, leave the document open to continue working. If not, save the file as directed by your instructor and close it.

» **Instructor materials available on the online learning center, www.mhhe.com/office2013skills**

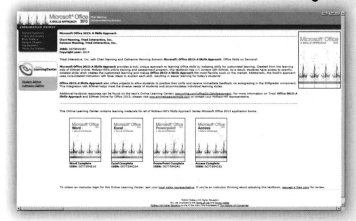

- Instructor Manual
- Instructor PowerPoints
- Test Bank

SIMnet for Office 2013 Online Training & Assessment

❱ Includes:
- Microsoft® Office Suite
- Computer Concepts
- Windows 7
- Internet Explorer 9

EASY TO USE

SIMnet is McGraw-Hill's leading solution for training and assessment of Microsoft Office skills and beyond. Completely online with no downloads for installation (besides requiring Adobe Flash Player), SIMnet is accessible for today's students through multiple browsers and is easy to use for all. Now, SIMnet offers SIMbook and allows students to go mobile for their student learning. Available with videos and interactive "Guide Me" pages to allow students to study MS Office skills on any device. Its consistent, clean user interface and functionality will help save you time and help students be more successful in their course.

LIFELONG LEARNING

SIMnet offers lifelong learning. SIMnet is designed with features to help students immediately learn isolated Microsoft Office skills on demand. Students can use SIMSearch and the Library to learn skills both in and beyond the course.

It's more than a resource; it's a tool they can use throughout their entire time at your institution.

MEASURABLE RESULTS

SIMnet provides powerful, measureable results for you and your students. See results immediately in our various reports and customizable gradebook. Students can also see measurable results by generating a custom training lesson after an exam to help determine exactly which content areas they still need to study. Instructors can use the dashboard to see detailed results of student activity, assignment completion, and more. SIMnet Online is your solution for helping students master today's Microsoft Office Skills.

SIMNET FOR OFFICE 2013

. . . Keep IT SIMple! To learn more, visit www.simnetkeepitsimple.com and also contact your McGraw-Hill representative.

office 2013

Essential Skills for Office 2013

In this chapter, you will learn the following skills:

- Learn about Microsoft Office 2013 and its applications Word, Excel, PowerPoint, and Access
- Demonstrate how to open, save, and close files
- Recognize Office 2013 common features and navigation elements
- Modify account information and the look of Office
- Create new files
- Use Microsoft Help

skills

introduction

This chapter introduces you to Microsoft Office 2013. You will learn about the shared features across the Office 2013 applications and how to navigate common interface elements such as the Ribbon and Quick Access Toolbar. You will learn how to open and close files as well as learn how to work with messages that appear when you first open files. You will become familiar with the Office account and learn how to modify the account as well as the look of Office 2013. Introductory features such as creating and closing files and using Office Help are explained.

Skill 1.1 Introduction to Microsoft Office 2013

Microsoft Office 2013 is a collection of business "productivity" applications (computer programs designed to make you more productive at work, school, and home). The most popular Office applications are:

Microsoft Word—A word processing program. Word processing software allows you to create text-based documents, similar to how you would type a document on a typewriter. However, word processing software offers more powerful formatting and design tools, allowing you to create complex documents, including reports, résumés, brochures, and newsletters.

FIGURE OF 1.1
Microsoft Word 2013

Microsoft Excel—A spreadsheet program. Originally, spreadsheet applications were viewed as electronic versions of an accountant's ledger. Today's spreadsheet applications can do much more than just calculate numbers—they include powerful charting and data analysis features. Spreadsheet programs can be used for everything from personal budgets to calculating loan payments.

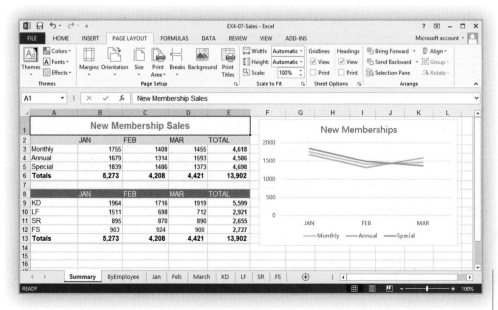

FIGURE OF 1.2
Microsoft Excel 2013

Microsoft PowerPoint—A presentation program. Such applications enable you to create robust, multimedia presentations. A presentation consists of a series of electronic slides. Each slide contains content, including text, images, charts, and other objects. You can add multimedia elements to slides, including animations, audio, and video.

Microsoft Access—A database program. Database applications allow you to organize and manipulate large amounts of data. Databases that allow you to relate tables and databases to one another are referred to as *relational* databases. As a database user, you usually see only one aspect of the database—a *form*. Database forms use a graphical interface to allow a user to enter record data. For example, when you fill out an order form online, you are probably interacting with a database. The information you enter becomes a record in a database *table*. Your order is matched with information in an inventory table (keeping track of which items are in stock) through a *query*. When your order is filled, a database *report* can be generated for use as an invoice or a bill of lading.

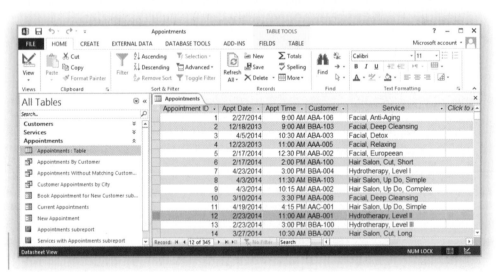

To open one of the Office applications using the Windows 8 operating system:

1. Display the **Start screen.**

2. In the *Pinned Apps* section, click the tile of the application you want to open.

To open one of the Office applications using the Windows 7 operating system:

1. Click the Windows **Start** button (located in the lower left corner of your computer screen).
2. Click **All Programs.**
3. Click the **Microsoft Office** folder.
4. Click the application you want to open.

tips & tricks

You can download a free trial version of Microsoft Office from Microsoft's Web site (http://office.microsoft.com). The trial allows you to try the applications before buying them. When your trial period ends, if you haven't purchased the full software license yet, you will no longer be able to use the applications (although you will continue to be able to open and view any files you previously created with the trial version).

tell me **more**

There are two main versions of Microsoft Office, each offering a different way to pay for the program:

Office 365—This version allows you to download and install Office and pay for it on a yearly or monthly subscription basis. It includes full versions of the different Office applications along with online storage services for your files. When the next version of Office is released, the subscription can be transferred to the new version. If you do not want to install the full version of Office on your computer, you can access limited versions of each application online with an Office 365 subscription.

Office 2013—This version allows you to install Office and pay for it once, giving you a perpetual license for the programs. This means that when the next version of Office is released, you will need to purchase the application suite again. You can associate a Windows Live account with Office 2013, giving you access to online storage for your files.

If you are a home user, business, or a student, there are different purchasing options for both Office 365 and Office 2013. Both versions require that you are running the Windows 7 or Windows 8 operating system.

Skill 1.2 Opening Files

Opening a file retrieves it from storage and displays it on your computer screen. The steps for opening a file are the same for Word documents, Excel spreadsheets, PowerPoint presentations, and Access databases.

To open an existing file from your computer:

1. Click the **File** tab to open Backstage view.
2. Click **Open.**
3. The *Open* page displays listing the recently opened files by default.
4. Click **Computer.**
5. A list of folders you have recently opened files from appears on the right. Click a folder to open the **Open** dialog with that folder displayed.

FIGURE OF 1.5

6. Select the file name you want to open in the large list box.
7. Click the **Open** button in the dialog.

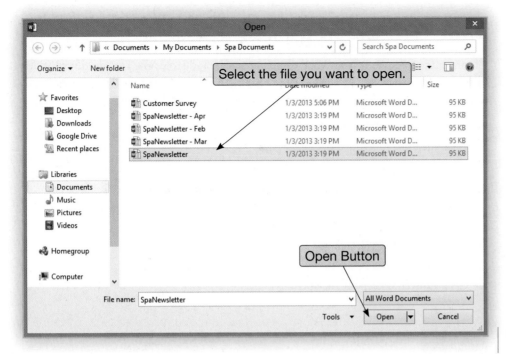

FIGURE OF 1.6

tips & tricks

If you do not see the folder containing the file you want to open, click the **Browse** button. The *Open* dialog will open to your *Documents* folder. Navigate to the location where the file you want to open is located, select the file, and click **Open.**

tell me **more**

The screen shot shown here is from Word 2013 running on the Microsoft Windows 8 operating system. Depending on the operating system you are using, the *Open* dialog will appear somewhat different. However, the basic steps for opening a file are the same regardless of which operating system you are using.

another **method**

To display the *Open* page in Backstage view, you can also press (Ctrl) + (O) on the keyboard.

To open the file from within the *Open* dialog, you can also:

❯ Press the (←Enter) key once you have typed or selected a file name.

❯ Double-click the file name.

let me **try**

Try this skill on your own:

1. Open the student data file **of1-SpaNewsletter.**

   NOTE: You may see a yellow security message at the top of the window. See the skill *Working in Protected View* to learn more about security warning messages.

2. Keep the file open to work on the next skill.

Skill 1.3 Closing Files

Closing a file removes it from your computer screen and stores the last-saved version for future use. If you have not saved your latest changes, most applications will prevent you from losing work by asking if you want to save the changes you made before closing.

To close a file and save your latest changes:

1. Click the **File** tab to open Backstage view.
2. Click the **Close** button.
3. If you have made no changes since the last time you saved the file, it will close immediately. If changes have been made, the application displays a message box asking if you want to save the changes you made before closing.

   Click **Save** to save the changes.

   Click **Don't Save** to close the file without saving your latest changes.

   Click **Cancel** to keep the file open.

FIGURE OF 1.7

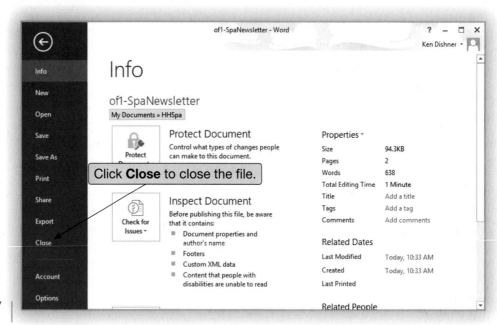

another method

To close a file, you can also press (Ctrl) + (W) on the keyboard.

let me try

If necessary, open the student data file **of1-SpaNewsletter** and try this skill on your own:
   Close the file.

Skill 1.4 Getting to Know the Office 2013 User Interface

THE RIBBON

If you have used a word processing or spreadsheet program in the past, you may be surprised when you open one of the Microsoft Office 2013 applications for the first time. Beginning with Office 2007, Microsoft redesigned the user experience—replacing the familiar menu bar/toolbar interface with a new Ribbon interface that makes it easier to find application functions and commands.

The **Ribbon** is located across the top of the application window and organizes common features and commands into tabs. Each **tab** organizes commands further into related **groups**.

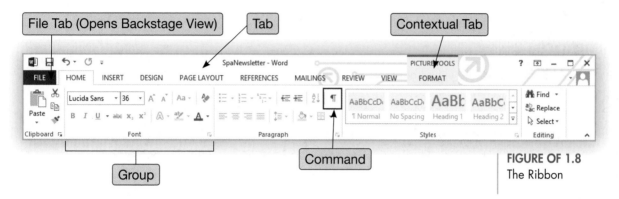

FIGURE OF 1.8
The Ribbon

When a specific type of object is selected (such as a picture, table, or chart), a contextual tab will appear. **Contextual tabs** contain commands specific to the type of object selected and are only visible when the commands might be useful.

Each application includes a **Home tab** that contains the most commonly used commands for that application. For example, in Word, the *Home* tab includes the following groups: *Clipboard, Font, Paragraph, Styles,* and *Editing,* while the Excel *Home* tab includes groups more appropriate for a spreadsheet program: *Clipboard, Font, Alignment, Number, Styles, Cells,* and *Editing.*

tips & tricks

If you need more space for your file, you can minimize the Ribbon by clicking the **Collapse the Ribbon** button in the upper-right corner of the Ribbon (or press Ctrl + F1). When the Ribbon is minimized, the tab names appear along the top of the window (similar to a menu bar). When you click a tab name, the Ribbon appears. After you select a command or click away from the Ribbon, the Ribbon hides again. To redisplay the Ribbon permanently, click the **Ribbon Display Options** button in the upper-right corner of the window and select **Show Tabs and Commands.** You can also double-click the active tab to hide or display the Ribbon.

BACKSTAGE

Notice that each application also includes a **File tab** at the far left side of the Ribbon. Clicking the *File* tab opens the **Microsoft Office Backstage view,** where you can access the commands for managing and protecting your files, including *Save, Open, Close, New,* and *Print.* Backstage replaces the Office Button menu from Office 2007 and the *File* menu from previous versions of Office.

To return to you file from Backstage view, click the **Back** button located in the upper left corner of the window.

KEYBOARD SHORTCUTS

Many commands available through the Ribbon and Backstage view are also accessible through keyboard shortcuts and shortcut menus.

Keyboard shortcuts are keys or combinations of keys that you press to execute a command. Some keyboard shortcuts refer to F keys or function keys. These are the keys that run across the top of the keyboard. Pressing these keys will execute specific commands. For example, pressing the F1 key will open Help in any of the Microsoft Office applications. Keyboard shortcuts typically use a combination of two keys, although some commands use a combination of three keys and others only one key. When a keyboard shortcut calls for a combination of key presses, such as (Ctrl) + (V) to paste an item from the *Clipboard,* you must first press the modifier key (Ctrl), holding it down while you press the (V) key on the keyboard.

Press and hold **Ctrl** and then press **V** to paste text or item in a file.

FIGURE OF 1.9

tell me **more**

Many of the keyboard shortcuts are universal across all applications—not just Microsoft Office applications. Some examples of universal shortcut keys include:

(Ctrl) + (C) = Copy

(Ctrl) + (X) = Cut

(Ctrl) + (V) = Paste

(Ctrl) + (Z) = Undo

(Ctrl) + (O) = Open

(Ctrl) + (S) = Save

SHORTCUT MENUS

Shortcut menus are menus of commands that display when you right-click an area of the application window. The area or object you right-click determines which menu appears. For example, if you right-click in a paragraph, you will see a shortcut menu of commands for working with text; however, if you right-click an image, you will see a shortcut menu of commands for working with images.

FIGURE OF 1.10
Right-Click Shortcut Menu

THE MINI TOOLBAR

The **Mini toolbar** gives you access to common tools for working with text. When you select text and then rest your mouse over the text, the Mini toolbar fades in. You can then click a button to change the selected text just as you would on the Ribbon.

another **method**

To display the Mini toolbar, you can also right-click the text. The Mini toolbar appears above the shortcut menu.

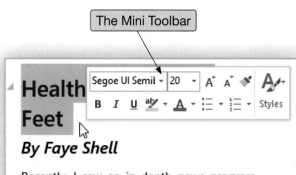

FIGURE OF 1.11

QUICK ACCESS TOOLBAR

The **Quick Access Toolbar** is located at the top of the application window above the *File* tab. The Quick Access Toolbar, as its name implies, gives you quick one-click access to common commands. You can add commands to and remove commands from the Quick Access Toolbar.

To modify the Quick Access Toolbar:

1. Click the **Customize Quick Access Toolbar** button located on the right side of the Quick Access Toolbar.

2. Options with checkmarks next to them are already displayed on the toolbar. Options with no checkmarks are not currently displayed.

3. Click an option to add it to or remove it from the Quick Access Toolbar.

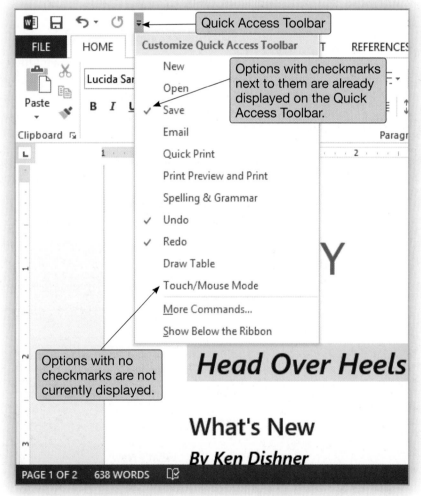

FIGURE OF 1.12

tips & tricks

If you want to be able to print with a single mouse click, add the *Quick Print* button to the Quick Access Toolbar. If you do not need to change any print settings, this is by far the easiest method to print a file because it doesn't require opening Backstage view first.

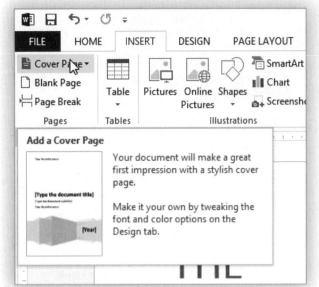

ENHANCED SCREENTIP

A **ScreenTip** is a small information box that displays the name of the command when you rest your mouse over a button on the Ribbon. An **Enhanced ScreenTip** displays not only the name of the command, but also the keyboard shortcut (if there is one) and a short description of what the button does and when it is used. Certain Enhanced ScreenTips also include an image along with a description of the command.

FIGURE OF 1.13
Cover Page
Enhanced ScreenTip

USING LIVE PREVIEW

The **Live Preview** feature in Microsoft Office 2013 allows you to see formatting changes in your file before actually committing to the change. When Live Preview is active, rolling over a command on the Ribbon will temporarily apply the formatting to the currently active text or object. To apply the formatting, click the formatting option.

Use Live Preview to preview the following:

Font Formatting—Including the font, font size, text highlight color, and font color

Paragraph Formatting—Including numbering, bullets, and shading

Quick Styles and Themes

Table Formatting—Including table styles and shading

Picture Formatting—Including correction and color options, picture styles, borders, effects, positioning, brightness, and contrast

SmartArt—Including layouts, styles, and colors

Shape Styles—Including borders, shading, and effects

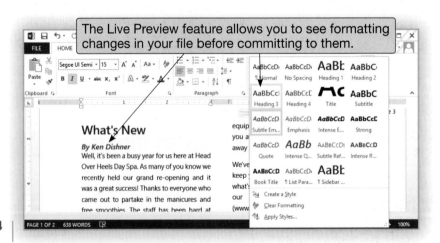

FIGURE OF 1.14

THE OPTIONS DIALOG

You can enable and disable some of the user interface features through the *Options* dialog.

1. Click the **File** tab to open Backstage view.

2. Click **Options.**

3. Make the changes you want, and then click **OK** to save your changes.

❯ Check or uncheck **Show Mini toolbar on selection** to control whether or not the Mini toolbar appears when you hover over selected text. (This does not affect the appearance of the Mini toolbar when you right-click.)

❯ Check or uncheck **Enable Live Preview** to turn the live preview feature on or off.

❯ Make a selection from the *ScreenTip style* list:

- **Show feature descriptions in ScreenTips** displays Enhanced ScreenTips when they are available.

- **Don't show feature descriptions in ScreenTips** hides Enhanced ScreenTips. The ScreenTip will still include the keyboard shortcut if there is one available.

- **Don't show ScreenTips** hides ScreenTips altogether, so if you hold your mouse over a button on the Ribbon, nothing will appear.

You can enable and disable some of the user interface features through the *Options* dialog.

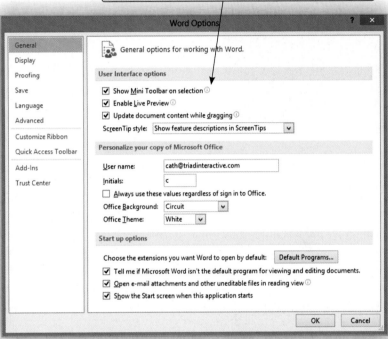

FIGURE OF 1.15

let me try

Open the student data file **of1-SpaNewsletter** and try this skill on your own:

1. Explore the Ribbon. Click on different tabs and note how commands are arranged together in groups.
2. Click the picture to display the *Picture Tools* contextual tab.
3. Click the **File** tab to display Backstage view. Click the **Back** button to return to the file.
4. Right-click an area of the file to display the shortcut menu.
5. Explore the Mini Toolbar at the top of the shortcut menu. Click away from the menu to hide it.
6. Click the **Customize Quick Access Toolbar** arrow to display the menu of items that can be displayed on the Quick Access Toolbar. Note the ones with checkmarks are the items currently displayed.
7. Click the **Insert** tab. In the *Pages* group, roll your mouse over the **Cover Page** button to display the Enhanced ScreenTip.
8. Click the **File** tab.
9. Click **Options** to open the *Options* dialog.
10. Disable **Live Preview.**
11. Change the ScreenTips so they don't show feature descriptions.
12. Close the file.

Skill 1.5 Using the Start Page

When you launch an Office 2013 application you are first taken to the **Start page**. The *Start* page gives you quick access to recently opened files and templates for creating new files in each of the applications.

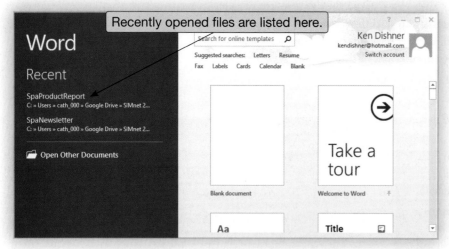

Recently opened files are listed here.

FIGURE OF 1.16

To open a recent file from the *Start* page:

1. Launch the application.
2. The *Start* page displays.
3. Click a file in the left pane to open the file.

tips & tricks

If you do not see the file you want to open in the list of recent files, click **Open Other Documents** at the bottom of the left pane. This will display the *Open* page that includes buttons for finding and opening files from other locations such as your computer or your OneDrive.

tell me **more**

In previous versions of Office when you launched an application, a blank file opened ready for you to begin working. If you want to start a new blank file, click the blank file template in the list of templates. It is always listed as the first option.

let me **try**

To try this skill on your own:

1. Launch **Microsoft Word.**
2. If you have files listed under *Recent,* click a file to open it.
3. Close the file.

from the perspective of . . .

A BUSY PARENT

Learning Microsoft Office was one of the best things I did to help manage my family's busy lifestyle. I use Word to write up and print a calendar of everyone's activities for the week. I keep a handle on the family finances with a budget of all expenses in an Excel spreadsheet. I've even learned how to use Excel to calculate loan payments and found the best offer when I had to buy a new family car. I used PowerPoint to create a presentation for my family of our summer vacation pictures. Once I became more familiar with Access, I used it to help organize my family's busy schedule. I created a database with one table for activities, another for parent contact information, another one for carpooling, and another one for the schedule. Being able to organize all the information in a database has been invaluable. I always thought Office was only for businesses, but now I can't imagine running my household without it!

Skill 1.6 Changing Account Information

Office 2013 includes an **Account page** that lists information for the user currently logged into Office. This account information comes from the Microsoft account you used when installing Office. From the *Account* page, you can update your user profile, including contact and work information. You can also change the picture associated with the user account.

To change the user information

1. Click the **File** tab.
2. Click **Account.**
3. The current user profile is listed under *User Information.*
4. Click the **Change photo** link.

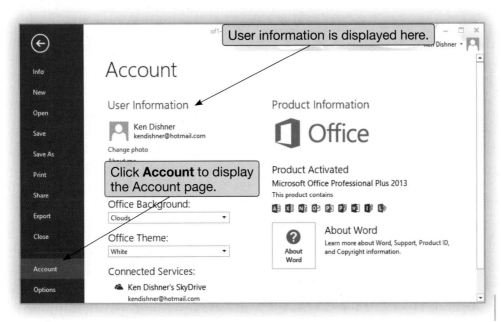

FIGURE OF 1.17

5. The *Profile* page on *live.com* is displayed in the browser window.
6. Click the **Change Picture** link.
7. On the *Picture* page, click the **Browse** button.
8. Navigate to the location of the picture you want to use for you profile and select it.
9. Click the **Open** button.
10. The picture appears on the page. Click the **Save** button to save the profile change.

From the *Profile* page, you can also edit your contact information and work information. Click the **Edit** link under each section to display the edit page. Fill in the form with your information and click the **Save** button.

FIGURE OF 1.18

tell me **more**

Depending on the version of Office 2013 you have, you can have multiple accounts use the same installation of Office. When you switch accounts, any personalization that person has done to Office will be applied. The account will also have access to that person's OneDrive account and all files that have been saved there. To learn more about OneDrive, see the skill *Saving Files to a OneDrive*.

another **method**

To change the user photo, you can also click the arrow next to the user name in the upper right corner of the window and click the **Change photo** link.

let me **try**

Open the student data file **of1-SpaNewsletter** and try this skill on your own:

1. Open the **Account** page in Backstage view.
   NOTE: If you are using this in class or in your school's computer lab, check with your instructor about permissions before completing the following steps.
2. Change the photo for the user account.
3. Change the picture using a photo of your choice.
4. Save the changes to the picture.
5. Close the browser window.
6. Keep this file open for working on the next skill.

Skill 1.7 Changing the Look of Office

In addition to managing the Office account, you can also control the look of Office from the *Account* page. Changing the Office background changes the background image that displays in the upper right corner of the window near the user profile. Changing the Office theme changes the color scheme for Office, affecting the look of the Ribbon and dialogs.

To change the look of Office:

1. Click the **File** tab to open Backstage view.
2. Click **Account.**
3. Click the **Office Background** drop-down list and select an option to display as the background.
4. Click the **Office Theme** drop-down list and select a color option for your applications.

FIGURE OF 1.19

let me try

If necessary, open the student data file **of1-SpaNewsletter** and try this skill on your own:

1. Open the **Account** page in Backstage view.
   NOTE: If you are using this in class or in your school's computer lab, check with your instructor about permissions before completing the following steps.
2. Change the Office background to the **Circuit** background.
3. Change the Office color to **Light Gray.**
4. Close the file.

Skill 1.8 Working in Protected View

When you download a file from a location that Office considers potentially unsafe, it opens automatically in **Protected View**. Protected View provides a read-only format that protects your computer from becoming infected by a virus or other malware. Potentially unsafe locations include the Internet, e-mail messages, or a network location. Files that are opened in Protected View display a warning in the Message Bar at the top of the window, below the Ribbon.

To disable Protected View, click the **Enable Editing** button in the Message Bar.

FIGURE OF 1.20

tips & tricks

To learn more about the security settings in Office 2013, open the Trust Center and review the options. We do not recommend changing any of the default Trust Center settings.

another method

You can also enable editing from the Info page in Backstage.
1. Click the **File** tab to open Backstage.
2. Click **Info.**
3. The Info page provides more information about the file. If you are sure you want to remove it from Protected View, click the **Enable Editing** button.

let me try

Open the student data file **of1-SpaNewsletter** and try this skill on your own:
1. If you downloaded the file from the Internet, the file will open in Protected View.
2. Click the **Enable Editing** button to begin working with the file.
3. Close the file.

Skill 1.9 Picking Up Where You Left Off

When you are working in a long document or a presentation and reopen it to work on it, you may not remember where you were last working. Office 2013 includes a new feature that automatically bookmarks the last location that was worked on when the file was closed.

To pick up where you left off in a document or presentation:

1. Open the document or presentation.

2. A message displays on the right side of the screen welcoming you back and asking if you want to pick up where you left off. The message then minimizes to a bookmark tag.

3. Click the **bookmark tag** to navigate to the location.

FIGURE OF 1.21

tips & tricks

The bookmark tag only displays until you navigate to another part of the document. If you scroll the document, the bookmark tag disappears.

tell me **more**

This feature is only available in Word and PowerPoint. Excel and Access do not give you the option of picking up where you left off when you open a file.

let me **try**

Open the student data file **of1-09-SpaNewsletter** and try this skill on your own:

1. Navigate to the location where the last location the file was at when last closed.

2. Close the file.

Skill 1.10 Creating a New Blank File

When you first open an Office application, the *Start* page displays giving you the opportunity to open an existing file or create a new blank file or one based on a template. But what if you have a file open and want to create another new file? Will you need to close the application and then launch it again? The **New command** allows you to create new files without exiting and reopening the program.

To create a new blank file:

1. Click the **File** tab to open Backstage view.

2. Click **New.**

3. The first option on the *New* page is a blank file. Click the **Blank document** thumbnail to create the new blank file.

FIGURE OF 1.22

tell me **more**

In addition to a blank file, you can create new files from templates from the *New* page.

another **method**

To bypass the Backstage view and create a new blank file, press ⌃Ctrl + Ⓝ on the keyboard.

let me **try**

Open the student data file **of1-SpaNewsletter** and try this skill on your own:

1. Create a new blank file.
2. Close the file but do not save it.

Skill 1.11 Using Help

If you don't know how to perform a task, you can look it up in the **Office Help** system. Each application comes with its own Help system with topics specifically tailored for working with that application.

To look up a topic using the Microsoft Office Help system:

1. Click the **Microsoft Office Help** button. It is located at the far right of the Ribbon.
2. Click in the *Search online help* **box** and type a word or phrase describing the topic you want help with.
3. Click the **Search** button.
4. A list of results appears.
5. Click a result to display the help topic.

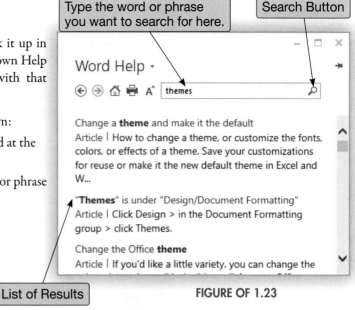

FIGURE OF 1.23

FIGURE OF 1.24

tips & tricks

To search for topics in Microsoft Office Help, you must have an active Internet connection. If you are working offline (not connected to *Office.com*), Help is still available, but it is limited to information about finding buttons of the Ribbon.

tell me **more**

The Help toolbar is located at the top of the Help window. This toolbar includes buttons for navigating between screens, changing the size of text, and returning to the *Help Home* page. Click the **printer icon** on the toolbar to print the current topic. Click the **pushpin icon** to keep the Help window always on top of the Microsoft Office application.

another **method**

To open the Help window, you can also press (F1) on the keyboard.

let me **try**

Open the student data file **of1-SpaNewsletter** and try this skill on your own:
1. Click the **Microsoft Office Help** button.
2. Search for topics about **themes.**
3. Click a link of your choice.
4. Close the **Help** window.
5. Keep this file open for working on the next skill.

Skill 1.12 Working with File Properties

File Properties provide information about a file such as the location of the file, the size of file, when the file was created and when it was last modified, the title, and the author. Properties also include keywords, referred to as **tags**, that are useful for grouping common files together or for searching. All this information about a file is referred to as **metadata**.

To view a file's properties, click the **File** tab to open Backstage view. Properties are listed at the far right of the *Info* tab. To add keywords to a file, click the text box next to *Tags* and type keywords that describe the file, separating each word with a comma. The Author property is added automatically using the account name entered when you installed and registered Office. You can change the author name or add more names by editing the Author property.

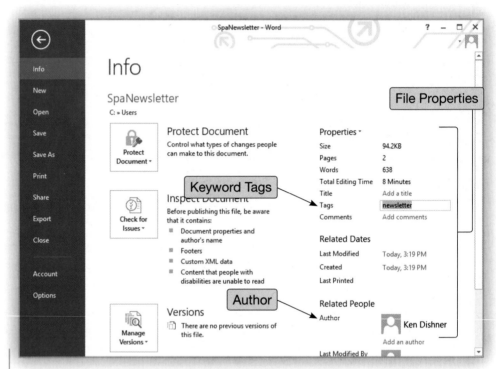

FIGURE OF 1.25

tips & tricks

Some file properties are generated automatically by Windows and cannot be edited by the user, such as the date the file was created and the size of the file.

let me try

If necessary, open the student data file **of1-SpaNewsletter** and try this skill on your own:
1. Add a tag to the document that reads **newsletter.**
2. Keep this file open for working on the next skill.

Skill 1.13 Saving Files to a Local Drive

As you work on a new file, it is displayed on-screen and stored in your computer's memory. However, it is not permanently stored until you save it as a file to a specific location. The first time you save a file, the *Save As* page in Backstage view will display. Here you can choose to save the file to your OneDrive, your local computer, or another location.

To save a file to a local drive:

1. Click the **Save** button on the Quick Access Toolbar.
2. The *Save As* page in Backstage view appears.
3. On the left side of the page, click **Computer** to save the file to a local drive.
4. Word displays a list of recent folders; select a folder where you want to save the file.

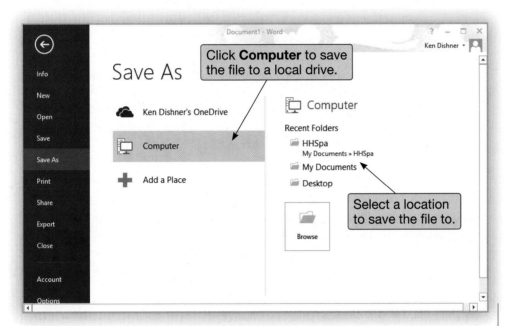

FIGURE OF 1.26

5. The *Save As* dialog opens.
6. If you want to create a new folder, click the **New Folder** button near the top of the file list. The new folder is created with the temporary name *New Folder.* Type the new name for the folder and press **Enter.**
7. Click in the **File name** box and type a file name.
8. Click the **Save** button.

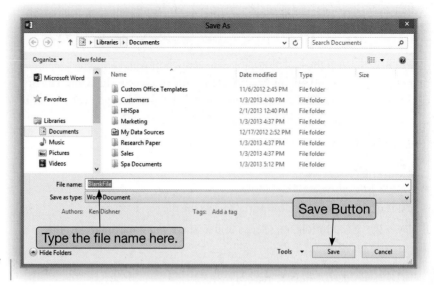

FIGURE OF 1.27

The next time you save this file, it will be saved with the same file name and to the same location automatically.

As you are working with files, be sure to **save often!** Although Office 2013 includes a recovery function, it is not foolproof. If you lose power or your computer crashes, you may lose all the work done on the file since the last save.

tips & tricks

If the location where you want to save the file is not listed under *Recent Folders,* click the **Browse** button to open the *Save As* dialog. Navigate to the location where you want to save the file.

another method

To save a file, you can also:

▶ Press Ctrl + S on the keyboard.

▶ Click the **File** tab, and then select **Save.**

▶ Click the **File** tab, and then select **Save As.**

let me try

Try this skill on your own:

1. Create a new blank file.
2. Save the file to the **My Documents** folder on your computer. Name the file **BlankFile.**
3. Close the file.

Skill 1.14 Saving Files to a OneDrive

NOTE: When Microsoft Office 2013 first published, this feature was named **SkyDrive**. It has since been renamed **OneDrive**.

OneDrive is Microsoft's free cloud storage where you can save documents, workbooks, presentations, videos, pictures, and other files and access those files from any computer or share the files with others. When you save files to your OneDrive, they are stored locally on your computer and then "synched" with your OneDrive account and stored in the "cloud" where you can then access the files from another computer or device that has OneDrive capability.

To save a file to your OneDrive:

1. Click the **File** tab.
2. Click **Save As.**
3. Verify the OneDrive account is selected on the left side of the page.
4. Under *Recent Folders,* click the **OneDrive** account you want to save to.
5. The *Save As* dialog opens to your OneDrive folder location on your computer.
6. Click in the **File name** box and type a file name.
7. Click the **Save** button.

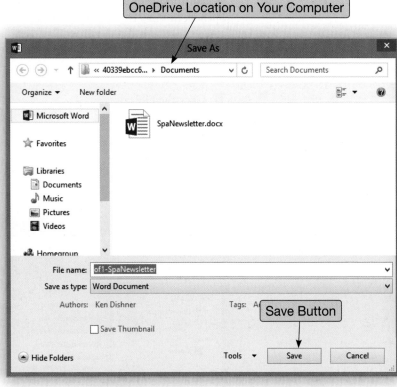

FIGURE OF 1.28

tips & tricks

By default, your OneDrive includes folders for documents, pictures, and files you want to make public. You can save your files in any of these folders or create your own. To create a new folder in your OneDrive, click the **New Folder** button near the top of the file list. The new folder is created with the temporary name *New Folder.* Type the new name for the folder and press ⏎ Enter .

tell me **more**

When you are working on an Excel or Word file that has been saved to your OneDrive, others can work on the file at the same time you are working the file. The application will mark the area being worked on as read only so others cannot modify the same information you are working on. However, if you are sharing a PowerPoint presentation, only one user at a time can work on the presentation.

let me **try**

If necessary, open the student data file **of1-SpaNewsletter** and try this skill on your own:

1. Save the file to the **Documents** folder on your OneDrive. **NOTE:** If you are using this in class or in your school's computer lab, check with your instructor before completing this step.
2. Keep this file open for working on the next skill.

Skill 1.15 Saving Files with a New Name

When working on files you may want to save a file but not overwrite the original file you opened. In this case, you should save the file with a new name. When you save a file with a new name, the original file still exists in its last saved state and the new file you save will include all the changes you made.

To save a file with a new name:

1. Click the **File** tab.
2. Click **Save As.**
3. Select a location to save the file, either your OneDrive or your local drive.
4. In the *Save As* dialog, click in the **File name** box, type a new name for the file, and click **Save.**

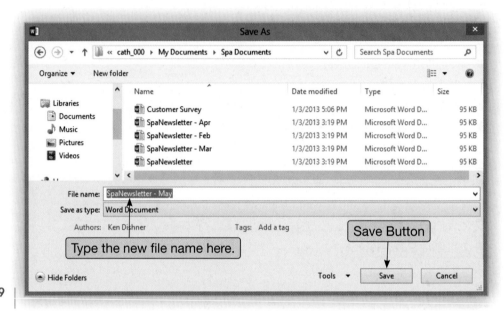

FIGURE OF 1.29

tell me **more**

Beginning with Office 2007, Microsoft changed the file format for Office files. If you want to share your files with people who are using Office 2003 or older, you should save the files in a different file format.

1. In the *Save As* dialog, click the arrow at the end of the *Save as type* box to expand the list of available file types.
2. To ensure compatibility with older versions of Office, select the file type that includes 97-2003 (for example, Word 97-2003 Document or Excel 97-2003 Workbook).

let me **try**

If necessary, open the student data file **of1-SpaNewsletter** and try this skill on your own:

1. Save the file to the **Documents** folder on your computer with the name **SpaNewsletter.**
2. Keep this file open for working on the next skill.

Skill 1.16 Closing the Application

When you close a file, the application stays open so you can open another file to edit or begin a new file. Often, when you are finished working on a file, you want to close the file and exit the application at the same time. In this case, you will want to close the application.

To close an application:

1. Click the **Close** button in the upper-right corner of the application.

2. If you have made no changes since the last time you saved the file, it will close immediately. If changes have been made, the application displays a message box asking if you want to save the changes you made before closing.
   Click **Save** to save the changes.
   Click **Don't Save** to close the file without saving your latest changes.
   Click **Cancel** to keep the file open.

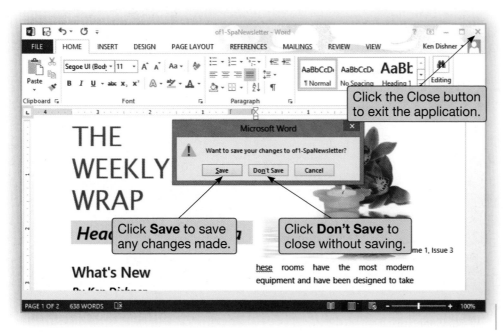

FIGURE OF 1.30

another method

To close the application, you can also:

❯ Right-click the title bar and select **Close.**

❯ Click the application icon in the upper-left corner of the application and select **Close.**

let me try

If necessary, open the student data file **of1-SpaNewsletter** and try this skill on your own:

   Close the application.

key terms

Microsoft Word
Microsoft Excel
Microsoft PowerPoint
Microsoft Access
Ribbon
Tab
Groups
Contextual tabs
Home tab
File tab
Backstage
Keyboard shortcuts
Shortcut menus
Mini toolbar

Quick Access Toolbar
ScreenTip
Enhanced ScreenTip
Live Preview
Start page
Account page
Protected View
New command
Office Help
File Properties
Tags
Metadata
OneDrive

concepts review

1. Microsoft _____ is a spreadsheet program.
   a. Word
   b. Excel
   c. Access
   d. PowerPoint

2. Click the _____ tab to display Backstage view.
   a. File
   b. Home
   c. View
   d. Contextual

3. To display a shortcut menu _____ an area of the file.
   a. left-click
   b. right-click
   c. double-click
   d. None of the above

4. If you have downloaded a file from the Internet and it opens in Protected View, you should never open the file.
   a. True
   b. False

5. The _____ is located across the top of the application window and organizes common features and commands into tabs.
   a. menu bar
   b. toolbar
   c. title bar
   d. Ribbon

6. The _____ provide(s) information about a file such as the location of the file, the size of file, when the file was created and when it was last modified, the title, and the author.

   a. file properties

   b. user profile

   c. account information

   d. Options dialog

7. When you save files to your OneDrive, they are available to access from other computers that have OneDrive capability. If you are working on an Excel or Word file, others can be working on the same file at the same time you are working on the file.

   a. True

   b. False

8. You can change user information from the _____ page in Backstage view.

   a. Account

   b. Options

   c. Share

   d. Info

9. To paste an item from the *Clipboard,* use the keyboard shortcut _____.

   a. Ctrl + C

   b. Ctrl + X

   c. Ctrl + V

   d. Ctrl + P

10. The _____ gives you quick one-click access to common commands and is located at the top of the application window above the *File* tab.

   a. Ribbon

   b. Quick Access Toolbar

   c. Options dialog

   d. Backstage view

word 2013

Getting Started with Word 2013

In this chapter, you will learn the following skills:

❯ Enter, select, and delete text

❯ Use the spelling and grammar features

❯ Use Undo and Redo

❯ Find and replace text in a document

❯ Cut, copy, and paste text

❯ Apply different paste options

❯ Use the Clipboard

❯ Change how the document displays in the window

❯ View Document Statistics

skills

introduction

This introductory chapter will teach students some of the basic editing features of Microsoft Word 2013, such as entering, selecting, and deleting text. Students will also learn how to correct spelling and grammar errors; find and replace text; and use the cut, copy, and paste commands. In addition, students will learn how to look up document statistics and to change the magnification of a document by using the *Zoom* feature.

Skill 1.1 Introduction to Word 2013

Microsoft Office Word 2013 is a word processing program that enables you to create many types of documents including letters, résumés, reports, proposals, Web pages, blogs, and more. Word's advanced editing capabilities allow you to quickly and easily perform tasks such as checking your spelling and finding text in a long document.

Robust formatting allows you to produce professional documents with stylized fonts, layouts, and graphics. Building Blocks and Quick Styles allow you to insert complex desktop publishing elements into your document. Printing and file management can be managed directly from the Word window. In short, everything you need to create polished professional and personal documents is available in Microsoft Word.

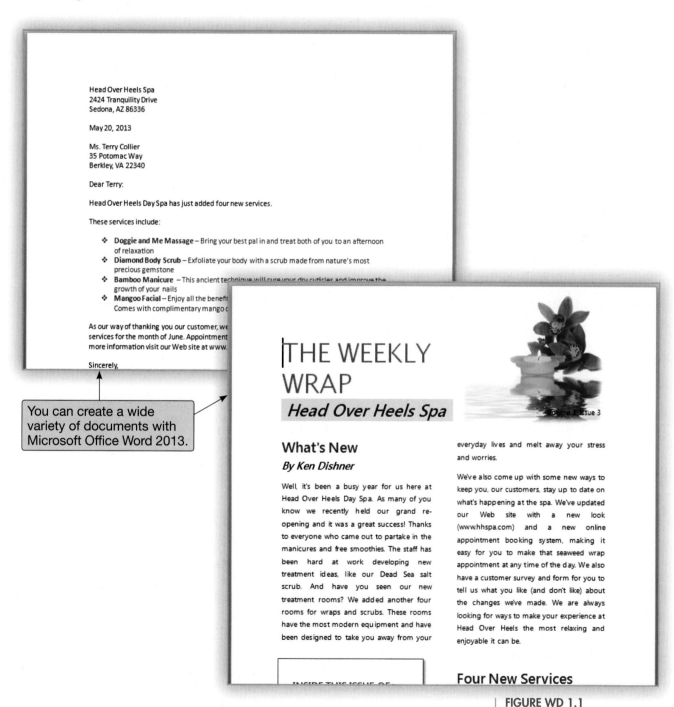

You can create a wide variety of documents with Microsoft Office Word 2013.

FIGURE WD 1.1

Here are some basic elements of a Word document:

Font—also called the typeface, refers to a set of characters of a certain design. You can choose from several preinstalled fonts available.

Paragraph—groups of sentences separated by a hard return. A hard return refers to pressing the ⌐← Enter ⌐ key to create a new paragraph. You can assign a paragraph its own style to help it stand out from the rest of the document.

Styles—complex formatting, including font, color, size, and spacing, that can be applied to text. Use consistent styles for headings, body text, notes, and captions throughout your document. Styles also can be applied to tables and graphics.

Tables—used to organize data into columns and rows.

Graphics—photographs, clip art, SmartArt, or line drawings that can be added to documents.

tips & tricks

Microsoft Office 2013 includes many other features that can further enhance your documents. If you would like to learn more about these features, click the **Help** icon ? in the upper-right corner of the Word window or visit Microsoft Office online through your Web browser.

tell me **more**

Some basic features of a word processing application include:

❱ *Word Wrap*—places text on the next line when the right margin of the page has been reached.

❱ *Find and Replace*—searches for any word or phrase in the document. Also, allows all instances of a word to be replaced by another word.

❱ *Spelling and Grammar*—checks for errors in spelling and grammar and offers solutions to the problem.

❱ *Document Formatting*—allows the enhancement of the appearance of the document.

Skill 1.2 Entering and Deleting Text

The basic function of a word processing application like Microsoft Word is to create written documents. Whether the documents are simple, such as a letter, or complex, such as a newsletter, one of the basic tasks you will perform in Word is entering text. **Word wrap** is a feature in Microsoft Word that automatically places text on the next line when the right margin of the document has been reached. There is no need to press (←─ Enter) to begin a new line in the same paragraph. Only press (←─ Enter) when you want to create a break and start a new paragraph.

To enter text in a document:

1. Place the cursor where you want the new text to appear.

2. Begin typing.

3. When the cursor reaches the end of the line, do not press (←─ Enter). Keep typing and allow word wrap to move the text to the next line.

If you make a mistake when entering text, you can press the (←─ Backspace) key to remove text to the left of the cursor, or press the (Delete) key to remove text to the right of the cursor.

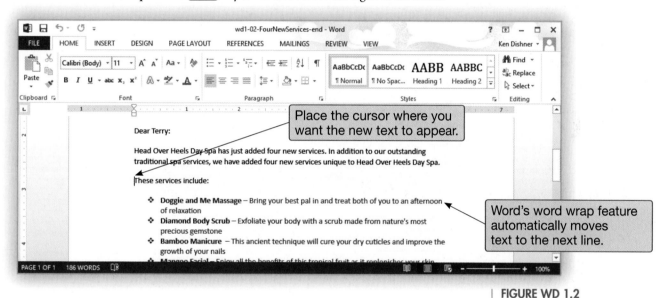

FIGURE WD 1.2

tips & tricks

If you want to edit text you have typed, click in the text to place the cursor anywhere in the document. When you begin typing, the new text will be entered at the cursor point, pushing out any existing text to the right. You can also use the arrow keys to move the cursor around in the document and then begin typing.

tell me **more**

The cursor indicates the place on the page where text will appear when you begin typing. There are a number of cursors that display, but the default text cursor is a blinking vertical line.

let me **try**

Open the student data file **wd1-02-FourNewServices** and try this skill on your own:

1. Place your cursor at the end of the first paragraph and type the following text: In addition to our outstanding traditional spa services, we have added four new services unique to Head Over Heels Day Spa.

2. Save the file as directed by your instructor and close it.

Skill 1.3 Selecting Text

When you select text in a document, a shaded background appears behind the selected text. You can then apply commands to the text as a group, such as changing the font or applying the bold effect.

There are several methods for selecting text in a document:

❯ Click and drag the cursor across the text.

❯ To select a single word: double-click the word.

❯ To select a paragraph: triple-click a word in the paragraph you want to select.

❯ To select a line of text: point to the left margin next to the line you want to select. When the cursor changes to an arrow, click once to select the line of text.

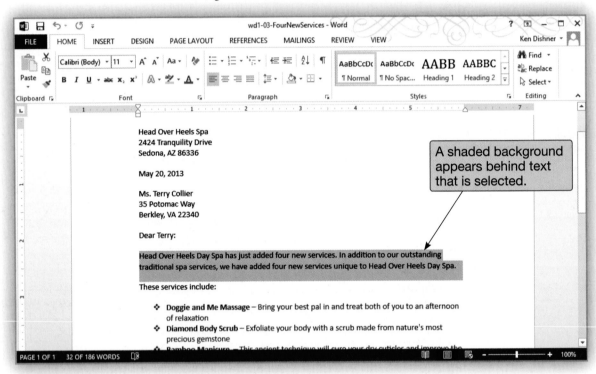

FIGURE WD 1.3

tips & tricks

To select all the text in the document, you can press Ctrl + A on the keyboard or triple-click the left margin of the document.

another method

To select a paragraph of text, you can also double-click in the left margin next to the paragraph you want to select.

let me try

Open the student data file **wd1-03-FourNewServices** and try this skill on your own:

1. Select the word **Sedona**.
2. Select the line **2424 Tranquility Drive**.
3. Select the **first paragraph of text**.
4. Close the file.

Skill 1.4 Checking Spelling and Grammar as You Type

Microsoft Word can automatically check your document for spelling and grammar errors while you type. Misspelled words, words that are not part of Word's dictionary, are indicated by a wavy red underline. Grammatical errors are similarly underlined in blue and are based on the grammatical rules that are part of Word's grammar checking feature. When you right-click either type of error, a shortcut menu appears with suggestions for correcting the error and other options.

To correct a misspelled word underlined in red:

1. Right-click the misspelled word.
2. Choose a suggested correction from the shortcut menu.

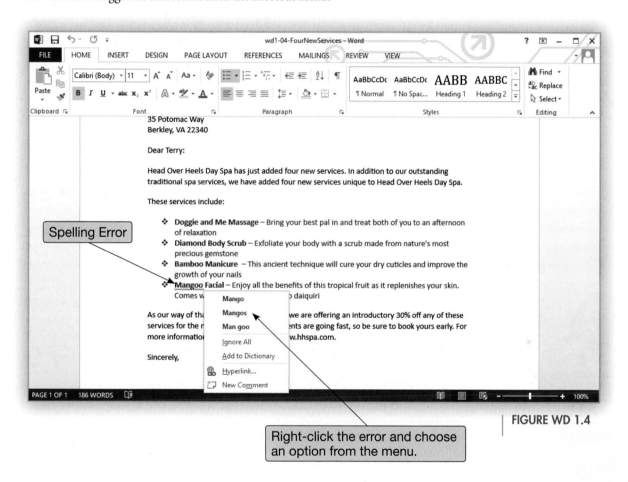

FIGURE WD 1.4

tips & tricks

Although checking spelling and grammar as you type is a useful tool when creating documents, there are times when you may find it distracting. You can choose to turn off checking spelling errors or grammar errors as you type. To turn the *Check Spelling as you type* and *Check Grammar as you type* features on and off:

1. Click the **File** tab.
2. Click the **Options** button.
3. In the *Word Options* dialog, click the **Proofing** button.
4. In the *When correcting spelling and grammar in Word* section, deselect the **Check spelling as you type** option for **Spelling Error** or the **Mark grammar errors as you type** option for grammatical errors.

tell me **more**

Word will not suggest spelling corrections if its dictionary does not contain a word with similar spelling, and Word will not always be able to display grammatical suggestions. In these cases, you must edit the error manually. If the word is spelled correctly, you can choose the **Add to Dictionary** command on the shortcut menu. When you add a word to the dictionary, it will no longer be marked as a spelling error.

let me **try**

Open the student data file **wd1-04-FourNewServices** and try this skill on your own:

1. Using the right-click method, replace the misspelled word **mangoo** with the correction **mango.**

2. Save the file as directed by your instructor and close it.

from the perspective of . . .

ADMINISTRATIVE ASSISTANT

It seems like every time I write up a memo or a letter, I use all the basic Word skills I learned when I first started using Word. Shortcuts like triple-clicking to select a paragraph of text and cutting and pasting to move text around in a document are tricks I use over and over every day. My boss has terrible eyesight, so every time I get a document in from him I have to take the zoom on the document down from 180% to 100% before I send it out. And trust me, I don't know where I would be without Word's Spelling and Grammar check, but no matter what, I always give my documents another read before sending them out to clients.

Skill 1.5 Checking Spelling

Regardless of the amount of work you put into a document, a spelling error or typo can make the entire document appear sloppy and unprofessional. All the Office applications include a built-in spelling checker. In Word, the *Spelling & Grammar* command analyzes your entire document for spelling errors. Spelling errors are presented in the *Spelling* task pane, enabling you to make decisions about how to handle each error or type of error in turn.

To check a file for spelling errors:

1. Click the **Review** tab. In the *Proofing* group, click the **Spelling & Grammar** button.
2. The first spelling error appears in the *Spelling* task pane.
3. Review the spelling suggestions and then select an action:
   - Click **Ignore** to make no changes to this instance of the word.
   - Click **Ignore All** to make no changes to all instances of the word.
   - Click **Add** to make no changes to this instance of the word and add it to the main dictionary, so future uses of this word will not show up as misspellings. When you add a word to the main dictionary, it is available for all of the Office applications.
   - Click the correct spelling in the list of suggestions, and click **Change** to correct just this instance of the misspelling in your document.
   - Click the correct spelling in the list of suggestions, and click **Change All** to correct all instances of the misspelling in your document.
4. After you select an action, the spelling checker automatically advances to the next suspected spelling error.
5. When the spelling checker finds no more errors, it displays a message telling you the check is complete. Click **OK** to close the dialog and return to your file.

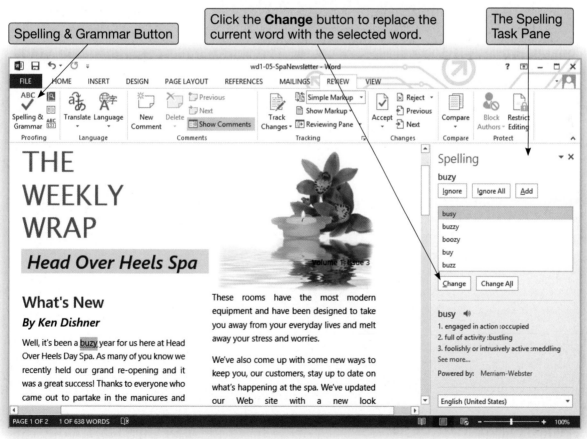

Spelling & Grammar Button

Click the **Change** button to replace the current word with the selected word.

The Spelling Task Pane

FIGURE WD 1.5

tips & tricks

> Whether or not you use the Spelling tool, you should always proofread your files. Spelling checkers are not infallible, especially if you misuse a word, yet spell it correctly—for instance, writing "bored" instead of "board."

> If you have repeated the same word in a sentence, Word will flag the second instance of the word as a possible error. In the *Spelling* task pane, the *Change* button will switch to a *Delete* button. Click the **Delete** button to remove the duplicate word.

tell me **more**

When you select an option in the list of suggestions, Word displays a list of words that have the same meaning as the selected word along with an audio file of the pronunciation of the word.

another **method**

To open the *Spelling* task pane, you can also press the [F7] key.

let me **try**

Open the student data file **wd1-05-SpaNewsletter** and try this skill on your own:

1. Open the **Spelling** task pane.
2. Change the word **buzy** to the suggestion **busy**.
3. Save the file as directed by your instructor and close it.

Skill 1.6 Using Undo and Redo

If you make a mistake when working, the **Undo** command allows you to reverse the last action you performed. The **Redo** command allows you to reverse the *Undo* command and restore the file to its previous state. The Quick Access Toolbar gives you immediate access to both commands.

To undo the last action taken, click the **Undo** button on the Quick Access Toolbar.
To redo the last action taken, click the **Redo** button on the Quick Access Toolbar.

To undo multiple actions at the same time:

1. Click the arrow next to the *Undo* button to expand the list of your most recent actions.

2. Click an action in the list.

3. The action you click will be undone, along with all the actions completed after that. In other words your document will revert to the state it was in before that action.

Click the **Undo** button to undo the last action taken.

Click the **Redo** button to redo the last action taken.

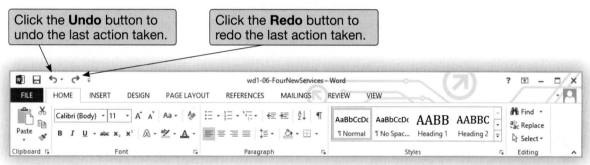

FIGURE WD 1.6

another method

To undo an action, you can also press (Ctrl) + (Z) on the keyboard.
To redo an action, you can also press (Ctrl) + (Y) on the keyboard.

let me try

Open the student data file **wd1-06-FourNewServices** and try this skill on your own:

1. In the first paragraph, select the word **unique**. Press the **Delete** key to delete the word.
2. Click the **Undo** button to restore the word to the document.
3. Click the **Redo** button to remove the word again.
4. Save the file as directed by your instructor and close it.

Skill 1.7 Finding Text

The **Find** command allows you to search a document for a word or phrase. In past versions of Microsoft Word, searching for text was performed through the *Find and Replace* dialog. In Word 2010, Microsoft introduced the *Navigation* task pane as the default method for searching for text in a document. When you search for a word or phrase in a document using the *Navigation* task pane, Word highlights all instances of the word or phrase in the document and displays each instance as a separate result in the pane.

To find a word or phrase in a document:

1. On the *Home* tab, in the *Editing* group, click the **Find** button.

2. The *Navigation* task pane appears.

3. Type the word or phrase you want to find in the *Search Document* box at the top of the task pane.

4. As you type, Word automatically highlights all instances of the word or phrase in the document and displays any results in the task pane.

5. Click a result to navigate to that instance of the word or phrase in the document.

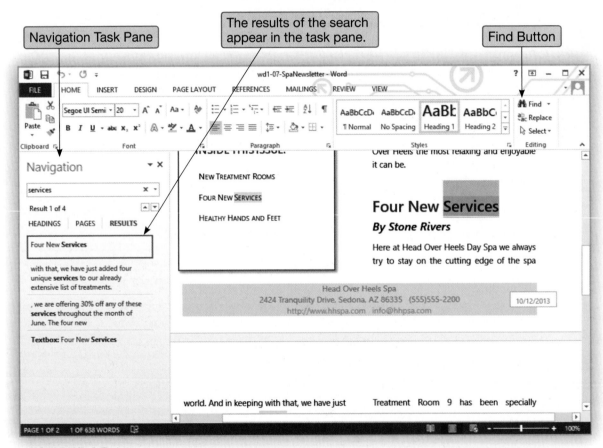

FIGURE WD 1.7

tips & tricks

If you are more comfortable using the *Find and Replace* dialog, you can still use it to search for text in your document. To open the *Find and Replace* dialog, start on the *Home* tab. In the *Editing* group, click the **Find** button arrow and select **Advanced Find...** The *Find and Replace* dialog opens with the *Find* tab displayed. Use the dialog to search for text just as you would in previous versions of Word.

tell me **more**

❯ The magnifying glass in the *Search Document* box gives you access to more search options. You can choose to only search specific elements in your document, such as tables, graphics, footnotes, or comments.

❯ Clicking the **X** next to a search word or phrase will clear the search, allowing you to perform a new search.

another **method**

To display the *Navigation* task pane with the *Results* section displayed, you can also:

❯ Click the **Find** button and select **Find** on the menu.

❯ Press (Ctrl) + (F) on the keyboard.

let me **try**

Open the student data file **wd1-07-SpaNewsletter** and try this skill on your own:

1. Open the **Navigation** task pane with the *Results* section displayed.
2. Search the document for instances of the word **services**.
3. Close the file.

Skill 1.8 Replacing Text

The **Replace** command in Word allows you to locate specific instances of text in your document and replace them with different text. With the *Replace* command, you can replace words or phrases one instance at a time or all at once throughout the document.

To replace instances of a word in a document:

1. On the *Home* tab, in the *Editing* group, click the **Replace** button.
2. Type the word or phrase you want to change in the *Find what* box.
3. Type the new text you want in the *Replace with* box.
4. Click **Replace** to replace just that one instance of the text.
5. Click **Replace All** to replace all instances of the word or phrase.
6. Word displays a message telling you how many replacements it made. Click **OK** in the message that appears.
7. To close the *Find and Replace* dialog, click the **Cancel** button.

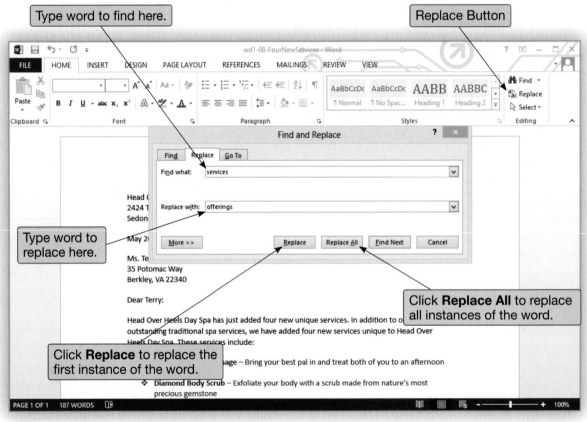

FIGURE WD 1.8

tips & tricks

In addition to text, the *Replace* command can also operate on formatting characters such as italicized text and paragraph marks. The *More >>* button in the *Find and Replace* dialog displays additional options, including buttons that allow you to select formatting and other special characters in the document.

tell me **more**

The *Go To* tab in the *Find and Replace* dialog allows you to quickly jump to any page, line, section, comment, or other object in your document.

another **method**

To open the *Find and Replace* dialog with the *Replace* tab displayed, you can also press Ctrl + H on the keyboard.

let me **try**

Open the student data file **wd1-08-FourNewServices** and try this skill on your own:

1. Open the **Find and Replace** dialog with the *Replace* tab displayed.
2. Replace all instances of **services** with **offerings**.
3. There will be 5 replacements. Click **OK** to close the message box.
4. Save the file as directed by your instructor and close it.

Skill 1.9 Using Copy and Paste

The **Copy** command places a duplicate of the selected text or object on the *Clipboard* but does not remove it from your document. You can then use the **Paste** command to insert the text or object into the same document, another document, or another Microsoft Office file, such as an Excel workbook or a PowerPoint presentation.

To copy text and paste it into the same document:

1. Select the text to be copied.
2. On the *Home* tab, in the *Clipboard* group, click the **Copy** button.
3. Place the cursor where you want to insert the text from the *Clipboard*.
4. On the *Home* tab, in the *Clipboard* group, click the **Paste** button.

These same steps apply whether you are copying and pasting text, pictures, shapes, video files, or any type of object in a Word file.

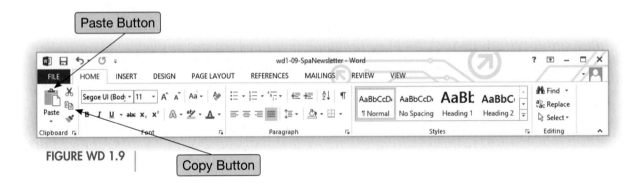

FIGURE WD 1.9

another method

To apply the *Copy* or *Paste* command, you can also use the following shortcuts:

Copy = Press (Ctrl) + (C) on the keyboard, or right-click and select **Copy**.

Paste = Press (Ctrl) + (V) on the keyboard, or right-click and select **Paste**.

let me try

Open the student data file **wd1-09-SpaNewsletter** and try this skill on your own:

1. In the first sentence of the first paragraph, select the text **Head Over Heels Day Spa** and copy it to the *Clipboard*.
2. Place the cursor before the word **staff** in the same paragraph. Paste the copied text. Be sure to check for the proper spacing between words.
3. Save the file as directed by your instructor and close it.

Skill 1.10 Using Cut and Paste

The *Copy* command is great if you want to duplicate content in your document, but what if you want to move content from one place to another? The **Cut** command is used to move text and other objects within a file and from one file to another. Text, or an object that is cut, is removed from the file and placed on the **Clipboard** for later use. You can then use the *Paste* command to insert the text or object into the same document, another document, or another Microsoft Office file.

To cut text and paste it into the same document:

1. Select the text to be cut.

2. On the *Home* tab, in the *Clipboard* group, click the **Cut** button.

3. Place the cursor where you want to insert the text from the *Clipboard*.

4. On the *Home* tab, in the *Clipboard* group, click the **Paste** button.

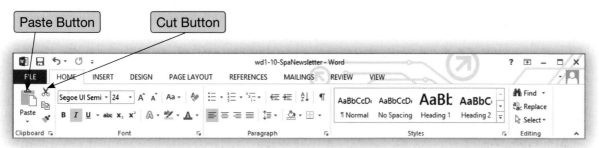

FIGURE WD 1.10

another method

To apply the *Cut* or *Paste* command, you can also use the following shortcuts:

❭ *Cut* = Press Ctrl + X on the keyboard, or right-click and select **Cut**.

❭ *Paste* = Press Ctrl + V on the keyboard, or right-click and select **Paste**.

let me try

Open the student data file **wd1-10-SpaNewsletter** and try this skill on your own:

1. In the *What's New* article, cut the sentence **And have you seen our new treatment rooms?** Be sure to include the space after the question mark.

2. Later in the same paragraph, place the cursor before the sentence that begins with **We added another four rooms**.

3. Paste the cut sentence.

4. Save the file as directed by your instructor and close it.

Skill 1.11 Using Paste Options

When you cut or copy an item, whether it be a piece of text, a chart, or an image, Word gives you a variety of ways to paste the item into your document. The *Paste* button has two parts—the top part of the button pastes the topmost contents of the *Clipboard* into the current file. If you click the bottom part of the button (the *Paste* button arrow), you can control how the item is pasted.

Each type of object has different **paste options**. For example, if you are pasting text, you may have options to keep the source formatting, merge the formatting of the source and the current document, or paste only the text without any formatting. Move your mouse over the icon for each paste option to see a preview of how the paste would look, and then click the **icon** for the paste option you want.

To paste text using paste options:

1. Place your cursor where you want to paste the text.
2. On the *Home* tab, in the *Clipboard* group, click the **Paste button arrow**.
3. Roll your mouse over each of the paste options to see how the text will appear when pasted.
4. Click an option to paste the text.

Click the **Paste** button arrow to display the *Paste Options* menu.

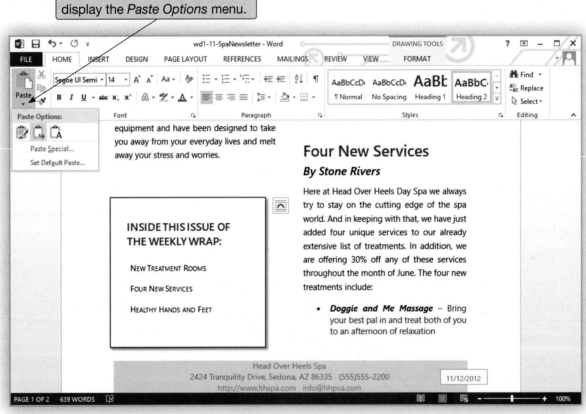

FIGURE WD 1.11

tips & tricks

When you paste text using the **Paste** button, Word pastes the text using the source formatting.

tell me **more**

There are three paste options for pasting text:

» *Source Formatting*—pastes the text and any formatting that was applied to the copied text.

» *Merge Formatting*—pastes the text to match the formatting of the surrounding text.

» *Keep Text Only*—pastes the text without any formatting that was applied to the copied text.

another **method**

To paste text using paste options, you can also right-click and select an option under *Paste Options* on the menu.

let me **try**

Open the student data file **wd1-11-SpaNewsletter** and try this skill on your own:

1. Select the newsletter title **THE WEEKLY WRAP**, and copy the text to the *Clipboard*.
2. Place the cursor before the colon in the *Inside this Issue of* text box.
3. Paste the text using the **Merge Formatting** paste command.
4. Save the file as directed by your instructor and close it.

Skill 1.12 Using the Clipboard

When you cut or copy items, they are placed on the *Clipboard*. The icons in the *Clipboard* identify the type of document from which each item originated (Word, Excel, Paint, etc.). A short description or thumbnail of the item appears next to the icon, so you know which item you are pasting into your document. The *Clipboard* can store up to 24 items for use in the current document or any other Office application.

To paste an item from the *Clipboard* into a document:

1. Place your cursor where you want to paste the item.
2. On the *Home* tab, in the *Clipboard* group, click the **Clipboard** dialog launcher.
3. The *Clipboard* task pane appears.
4. To paste an item from the *Clipboard* into your document, click the item you want to paste.

Click the dialog launcher to open the *Clipboard* task pane.

Copied items appear in the *Clipboard*, with the most recent at the top of the list.

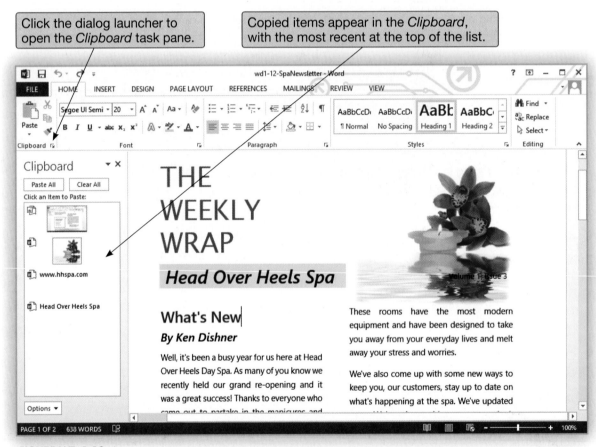

FIGURE WD 1.12

tips & tricks

The *Clipboard* is common across all Office applications—so you can cut text from a Word document and then paste that text into an Excel spreadsheet or copy a chart from Excel into a PowerPoint presentation.

tell me **more**

> To remove an item from the *Clipboard*, point to the item, click the arrow that appears, and select **Delete**.

> To add all the items in the *Clipboard* at once, click the **Paste All** button at the top of the task pane.

> To remove all the items from the *Clipboard* at once, click the **Clear All** button at the top of the task pane.

another **method**

To paste an item, you can also point to the item in the *Clipboard* task pane, click the arrow that appears, and select **Paste**.

let me **try**

Open the student data file **wd1-12-SpaNewsletter** and try this skill on your own:

1. Display the **Clipboard**.
2. In the first sentence of the *What's New* article, select the text **Head Over Heels Day Spa** and copy it to the *Clipboard*.
3. Click the picture of the flower at the top of the document to select it. Click the **Copy** button to copy it to the *Clipboard*.
4. Place the cursor before the word **staff** in the first paragraph of the *What's New* article. Paste the copied text from the *Clipboard*.
5. Save the file as directed by your instructor and close it.

Skill 1.13 Zooming a Document

When you first open a document, you may find that the text is too small to read, or that you cannot see the full layout of a page. Use the **zoom slider** in the lower-right corner of the window to zoom in and out of a document, changing the size of text and images on-screen. Zooming a document only affects how the document appears on-screen. It does not affect how the document will print.

To zoom in on a document, making the text and graphics appear larger:

❱ Click and drag the **zoom slider** to the right.

❱ Click the **Zoom In** button (the button with the plus sign on it) on the slider.

To zoom out of a document, making text and graphics appear smaller:

❱ Click and drag the **zoom slider** to the left.

❱ Click the **Zoom Out** button (the button with the minus sign on it) on the slider.

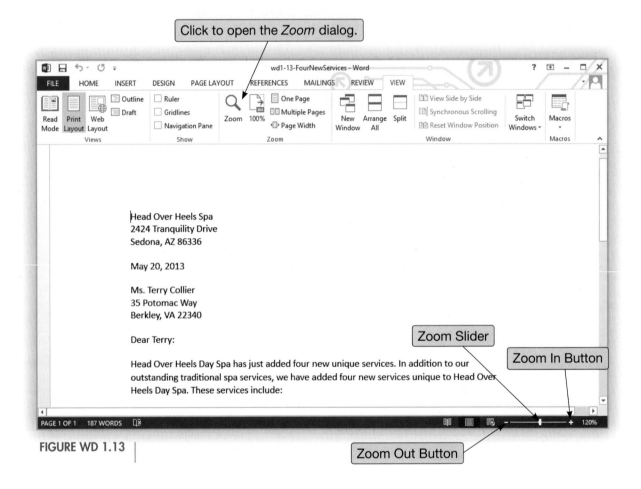

FIGURE WD 1.13

tips & tricks

As you move the slider, the zoom level displays the percentage the document has been zoomed in or out. When zooming a document, 100% is the default zoom level. If you change the zoom percentage and then save and close the document, the next time you open the document, it will display at the last viewed zoom percentage. If you work on a large monitor at a high resolution and need to display your document at a higher zoom percentage, it is a good idea to return the document back to 100% before sending it out to others.

tell me **more**

You can use the *Zoom* dialog to apply a number of display presets:

❯ *Page width*—changes the zoom so the width of the page including margins fills the screen.

❯ *Text width*—changes the zoom so the width of the page not including margins fills the screen.

❯ *Whole page*—changes the zoom so the entire page, both vertically and horizontally, displays on the screen. This is a helpful view when working with a page's layout.

❯ *Many pages*—changes the zoom to display anywhere from one to six pages on the screen at once.

another **method**

You also can change the zoom level through the *Zoom* dialog. To open the *Zoom* dialog:

1. Click the **zoom level number** next to the zoom slider OR click the **View** tab. In the *Zoom* group, click the **Zoom** button.
2. Click a **zoom preset** or type the **zoom percentage** in the *Percent* box.
3. Click **OK**.

let me **try**

Open the student data file **wd1-13-FourNewServices** and try this skill on your own:

1. Change the zoom level of the document to 90%.
2. Change the zoom level of the document back to 100%.
3. Close the file.

Skill 1.14 Using Word Count

Have you ever had to write a 250-word essay or submit a 3,000-word article? You don't need to guess if your Word document is long enough (or too long). Word's **Word Count** feature provides the current statistics of the document you are working on, including the number of pages, number of words, number of characters (with and without spaces), number of paragraphs, and number of lines.

To view document statistics:

1. From the *Review* tab, in the *Proofing* group, click the **Word Count** button.
2. The *Word Count* dialog opens and displays the statistics for the document.
3. By default, the document statistics include the text in text boxes, footnotes, and endnotes. To exclude text in these areas, click the **Include textboxes, footnotes, and endnotes** check box to remove the checkmark.
4. Click **Close** to close the dialog.

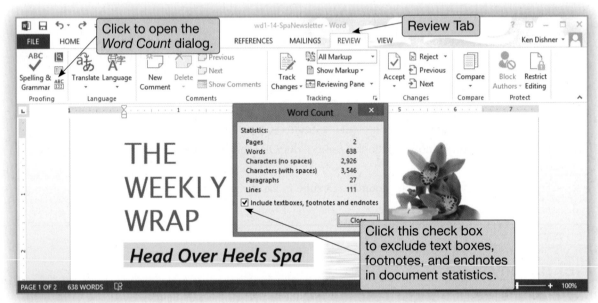

FIGURE WD 1.14

tips & tricks

The number of words and the number of pages in the document are also displayed as part of the document properties available from the *Info* tab in Backstage view. They are also displayed on the status bar at the bottom of the Word window.

another method

To open the *Word Count* dialog, you can also click **Words** on the status bar at the bottom of the Word window.

let me try

Open the student data file **wd1-14-SpaNewsletter** and try this skill on your own:

1. Open the **Word Count** dialog.
2. Note the number of words in the newsletter along with other document statistics.
3. Close the **Word Count** dialog.
4. Close the file.

Font   Replace
Paragraph   Copy
Styles   Paste
Tables   Cut
Graphics   Clipboard
Word wrap   Paste options
Undo   Icon
Redo   Zoom slider
Find   Word Count

concepts review

1. To select a paragraph of text, you can _____.

   a. single-click the paragraph

   b. double-click the paragraph

   c. triple-click the paragraph

   d. click in the left margin next to the paragraph

2. Grammatical errors in a document are represented by a _____.

   a. red wavy underline

   b. blue wavy underline

   c. green wavy underline

   d. purple wavy underline

3. The feature in Word that automatically places text on the next line when the right margin of the document has been reached is called _____.

   a. styles

   b. zoom slider

   c. word wrap

   d. status bar

4. To copy text to the Clipboard and remove it from the document, you would use the _____ command.

   a. Copy

   b. Cut

   c. Undo

   d. Redo

5. To paste text with the original formatting of the copied text, you would use the _____ paste option.

   a. Keep Source Formatting

   b. Merge Formatting

   c. Keep Text Only

   d. None of these

6. To replace all instances of a word with another word, you would use the _____ command.

   a. Find

   b. Replace

   c. Replace All

   d. Paste All

7. The primary method for finding text in a document is to use the _____.

   a. Find and Replace dialog

   b. Navigation pane

   c. Clipboard pane

   d. Go To dialog

8. To change one instance of a misspelled word, click the _____ in the *Spelling* task pane.

   a. Add button

   b. Change button

   c. Change All button

   d. Spelling button

9. To magnify the text on-screen, making the text appear larger, you would use the _____.

   a. Zoom Out button

   b. Zoom In button

   c. Page Width command

   d. 100% command

10. In addition to the number of words in a document, the Word Count dialog also displays _____.

   a. the number of tables

   b. the number of charts

   c. the number of pages

   d. the number of images

projects

In this project you will be editing the text of a brochure for Suarez Marketing.

Skills needed to complete this project:

- Zooming a Document (Skill 1.13)
- Entering and Deleting Text (Skill 1.2)
- Selecting Text (Skill 1.3)
- Checking Spelling and Grammar as You Type (Skill 1.4)
- Using Cut and Paste (Skill 1.10)
- Using Word Count (Skill 1.14)

1. Open the **WD2013-SkillReview-1-1** document.

2. Save this document as: **[your initials]WD-SkillReview-1-1**

3. Change how the document is displayed on your computer by clicking the **zoom slider** and dragging it to the 90% magnification.

4. Add text to the document.

   a. Place the cursor on the empty line following the phone number.

   b. Type the following heading: `Mission Statement`

   c. Press **Enter.**

   d. Type the following text: `I am dedicated to listening to your needs and providing you with prompt and excellent service to exceed your expectations.`

5. Select and delete text from the document.

   a. In the paragraph under the *Experience* heading, select the text **hard earned** by clicking and dragging the mouse across the words. Be sure to include the space after the word *earned*.

   b. Press the **Delete** key to remove the text.

6. Check spelling and grammar as you type. Notice how words that Word does not recognize are underlined in red and potential grammar errors are underlined in blue.

   a. Right-click the word **markats** in the *Why I Do What I Do* section. A list of suggested changes is shown.

   b. Click **markets**. Word corrects the spelling of this word.

   c. Right-click the word **communication** in the *Why I Do What I Do* section.

   d. Click **Communication**.

7. Cut and paste text from one part of the document to another.

   a. Select the text **"Putting your needs first"** at the end of the document.

   b. On the *Home* tab, in the *Clipboard* group, click the **Cut** button to remove the text and copy it to the *Clipboard*.

   c. Navigate back to the top of the first page and place the cursor on the empty line before the phone number.

   d. On the *Home* tab, in the *Clipboard* group, click the **Paste** button to paste the text. If an empty line is pasted in with the text, delete the empty line.

8. View the statistics for the document.

    a. Click the **Review** tab.

    b. In the *Proofing* group, click the **Word Count** button.

    c. Review the number of pages, words, and paragraphs in the document. Click the **Close** button to close the *Word Count* dialog.

9. Save and close the document.

skill review 1.2

In this project you will be editing an employment offer from Modern Dynamics International.

Skills needed to complete this project:

- Finding Text (Skill 1.7)
- Replacing Text (Skill 1.8)
- Checking Spelling (Skill 1.5)
- Using Copy and Paste (Skill 1.9)
- Using Paste Options (Skill 1.11)
- Using Undo and Redo (Skill 1.6)

1. Open the **WD2013-SkillReview-1-2** document.

2. Save this document as: **[your initials]WD-SkillReview-1-2**

3. Use the *Navigation* pane to find a word in the document.

    a. On the *Home* tab, in the *Editing* group, click the **Find** button. The *Navigation* pane is displayed on the right side of the Word window. *Ctrl + F* also will open the *Find* feature in the *Navigation* pane.

    b. In the *Search Document* box type: `Vision`

    c. Press **Enter**. Only one occurrence is found.

    d. In the document, select the entire line by clicking to the left of the lettered item outside of the left margin. The entire line will be selected.

    e. Press **Delete** to delete this line.

    f. Click the **X** in the upper-right corner of the *Navigation* pane to close it.

4. Use the **Find and Replace** feature to replace **MoDyInt** with **Modern Dynamics International**.

    a. Press **Ctrl + Home** to move to the top of the document.

    b. On the *Home* tab, in the *Editing* group, click the **Replace** button. The *Find and Replace* dialog will open. *Ctrl + H* also will open the *Find and Replace* dialog.

    c. In the *Find what* box type: `MoDyInt`

    d. In the *Replace with* box type: `Modern Dynamics International`

    e. Click the **Replace** button. The first occurrence of this word is selected in the document.

    f. Click **Replace** to replace **MoDyInt** with **Modern Dynamics International**. The next occurrence will be selected.

    g. Click **Replace All** to replace all occurrences in the document.

    h. Click **OK** to finish the find and replace process.

    i. Click **Close** to close the *Find and Replace* dialog.

5. Spell check the entire document.

   a. Press **Ctrl + Home** to move to the top of the document.

   b. Click the **Review** tab.

   c. Click the **Spelling & Grammar** button in the *Proofing* group. The *Spelling* task pane will open.

   d. For the first error, fix the misspelling to read **historically**.

   e. For the second error, ignore the error and do not change the spelling of the last name *Lumita*.

   f. Click **OK** when finished.

6. Copy and paste text.

   a. Triple-click in the last paragraph of the letter to select it. The paragraph begins with *We are excited about you joining*.

   b. On the *Home* tab, in the *Clipboard* group, click the **Copy** button.

   c. Navigate to the beginning of the document and place the cursor at the beginning of the first paragraph. The paragraph begins with *I am pleased to formally extend to you*.

   d. On the *Home* tab, in the *Clipboard* group, click the **Paste** button arrow and select **Keep Text Only** to paste the paragraph without formatting.

7. Click the **Undo** button on the *Quick Access Toolbar* to undo the previous command.

8. Save and close the document.

challenge yourself **1.3**

In this project you will be editing the *Notice of Privacy Practices* document from Courtyard Medical Plaza.

Skills needed to complete this project:

- Zooming a Document (Skill 1.13)
- Entering and Deleting Text (Skill 1.2)
- Selecting Text (Skill 1.3)
- Using Cut and Paste (Skill 1.10)
- Replacing Text (Skill 1.8)
- Checking Spelling (Skill 1.5)

1. Open the **WD2013-ChallengeYourself-1-3** document.

2. Save this document as: **[your initials]WD-Challenge-1-3**

3. Change the zoom level to view the document at 120% magnification.

4. Enter and delete text in the document.

   a. On the fourth line on the first page, select **Courtyard Medical Plaza** and delete this entire line.

   b. Click in front of *Notice of Privacy Practices* on the first line of the document, and type `Courtyard Medical Plaza` and press **Enter**.

   c. Click at the end of the first numbered item on the first page.

   d. Press **Enter**.

   e. Type the following text: `tell you about your rights and our legal duties with respect to your protected health information, and`

f. If Word automatically capitalized *tell,* change it back to lowercase.

g. Click at the end of the second bulleted item.

h. Replace the period with a semicolon, space once, and type and

i. Press **Enter** and type the following text: `Information about your relationship with Courtyard Medical Plaza such as medical services received, claims history, and information from your benefits plan sponsor or employer about group health coverage you may have.`

5. Cut and paste text in the document.

  a. Select the paragraph in all caps that starts *THIS NOTICE DESCRIBES*

  b. Cut the paragraph and paste it above the heading *Notice of Privacy Practices.*

6. Use Find and Replace.

  a. Use *Find and Replace* to replace **protected health information** with **PHI**. Ignore any occurrences of this information in headings (all caps bolded text). Click **Find Next** to skip an occurrence.

  b. Use *Find and Replace* to replace all instances of **Privacy and Compliance Office** with **Office of Privacy & Compliance**.

  c. Use the *Find* feature to find the word **utilization**.

7. Check the spelling and grammar on the entire document.

  a. Ignore the section heading text that is marked as a potential grammatical error (e.g., *Your*).

  b. Ignore all proper nouns.

  c. Ignore the lowercase letters at the beginning of the numbered list.

8. Save and close the document.

challenge yourself 1.4

In this project you will be editing a personal training program document from American River Cycling Club.

Skills needed to complete this project:

- Zooming a Document (Skill 1.13)
- Entering and Deleting Text (Skill 1.2)
- Selecting Text (Skill 1.3)
- Checking Spelling and Grammar as You Type (Skill 1.4)
- Replacing Text (Skill 1.8)
- Using Copy and Paste (Skill 1.9)
- Using Paste Options (Skill 1.11)
- Using Undo and Redo (Skill 1.6)
- Checking Spelling (Skill 1.5)
- Using Word Count (Skill 1.14)

1. Open the **WD2013-ChallengeYourself-1-4** document.

2. Save this document as: `[your initials]WD-Challenge-1-4`

3. Change the zoom level to view the document at 120%.

4. In the *Training Intensity and Heart Rate* section, select and delete the **second paragraph**.

5. Use the right-click method to fix the **grammar error** in the **second bulleted item** in the *General Guidelines* section.

6. Replace all occurrences of **heartrate** (one word) with **heart rate** (two words).

7. Copy the heading **General Guidelines** to the *Clipboard*.

8. Paste the text at the end of the *More about Long Rides* heading. Use the **Keep Text Only** paste option.

9. Use the **Undo** command to remove the pasted text.

10. Check the spelling and grammar on the entire document. Ignore the word *criterium*.

11. Use the *Word Count* dialog to review the number of words, paragraphs, and pages in the document.

12. Save and close the document.

on your own 1.5

In this project you will be editing the online learning plan for Fairlawn Community College.

Skills needed to complete this project:
- Zooming a Document (Skill 1.13)
- Replacing Text (Skill 1.8)
- Entering and Deleting Text (Skill 1.2)
- Selecting Text (Skill 1.3)
- Finding Text (Skill 1.7)
- Using Copy and Paste (Skill 1.9)
- Using the Clipboard (Skill 1.12)
- Using Undo and Redo (Skill 1.6)
- Checking Spelling (Skill 1.5)
- Using Word Count (Skill 1.14)

1. Open the **WD2013-OnYourOwn-1-5** document.

2. Save this document as: **[your initials]WD-OnYourOwn-1-5**

3. Change the zoom level to your preference.

4. Replace occurrences of **online learning** with **OL**. Make sure you look at the context of the sentence to make sure the replacement is appropriate. Do not make this replacement in headings.

5. In the *Planning Process* section, select and delete the last paragraph and the four bulleted items beneath it.

6. Locate **learning management system** in the body of the document and put the acronym in parentheses after these words. Use proper spacing.

7. In the *PURPOSE OF THIS PLAN* section, type the following as the first sentence in the paragraph: The Online Learning Task Force was formed in February 2005 to develop an Online Learning Strategic Plan for Fairlawn Community College.

8. Copy several pieces of text to the *Clipboard*. Paste a text piece into the document and then undo the action.

9. The current success rate for online courses is 72 %. Find and make this change.

10. Check the spelling and grammar on the entire document and make appropriate changes.

11. Check the number of words and pages in the document.

12. Save and close the document.

fix it 1.6

In this project you will be editing a disclosure letter from Placer Hills Real Estate.

Skills needed to complete this project:

- Zooming a Document (Skill 1.13)
- Entering and Deleting Text (Skill 1.2)
- Selecting Text (Skill 1.3)
- Replacing Text (Skill 1.8)
- Using Cut and Paste (Skill 1.10)
- Checking Spelling and Grammar as You Type (Skill 1.4)
- Checking Spelling (Skill 1.5)
- Using Word Count (Skill 1.14)

1. Open the **WD2013-FixIt-1-6** document.

2. Save this document as: **[your initials]WD-FixIt-1-6**

3. Change the zoom level to your preference.

4. Change the inside address of this block format business letter to:

   ```
   David and Sharon Wing
   4685 Orange Grove Rocklin,
   CA 97725
   ```

5. Make the necessary change to the salutation of the letter.

6. Find and replace all occurrences of **release** with **disclosure**.

7. Add the following sentence as the first sentence in the last body paragraph.
   ```
   Please complete the enclosed disclosure statement by
   March 1, 2014 and return it to me.
   ```

8. Whenever a letter refers to an attached or enclosed document, it is proper to include an Enclosure notation below the reference initials. Cut the word **Enclosure** and paste it in the proper place.

9. Proofread the document carefully and make any necessary spelling and grammar changes.

10. Check the number of words in the document.

11. Save and close the document.

chapter 2

Formatting Text and Paragraphs

In this chapter, you will learn the following skills:

❭ Apply fonts and style to text

❭ Copy and paste formatting using the Format Painter

❭ Use bulleted and numbered lists to organize information

❭ Use Quick Styles and text effects to format text

❭ Change paragraph alignment and spacing to effectively use white space

❭ Set and use tabs and indents to improve document layout

Skill **2.1** Using Bold, Italic, and Underline

Skill **2.2** Changing Fonts

Skill **2.3** Changing Font Sizes

Skill **2.4** Changing Text Case

Skill **2.5** Changing Font Colors

Skill **2.6** Applying Highlights

Skill **2.7** Applying Text Effects

Skill **2.8** Using Format Painter

Skill **2.9** Clearing Formatting

Skill **2.10** Creating Bulleted Lists

Skill **2.11** Creating Numbered Lists

Skill **2.12** Using Quick Styles

Skill **2.13** Changing Paragraph Alignment

Skill **2.14** Changing Line Spacing

Skill **2.15** Revealing Formatting Marks

Skill **2.16** Adding Space Before and After Paragraphs

Skill **2.17** Changing Indents

Skill **2.18** Displaying the Ruler

Skill **2.19** Using Tab Stops

skills

introduction

This chapter will cover character and paragraph formatting and alignment to enhance the presentation, professionalism, and readability of documents. Students will apply fonts and styles, incorporate lists, use Quick Styles, change paragraph alignment and spacing, and use tabs and indents.

Skill 2.1 Using Bold, Italic, and Underline

You can call attention to text in your document by using the **bold,** *italic,* or <u>underline</u> effects. These effects are called character effects because they are applied to individual characters or words rather than paragraphs. Remember that these effects are used to emphasize important text and should be used sparingly—they lose their effect if overused.

You can apply these effects using similar steps:

1. Select the text you want to emphasize.

2. On the *Home* tab, in the *Font* group, click the button of the effect you want to apply:

   B **Bold**—gives the text a heavier, thicker appearance.

   I **Italic**—makes text slant to the right.

   <u>U</u> ▾ **Underline**—draws a single line under the text.

Some of the other character effects available from the Ribbon include:

   a̶b̶c̶ **Strikethrough**—draws a horizontal line through the text.

   x₂ **Subscript**—draws a small character below the bottom of the text.

   x² **Superscript**—draws a small character above the top of the text.

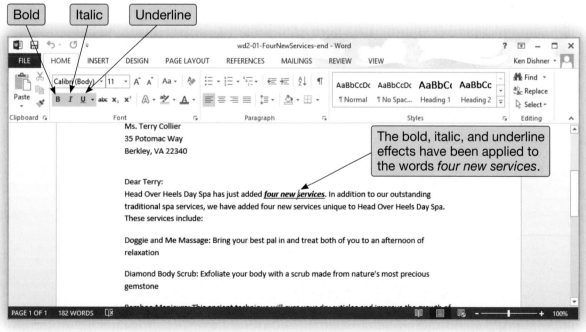

FIGURE WD 2.1

tips & tricks

The *Font* dialog contains other character formatting options not available from the Ribbon. These effects include **Shadow** and **Outline** among others. To open the *Font* dialog, on the *Home* tab, in the *Font* group, click the dialog launcher. Select an option in the *Effects* section and click **OK** to apply the character effect to the text.

tell me **more**

When text is bolded, italicized, or underlined, the button appears highlighted on the Ribbon. To remove the effect, click the highlighted button, or press the appropriate keyboard shortcut.

another **method**

> The following keyboard shortcuts can be used to apply the bold, italic, and underline effects:
>   - Bold = Ctrl + B
>   - Italic = Ctrl + I
>   - Underline = Ctrl + U
>
> To access the bold, italic, or underline commands, you can also right-click the selected text and click the **Bold** or **Italic** button on the Mini toolbar.
>
> To apply an underline style, click the **Underline** button arrow and select a style.

let me **try**

Open the student data file **wd2-01-FourNewServices** and try this skill on your own:

1. Select the text **four new services** in the first paragraph.
2. Apply the **Bold, Italic,** and **Underline** character formatting to the text.
3. Save the file as directed by your instructor and close it.

Skill 2.2 Changing Fonts

A **font**, or typeface, refers to a set of characters of a certain design. The font is the shape of a character or number as it appears on-screen or in a printed document.

To change the font:

1. Select the text to be changed.

2. On the *Home* tab, click the arrow next to the *Font* box.

3. As you roll over the list of fonts, the Live Preview feature in Word changes the look of the text in your document, giving you a preview of how the text will look with the new font applied.

4. Click a font name from the menu to apply it to the text.

Word offers many fonts. **Serif fonts**, such as Cambria and Times New Roman, have an embellishment at the end of each stroke. **Sans serif fonts**, such as Calibri and Arial, do not have an embellishment at the end of each stroke. Sans serif fonts are easier to read on-screen and should be used for the main body text for documents that will be delivered and read electronically, such as a blog. Serif fonts are easier to read on the printed page and should be used for documents that will be printed, such as a report.

> Cambria is a serif font.
> Calibri is a sans serif font.

FIGURE WD 2.2

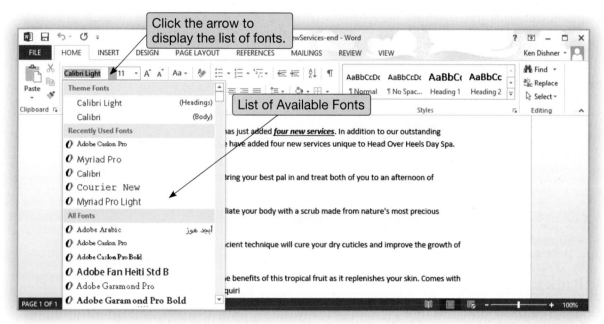

FIGURE WD 2.3

tips & tricks

If you want to change the font of an individual word, you can place your cursor in the word you want to modify, then select the new font.

another method

To change the font you can also right-click the text, click the arrow next to the *Font* box on the Mini toolbar, and select a font from the list.

let me try

Open the student data file **wd2-02-FourNewServices** and try this skill on your own:

1. Select **the address** at the top of the document.
2. Change the font to **Calibri**.
3. Save the file as directed by your instructor and close it.

Skill 2.3 Changing Font Sizes

When creating a document it is important to not only choose the correct font, but also to use the appropriate font size. Fonts are measured in **points**, abbreviated "pt." On the printed page, 72 points equal one inch. Different text sizes are used for paragraphs and headers in a document. Paragraphs typically use 10 pt., 11 pt., and 12 pt. fonts. Headers often use 14 pt., 16 pt., and 18 pt. fonts.

To change the size of the text:

1. Select the text to be changed.

2. On the *Home* tab, in the *Font* group, click the arrow next to the *Font Size* box.

3. Scroll the list to find the new font size.

4. Click the size you want.

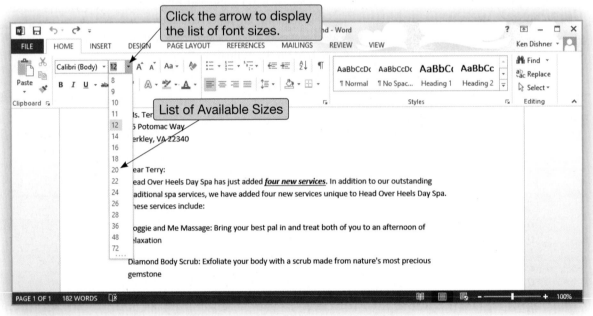

FIGURE WD 2.4

tips & tricks

Sometimes when you are formatting text, you may not be sure of the exact size you want your text to be. You can experiment with the look of text in your document by incrementally increasing and decreasing the size of the font. Use the **Grow Font** A⌃ or **Shrink Font** A⌄ button, available in the *Font* group, to change the font size by one increment.

another method

To change the font you can also right-click the text, click the arrow next to the *Font Size box* on the Mini toolbar, and select a font size from the list.

let me try

Open the student data file **wd2-03-FourNewServices** and try this skill on your own:

1. Select **the date.**

2. Change the font size to **12 pt.**

3. Save the file as directed by your instructor and close it.

Skill 2.4 Changing Text Case

When you type on a keyboard you use the ⟨↑ Shift⟩ key to capitalize individual letters and the ⟨Caps lock⟩ key to type in all capital letters. Another way to change letters from lowercase to uppercase, and vice versa, is to use the *Change Case* command. When you use the **Change Case** command in Word, you are manipulating the characters that were typed, changing how the letters are displayed. There are five types of text case formats you can apply to text:

Sentence case—formats text as a sentence with the first word being capitalized and all remaining words beginning with a lowercase letter.

lowercase—changes all letters to lowercase.

UPPERCASE—changes all letters to uppercase, or capital letters.

Capitalize Each Word—formats text so each word begins with a capital letter.

tOGGLE cASE—formats text in the reverse of the typed format, converting uppercase letters to lowercase and lowercase letters to uppercase.

To apply text case formatting to text:

1. Select the text you want to change.
2. On the *Home* tab, in the *Font* group, click the **Change Case** button.
3. Select a text case option from the menu to apply it to the text.

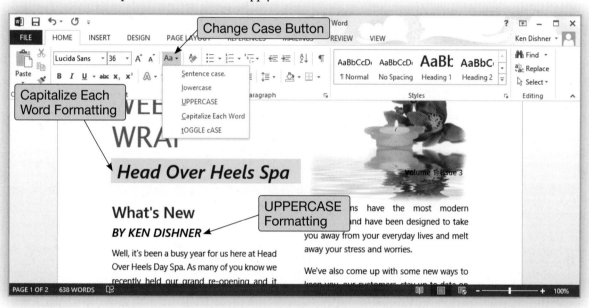

FIGURE WD 2.5

tips & tricks

Headers and titles often use the *Capitalize Each Word* format. One way to ensure that your headers and titles are consistent in text case is to use the *Change Case* command.

tell me **more**

From the *Font* dialog, you can apply the *All caps* or *Small caps* character formatting to text. Although the *All caps* command has the same effect as the *UPPERCASE* case command, *All caps* applies character formatting, while *UPPERCASE* changes the underlying text that was typed.

let me **try**

Open the student data file **wd2-04-SpaNewsletter** and try this skill on your own:

1. Select the **what's new** article title.
2. Use the **Change Case** command to capitalize each word.

3. Select the text **by ken dishner** below the *What's New* article title.
4. Use the **Change Case** command to change the text to all uppercase letters.
5. Save the file as directed by your instructor and close it.

Skill 2.5 Changing Font Colors

In the past, creating black-and-white documents was the standard for most business purposes. This was mostly because printing color documents was cost prohibitive. Today, color printing is more affordable and accessible. Business documents typically include graphics, illustrations, and color text. Adding color to text in your document adds emphasis to certain words and helps design elements, such as headers, stand out for your reader. It is important to be selective when adding color to your document. Using too many colors can often be distracting to the reader.

To change the color of the text:

1. Select the text to be changed.
2. On the *Home* tab, in the *Font* group, click the arrow next to the *Font Color* button.
3. Click the color you want from the color palette.

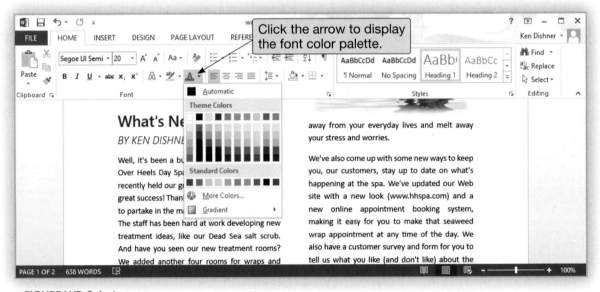

FIGURE WD 2.6

tips & tricks

When you change the color of text, the *Font Color* button changes to the color you selected. Click the **Font Color** button to quickly apply the same color to other text in the document.

tell me **more**

A color theme is a group of predefined colors that works well together in a document. You can apply a color theme to change the color of a number of elements at once. When you change the color theme, the color palette changes and displays only colors that are part of the color theme.

another method

You can change the font color from the Mini toolbar. To display the Mini toolbar, right-click in the text you want to change. Click the arrow next to the *Font Color* button and select the color you want.

let me try

Open the student data file **wd2-05-SpaNewsletter** and try this skill on your own:

1. Select the text **BY KEN DISHNER** below the *What's New* article title.
2. Change the text to the **Dark Blue** standard color.
3. Save the file as directed by your instructor and close it.

Skill 2.6 Applying Highlights

Text in a Word document can be highlighted to emphasize or call attention to it. The effect is similar to that of a highlighting marker. When text is highlighted, the background color of the selected area is changed to make it stand out on the page.

Highlighting is very useful when you are sharing a document with coworkers or reviewers. It calls the other person's attention to elements that most need his or her attention. However, highlighting can sometimes be distracting as well. Be careful when using the highlighter in Word; only use it for small amounts of text.

To highlight text in a document:

1. Select the text to be highlighted.
2. On the *Home* tab, in the *Font* group, click the arrow next to the *Text Highlight Color* button.
3. Click the color you want to use.

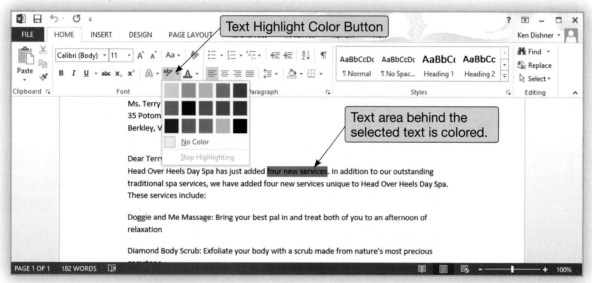

FIGURE WD 2.7

tips & tricks

Be careful when selecting colors to use for highlighting. If both the color of the text and the highlight color are dark, the text will be hard to read. If the highlight color is too light, it may not give the text enough emphasis.

tell me **more**

Rather than applying highlighting to text you have already selected, you can use the highlighter to apply highlighting to text throughout your document. Click the **Text Highlight Color** button without selecting any text first. Your cursor changes to a highlighter shape. Click and drag across text with the highlighter cursor to highlight text. To change your cursor back, click the **Text Highlight Color** button again.

another **method**

You can highlight text from the Mini toolbar. First, select the text you want to highlight; right-click the selected text to display the Mini toolbar. Click the arrow next to the *Text Highlight Color* button and select the color you want.

let me **try**

Open the student data file **wd2-06-FourNewServices** and try this skill on your own:

1. Select the text **four new services** in the first paragraph.
2. Apply the **Pink** highlighting to the text.
3. Save the file as directed by your instructor and close it.

Skill 2.7 Applying Text Effects

Sometimes you will want to draw attention to text you have added to your document. You could format the text using character formatting and changing the font color, or if you want the text to really stand out, use **text effects**. As with other robust text formatting options, be sure to limit the use of text effect to a small amount of text—like a newsletter banner or report title. Overuse of text effects can be distracting to your readers.

Text effects are predefined graphic styles you can apply to text. These styles include a combination of color, outline, shadow, reflection, and glow effects.

To apply text effects:

1. Select the text you want to apply the text effects to.

2. On the *Home* tab, in the *Font* group, click the **Text Effects** button.

3. Select a pre-designed option from the gallery.

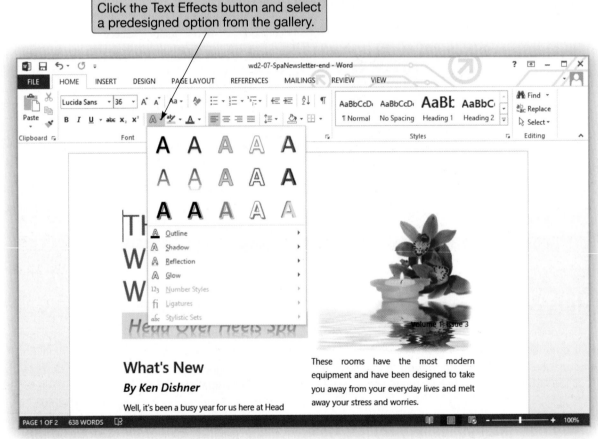

Click the Text Effects button and select a predesigned option from the gallery.

FIGURE WD 2.8

tips & tricks

You can adjust individual effects from the *Text Effects* gallery. Point to a menu item listed below the pre-designed effects in the gallery to display sub-galleries for each effect option. You can then select an option form the sub-gallery to adjust that individual effect. In Word 2013, Microsoft added the ability to control number styles, ligatures, and style sets of text through the *Text Effects* gallery.

tell me **more**

When you add text to a document using the text effects command, it is treated as formatted text. The *WordArt* gallery allows you to add text to a document using the same styles, but when you add WordArt to a document it is treated as a drawing object. Clicking on WordArt in a document will display the *Drawing* contextual tab. Clicking on text with text effects applied will not display the *Drawing* contextual tab.

another **method**

You can also apply text effects through the *Font* dialog:

1. On the *Home* tab, in the *Font* group, click the **Dialog launcher.**
2. In the *Font* dialog, click the **Text Effects...** button.
3. Click the **Text Effects** button at the top of the dialog to select options to apply to text.

let me **try**

Open the student data file **wd2-07-SpaNewsletter** and try this skill on your own:

1. Select the text **Head Over Heels Spa** under the newsletter title *The Weekly Wrap.*
2. Apply the **Gradient Fill–Olive Green, Accent 1, Reflection** text effect to the text. It is the second item in the second row of the gallery.
3. Save the file as directed by your instructor and close it.

Skill 2.8 Using Format Painter

When you want to copy text from one part of your document to another, you use the **Copy** and **Past**e commands. What if you don't want to copy the text but instead copy all the formatting from text in one part of your document to text in another part of your document? The **Format Painter** tool allows you to copy formatting styles that have been applied to text. You can then "paste" the formatting, applying it to text anywhere in the document.

To use *Format Painter:*

1. Select the text that has the formatting you want to copy.
2. On the *Home* tab, in the *Clipboard* group, click the **Format Painter** button.
3. Select the text that you want to apply the formatting to.
4. The formats are automatically applied to the selected text.

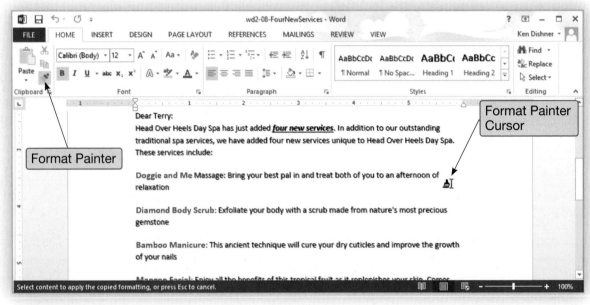

FIGURE WD 2.9

tips & tricks

If the text you are copying the formatting from is formatted using a paragraph *style,* then you don't need to select the entire paragraph. Just place the cursor anywhere in the paragraph and click the **Format Painter** button. To apply the same paragraph style formatting to another paragraph, click anywhere in the paragraph to which you want to apply the formatting.

tell me **more**

If you want to apply the formats more than once, double-click the **Format Painter** button when you select it. It will stay on until you click the **Format Painter** button again or press (Esc) to deselect it.

another **method**

To activate *Format Painter,* you can right-click the text with formatting you want to copy and click the **Format Painter** button on the Mini toolbar.

let me **try**

Open the student data file **wd2-08-FourNew Services** and try this skill on your own:

1. Use the **Format Painter** to copy the formatting of the text **Doggie and me.**
2. Apply the copied formatting to the text **Massage:.**
3. Save the file as directed by your instructor and close it.

word 2013   chapter 2 Formatting Text and Paragraphs

Skill 2.9 Clearing Formatting

After you have applied a number of character formats and effects to text, you may find that you want to return your text to its original formatting. You could perform multiple undo commands on the text, or you could use the *Clear Formatting* command. The **Clear Formatting** command removes any formatting that has been applied to text, including character formatting, text effects, and styles, and leaves only plain text.

To remove formatting from text:

1. Select the text you want to remove the formatting from.
2. On the *Home* tab, in the *Font* group, click the **Clear Formatting** button.

FIGURE WD 2.10

tips & tricks

If you clear the formatting from text and then decide that you want to keep the formatting that was removed, you can use the **Undo** command to apply the previous formatting to the text.

another method

To clear the formatting from text, you can also:

1. On the *Home* tab, in the *Styles* group, click the **More** button.
2. Click **Clear Formatting.**

tell me more

The *Clear Formatting* command does not remove highlighting that has been applied to text. In order to remove highlighting from text, you must click the **Text Highlighting Color** button and select **No Color.**

let me try

Open the student data file **wd2-09-SpaNewsletter** and try this skill on your own:

1. Select the text **By Ken Dishner** below the *What's New* article title.
2. Clear the formatting from the text.
3. Save the file as directed by your instructor and close it.

Skill 2.10 Creating Bulleted Lists

When typing a document you may want to include information that is best displayed in list format rather than paragraph format. If your list does not include items that need to be displayed in a specific order, use a bulleted list to help information stand out from surrounding text. A bullet is a symbol that is displayed before each item in a list. When a bullet appears before a list item, it indicates that the items in the list do not have a particular order to them.

To create a bulleted list:

1. Select the text you want to change to a bulleted list. In order to appear as separate items within a bulleted list, each item must be followed by a hard return (press ⏎ Enter).

2. On the *Home* tab, in the *Paragraph* group, click the **Bullets** button.

3. Click outside the list to deselect it.

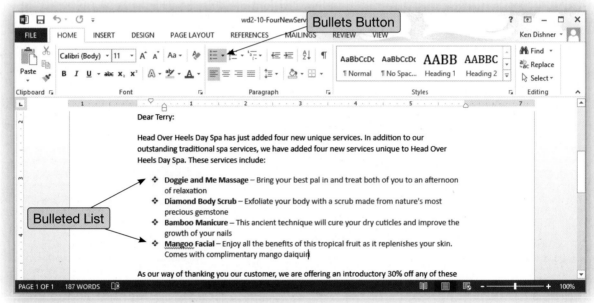

FIGURE WD 2.11

tips & tricks

> Sometimes you will want to add more items to an existing list. Place your cursor at the end of a list item and press ⏎ Enter to start a new line. A bullet will automatically appear before the list item.

> You can turn off the **Bullets** formatting feature by pressing ⏎ Enter twice.

tell me **more**

To change the bullet type, click the **Bullets** button arrow and select an option from the *Bullet Library*. You can create new bullets by selecting **Define New Bullet...**

another **method**

You can start a bulleted list by:

> Typing an asterisk, a space, and your list item, then pressing the ⏎ Enter key.

You can convert text to a bulleted list by right-clicking the selected text, pointing to **Bullets,** and selecting an option.

let me **try**

Open the student data file **wd2-10-FourNew Services** and try this skill on your own:

1. Select the text for the **four new services** in the letter.

2. Apply the **four diamond** bullet style to the text.

3. Save the file as directed by your instructor and close it.

Skill 2.11 Creating Numbered Lists

Some lists, such as directions to complete a task, need to have the items displayed in a specific order. **Numbered lists** display a number next to each list item and display the numbers in order. Numbered lists help you organize your content and display it in a clear, easy-to-understand manner.

To create a numbered list:

1. Select the text you want to change to a numbered list. As with bulleted lists, in order to appear as separate items within a numbered list, each item must be followed by a hard return (press `← Enter`).

2. Click outside the list to deselect it.

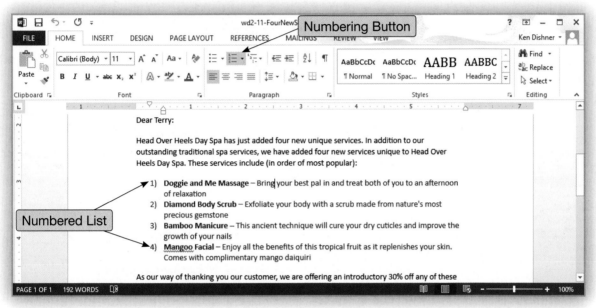

FIGURE WD 2.12

tips & tricks

> Sometimes you will want to add more items to an existing list. To add another item to the list, place your cursor at the end of an item and press `← Enter` to start a new line. The list will renumber itself to accommodate the new item.

> You can turn off the numbering feature by pressing `← Enter` twice.

tell me more

To change the numbering list type, click the **Numbering** button arrow and select an option from the *Numbering Library*. You can create new numbered list styles by selecting **Define New Number Format...**

another method

You can start a numbered list by:

> Typing a 1, a space, and your list item, then pressing the `← Enter` key.

> Clicking the **Numbering** button, typing your list item, then pressing the `← Enter` key.

You can convert text to a numbered list by right-clicking the selected text, pointing to **Numbering,** and selecting an option.

let me try

Open the student data file **wd2-11-FourNewServices** and try this skill on your own:

1. Select the text for the four new services in the letter.

2. Apply the **1), 2), 3)** number style to the text.

3. Save the file as directed by your instructor and close it.

Skill 2.12 Using Quick Styles

A **Quick Style** is a group of formatting, including character and paragraph formatting, that you can easily apply to text in your document. Quick Styles can be applied to body text, headers, quotes, or just about any type of text you may have in your document.

It is a good idea to use Quick Styles to format text in your documents. When you use Quick Styles to format text, you can quickly change the look of that style across your document by changing the document's theme. Certain Quick Styles, such as headings, are also used by other features in Word, such as creating a table of contents and the Navigation task pane.

To apply a Quick Style to text:

1. Select the text you want to change.
2. On the *Home* tab, in the *Styles* group, click the **More** button .
3. Select a **Quick Style** from the *Quick Styles* gallery.

Click the More button to expand the gallery and view more Quick Styles.

Click a Quick Style to apply it to text.

FIGURE WD 2.13

word 2013 chapter 2 Formatting Text and Paragraphs

tips & tricks

If you modify a Quick Style, you can save the style with a new name and then use it throughout your document. To save a new text Quick Style, open the *Quick Styles* gallery and select **Save Selection as a New Quick Style...**

tell me **more**

When you select a new Quick Style, it replaces the style for the text. If you want to clear all the formatting for text, open the *Quick Styles* gallery and select **Clear Formatting.**

another **method**

The *Styles* group on the *Home* tab displays the latest Quick Styles you have used. If you want to apply a recently used Quick Style, you can click the option directly from the Ribbon without opening the *Quick Styles* gallery.

let me **try**

Open the student data file **wd2-12-SpaNewsletter** and try this skill on your own:

1. Select the **What's New** article title.
2. Apply the **Heading 1** Quick Style to the text.
3. Save the file as directed by your instructor and close it.

from the perspective of . . .

COLLEGE GRADUATE

When creating my résumé to send out to potential employers, I always make sure I use the right combination of fonts and styles to create the most eye-catching and professional document. I use tab stops and indents to align text just the way I want it and add space before and after paragraphs to control the layout on the page. I learned my lesson with the first résumé I sent out. Apparently, using a different color font for each section and applying an "eye popping" text effect to my name was not the way to land an interview at the firm I applied to.

Skill 2.13 Changing Paragraph Alignment

Paragraph alignment refers to how text is aligned with regard to the left and right margins.

> **Left alignment** aligns the text on the left side, leaving the right side ragged.
> **Center alignment** centers each line of text relative to the margins.
> **Right alignment** aligns the text on the right side, leaving the left side ragged.
> **Justified alignment** evenly spaces the words, aligning the text on the right and left sides of the printed page.

It is important to understand common uses of different alignments. Paragraph text and headers are typically left aligned, but titles are often centered. Newspaper columns are often justified, and columns of numbers are typically right aligned.

To change the alignment of text:

1. Click in the paragraph you want to change.
2. On the *Home* tab, in the *Paragraph* group, click an alignment button—**Align Text Left, Center, Align Text Right,** or **Justify.**

FIGURE WD 2.14

another method

The following keyboard shortcuts can be used to apply horizontal alignment:

- Align Left = Ctrl + L
- Center = Ctrl + E
- Align Right = Ctrl + R
- Justify = Ctrl + J

let me try

Open the student data file **wd2-13-SpaNewsletter** and try this skill on your own:

1. Select **all the text** in the *What's New* article. The article includes three paragraphs of text.
2. Change the paragraph text so it is **justified.**
3. Save the file as directed by your instructor and close it.

Skill 2.14 Changing Line Spacing

Line spacing is the white space between lines of text. The default line spacing in Microsoft Word 2013 is 1.08 spacing. This gives each line the height of single spacing with a little extra space at the top and bottom. This line spacing is a good choice to use for the body of a document. Other commonly used spacing options include single spacing, double spacing, and 1.5 spacing.

To change line spacing:

1. Select the text you want to change.
2. On the *Home* tab, in the *Paragraph* group, click the **Line Spacing** button.
3. Select the number of the spacing you want.

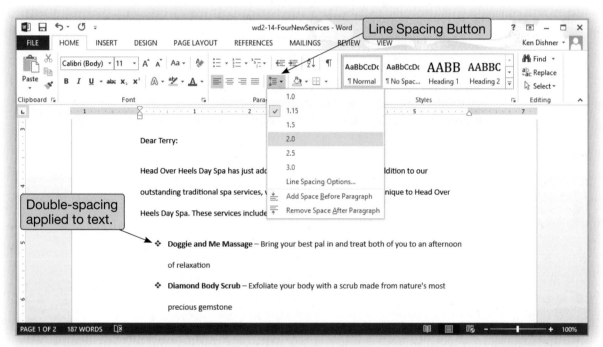

FIGURE WD 2.15

tell me **more**

In Word 2007, Microsoft changed the default line spacing from single space to 1.15 lines. In Word 2013, this default has been changed to 1.08 lines. This new default line spacing is designed to help with readability of online documents on a number of devices, including traditional desktop and laptop computers, tablets, and smart phones.

another **method**

▶ To apply single spacing, you can also press Ctrl + 1 on the keyboard.

▶ To apply double spacing, you can also press Ctrl + 2 on the keyboard.

let me **try**

Open the student data file **wd2-14-FourNewServices** and try this skill on your own:

1. Press Ctrl + A on the keyboard to select **all the text** in the document.
2. Change the line spacing from double spaced to **1.15 spacing.**
3. Save the file as directed by your instructor and close it.

Skill 2.15 Revealing Formatting Marks

When creating a document it is important to use consistent formatting, such as a single space after the period at the end of a sentence. As you create a document, Word adds **formatting marks** that are hidden from view. For example, a paragraph mark, ¶, is created every time the ⌨ Enter key is pressed. When creating professional documents, it is considered bad practice to use extra line breaks to add space between paragraphs in a document. By displaying formatting marks, you can quickly see where these extra line breaks occur in your documents and then easily delete them.

To display formatting marks in a document:

1. On the *Home* tab, in the *Paragraph* group, click the **Show/Hide** button.
2. The formatting marks are displayed in the document.
3. Click the **Show/Hide** button again to hide the formatting marks. Formatting marks include symbols that represent spaces, nonbreaking spaces, tabs, and paragraphs. Table 2.1 shows examples of formatting marks.

TABLE WD 2.1 Formatting Marks

CHARACTER	FORMATTING MARK
Space	.
Nonbreaking Space	o
Tab	→
Paragraph	¶

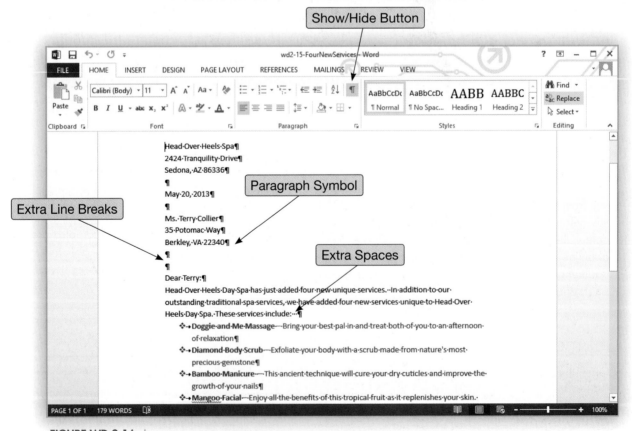

FIGURE WD 2.16

word 2013   chapter 2 Formatting Text and Paragraphs

tips & tricks

You can choose to always show specific formatting marks on-screen even when the **Show/Hide** button is inactive. To show specific formatting marks:

1. Click the **File** tab and select **Options.**
2. In the *Word Options* dialog, click the **Display** category.
3. Select the formatting marks you want to display in the *Always show these formatting marks on the screen* section.
4. Click **OK.**

tell me **more**

❱ Formatting marks appear on-screen, but they do not appear in the printed document.

❱ A nonbreaking space is a space between two words that keeps the words together and prevents the words from being split across two lines.

another **method**

To show formatting marks, you can press Ctrl + ↑ Shift + 8 .

let me **try**

Open the student data file **wd2-15-FourNewServices** and try this skill on your own:

1. Show the formatting marks in the document.
2. Remove any extra blank lines in the document.
3. There should only be one space after a period and no spaces after punctuation at the end of a line. Remove the extra spaces from the document.
4. Hide the formatting marks.
5. Save the file as directed by your instructor and close it.

Skill 2.16 Adding Space Before and After Paragraphs

The default spacing after paragraphs in Word is 8 pt. This setting results in a very evenly spaced document, with some space between paragraphs to set them apart. To help differentiate between paragraphs even more, you can add space before a paragraph. If you want to tighten up a document, you can remove space after the paragraph.

To increase the space before a paragraph and to decrease the space after a paragraph:

1. Click in the paragraph you want to change.

2. On the *Home* tab, in the *Paragraph* group, click the **Line Spacing** button.

3. Choose one of the following options:

> ❯ Click **Add Space Before Paragraph** to add space above the first line of the paragraph.

> ❯ Click **Remove Space After Paragraph** to remove space from below the last line of the paragraph.

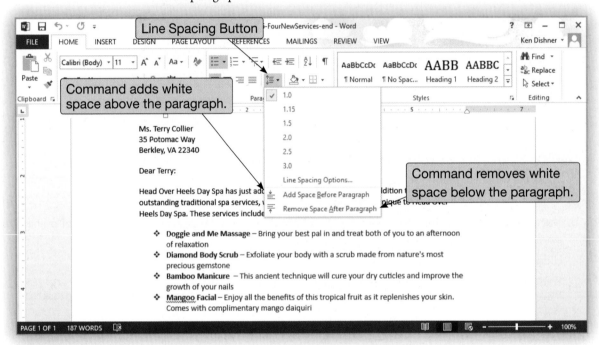

FIGURE WD 2.17

tips & tricks

After you have added space before a paragraph, the command on the menu changes to *Remove Space Before Paragraph* so you can easily remove the space you added. Similarly, when you remove space after a paragraph, the command changes to **Add Space After Paragraph** to add back in the space you removed.

tell me **more**

Many of the Quick Styles available in the *Styles* group on the *Home* tab include spacing before and after paragraphs. Use Quick Styles to add text that includes text and paragraph formatting.

let me try

Open the student data file **wd2-16-FourNewServices** and try this skill on your own:

1. Add space before the **first paragraph in the letter.**

2. Save the file as directed by your instructor and close it.

Skill 2.17 Changing Indents

When you create a document, the margins control how close the text comes to the edge of a page. But what if you don't want all your paragraphs to line up? Indenting paragraphs increases the left margin for a paragraph, helping it stand out from the rest of your document.

To change the indentation of a paragraph:

1. Place the cursor anywhere in the paragraph you want to change.
2. To increase the indent of the paragraph by one level, on the *Home* tab, in the *Paragraph* group, click the **Increase Indent** button.
3. To reduce the indent of the paragraph and bring it closer to the edge of the page by one level, click the **Decrease Indent** button.

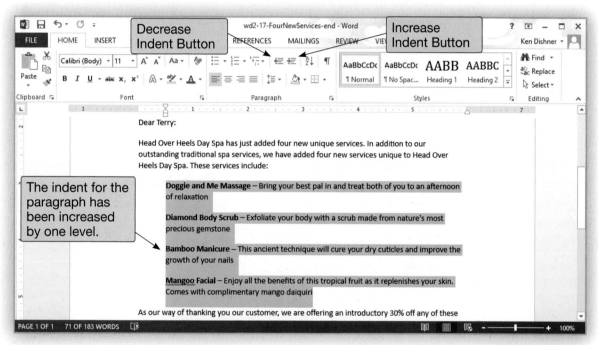

FIGURE WD 2.18

tell me **more**

The *Indent* commands indent all lines in a paragraph the same amount. If you want only the first line of a paragraph to be indented and the remainder of the paragraph to be left-aligned, use a **First Line Indent.** If you want the first line of a paragraph to be left-aligned and the remainder of the paragraph to be indented, use a **Hanging Indent.** In the *Format Paragraph* dialog, you can precisely set options for first line indents and hanging indents. To open the *Format Paragraph* dialog, click the **Dialog Launcher** in the *Paragraph* group on the *Home* tab or in the *Paragraph* group on the *Page Layout* tab.

tips & tricks

You can increase indents by one increment (one tenth of an inch) rather than by one level:

1. Click the **Page Layout** tab.
2. In the *Paragraph* group, click the arrows next to *Left* and *Right* to move paragraphs by one increment for each click.

let me try

Open the student data file **wd2-17-FourNew Services** and try this skill on your own:

1. Select the text for the **four new services** in the letter.
2. Increase the indent for the text by one level.
3. Save the file as directed by your instructor and close it.

Skill 2.18 Displaying the Ruler

When working with documents, it is helpful to display the **ruler**. The ruler displays horizontally across the top of the window just below the Ribbon and vertically along the left side of the window. The ruler gives you a quick view of the margins and position of elements in your document. From the ruler you can also control other document layout controls such as tabs, first line indents, and hanging indents.

To display the ruler:

1. Click the **View** tab.
2. In the *Show* group, click the check box next to **Ruler** so a checkmark appears.
3. To hide the ruler, click the check box again so the checkmark disappears.

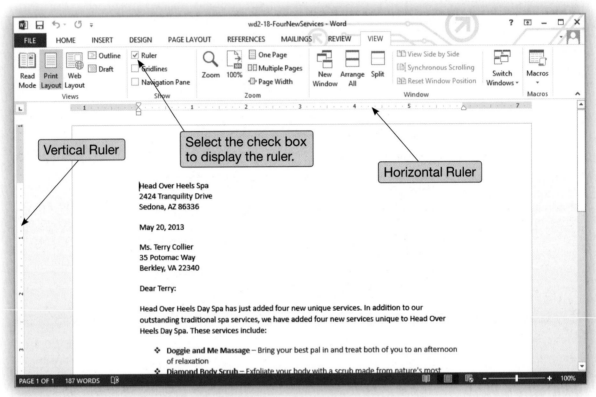

FIGURE WD 2.19

tips & tricks

Double-click the ruler to open the *Page Setup* dialog where you can control page layout elements such as margins and page orientation.

tell me **more**

Gridlines are a series of vertical and horizontal lines that divide the page into small boxes, giving you visual markers for aligning graphics, tables, and other elements on the page.

let me try

Open the student data file **wd2-18-FourNewServices** and try this skill on your own:

1. Show the ruler and then hide the ruler again.
2. Close the file.

word 2013   chapter 2 Formatting Text and Paragraphs

Skill 2.19 Using Tab Stops

A **tab stop** is a location along the horizontal ruler that indicates how far to indent text when the Tab key is pressed.

There are five types of tab stops:

Left—Displays text to the right of the tab stop

Center—Displays text centered over the tab stop

Right—Displays the text to the left of the tab stop

Decimal—Aligns the text along the decimal point

Bar—Displays a vertical line through the text at the tab stop

To set a tab stop:

1. Select the paragraph in which you want to set a tab stop.
2. Click the **tab selector** at the far left of the horizontal ruler until it changes to the type of tab you want.
3. Click the horizontal ruler where you want to set a tab stop.

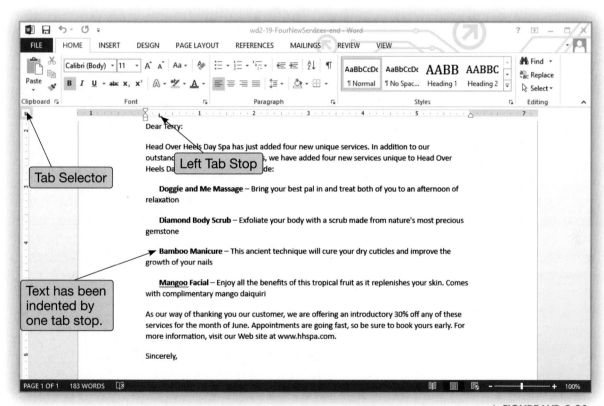

FIGURE WD 2.20

tips & tricks

To clear a tab stop:
Drag the tab marker down from the horizontal ruler to remove it.

To move a tab stop:
Drag the tab marker to the right or left along the horizontal ruler to its new position.

tell me **more**

The tab selector also includes two options for adding indents to your document. The **First Line Indent** controls where the first line of a paragraph begins. The **Hanging Indent** controls where the remainder of the paragraph is indented.

another **method**

You can set tab stops in the *Tabs* dialog:

1. Double-click the ruler to open the *Tabs* dialog.
2. In the *Tab stop position:* box, type the number of where you want the tab stop to appear.
3. Click a radio button in the *Alignment* section.
4. Click **OK.**

let me **try**

Open the student data file **wd2-19-FourNewServices** and try this skill on your own:

1. Select the text for the **four new services** in the letter.
2. Add a **left tab stop** at the **.25" mark** on the ruler.
3. Use the (Tab ⇄) key to indent each of the following by one tab stop: **Doggie and Me Massage:, Diamond Body Scrub, Bamboo Manicure,** and **Mangoo Facial.**
4. Save the file as directed by your instructor and close it.

Bold
Italic
Underline
Font
Serif fonts
Sans serif fonts
Points
Change Case command
Highlighting
Text effects

Format Painter
Bullet
Numbered list
Quick Style
Paragraph alignment
Line spacing
Formatting marks
Ruler
Tab stop

concept review

1. A _____ font has an embellishment at the end of each stroke to lead the eye from one character to the next.

   a. sans serif

   b. serif

   c. theme

   d. heading

2. Use the _____ command to copy the styles from one word to another.

   a. text effects

   b. styles

   c. Format painter

   d. Text Highlighting Color

3. _____ tab stops display the text to the left of the tab stop.

   a. Left

   b. Right

   c. Center

   d. Decimal

4. Use the _____ command to change text from uppercase to having each word capitalized.

   a. Change Font

   b. Grow Font

   c. Shrink Font

   d. Change Case

5. To evenly space words, aligning the text on the right and left sides of the printed page use the _____ command.

   a. Align Left

   b. Center

   c. Align Right

   d. Justify

6. To display a list of items that do not need to be in a certain order, use a _____.
   a. bulleted list
   b. numbered list
   c. multilevel list
   d. justified list

7. Use _____ to ensure parts of your document, such as headings, all use the same formatting.
   a. Quick Styles
   b. Text Effects
   c. Font Styles
   d. Character Styles

8. The _____ command displays hidden formatting marks in a document, including paragraph and space marks.
   a. Clear Formatting
   b. Styles
   c. Format Painter
   d. Show/Hide

9. To call attention to text by coloring the background behind the text, use the _____ command.
   a. Font Color
   b. Text Highlight Color
   c. Text Effects
   d. Styles

10. Use _____ to apply combinations of shadows, outlines, and glows to text with one command.
    a. Font Color
    b. text Highlighting Color
    c. Text Effects
    d. character effects

projects

skill review 2.1

In this project you will be editing the **WD2013-SkillReview-2-1** document from Suarez Marketing.

Skills needed to complete this project:
- Clearing Formatting (Skill 2.9)
- Changing Fonts (Skill 2.2)
- Changing Font Sizes (Skill 2.3)
- Changing Line Spacing (Skill 2.14)
- Revealing Formatting Marks (Skill 2.15)
- Using Quick Styles (Skill 2.12)
- Adding Space Before and After Paragraphs (Skill 2.16)
- Using Bold, Italic, and Underline (Skill 2.1)
- Changing Font Colors (Skill 2.5)
- Using Format Painter (Skill 2.8)
- Apply Text Effects (Skill 2.7)
- Creating Numbered Lists (Skill 2.11)
- Changing Indents (Skill 2.17)
- Creating Bulleted Lists (Skill 2.10)
- Changing Paragraph Alignment (Skill 2.13)

1. Open the **WD2013-SkillReview-2-1** document.
2. Save this document as: **[your initials]WD-SkillReview-2-1**
3. Clear the formatting on text.
   a. Select the **first two lines of text** in the document.
   b. On the *Home* tab, in the *Font* group, click the **Clear Formatting** button.
4. Change the font and size on **all of the text** in the body of the document.
   a. Press Ctrl + A to select **all text** in the body of the brochure.
   b. On the *Home* tab, in the *Font* group, click the arrow next to the *Font* box.
   c. Choose **Calibri** as the font to use on the selected text.
   d. In the *Font* group, click the arrow next to the **Font Size** box.
   e. Choose **11** as the font size.
5. Change the line spacing for each paragraph.
   a. With the entire document still selected, in the *Paragraph* group, click the **Line and Paragraph Spacing** button.
   b. Click **1.15** to change the line spacing.
6. On the *Home* tab, in the *Paragraph* group, click the **Show/ Hide** button to reveal formatting marks in the document.

7. Delete all of the extra blank lines between paragraphs in the document. Click the **Show/Hide** button again to hide the formatting marks.

8. Use Quick Styles to apply a heading format to a section heading in the document.

   a. Select the **Mission Statement** heading on the first page.

   b. On the *Home* tab, in the *Styles* group, click the **Heading 1** style. The Heading 1 style is applied to the selected section heading.

   c. Apply the *Heading 1* style to the following lines of text:
   - **Experience**
   - **Why I Do What I Do**
   - **What Clients are Saying**
   - **Professional Credentials**
   - **Education & Training**
   - **The Suarez Marketing Belief System**

9. Change the spacing before paragraph on the selected heading.

   a. Select the **Mission Statement** heading on the first page.

   b. Click the **Line and Paragraph Spacing** button.

   c. Select the **Remove Space Before Paragraph** option.

   d. Use this method to remove space before all the headings in the brochure.

10. Change the character formatting, font, and color of text.

   a. Select the text **Maria Suarez** at the top of the document.

   b. On the *Home* tab, in the *Font* group, click the **Bold** button.

   c. In the *Font* group, click the arrow next to the **Font** box and select **Cambria.**

   d. In the *Font* group, click the **Font Color** button and select **Blue-Gray, Text 2** (it is the fourth color in the first row under *Theme Colors*).

11. Use the **Format Painter** to change the format of text.

   a. With the text **Maria Suarez** still selected, on the *Home* tab, in the *Clipboard* group, click the **Format Painter** button.

   b. Select the text **Suarez Marketing** to apply the copied formatting.

12. Apply text effects to text.

   a. Select the tag line **"Putting Your Needs First"**

   b. On the *Home* tab, in the *Font* group, click the **Text Effects** button.

   c. Select the **Fill–Blue, Accent 1, Shadow** effect (it is the second option in the first row of the gallery).

13. Add a numbered list to and decrease the indent on a section of the brochure.

   a. In the *Why I Do What I Do* section, select all of the text.

   b. On the *Home* tab, in the *Paragraph* group, click the **Numbering** button. Numbering is applied to this section and it is indented.

   c. Click the **Decrease Indent** button once to change the left indent to 0".

14. Add a bulleted list to and decrease the indent on a section of the brochure.

   a. In the *The Suarez Marketing Belief System* section, select all of the text.

   b. On the *Home* tab, in the *Paragraph* group, click the **Bullets** button. Bullets are applied to this section and it is indented.

   c. Click the **Decrease Indent** button once to change the left indent to 0".

15. Apply a Quick Style to and change the paragraph alignment on selected text.

    a. In the *What Clients Are Saying* section, select **the first quote and include the quotation marks.**

    b. On the *Home* tab, in the *Styles* group, apply the **Quote** style. You will have to click the **More** button to locate this style.

    c. Use the **Format Painter** to apply this format to the **second quote in this section.**

    d. Select–**Allison Palmer, Creve Couer, MO.**

    e. On the *Home* tab, in the *Paragraph* group, click the **Align Right** button.

    f. Select and right align–**Scott Morris and Associates, St. Louis, MO.**

16. Save and close the document.

skill review 2.2

In this project you will be editing the **WD2013-SkillReview-2-2** document from Tri-State Book Festival.

Skills needed to complete this project:

- Changing Fonts (Skill 2.2)
- Changing Font Sizes (Skill 2.3)
- Changing Line Spacing (Skill 2.14)
- Revealing Formatting Marks (Skill 2.15)
- Using Quick Styles (Skill 2.12)
- Applying Highlights (Skill 2.6)
- Changing Font Colors (Skill 2.5)
- Changing Paragraph Alignment (Skill 2.13)
- Creating Bulleted Lists (Skill 2.10)
- Using Bold, Italic, and Underline (Skill 2.1)
- Using Format Painter (Skill 2.8)
- Displaying the Ruler (Skill 2.18)
- Using Tab Stops (Skill 2.19)
- Changing Indents (Skill 2.17)
- Changing Text Case (Skill 2.4)

1. Open the **WD2013-SkillReview-2-2** document.

2. Save this document as: **[your initials]WD-SkillReview-2-2**

3. Change font, font size, and line spacing on the entire document.

    a. Press **Ctrl + A** to select the entire document.

    b. On the *Home* tab, in the *Font* group, click the arrow next to the **Font** box.

    c. Choose **Arial** as the font to use on the selected text.

    d. In the *Font* group, click the arrow next to the **Font Size** box.

    e. Choose **11** as the font size.

    f. In the *Paragraph* group, change the line spacing to **2.0.**

4. On the *Home* tab, in the *Paragraph* group, click the **Show/Hide** button to reveal formatting marks in the document.

5. Delete all of the extra blank lines between paragraphs in the document. Click the **Show/Hide** button again to hide the formatting marks.

6. Apply a style to text and change paragraph alignment.

   a. Select the text **Tri-State Book Festival** at the top of the document.

   b. On the *Home* tab, in the *Styles* group, select the **Title** style. You might have to click the **More** button to locate this style.

   c. In the *Paragraph* group, click the **Center** button to center align the text on the page.

7. Apply highlighting to text.

   a. In the second paragraph, select the text **Tuesday, August 23.**

   b. On the *Home* tab, in the *Font* group, click the **Text Highlight Color** button. Select the **Yellow** option.

8. Change the color of text.

   a. Select the line of text that reads **Fiction Writers Association of the Tri-State Region.**

   b. On the *Home* tab, in the *Font* group, click the **Font Color** arrow.

   c. Select the **Dark Blue** option under *Standard Colors.*

9. Add bullets and apply character formatting to selected lines of text.

   a. Select the **five lines of text** under *Agency Name:.*

   b. On the *Home* tab, in the *Paragraph* group, click the **Bullets** button arrow.

   c. Select the **open circle bullet.**

   d. On the *Home* tab, in the *Font* group, click the **Bold** button.

10. Use Format Painter to copy and paste styles.

    a. With the bulleted list you just created still selected, on the *Home* tab, in the *Clipboard* group, double-click the **Format Painter** button.

    b. Apply the styles to the following lines:

       - **Non-smoking**
       - **Smoking**
       - **King**
       - **Two Doubles**
       - **Flying: Arrival time:** _____
       - **Driving**
       - **Yes, I would like to participate in the cooking demonstration.**
       - **No, I will not be participating in the cooking demonstration.**

11. Set a tab stop and use the tab to indent lines of text.

    a. If the ruler is not displayed, click the **View** tab. In the *Show* group, click the **Ruler** check box so a checkmark appears in the box.

    b. Place the cursor at the beginning of the line **I need a shuttle to Westfield Hotel & Spa from the airport.**

    c. Add a left tab stop at **1.25″.**

    d. Press the ⟨Tab ⇆⟩ key on the keyboard.

    e. Apply the same tab to the line that reads **I need directions to Westfield Hotel & Spa from:.** _____

12. Apply bullets and indents to text.

    a. Place the cursor at the beginning of the line **I need a shuttle to Westfield Hotel & Spa from the airport.**

    b. On the *Home* tab, in the *Paragraph* group, click the **Bullets** button arrow.

    c. Select the **open circle** option.

    d. In the *Paragraph* group, click the **Decrease Indent** button.

    e. Apply the same bullet style to the text **I need directions to Westfield Hotel & Spa from:. _____**

13. Change font case text.

    a. Select the line of text that reads **Fax or E-Mail This Form to.**

    b. On the *Home* tab, in the *Font* group, click the **Change Case** button and select **UPPERCASE.**

14. Save and close the document.

challenge yourself **2.3**

In this project you will be editing the **WD2013-ChallengeYourself-2-3** document from Spring Hills Community.

Skills needed to complete this project:

- Using Bold, Italic, and Underline (Skill 2.1)
- Changing Fonts (Skill 2.2)
- Changing Font Sizes (Skill 2.3)
- Changing Line Spacing (Skill 2.14)
- Revealing Formatting Marks (Skill 2.15)
- Changing Text Case (Skill 2.4)
- Using Quick Styles (Skill 2.12)
- Changing Paragraph Alignment (Skill 2.13)
- Using Format Painter (Skill 2.8)
- Adding Space Before and After Paragraphs (Skill 2.16)
- Creating Bulleted Lists (Skill 2.10)
- Changing Indents (Skill 2.17)
- Creating Numbered Lists (Skill 2.11)

1. Open the **WD2013-ChallengeYourself-2-3** document.

2. Save this document as: **[your initials]WD-Challenge-2-3**

3. Change font, font size, line spacing, and paragraph spacing on entire document.

    a. Select all the text in the document.

    b. Change the font to **Calibri** and the size to **11 pt.**

    c. Change the line spacing to **1.15 spacing.**

4. Display the paragraph marks for the document and delete all of the extra blank lines between paragraphs in the document. When you are finished, hide the paragraph marks.

5. Customize the title of the document.

   a. Apply the **Document Heading** style to the title of the document.

   b. Change the font size to **18 pt.**

   c. **Center** the title.

6. Customize the first section heading in the document (*Tips for staying safe*).

   a. Apply the **Document Section** style to the text.

7. Use the **Format Painter** to apply the formatting of the first section heading to the other two section headings in the document.

8. Use the **Add Space Before Paragraph** command to add space above each section heading in the document.

9. Change the case of all the section headings to **Capitalize Each Word.**

10. Apply character formatting.

    a. Select the text **basic safety strategy** in the first paragraph.

    b. Bold and italicize the text.

11. Convert the text in the **Basic Tips For Staying Safe** section to a bulleted list.

    a. Select all the lines in this section.

    b. Apply the **closed circle bullet** style.

    c. Decrease the indent of the bulleted list so the bullets are at the left margin.

12. Convert the text in the **What Electronics Are Being Targeted** section to a numbered list.

    a. Select all the five targeted electronic items in this section.

    b. Apply the **1.,2.,3.** number format to the text.

13. Save and close the document.

challenge yourself 2.4

In this project you will be editing the **WD2013-ChallengeYourself-2-4** document from Fairlawn Community College.

Skills needed to complete this project:

- Changing Fonts (Skill 2.2)
- Changing Font Sizes (Skill 2.3)
- Changing Line Spacing (Skill 2.14)
- Revealing Formatting Marks (Skill 2.15)
- Applying Text Effects (Skill 2.7)
- Using Bold, Italic, and Underline (Skill 2.1)
- Changing Font Colors (Skill 2.5)
- Clearing Formatting (Skill 2.9)
- Using Quick Styles (Skill 2.12)
- Using Format Painter (Skill 2.8)
- Displaying the Ruler (Skill 2.18)
- Using Tab Stops (Skill 2.19)
- Creating Bulleted Lists (Skill 2.10)

1. Open the **WD2013-ChallengeYourself-2-4** document.

2. Save this document as: **[your initials]WD-Challenge-2-4**

3. Change the font on the entire document to **Calibri** and **12 pt**.

4. Change the line spacing for the entire document to **1.5** line spacing.

5. Display the paragraph marks for the document.

   a. Delete all of the extra blank lines between paragraphs in the document.

   b. There should only be one space between sentences and no spaces after a period in the last sentence in a paragraph. Fix all the spacing issues in the document.

   c. When you are finished, hide the paragraph marks.

6. Apply text effects to the title of the document and change the size of the text.

   a. Select the text **Fairlawn Community College Social Software Strategic Initiative** at the top of the document.

   b. Apply the **Fill–Blue, Accent 1, Shadow** text effect to the text. It is the second option in the first row of the gallery.

   c. Change the text size to **18 pt**.

7. Underline, change the color, and clear formatting from text.

   a. Select the first heading section (**Strategic Goal: Student Success**) in the document.

   b. Underline the text.

   c. Change the color of the text to **Blue-Gray–Text 2**.

   d. Clear the formatting from the text.

8. Customize the section headings of the document.

   a. Apply the **Heading 2** Quick Style to the first section heading (**Strategic Goal: Student Success**) in the document.

   b. Use the **Format Painter** to apply this formatting to the remaining headings in the document (**Initiative: Collaboration using Social Software:, Background:, Scope:, Deliverables:, Benefits:, Risks:, and Timeline:**).

9. Set tab stops in the document.

   a. Display the ruler.

   b. Select all the text in the document.

   c. Set a left tab stop at the **.25″** mark.

   d. Using the (Tab ⇆) key, indent the first paragraph under each section to the **.25″** tab stop.

10. Convert text to a bulleted list.

    a. Select the list items in the **Background** section (**Our basic Blog, Wiki, Discussion Board tools**).

    b. Apply the **open circle bullet** style to the list.

11. Save and close the document.

on your own 2.5

In this project you will be editing the **WD2013-OnYourOwn-2-5** document from Penn-mark Management Company.

Skills needed to complete this project:

- Clearing Formatting (Skill 2.9)
- Changing Fonts (Skill 2.2)
- Changing Font Sizes (Skill 2.3)
- Changing Line Spacing (Skill 2.14)
- Displaying the Ruler (Skill 2.18)
- Using Tab Stops (Skill 2.19)
- Revealing Formatting Marks (Skill 2.15)
- Using Quick Styles (Skill 2.12)
- Changing Text Case (Skill 2.4)
- Changing Paragraph Alignment (Skill 2.13)
- Applying Highlights (Skill 2.6)
- Using Bold, Italic, and Underline (Skill 2.1)
- Using Format Painter (Skill 2.8)
- Adding Space Before and After Paragraphs (Skill 2.16)
- Creating Numbered Lists (Skill 2.11)

1. Open the **WD2013-OnYourOwn-2-5** document.
2. Save this document as: **[your initials]WD-OnYourOwn-2-5**
3. Select the entire document and make the following formatting changes:
   a. Clear all formatting.
   b. Change the font to **Arial** and **11 pt.**
   c. Change the line spacing to **1.15** spacing.
   d. Set a left tab at **3.5″.**
4. Delete all extra blank lines in the document.
5. Select the first line of the document and make the following changes:
   a. Apply the **Heading 1** style.
   b. Change the case to **UPPERCASE.**
   c. Right-align the heading.
6. Select the next line of the document (**Contractor's Questionnaire**) and apply the **Heading 2** style.
7. In the next line of the document, apply a highlight of your choice to the text **Please read carefully.**
8. Select the *Contractor's Information* line in the document. Bold and italicize the text. Change the font color to **Blue–Gray, Text 2.**
9. Apply the formatting from **Contractor's Information** heading to the following lines (the last three lines in the document): **Signature of Applicant, Company,** and **Date of Application.**
10. Add space before each of the following lines: **Signature of Applicant, Company,** and **Date of Application.**

11. Press (Tab ⇆) to move the last three lines of text to the **3.5″** tab stop.

12. Select the items under *Contractor's Information* (from **Applicant:** to **Geographical Area of Operation:**) and change the line spacing to **2.0.**

13. Convert the **questions in the questionnaire** to a numbered list and change the line spacing to **2.0.**

14. Select the **entire document** and change the paragraph alignment to **Justify.**

15. Save and close the document.

fix it 2.6

In this project you will be editing the **WD2013-FixIt-2-6** document. This document is a résumé of an applicant for a project assistant position.

Skills needed to complete this project:

- Clearing Formatting (Skill 2.9)
- Revealing Formatting Marks (Skill 2.15)
- Changing Fonts (Skill 2.2)
- Changing Font Sizes (Skill 2.3)
- Using Quick Styles (Skill 2.12)
- Changing Paragraph Alignment (Skill 2.13)
- Adding Space Before and After Paragraphs (Skill 2.16)
- Changing Font Colors (Skill 2.5)
- Using Format Painter (Skill 2.8)
- Displaying the Ruler (Skill 2.18)
- Using Tab Stops (Skill 2.19)
- Using Bold, Italic, and Underline (Skill 2.1)
- Creating Bulleted Lists (Skill 2.10)
- Changing Indents (Skill 2.17)
- Changing Text Case (Skill 2.4)
- Changing Line Spacing (Skill 2.14)

1. Open the **WD2013-FixIt-2-6** document.

2. Save this document as: **[your initials]WD-FixIt-2-6**

3. Clear the formatting from all the text in the document.

4. Reveal the formatting marks in the document and remove any extra line spaces.

5. Change the font and font size for the text in the document.

6. Select the **name at the top of the document** and apply a **Heading 1** Quick Style of your choice. Center the text.

7. Place your cursor in the first line of the address and remove the space after the paragraph.

8. Select the first section heading (**Summary**) and apply a **Heading 2** Quick Style of your choice and then change the font color of the text.

9. Use the **Format Painter** to copy and paste the formatting from the first section heading to the other section headings (**Computer Skills, Experience,** and **Education**).

10. Display the ruler and set a .75" tab stop to indent the first paragraph under the **Summary** section.

11. In the *Experience* section, bold the **dates** and italicize the **position titles and the company name.**

12. Change the items under *Computer Skills* into a bulleted list using a round filled circle bullet style.

13. Apply the same bulleted list style to items listed under each job experience.

14. Increase the indent on the lines under each degree by one level (the **school name** and the **GPA**).

15. Change the text case on both instances of **Gpa** to be **UPPERCASE.**

16. Adjust the line spacing and remove space before and after paragraphs to fit the text on one page.

17. Save and close the document.

chapter 3

Formatting and Printing Documents

In this chapter, you will learn the following skills:

❱ Add consistency to document fonts and colors by using themes

❱ Use headers and footers to display page numbering and the date/time

❱ Control document layout by adjusting margins and using page breaks

❱ Enhance document formatting by using page borders, watermarks, and hyperlinks

❱ Use building blocks, Quick Parts, and property controls to save time and provide consistency for

❱ Print multiple copies of a document and specific pages within a document

skills

introduction

This chapter provides you with the skills needed to format and print documents. The first step is to apply and work with document themes. Once you have applied themes, you will add document elements, including headers, footers, page numbers, and automatic dates. Next, you will add building blocks and property controls as well as hyperlinks. You'll learn how to modify the layout of a document by adding breaks and adjusting the margins. You will add a cover page and page borders to add graphic elements to the document. Finally, you will preview and print the document, including printing multiple copies and specific page ranges.

Skill 3.1 Applying Document Themes

A **theme** is a group of formatting options that you apply to an entire document. Themes include font, color, and effect styles that are applied to specific elements of a document. Theme colors control the colors available from the color palette for fonts, borders, and backgrounds. Theme fonts change the fonts used for built-in styles—such as Normal style and headings. Theme effects control the way graphic elements in your document appear. Applying a theme to your document is a quick way to take a simple piece of text and change it into a polished, professional-looking document.

To apply a theme to a document:

1. Click the **Design** tab.
2. In the *Document Formatting* group, click the **Themes** button.
3. Click a theme option to apply it to your document.

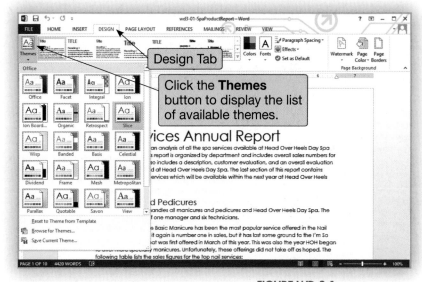

FIGURE WD 3.1

tell me **more**

You can modify any of the existing themes and save it as your own custom theme. The file will be saved with the *thmx* file extension. The theme will be saved in the *Document Themes* folder and will be available from Excel, PowerPoint, and Outlook as well as Word.

let me **try**

Open the student data file **wd3-01-SpaProductsReport** and try this skill on your own:

1. Change the theme of the document to the **Office** theme.
2. Save the file as directed by your instructor and close it.

Skill 3.2 Applying Style Sets

Each theme comes with a number of style sets you can choose from. A **style set** changes the font and paragraph formatting for an entire document. Style sets apply formatting based on styles. So, in order to see your changes, the text in your document must be formatted using styles. To learn more about applying styles to text, see *Using Quick Styles* in Chapter 2. The *Style Set* gallery displays thumbnails of how the text will appear when the style set is applied.

To change the style set:

1. Click the **Design** tab.
2. In the *Document Formatting* group, click the **More** button to open the *Style Set* gallery.
3. Click a style set from the gallery to apply it to the document.

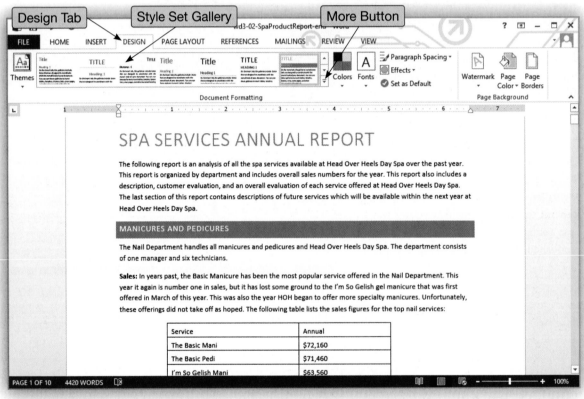

FIGURE WD 3.2

tips & tricks

Click the **More** button in the *Style Set* gallery to see more options to choose from.

tell me **more**

The first thumbnail in the *Style Set* gallery displays the style set that is currently in use for the document.

let me **try**

Open the student data file **wd3-02-SpaProductReport** and try this skill on your own:

1. Apply the **Shaded** style set to the document.
2. Save the file as directed by your instructor and close it.

Skill 3.3 Using Color Themes

When creating a document, it can sometimes be difficult to choose colors that work well together. Documents can end up monochromatic or with too many colors that don't work well together. A **color theme** is a set of colors that are designed to work well together in a document. A color theme will change the color of text, tables, and drawing objects in a document. When you apply a theme to a document it includes a color theme, which has default theme colors for document elements. You can change the color theme without affecting the other components of the theme.

To apply a color theme to a document:

1. Click the **Design** tab.
2. In the *Document Formatting* group, click the **Colors** button.
3. Click a color theme option to apply it to your document.

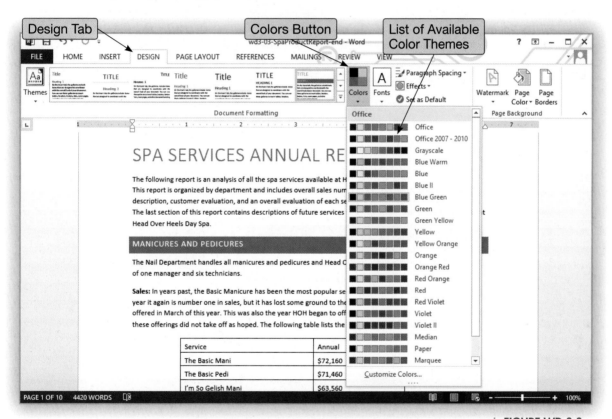

FIGURE WD 3.3

tell me **more**

When you change the color theme for a document, the color options for document elements will change. The theme colors will appear in the *Font Color* menu, as well as in the *Table Styles* and *Shape Styles* galleries. Choose your colors from these preset theme colors to ensure your document has a consistent color design.

let me try

Open the student data file **wd3-03-SpaProductReport** and try this skill on your own:

1. Change the color theme to the **Blue Green.**
2. Save the file as directed by your instructor and close it.

Skill 3.4 Using Font Themes

There are thousands of fonts for you to choose from to use in your documents. Some fonts are designed to work well as header text, such as Calibri Light and Cambria, and others are designed to work well as body text, such as Calibri. When you apply a theme to a document, this includes a **font theme**, which includes default fonts for body text and header text. As with color themes, you can change the font theme without affecting the other components of the theme.

To apply a font theme to a document:

1. Click the **Design** tab.
2. In the *Document Formatting* group, click the **Fonts** button.
3. Click a font theme option to apply it to your document.

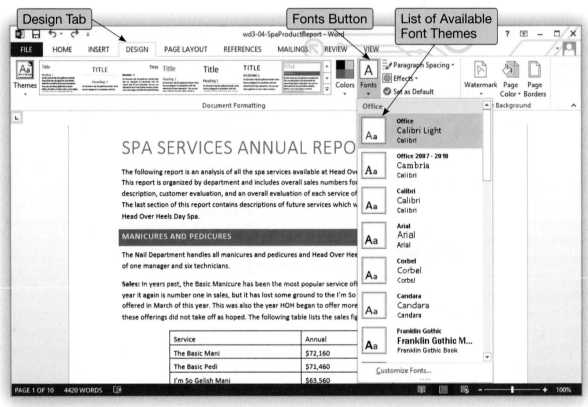

FIGURE WD 3.4

tell me **more**

The font theme menu displays a preview of the header font (on top) and the body font (on bottom). Notice that some themes include two different fonts, but others include the same font, only in different sizes. The default font theme for Word 2013 is the *Office Calibri Light/Calibri* font theme.

let me **try**

Open the student data file **wd3-04-SpaProductReport** and try this skill on your own:

1. Change the font theme to **Corbel.**
2. Save the file as directed by your instructor and close it.

word 2013 chapter 3 Formatting and Printing Documents

Skill 3.5 Creating Watermarks

A **watermark** is a graphic or text that appears as part of the page background. Watermarks appear faded so the text that appears on top of the watermark is legible when the document is viewed or printed.

There are three categories of watermarks:

Confidential—Includes the text "Confidential" or "Do Not Copy" in different layouts.

Disclaimers—Include the text "Draft" or "Sample" in different layouts.

Urgent—Includes the text "ASAP" or "Urgent" in different layouts.

To add a watermark to a document:

1. Click the **Design** tab.

2. In the *Page Background* group, click the **Watermark** button and select an option from the gallery.

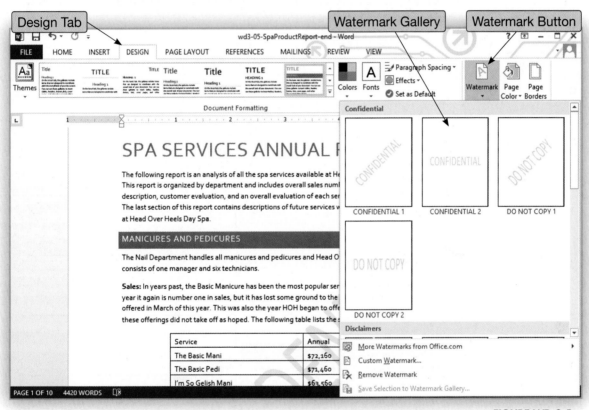

FIGURE WD 3.5

tips & tricks

You do not have to use one of the built-in watermarks from the *Watermark* gallery. You can create your own custom watermark, displaying whatever text or image you like. Click the **Custom Watermark**... command to open the *Printed Watermark* dialog and choose different options for the text watermark. You can add pictures as watermarks from this dialog. When you add a picture as a watermark, it appears faded so any text on top of it is still legible.

let me try

Open the student data file **wd3-05-SpaProduct Report** and try this skill on your own:

1. Apply the **Confidential 1** watermark to the document.

2. Save the file as directed by your instructor and close it.

Skill 3.6 Adding Headers

A **header** is text that appears at the top of every page, just below the top margin. Typically, headers display dates, page numbers, document titles, or authors' names. Word 2013 comes with a number of predesigned headers that you can add to your document and then modify to suit your needs.

To add a header to a document:

1. Click the **Insert** tab.

2. In the *Header & Footer* group, click the **Header** button and select a header format from the gallery.

3. Word displays the *Header & Footer Tools* contextual tab and inserts a header with content controls for you to enter your own information. Click a content control and enter the information for your header.

4. To close the header and return to your document, click the **Close Header and Footer** button on the contextual tab.

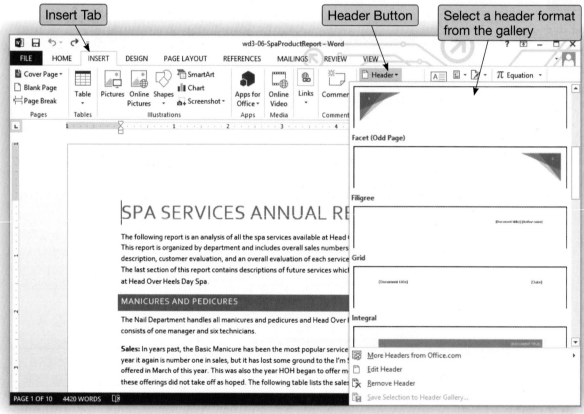

FIGURE WD 3.6

If the first page of your document is a title page, you won't want the header text to display on the page. To display a header on the first page of the document that is different from the header in the rest of the document, display the *Header & Footer Tools* tab. In the *Options* group, select the **Different First Page** check box.

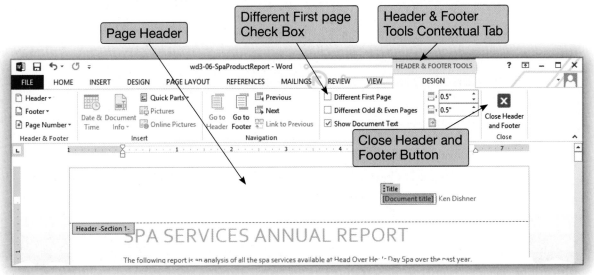

FIGURE WD 3.7

tips & tricks

Headers appear faded out in *Print Layout* view. If you want to edit a header, double-click it and make your changes. Click the **Close Header and Footer** button to return to the document.

another method

You can also add headers through the *Building Blocks Organizer*.

let me try

Open the student data file **wd3-06-SpaProductReport** and try this skill on your own:

1. Add a header to the document using the **Filigree** style.
2. Click the **[Document title]** control and type **Spa Services Annual Report**
3. Have the header display differently on the first page of the document.
4. Close the header and footer.
5. Scroll to the top of page 2 to see the header.
6. Save the file as directed by your instructor and close it.

Skill 3.7 Adding Footers

A **footer** is text that appears at the bottom of every page, just below the bottom margin. Typically, footers display dates, page numbers, or disclaimers. Word 2013 comes with a number of predesigned footers that you can add to your document and then modify to suit your needs.

To add a footer to a document:

1. Click the **Insert** tab.

2. In the *Header & Footer* group, click the **Footer** button and select a footer format from the gallery.

3. Word displays the *Header & Footer Tools* contextual tab and inserts a footer with content controls for you to enter your own information. Click a content control and enter the information for your footer.

4. To close the header and return to your document, click the **Close Header and Footer** button on the contextual tab.

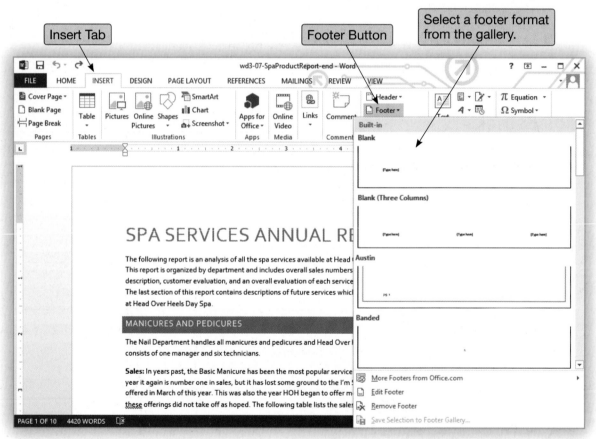

FIGURE WD 3.8

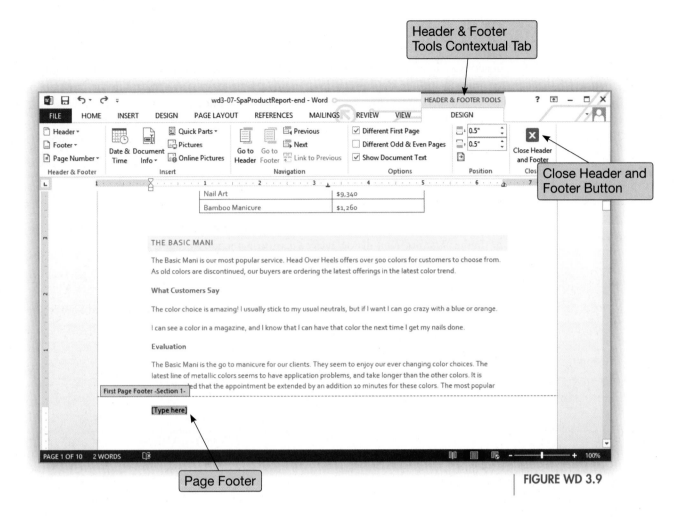

Header & Footer Tools Contextual Tab

Close Header and Footer Button

First Page Footer -Section 1-

[Type here]

Page Footer

FIGURE WD 3.9

tips & tricks

When you add a header or footer to your document, the *Design* tab under *Header & Footer Tools* displays. This is called a contextual tab because it only displays when a header or footer is the active element. Click the **Design** tab to modify the header or footer properties.

another method

You can also add footers through the *Building Blocks Organizer.*

let me try

Open the student data file **wd3-07-SpaProductReport** and try this skill on your own:

1. Add a footer to the document using the **Blank** style.
2. Click the **[Type here]** control and type **Not for disclosure outside Head Over Heels Day Spa**.
3. Close the header and footer.
4. Save the file as directed by your instructor and close it.

Skill 3.8 Adding an Automatic Date Stamp

In addition to information such as the company name and page numbers, headers and footers typically include the current date. You could manually type the date in the header or footer and then update the date every time you work on the document, or you could add an **automatic date stamp.** This pulls the current date from the computer's system clock and displays the date in the document. The date is then automatically updated when the computer's date changes.

To add an automatic date stamp to the header of a document:

1. Double-click the header to switch to header view.
2. Under the *Header & Footer Tools,* in the *Insert* group, click the **Date & Time** button.
3. In the *Date and Time* dialog, select a date format in the *Available formats* list.
4. Select the **Update automatically** check box.
5. Click **OK.**
6. To close the header and return to your document, click the **Close Header and Footer** button on the contextual tab.

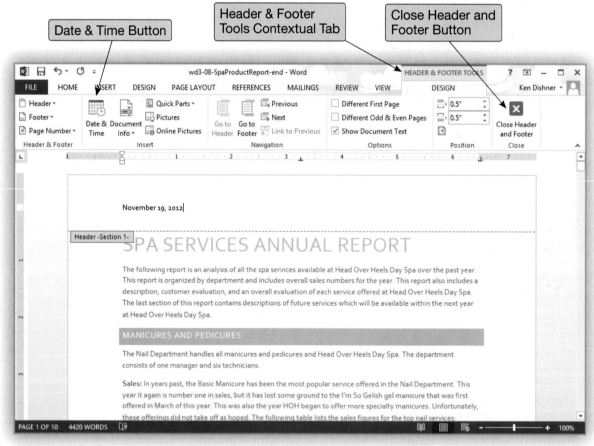

FIGURE WD 3.10

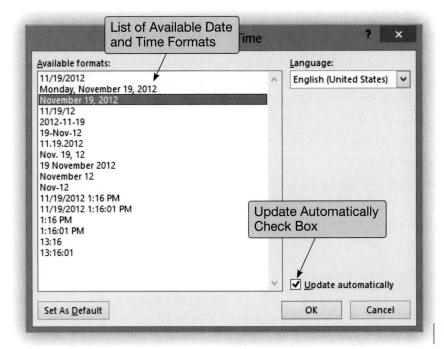

List of Available Date and Time Formats

Update Automatically Check Box

FIGURE WD 3.11

tips & tricks

To update the date in your document, click the date and then select the **Update automatically** check box. Word will automatically display the computer's current date. If you did not select the *Update automatically* check box when you inserted the date, the computer will not automatically update the date in your document.

another method

You can also use *Quick Parts* to add the date and time to the header or footer of your document:

1. Double-click the header to make it active.
2. Under the *Header &Footer Tools,* in the *Insert* group, click the **Quick Parts** button and select **Field**...
3. In the *Field* dialog, click the **CreateDate** or the **Date** field.
4. Select a format for the date.
5. Click **OK.**

let me try

Open the student data file **wd3-08-SpaProductReport** and try this skill on your own:

1. Double-click the header area to switch to header view.
2. Open the **Date and Time** dialog.
3. Add a date that will update automatically the uses the format **Month Day, Year.** For example, January 1, 2014**.**
4. Close the header and footer.
5. Save the file as directed by your instructor and close it.

Skill 3.9 Inserting Page Numbers

Headers and footers often include page numbers, but they also include other information, such as author name, date, and document title. If all you want to do is add page numbers to a document, you don't need to use the header and footer feature. Instead, you can insert simple page numbers to a document through the *Page Number* gallery.

To add page numbers to the bottom of pages of a document:

1. Click the **Insert** tab.
2. In the *Header & Footer* group, click the **Page Number** button. Point to **Bottom of Page.**
3. Click a page number format from the gallery.

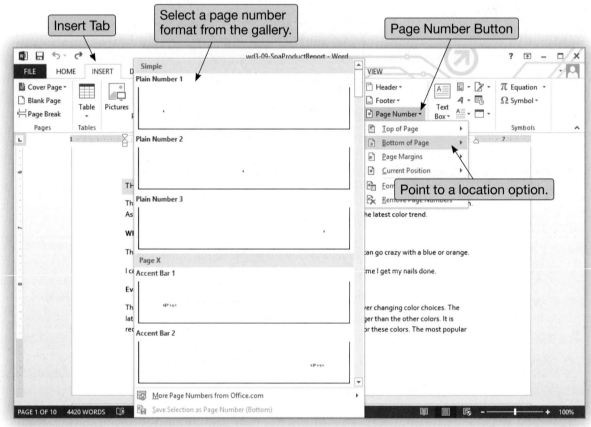

FIGURE WD 3.12

To remove a page number:

1. On the *Header & Footer Tools Design* tab, in the *Header & Footer* group, click the **Page Number** button.
2. Select **Remove Page Numbers.**

Page Number Button

Header & Footer Tools Contextual Tab

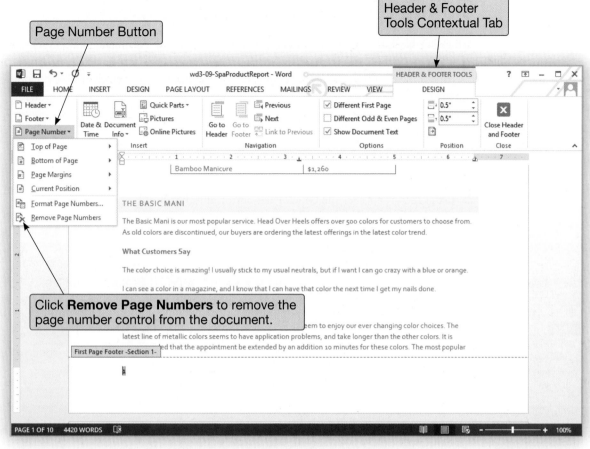

Click **Remove Page Numbers** to remove the page number control from the document.

tips & tricks

When adding page numbers to a document, you should always use Word's built-in building block. If you type page numbers into your document manually, they will not update when you add or remove pages.

tell me **more**

Traditionally, page numbers appear in the header or footer of the document. However, you can choose to display page numbers in the margin or at the current location of the cursor in the document.

another **method**

You can also add a page number through the *Building Blocks Organizer*.

let me **try**

Open the student data file **wd3-09-SpaProductReport** and try this skill on your own:

1. Add a page number to the bottom of the page using the **Plain Number 1** format.
2. Remove the **page number.**
3. Save the file as directed by your instructor and close it.

Skill 3.10 Inserting Building Blocks

A **building block** is a piece of content that is reusable in any document. Building blocks can be text, such as AutoText, or they can include graphics, such as a cover page. You can insert building blocks from specific commands on the Ribbon or from the **Building Blocks Organizer**. The *Building Blocks Organizer* lists the building blocks in alphabetical order by which gallery they appear in and includes *Bibliographies, Cover Pages, Equations, Footers, Headers, Page Numbers, Table of Contents, Tables, Text Boxes,* and *Watermarks*.

To insert a building block from the *Building Blocks Organizer:*

1. Click the **Insert** tab.
2. In the *Text* group, click the **Quick Parts** button and click **Building Blocks Organizer**...
3. Select a building block in the list and click the **Insert** button.

FIGURE WD 3.14

Building Blocks List

Insert Button

FIGURE WD 3.15

tips & tricks

If you find that the list of building blocks is too long, you can remove building blocks you don't use. To remove a building block from the *Building Blocks Organizer,* select a building block and click the **Delete** button. Be aware that the *Building Blocks Organizer* is used across all of Word 2013. If you delete a building block from the *Building Blocks Organizer,* it will no longer be available when you are working on other documents.

tell me **more**

You can sort the list of building blocks by clicking the *Name, Gallery, Category,* or *Template* button at the top of the *Building Blocks Organizer.* You can also modify the properties of a building block, changing properties such as the name or which gallery the building block appears in.

let me try

Open the student data file **wd3-10-SpaProductReport** and try this skill on your own:

1. Open the **Building Blocks Organizer**... dialog.
2. Insert a cover page using the **Austin building block.**
3. Save the file as directed by your instructor and close it.

Skill 3.11 Inserting Property Controls

A **property control** is an element you can add to your document to save time entering the same information over and over again. When you insert a property control and then replace the text with your own information, any time you add that control again it will include your custom text. Property controls can be used as shortcuts for entering long strings of text that are difficult to type. For example, instead of typing the company name Head Over Heels Day Spa, you can insert the *Company* property control. Word will add the text to the document and update the text automatically if any changes are made to the property control. By using property controls, you can be assured that all the information throughout the document is consistent.

> The *Company* property control inserts the same text each time it is used in the document.

SPA SERVICES ANNUAL REPORT
Company

The following report is an analysis of all the spa services available at Head Over Heels Day Spa over the past year. This report is organized by department and includes overall sales numbers for the year. This report also includes a description, customer evaluation, and an overall evaluation of each service offered at Head Over Heels Day Spa. The last section of this report contains descriptions of future services which will be available within the next year at Head Over Heels Day Spa.

MANICURES AND PEDICURES

The Nail Department handles all manicures and pedicures and Head Over Heels Day Spa. The department consists of one manager and six technicians.

Sales: In years past, the Basic Manicure has been the most popular service offered in the Nail Department. This year it again is number one in sales, but it has lost some ground to the I'm So Gelish gel manicure that was first offered in March of this year. This was also the year HOH began to offer more specialty manicures. Unfortunately, these offerings did not take off as hoped. The following table lists the sales figures for the top nail services:

FIGURE WD 3.16

To add a property control to a document:

1. Click the **Insert** tab.
2. In the *Text* group, click the **Quick Parts** button, point to **Document Property,** and select a control.
3. Type your text in the control. When you insert a property control, you may need to add a space between the control and the surrounding text.
4. Select the same control from the *Document Property* menu to add the same text to the document.

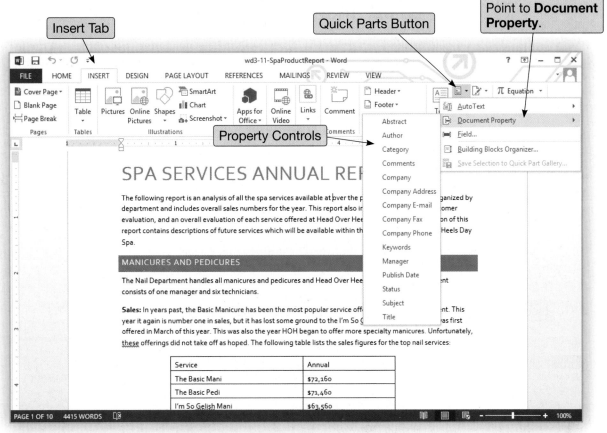

FIGURE WD 3.17

tips & tricks

If you need to update a property control, you only need to type the change once in the document. As you update any property control, all the other controls created from the same property control will update.

tell me more

Many of the built-in property controls, such as company name and author, pull their information from the document's properties. If you add a property control and modify the information, the document's related property will be updated as well.

let me try

Open the student data file **wd3-11-SpaProductReport** and try this skill on your own:

1. Click between the words **at** and **over** in the first sentence of the first paragraph of the document.

2. Insert a **document property** property control.

3. Type **Head Over Heels Day Spa.** Add a space between the property control and the surrounding text to fix any spacing issue.

4. Save the file as directed by your instructor and close it.

Skill 3.12 Inserting Hyperlinks

A **hyperlink** is text or a graphic that, when clicked, opens another page or file. You can use hyperlinks to link to a section in the same document, to a new document, or to an existing document, such as a Web page.

To insert a hyperlink:

1. Select the text or graphic you want to use as the link.
2. Click the **Insert** tab.
3. In the *Links* group, click the **Add a Hyperlink** button to open the *Insert Hyperlink* dialog.
4. Select an option under *Link to* and select the file to which you want to link.
5. Type the text of the link in the *Text to display* box.
6. Click **OK** to insert the hyperlink into your document.

FIGURE WD 3.18

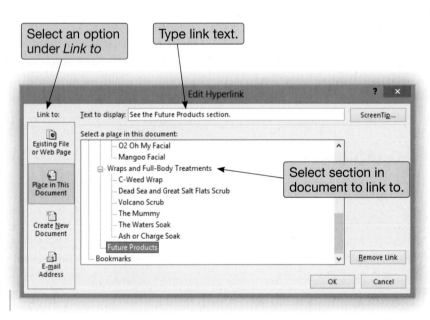

FIGURE WD 3.19

To edit a hyperlink, right-click the link and select **Edit Hyperlink...** from the menu. Make any changes in the *Edit Hyperlink* dialog.

To remove a hyperlink, right-click the link and select **Remove Hyperlink** from the menu.

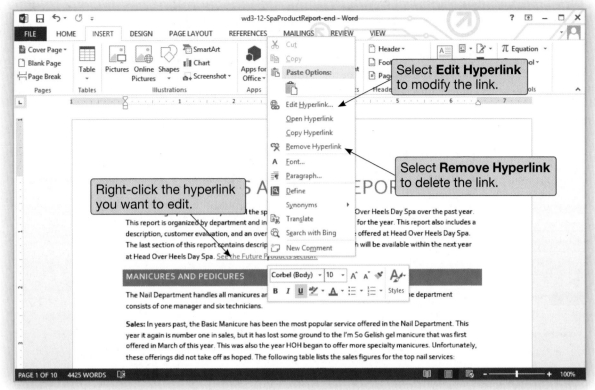

Right-click the hyperlink you want to edit.

Select **Edit Hyperlink** to modify the link.

Select **Remove Hyperlink** to delete the link.

FIGURE WD 3.20

tell me **more**

Some hyperlinks include ScreenTips. A ScreenTip is a bubble that appears when the mouse is placed over the link. Add a ScreenTip to include a more meaningful description of the hyperlink.

another **method**

To open the *Insert* Hyperlink dialog, you can:

❭ Right-click the text or object you want as the link and select **Hyperlink**... from the shortcut menu.

❭ Press (Ctrl) + (K) on the keyboard.

let me **try**

Open the student data file **wd3-12-SpaProductReport** and try this skill on your own:

1. Place the cursor at the end of the first paragraph. Press the spacebar one time.
2. Open the **Insert Hyperlink** dialog.
3. Add a link to the **Future Products** section of the document.
4. Change the link text to read **See the Future Products section** and add the hyperlink.
5. Save the file as directed by your instructor and close it.

Skill 3.13 Adjusting Margins

Margins are the blank spaces at the top, bottom, left, and right of a page. Word's default margins are typically 1 inch for the top and bottom and 1 inch for the left and right. Word 2013 comes with a number of predefined margin layout options for you to choose from, including normal, narrow, wide, and mirrored.

To adjust the margins for a document:

1. Click the **Page Layout** tab.
2. In the *Page Setup* group, click the **Margins** button, and select an option for the page layout.

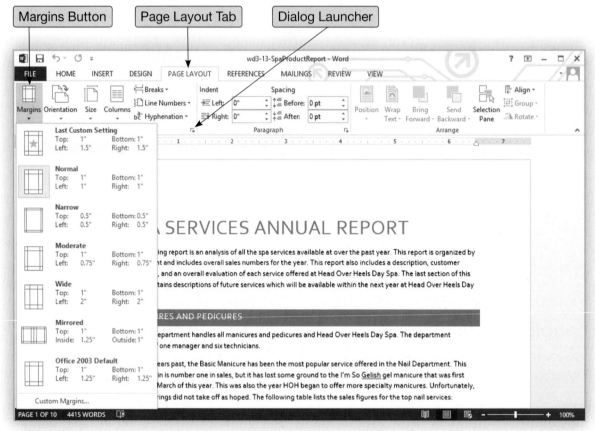

FIGURE WD 3.21

If you don't want to use one of Word's preset margins, you can set your own margin specifications in the *Page Setup* dialog.

To set custom margins:

1. On the *Page Layout* tab, in the *Page Setup* group, click the dialog launcher.
2. The *Page Setup* dialog opens.
3. Click the up and down arrows next to each margin (*Top, Bottom, Left,* and *Right*) to adjust the width and height of the margins.
4. Click **OK** to close the dialog.

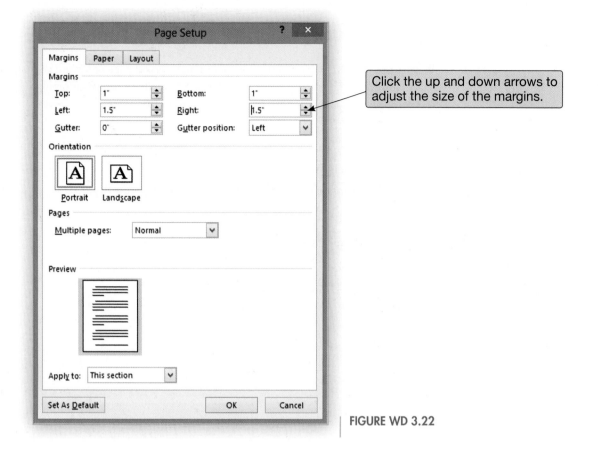

Click the up and down arrows to adjust the size of the margins.

FIGURE WD 3.22

tips & tricks

While most documents you create will use the *Normal* or *Moderate* settings for margins, some documents will require either less or more space around the text. If you have a large exhibit or table, you may want to make the margins narrow so the content will still fit in portrait orientation. On the other hand, if you are writing a letter, you may want to increase your margins to accommodate preprinted stationery.

tell me **more**

A gutter is additional space you can add to one side of the document when you plan to have the document bound. You can enter the amount of extra space you need for binding in the *Gutter* box in the *Page Setup* dialog. You can then choose how your document will be bound—along the left side or along the top.

another **method**

❯ To open the *Page Setup* dialog, you can also click the **Margins** button and select **Custom Margins**…

❯ To adjust margins in the *Page Setup* dialog, you can also type the number in the box.

let me **try**

Open the student data file **wd3-13-SpaProductReport** and try this skill on your own:

1. Change the margins for the document to use the **Wide** margin settings.
2. Open the **Page Setup** dialog.
3. Change the left margin to **1.5"**. Change the right margin to **1.5"**.
4. Save the file as directed by your instructor and close it.

Skill 3.14 Inserting Page Breaks

When text or graphics have filled a page, Word inserts a soft page break and goes on to a new page. However, at times you may want to manually insert a **hard page break**—forcing the text to a new page no matter how much content is on the present page. Typically hard page breaks are used to keep certain information together.

To insert a hard page break:

1. Click the **Page Layout** tab.
2. In the *Page Setup* group, click the **Breaks** button, and select **Page.**

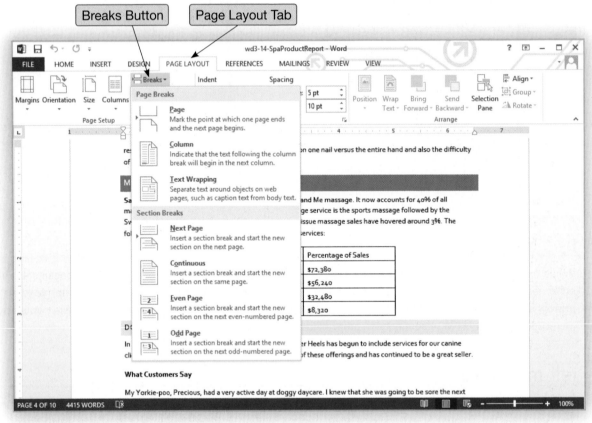

FIGURE WD 3.23

When you insert a page break, any remaining content in the document appears at the top of the next page. If you want an empty page to appear after the break, you can insert a blank page. When you insert a blank page, Word places a hard break, followed by a blank page, followed by the remaining content of the document.

To insert a blank page:

1. Click the **Insert** tab.
2. In the *Pages* group, click the **Blank Page** button.

tips & tricks

If you want to remove a hard page break, switch to *Draft* view so you can see where the break is. Place your cursor below the break and press **Delete** on the keyboard.

tell me more

There are two basic types of breaks you can add to a document:

Page Break—These breaks create visual breaks in your document but keep the content in the same section. Page breaks include *Page, Column,* and *Text Wrapping.*

Section Breaks—These breaks create new sections in your document. Section breaks include *Next Page, Continuous, Even Page,* and *Odd Page.*

another method

To insert a hard page break:

❯ On the *Insert* tab, in the *Pages* group, click the **Page Break** button.

❯ Press Ctrl + ←Enter on the keyboard.

let me try

Open the student data file **wd3-14-SpaProductReport** and try this skill on your own:

1. Place the cursor at the end of the paragraph before the **Massage Services** section. It is located near the top of page 4.
2. Insert a **page break.**
3. Save the file as directed by your instructor and close it.

Skill 3.15 Adding Page Borders

Page borders are graphic elements that can give your document a more polished look. **Page borders** draw a decorative graphic element along the top, right, bottom, and left edges of the page. Borders can be simple lines or 3-D effects and shadows. You can modify borders by changing the style and color. You can apply a border to the entire document or parts of a section.

To add a border to a document:

1. Click the **Design** tab.
2. In the *Page Background* group, click the **Page Borders** button.
3. The *Borders and Shading* dialog opens with the *Page Border* tab displayed.
4. Click a setting for the border.
5. Select a style, color, and width for the page border.
6. The *Preview* area shows how the border will look.
7. Click **OK** to accept your changes and add the page border to the document.

FIGURE WD 3.24

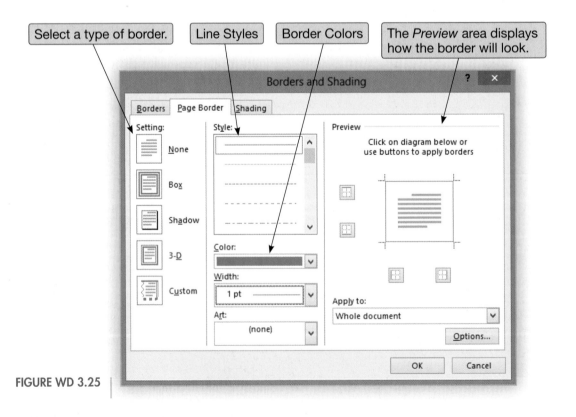

FIGURE WD 3.25

tips & tricks

You can further adjust the look of page borders from the *Borders and Shading* dialog:

❭ Click on the **Preview** area diagram to add or remove parts of the border.

❭ Click the **Art** drop-down menu to select graphic elements for the border.

another method

You can also open the *Borders and Shading* dialog from the *Home* tab. In the *Paragraph* group, click the arrow next to the *Borders* button and select **Borders and Shading**...

let me try

Open the student data file **wd3-15-SpaProductReport** and try this skill on your own:

1. Open the **Borders and Shading** dialog.
2. Change the border to use the **Box** style. Apply the **Aqua, Accent 1** color. Change the width of the border to **1 pt.**
3. Save the file as directed by your instructor and close it.

from the perspective of . . .

MARKETING MANAGER

When writing a report, I use Word's built-in themes and style sets to create a cohesive document. A cover page and page borders add visual zing to my report that really grabs the attention of my readers. Before I send it out for review, I always add a footer and watermark to the report to let others know not to share the information outside our organization. Using the *Company* property control has been invaluable, especially when I realized I misspelled our company name in the report! And when it comes to printing, I am often printing at least 10 copies to hand out, but then can easily reprint an individual page when minor edits come in from my boss—which they always do.

Skill 3.16 Adding a Cover Page

When creating documents such as reports, proposals, or business plans, it is a good idea to include a **cover page** that contains the title of the document and the date. You can also add other information such as a subtitle, a short description of the document, and company information. Word 2013 comes with a number of prebuilt cover pages that you can quickly and easily add to your documents.

To add a cover page:

1. Click the **Insert** tab.

2. In the *Pages* group, click the **Cover Page** button and select an option.

3. Word inserts a cover page with content controls for you to enter your own information. Click a content control and enter the information for your document.

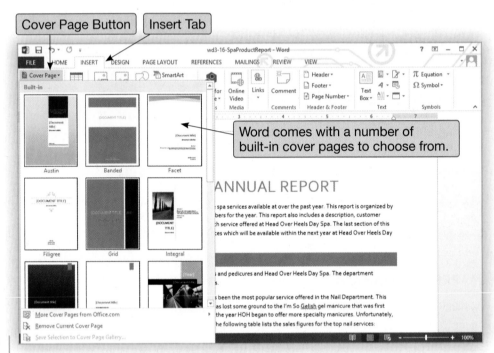

FIGURE WD 3.26

tips & tricks

Most content controls include instructions for adding text to the cover page. However, some content controls, such as the author, do not include text and are hidden from view. One way to see all the fields available in a cover page is to use the *Select All* command by pressing Ctrl + A on the keyboard.

tell me **more**

When you click a date content control, you will notice a calendar icon next to the text area. Click the icon to display the calendar to select a date to add to the cover page.

let me try

Open the student data file **wd3-16-SpaProductReport** and try this skill on your own:

1. Insert a cover page using the **Facet** style.

2. Delete the **Subtitle** content control from the cover page.

3. In the **Email address** content control, add the text **kdishner@hhspa.com.**

4. Save the file as directed by your instructor and close it.

Skill 3.17 Previewing and Printing a Document

In Word 2013, all the print settings are combined in a single page along with a preview of how the printed document will look. From the *Print* page in Backstage view, you can preview and print all the pages in your document.

To preview and print a document:

1. Click the **File** tab to open Backstage view.
2. Click **Print.**
3. At the right side of the page is a preview of how the printed document will look. Beneath the preview there is a page count. If there are multiple pages, click the next and previous arrows to preview all the pages in the document.
4. Verify that the correct printer name is displayed in the *Printer* section.
5. Click the **Print** button to print.

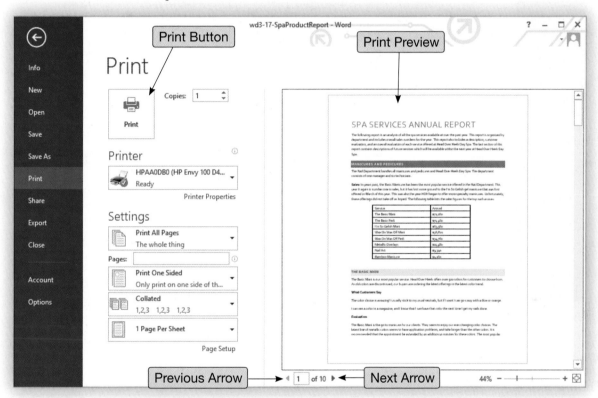

FIGURE WD 3.27

another method

To display the *Print* page, you can also press (Ctrl) + (P).

let me try

Open the student data file **wd3-17-SpaProductReport** and try this skill on your own:

1. Display the **Print** page in Backstage view.
2. Click the next and previous arrows to view how the document will look when it is printed.
3. Print the document. **NOTE:** If you are using this in class or in your school's computer lab, check with your instructor about printing permissions before completing this step.
4. Save the file as directed by your instructor and close it.

Skill 3.18 Printing Multiple Copies of a Document

When creating documents, sometimes you will only need one printed copy, but other times you will need to print more than a single copy. From the *Print* page in Backstage view, you can print multiple copies of a document.

To print multiple copies a document:

1. Click the **File** tab to open Backstage view.
2. Click **Print.**
3. Type the number of copies you want to print in the **Copies** box.
4. Click the **Print** button to print.

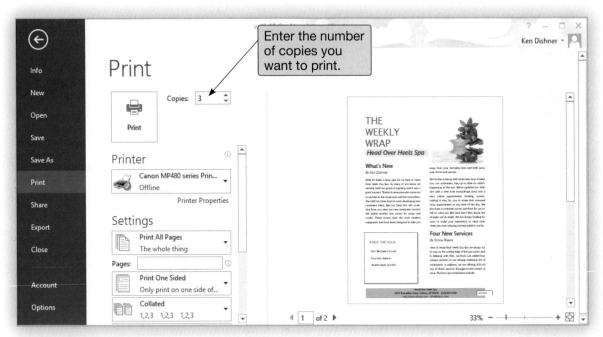

FIGURE WD 3.28

another method

You can also change the number of copies to print by clicking the up and down arrows next to the *Copies* box.

let me try

Open the student data file **wd3-18-SpaNewsletter** and try this skill on your own:

1. Display the **Print** page in Backstage view.
2. **Print** three copies of the document. **NOTE:** If you are using this in class or in your school's computer lab, check with your instructor about printing permissions before completing this step.
3. Save the file as directed by your instructor and close it.

Skill 3.19 Printing Page Ranges

When designating which pages to print, you can print a range of pages or individual pages. To print sequential pages type the number of the first page you want to print, followed by a hyphen, followed by the last page you want to print. For example, if you want to print pages 3 through 8 in your document, type **3-8** in the *Pages* box. To print individual pages, type each page number you want to print separated by a comma or semicolon. For example, if you want to print page 3, page 5, page 8, and page 10, type **3,5,8,10** in the *Pages* box.

To print specific pages in a document:

1. Click the **File** tab to open Backstage view.

2. Click **Print.**

3. In the *Settings* section, click in the **Pages** box and type the range of pages you want to print.

4. Click the **Print** button to print.

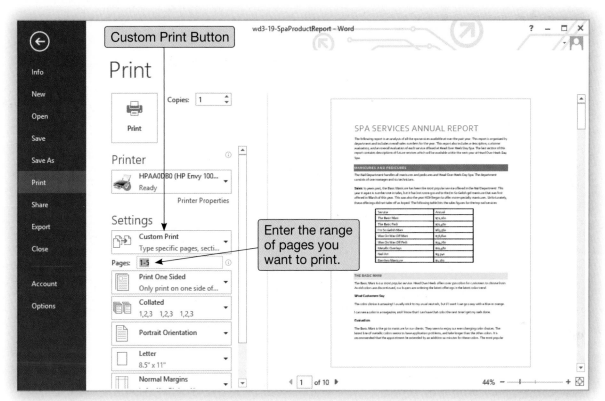

FIGURE WD 3.29

tell me **more**

When you enter a range of pages in the *Pages* box, the first button under *Settings* automatically changes to *Custom Print.*

let me try

Open the student data file **wd3-19-SpaProductReport** and try this skill on your own:

1. Display the **Print** page in Backstage view.
2. Print the first five pages of the document.
3. Now print pages 3 and 5. **NOTE:** If you are using this in class or in your school's computer lab, check with your instructor about printing permissions before completing this step.
4. Save the file as directed by your instructor and close it.

key terms

Theme	Building Blocks Organizer
Style set	Property control
Color theme	Hyperlink
Font theme	ScreenTip
Watermark	Margins
Header	Hard page break
Footer	Page borders
Automatic date stamp	Cover page
Building block	

concepts review

1. A group of formatting elements you apply to a document is known as a _____.

   a. building block

   b. property control

   c. theme

   d. style

2. A _____ changes the font and paragraph formatting for an entire document based on styles.

   a. font theme

   b. style set

   c. color theme

   d. effects theme

3. A _____ is a graphic or text that appears as part of the page background and is usually faded in appearance.

   a. watermark

   b. cover page

   c. margin

   d. property control

4. Text that appears at the top of every page, just below the top margin is known as the _____.

   a. header

   b. footer

   c. title

   d. cover page

5. A piece of content that is reusable in any document, such as a cover page or a watermark, is known as a _____.

   a. property control

   b. building block

   c. field

   d. style set

6. A _____ is an element you can add to your document to save time entering the same information over and over again.

   a. style set

   b. theme

   c. property control

   d. building block

7. The blank spaces at the top, bottom, left, and right of a page are known as _____.

   a. margins

   b. borders

   c. page breaks

   d. columns

8. A _____ is text or a graphic that, when clicked, opens another page or file.

   a. building block

   b. field

   c. property control

   d. hyperlink

9. To force text on to a new page, insert a _____.

   a. cover page

   b. page border

   c. page break

   d. column

10. To print only the third and fifth page in a document, type _____ in the *Pages* box on the *Print* page.

    a. 3-5

    b. 3,5

    c. 3:5

    d. 35

projects

Data files for projects can be found on
www.mhhe.com/office2013skills

skill review 3.1

In this project you will be formatting and printing a brochure for Suarez Marketing.

Skills needed to complete this project:

- Applying Document Themes (Skill 3.1)
- Applying Style Sets (Skill 3.2)
- Using Color Themes (Skill 3.3)
- Using Font Themes (Skill 3.4)
- Inserting Property Controls (Skill 3.11)
- Adjusting Margins (Skill 3.13)
- Inserting Page Breaks (Skill 3.14)
- Adding Page Borders (Skill 3.15)
- Adding Headers (Skill 3.6)
- Previewing and Printing a Document (Skill 3.17)
- Printing Multiple Copies of a Document (Skill 3.18)

1. Open the **WD2013-SkillReview-3-1** document.
2. Save this document as: **[your initials]WD-SkillReview-3-1**
3. Apply a theme to a document and change the style set.
   a. Click the **Design** tab.
   b. In the *Document Formatting* group, click the **Themes** button and select **Ion.**
   c. In the *Style Set* gallery, click the **Lines (Simple)** option.
4. Change the color theme.
   a. On the *Design* tab, in *Document Formatting* group, click the **Colors** button.
   b. Select the **Blue Warm** color theme.
5. Change the font theme.
   a. On the *Design* tab, in *Document Formatting* group, click the **Fonts** button.
   b. Select the **Corbel** font theme.
6. Add a company property control.
   a. Place the cursor in the empty line below *Maria Suarez*.
   b. Click the **Insert** tab.
   c. In the *Text* group, click the **Quick Parts** button. Point to *Document Property* and select **Company.**
   d. If a company name appears in the property control, delete the name. Type **Suarez Marketing** in the control. Click outside the control to deselect it.
7. Change the margins for the document.
   a. Click the **Page Layout** tab. In the *Page Setup* group, click the **Margins** button and select **Moderate.**
   b. In the *Page Setup* group, click the dialog launcher to open the *Page Setup* dialog.
   c. Type **.9″** in the *Left* box. Type **.9″** in the *Right* box. Click **OK.**

8. Add a page break.

   a. Click before the heading *Professional Credentials.*

   b. On the *Page Layout* tab, in the *Page Setup* group, click the **Breaks** button and select **Page.**

9. Add a page border to the document.

   a. Navigate to the top of the document.

   b. Click the **Design** tab. In the *Page Background* group, click the **Page Borders** button.

   c. Under *Setting,* change the option to **Box.** Click the **Color** arrow and select **Gray–50%, Accent 6** (it is the last option in the first row under *Theme Colors*). Click the **Width** arrow and select **1 ½ pt.** Click **OK.**

10. Add a header to the document.

    a. Click the **Insert** tab.

    b. In the *Header & Footer* group, click the **Header** button and select **Filigree** header option.

    c. On the *Design* tab, click the **Close Header and Footer** button.

11. Print multiple copies of the document.

    a. Click the **File** tab and click **Print.**

    b. Click the **Copies** up arrow two times, so **3** appears in the box.

    c. Click the **Print** button. **NOTE:** If you are using this in class or in your school's computer lab, check with your instructor about printing permissions before completing this step.

12. Save and close the document.

skill review 3.2

In this project you will be formatting and editing a paper on alternate assessments for students.

Skills needed to complete this project:

- Applying Document Themes (Skill 3.1)
- Applying Style Sets (Skill 3.2)
- Adding Footers (Skill 3.7)
- Inserting Property Controls (Skill 3.11)
- Inserting Page Numbers (Skill 3.9)
- Inserting Hyperlinks (Skill 3.12)
- Creating Watermarks (Skill 3.5)
- Inserting Page Breaks (Skill 3.14)
- Adding a Cover Page (Skill 3.16)
- Previewing and Printing a Document (Skill 3.17)
- Printing Page Ranges (Skill 3.19)

1. Open the **WD2013-SkillReview-3-2** document.

2. Save this document as: **[your initials]WD-SkillReview-3-2**

3. Apply a theme to a document and change the style set.

   a. Click the **Design** tab.

   b. In the *Document Formatting* group, click the **Themes** button and select **Mesh.**

   c. In the *Style Set* gallery, click the **Basic (Simple)** option.

4. Add footer text.

   a. Click the **Insert** tab.

   b. In the *Header & Footer* group, click the **Footer** button and select **Blank (Three Columns).**

   c. Click the **[Type here]** control at the far left side.

   d. Type `Alternate Assessment`

   e. Click the **[Type here]** control in the middle and press **Delete.**

5. Insert a property control.

   a. In the footer, click the **[Type here]** control at the far right side.

   b. Click the **Insert** tab.

   c. In the *Text* group, click the **Quick Parts** button, point to **Document Property,** and select **Author.**

   d. Type `Kelly Morehead`

   e. Click the **Header & Footer Tools Design** tab.

   f. Click the **Close Header and Footer** button.

6. Insert page numbers and display a different first page for the header.

   a. Click the **Insert** tab.

   b. In the *Header & Footer* group, click the **Page Number** button, point to **Top of Page,** and select **Plain Number 3.**

   c. On the *Header & Footer Tools Design* tab, in the *Options* group, select the **Different First Page** check box.

   d. Click the **Close Header and Footer** button.

7. Add a hyperlink to another place in the document.

   a. Navigate to the **Modified Achievement Standards** section.

   b. Place the cursor after the third sentence (ending in *to receive an alternate assessment.*) and press the spacebar one time.

   c. Click the **Insert** tab.

   d. In the *Links* group, click the **Hyperlink** button.

   e. Under *Link to* select **Place in This Document.**

   f. Select **Student Eligibility.**

   g. In the *Text to display* box, type `(See the Student Eligibility section)`

   h. Click **OK.**

8. Add a watermark to the document.

   a. Click the **Design** tab.

   b. In the *Page Background* section, click the **Watermark** button and select **DRAFT 1.**

9. Insert a page break.

   a. Navigate to the **Conclusion** heading and place the cursor at the beginning of the line.

   b. Click the **Page Layout** tab.

   c. In the *Page Setup* group, click the **Breaks** button and select **Page.**

10. Add a cover page.

    a. Click the **Insert** tab.

    b. In the *Pages* group, click the **Cover Page** button and select **Banded.**

    c. Select the **[Document Title]** control and type **Alternate Assessment**

    d. Select the **[Company address]** control and press **Delete.**

11. Preview and print a specific page range.

    a. Click the **File** tab.

    b. Click **Print. NOTE:** If you are using this in class or in your school's computer lab, check with your instructor about printing permissions before completing this step.

    c. Use the next and previous arrows to page through the preview of the document.

    d. In the *Pages* box, type **2-6.**

    e. Verify the name of your printer appears under *Printer.*

    f. Click the **Print** button. **NOTE:** If you are using this in class or in your school's computer lab, check with your instructor about printing permissions before completing this step.

12. Save and close the document.

challenge yourself 3.3

In this project you will be formatting and editing a document for the Tri-State Book Festival.

Skills needed to complete this project:

- Applying Document Themes (Skill 3.1)
- Applying Style Sets (Skill 3.2)
- Using Color Themes (Skill 3.3)
- Using Font Themes (Skill 3.4)
- Adding Headers (Skill 3.6)
- Adding Footers (Skill 3.7)
- Inserting Property Controls (Skill 3.11)
- Adjusting Margins (Skill 3.13)
- Inserting Page Breaks (Skill 3.14)
- Adding Page Borders (Skill 3.15)
- Previewing and Printing a Document (Skill 3.17)
- Printing Multiple Copies of a Document (Skill 3.18)

1. Open the **WD2013-ChallengeYourself-3-3** document.

2. Save this document as: **[your initials]WD-ChallengeYourself-3-3**

3. Apply a theme to a document and change the style set.

    a. Apply the **Facet** theme to the document.

    b. Change the style set to **Shaded.**

4. Change the color theme to **Blue Warm.**

5. Change the font theme to **Century Gothic.**

6. Add a header to the document.

    a. Add a header using the **Banded** format.

    b. Change the header so the first page is different from the rest of the document.

    c. Close the **Header and Footer** contextual tab.

7. Add a footer and a property control.

    a. Add a footer using the **Blank** format.

    b. Replace the [**Type here**] control with an author property control.

    c. Close the **Header and Footer** contextual tab.

8. Change the margins for the document to the following:
   - *Top:* **1.1"**
   - *Bottom:* **1.1"**
   - *Left:* **1.25"**
   - *Right:* **1.25"**

9. Place the cursor above the *Tuesday October 11* heading in the *Agenda* section. Add a page break. Delete the extra line above the heading.

10. Add a page border to the document with the following settings:
    - *Setting:* **Box**
    - *Style:* **Solid line** (default option)
    - *Color:* **Blue, Accent 3**
    - *Width:* **1 pt**

11. Print two copies of the document. **NOTE:** If you are using this in class or in your school's computer lab, check with your instructor about printing permissions before completing this step.

12. Save and close the document.

challenge yourself **3.4**

In this project you will be editing the text of a safety memo from the Spring Hills Association.

Skills needed to complete this project:
- Applying Document Themes (Skill 3.1)
- Applying Style Sets (Skill 3.2)
- Using Color Themes (Skill 3.3)
- Adding Footers (Skill 3.7)
- Adding Headers (Skill 3.6)
- Adding an Automatic Date Stamp (Skill 3.8)
- Inserting Hyperlinks (Skill 3.12)
- Creating Watermarks (Skill 3.5)
- Inserting Page Breaks (Skill 3.14)
- Adding a Cover Page (Skill 3.16)
- Previewing and Printing a Document (Skill 3.17)
- Printing Multiple Copies of a Document (Skill 3.18)
- Printing Page Ranges (Skill 3.19)

1. Open the **WD2013-ChallengeYourself-3-4** document.
2. Save this document as: **[your initials]WD-ChallengeYourself-3-4**
3. Apply a theme to a document and change the style set.

   a. Apply the **Wisp** theme to the document.

   b. Change the style set to **Lines (Simple)**.

4. Change the color theme to **Green.**
5. Add a footer using the **Ion (Light)** format. Close the **Header & Footer** contextual tab.
6. Add a header using the **Facet (Even Page)** format and display a different first page for the header.

7. Add an automatic date stamp to the right side of the header using the **MM/DD/YYYY** format. Be sure the date will update automatically. Close the **Header & Footer** contextual tab.

8. Add a hyperlink to another place in the document.

   a. Navigate to the **Our Safety Vision** section.

   b. Place the cursor after the second sentence (ending in *overlapping shifts.*) and press the spacebar one time.

   c. Add a hyperlink to the **Full Time Officers** section of the document. Have text for the link read (See the list of officers)

9. Add a watermark using the **SAMPLE 1.**

10. Insert a page break before the **Our Safety Vision** section.

11. Add a cover page.

    a. Insert a cover page using the **Retrospect** design.

    b. Change the **Document subtitle** to read **KEEPING OUR COMMUNITY SAFE**

    c. Delete the **COMPANY ADDRESS** control on the cover page.

12. Print three copies of the second, third, and fourth pages of the document. **NOTE:** If you are using this in class or in your school's computer lab, check with your instructor about printing permissions before completing this step.

13. Save and close the document.

on your own 3.5

In this project you will be editing the text of a brochure for Suarez Marketing.

Skills needed to complete this project:

- Applying Document Themes (Skill 3.1)
- Applying Style Sets (Skill 3.2)
- Using Color Themes (Skill 3.3)
- Using Font Themes (Skill 3.4)
- Inserting Page Numbers (Skill 3.9)
- Adding an Automatic Date Stamp (Skill 3.8)
- Adjusting Margins (Skill 3.13)
- Inserting Page Breaks (Skill 3.14)
- Adding Page Borders (Skill 3.15)
- Adding a Cover Page (Skill 3.16)
- Previewing and Printing a Document (Skill 3.17)
- Printing Multiple Copies of a Document (Skill 3.18)
- Printing Page Ranges (Skill 3.19)

1. Open the **WD2013-OnYourOwn-3-5** document.

2. Save this document as: **[your initials]WD-OnYourOwn-3-5**

3. Apply a theme of your choice to the document.

4. Change style set, color theme, and font theme.

5. Add a page number to the bottom of the document. Use a format of your choice.

6. Add an automatic date stamp to the footer of the document. Use a format of your choice.

7. Adjust the margins for optimal layout.

8. Insert page breaks so no heading section is broken across a page. **NOTE:** Depending on the margin settings you used, you may not need to insert a page break.

9. Add a page border of your choice. Modify the color and width of the border.

10. Add a cover page of your choice to the document. Enter document information and delete controls that are not used.

11. Print two copies of the document. **NOTE:** If you are using this in class or in your school's computer lab, check with your instructor about printing permissions before completing this step.

12. Save and close the document.

fix it **3.6**

In this project you will be editing the text of a brochure for Suarez Marketing.

Skills needed to complete this project:
- Inserting Page Numbers (Skill 3.9)
- Adding Footers (Skill 3.7)
- Adding an Automatic Date Stamp (Skill 3.8)
- Applying Document Themes (Skill 3.1)
- Applying Style Sets (Skill 3.2)
- Using Font Themes (Skill 3.4)
- Adjusting Margins (Skill 3.13)
- Inserting Page Breaks (Skill 3.14)
- Creating Watermarks (Skill 3.5)
- Previewing and Printing a Document (Skill 3.17)
- Printing Multiple Copies of a Document (Skill 3.18)

1. Open the **WD2013-FixIt-3-6** document.

2. Save this document as: **[your initials]WD-FixIt-3-6**

3. The author David Gonzalez typed his name and a page number at the top of each page. Delete this line from the top of each page. There are five instances of this mistake. **NOTE:** After you have deleted the first two instances of this mistake, the remaining instances will no longer appear at the top of the following pages.

4. Add the **Plain Number 3** page number to the top of **pages 2 through 5.**

5. Add a footer to the document using the **Facet (Even Page)** design.

6. Click after the author's name in the footer and insert an automatic time stamp using the **Month Day, Year** format (January 1, 2014). Close the **Header & Footer Tools** contextual tab.

7. Change the document theme to **View.**

8. Change the style set to **Basic (Simple).**

9. Change the font theme to **Office.**

10. Change the margins to use the **Normal** preset.

11. Insert a page break before the *V. Collect and evaluate the result* section.

12. Add a watermark using the **CONFIDENTIAL 1** format.

13. Print three copies of the document. **NOTE:** If you are using this in class or in your school's computer lab, check with your instructor about printing permissions before completing this step.

14. Save and close the document.

chapter 4

Working with Pictures, Tables, and Charts

In this chapter, you will learn the following skills:

❭ Insert pictures from an online source or from a file

❭ Resize, move, and change the layout of pictures

❭ Apply Quick Styles to objects

❭ Insert SmartArt, shapes, WordArt, and an online video

❭ Create a table

❭ Enter data in a table

❭ Modify the structure of a table

❭ Sort data in a table

❭ Add borders to a table

❭ Create and modify a chart

skills

introduction

This chapter provides you with the skills to add and modify pictures, graphic elements, tables, and charts. You will learn to insert pictures from an online source as well as from your own computer. Once you have added pictures to a document, you will manipulate them by resizing, positioning, and changing the text wrapping. You will then stylize pictures using Quick Styles. You will learn about other graphic objects you can add to documents including shapes, WordArt, and SmartArt diagrams. You will create and enter data in a table and then modify the table by adding and deleting rows and columns. You will change the display of data in a table by merging and splitting cells and sorting the data within a table. You will modify the look of a table by applying a table Quick Style and then changing the display of table borders. Finally, you will add a chart to a document and then modify the look of that chart.

Skill 4.1 Inserting Online Pictures

A new feature in Word 2013 is the ability to add **online pictures.** You can search for pictures from *Office.com Clip Art,* through a *Bing Image Search,* or from your SkyDrive. When you search on *Office.com,* you will be searching through Microsoft Office's royalty-free **clip art** collection. Word will display results of **clips** for you to use in your document. These clips refer to files from another source and include photographs and illustrations. If you use the *Bing Image Search,* you will be searching for images from across the Internet. Searching for images on your SkyDrive will return images that you have added to your SkyDrive for use in document.

To insert clip art from *Office.com:*

1. Click the **Insert** tab.
2. In the *Illustrations* group, click the **Online Pictures** button.

Insert Tab   Online Pictures Button   **FIGURE WD 4.1**

3. The *Insert Pictures* dialog opens.
4. Type a word describing the clip you want to search for in the **Office.com Clip Art** box and click the **Search** button.

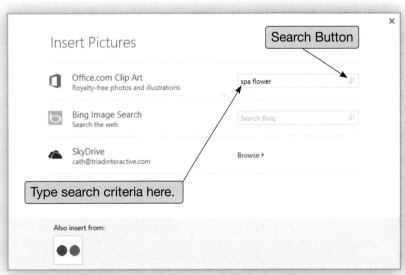

FIGURE WD 4.2

5. Word displays thumbnail results that match the search criteria.

6. Click a thumbnail to select it, and click the **Insert** button to add the image to your document.

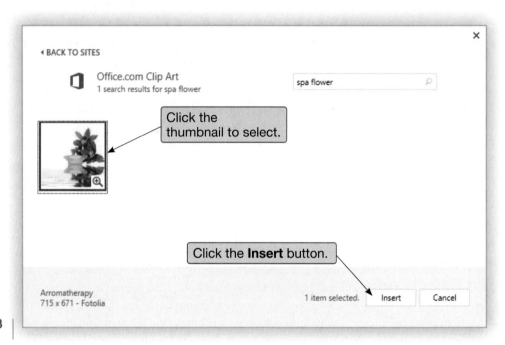

FIGURE WD 4.3

tips & tricks

If you use the *Office.com Clip Art* search, all the results that are returned are royalty-free images. This means you can use them freely in your document without worry of violating a copyright on an image. If you use the *Bing Image Search*, you will be searching the Internet for images and the results may not include images that are royalty free. You should only use images in your documents that you know you have the proper rights to use.

tell me **more**

In previous versions of Word, you searched for clips using the *Clip Art* task pane. In Word 2013, the *Clip Art* task pane has been replaced with the *Online Pictures* dialog. In the *Clip Art* task pane, you had the ability to filter the search results by type of image—photograph or illustration. The Online Pictures dialog does not have this feature.

let me try

Open the student data file **wd4-01-SpaNewsletter** and try this skill on your own:

1. Place the cursor at the end of the title **The Weekly Wrap.**
2. Open the **Insert Pictures** dialog.
3. Search **Office.com Clip Art** for **spa flower.**
4. Insert the picture of the purple flower with a candle. *Note:* If you do not see an image of a purple flower with a candle, insert an image of your choice.
5. Save the file as directed by your instructor and close it.

Skill 4.2 Resizing Pictures

When you first add an image to a document, you may find it is not the right size. The image may be too large for the page, or it may be too small for the page layout. You can resize images in a document by either manually entering the values for the size of the picture or by dragging a **resize handle** on the image to resize it.

To resize a picture by manually entering values:

1. Select the picture you want to resize.
2. Click the **Picture Tools Format** tab.
3. In the *Size* group, type a value in the *Width* or *Height* box to resize the picture.
4. Press ⏎ Enter to resize the picture.

To resize a picture by dragging:

1. Select the picture you want to change.
2. To resize a picture, click a **resize handle** and drag toward the center of the image to make it smaller or away from the center of the image to make it larger.

FIGURE WD 4.4

tips & tricks

When resizing by dragging, be sure to use one of the resize handles on the four corners of the picture to maintain the aspect ratio of the picture. If you use a resize handle along one of the sides of the picture, you will be resizing the width of the picture only. If you use a resize handle along the top or bottom of the picture, you will be resizing the height of the picture only.

When you enter a value in the *Width* or *Height* box on the Ribbon, the value in the other box will change to maintain the aspect ratio for the picture.

tell me **more**

When resizing a picture, you will most likely want the aspect ratio of the picture to stay the same. This means that as the width is increased or decreased, the height of the image is increased or decreased proportionally. If the aspect ratio did not remain the same, the image would appear stretched when you resized it.

let me try

Open the student data file **wd4-02-SpaNewsletter** and try this skill on your own:

1. Select the image of the flowers and candle.
2. Resize the image so it is **2.82"** in height and **3"** in width.
3. Save the file as directed by your instructor and close it.

Skill 4.3 Changing Picture Layouts

When you first add a picture to your document, Word inserts the picture at the insertion point and displays the picture in line with the text. This causes the picture to be treated as its own paragraph. But what if you want the text in your document to wrap around the picture? Word comes with a number of layout options for you to choose from. When a picture is selected, you will see the **Layout Options** button. This button gives you one-click access to text layout options for the picture.

To adjust the layout of a picture:

1. Click the image to select it.

2. Click the **Layout Options** button.

3. Select a wrapping option.

FIGURE WD 4.5

tips & tricks

As you roll the mouse over each layout option, Live Preview will display how the document will look with the text wrapping applied.

another method

To change the layout of pictures, you can also click the **Picture Tools Format** tab. In the *Arrange* group, click the **Wrap Text** button and select an option.

let me try

Open the student data file **wd4-03-SpaNewsletter** and try this skill on your own:

1. Select the image of the flowers and candle.
2. Change the layout option of the image of the flowers and candle so it appears behind text.
3. Save the file as directed by your instructor and close it.

Skill 4.4 Moving Pictures

When you first add an image to a document, you may find it is not positioned where you want it. You can change the position of images by dragging and dropping the image where you want it on the page.

Word 2013 now includes alignment guides for helping with picture layout. When you drag a picture, you will see horizontal and vertical green lines called the **alignment guides.** They appear when the picture's edge is aligned with another element on the page.

To move pictures in a document:

1. Select the picture you want to move.

2. Rest your mouse over the picture.

3. When the cursor changes to the **move cursor**, click and drag the image to the new location.

4. When an alignment guide appears aligning it with the desired element on the page, release the mouse button to snap the image in place and align it on the page.

FIGURE WD 4.6

tips & tricks

To turn off alignment guides, click the **Picture Tools Format** tab. In the *Arrange* group, click the **Align** button and select **Use Alignment Guides** so a checkmark does not appear next to the menu item.

let me try

Open the student data file **wd4-04-SpaNewsletter** and try this skill on your own:

1. Move the image of the flowers and candle to the upper right corner of the page, so the bottom of the image is aligned with the bottom of the gray banner (Volume 1, Issue 3).

2. Save the file as directed by your instructor and close it.

Skill 4.5 Inserting a Picture

You can insert pictures that you created in another program into your document. There are a number of graphic formats you can insert into a Word document. Some of the more common file types include JPEG, PNG, BMP, and GIF. By default, Word inserts images as embedded objects, meaning they become part of the new document. Changing the source file will not change or affect the newly inserted image.

To insert a picture from a file:

1. Click the **Insert** tab.
2. In the *Illustrations* group, click the **Pictures** button.

FIGURE WD 4.7

3. The *Insert Picture* dialog opens.
4. Navigate to the file location, select the file, and click **Insert.**

To delete a picture, select it and press the **Delete** key on the keyboard.

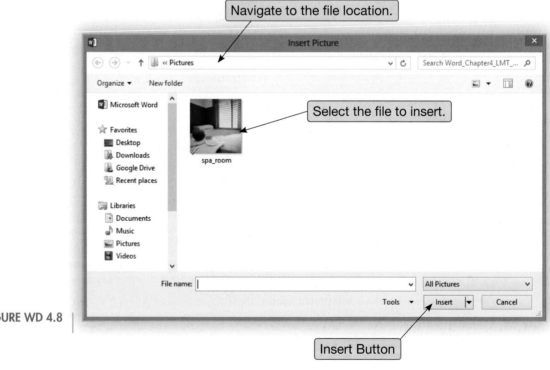

FIGURE WD 4.8

tell me **more**

When you insert a picture to a document, the *Format* tab under *Picture Tools* displays. This tab is called a contextual tab because it only displays when a picture is the active element. The *Format* tab contains tools to change the look of the picture, such as picture style, brightness and contrast, cropping, and placement on the page.

another **method**

To insert the file from the *Insert Picture* dialog, you can also click the **Insert** button arrow and select **Insert.**

let me **try**

Open the student data file **wd4-05-SpaNewsletter** and try this skill on your own:

1. Place the cursor at the end of the **Four New Services** article (below the *Mangoo Facial* bullet on page 2 of the student data file).
2. Open the **Insert Picture** dialog.
3. Navigate to the location where you saved the data files for this book.
4. Insert the **spa_room** picture.
5. Save the file as directed by your instructor and close it.

from the perspective of . . .

A COMMUNITY NEWSPAPER INTERN

When I first started working for the newspaper, articles were text with all the photographs arranged either above or below the text of the article. The text was well formatted, but didn't convey the information in an exciting, visual manner. We do the layout in Word for delivery either in print or online. So, one of the things I thought of was adding video to the online version of the newspaper. I can search for online videos and embed them in articles to be viewed by our readers. I also love playing with Word's picture layout and design tools, so now the newspaper layout has a more dynamic flow.

Skill 4.6 Positioning Pictures

When you first add a picture to your document, Word inserts the picture at the insertion point and displays the picture in line with the text. More often than not, you will want to place the picture somewhere else on the page. Word comes with a number of preset image positions that place the picture at a specific location on the page with text wrapping applied.

To position a picture on a page with text wrapping:

1. Click the **Picture Tools Format** tab.
2. In the *Arrange* group, click the **Position Object** button.
3. In the *With Text Wrapping* section, select an option. The image is placed on the page according to the option you chose.

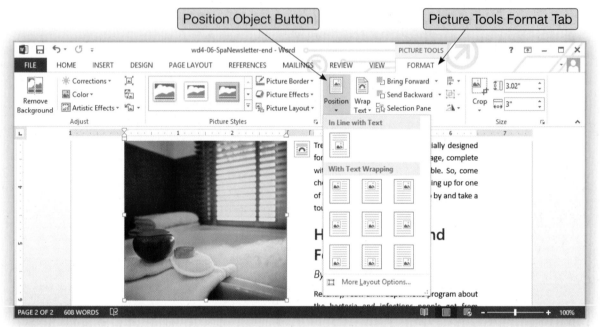

FIGURE WD 4.9

tips & tricks

When you position a picture, the location you choose is for the page the picture is on. If you want the picture to appear on another page, move the picture to that page and then use the **Position Object** command to place it.

another method

You can also position pictures on the page from the *Page Layout* tab. In the *Arrange* group, click the **Position Object** button and select an option.

let me try

Open the student data file **wd4-06-SpaNewsletter** and try this skill on your own:

1. Select the picture on page 2 of the student data file.
2. Position the picture so it is in the middle of the page aligned along the left side.
3. Save the file as directed by your instructor and close it.

Skill 4.7 Applying Quick Styles to Pictures

Quick Styles are a combination of formatting that gives elements of your document a more polished, professional look without a lot of work. Quick Styles for pictures include a combination of borders, shadows, reflections, and picture shapes, such as rounded corners or skewed perspective. Instead of applying each of these formatting elements one at a time, you can apply a combination of elements at one time using a preset Quick Style.

To apply a Quick Style to a picture:

1. Select the picture you want to apply the Quick Style to.
2. Click the **Picture Tools Format** tab.
3. In the *Picture Styles* group, click the **More** button.
4. In the *Picture Quick Styles* gallery, click an option to apply it to the picture.

Choose a formatting style from the *Picture Quick Styles* gallery.

Picture Tools Format Tab

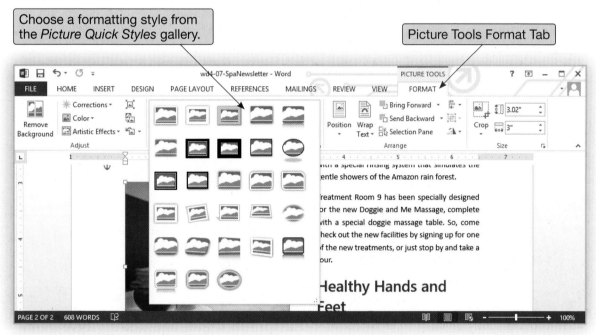

FIGURE WD 4.10

tell me **more**

The same steps for applying Quick Styles to pictures can be used to apply Quick Styles to other drawing objects, such as shapes.

another **method**

To apply a Quick Style to a picture, you can also right-click the picture, click the **Picture** button, and select a Quick Style from the gallery.

let me **try**

Open the student data file **wd4-07-SpaNewsletter** and try this skill on your own:

1. Select the picture on page 2 of the student data file.
2. Apply the **Reflected Rounded Rectangle** Quick Style to the picture (it is the fifth option in the first row of the gallery).
3. Save the file as directed by your instructor and close it.

Skill 4.8 Inserting SmartArt

SmartArt is a way to make your ideas visual. Where documents used to have plain bulleted and ordered lists, now they can have SmartArt, which are visual diagrams containing graphic elements with text boxes in which you can enter your information. Using SmartArt not only makes your document look better, but it helps convey the information in a more meaningful way.

To add SmartArt to a document:

1. Click the **Insert** tab.

2. Click the **SmartArt** button.

FIGURE WD 4.11

3. In the *Choose a SmartArt Graphic* dialog, click a **SmartArt** option and click **OK**.

4. The Smart Art is added to your document.

5. Click in the first item of the *SmartArt Text* pane and type your first item.

6. Enter the text for each item.

7. Click outside the SmartArt graphic to hide the *Text* pane.

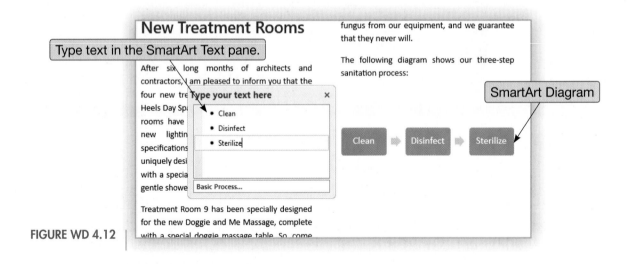

FIGURE WD 4.12

There are eight categories of SmartArt for you to choose from:

List—Use to list items that do not need to be in a particular order.

Process—Use to list items that do need to be in a particular order.

Cycle—Use for a process that repeats over and over again.

Hierarchy—Use to show branching, in either a decision tree or an organization chart.

Relationship—Use to show relationships between items.

Matrix—Use to show how an item fits into the whole.

Pyramid—Use to illustrate how things relate to each other with the largest item on the bottom and the smallest item on the top.

Picture—Use to show a series of pictures along with text in the diagram.

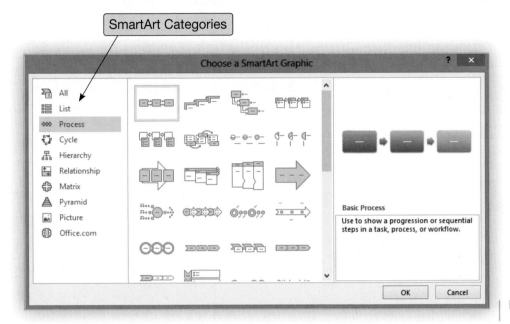

FIGURE WD 4.13

tips & tricks

When choosing a SmartArt diagram, it is important that the diagram type suits your content. In the *Choose a SmartArt Graphic* dialog, click a SmartArt type to display a preview of the SmartArt to the right. The preview displays not only what the diagram will look like, but also includes a description of the best uses for the diagram type.

another method

To enter text in SmartArt, you can click in a text box on the SmartArt diagram and type your text.

let me try

Open the student data file **wd4-08-SpaNewsletter** and try this skill on your own:

1. Place the cursor at the end of the *Healthy Hands and Feet* article (at the end of the second column on the second page).
2. Open the **Choose a SmartArt Graphic** dialog box.
3. Insert a **Basic Process** diagram.
4. Enter **Clean** in the first box.
5. Enter **Disinfect** in the second box.
6. Enter **Sterilize** in the third box.
7. Click outside the diagram to deselect it.
8. Save the file as directed by your instructor and close it.

Skill 4.9 Inserting a Shape

A **shape** is a drawing object that you can quickly add to your document. Word comes with a number of shapes for you to choose from, including lines, block arrows, callouts, and basic shapes such as smiley faces, rectangles, and circles.

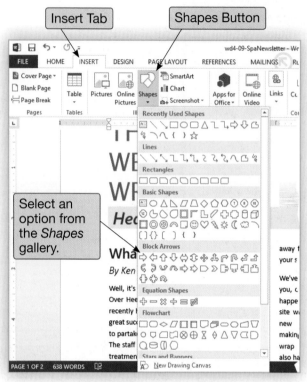

Insert Tab

Shapes Button

Select an option from the *Shapes* gallery.

FIGURE WD 4.14

To add a shape to a document:

1. Click the **Insert** tab.
2. In the *Illustrations* group, click the **Shapes** button and select an option from the *Shapes* gallery.
3. The cursor changes to a crosshair.
4. Click and drag anywhere on the document. As you are dragging, you will see an outline of the shape. When the shape is the size you want, release the mouse button.

tell me **more**

When you insert a shape into a document, the *Drawing Tools Format* tab displays. This is called a contextual tab because it only displays when a drawing object is the active element. The *Format* tab contains tools to change the look of the shape, such as shape styles, effects, and placement on the page. You can apply Quick Styles to shapes by selecting an option in the *Shape Quick Styles* gallery in the *Shape Styles* group. Click the **More** button for the gallery to expand it and view all the Quick Style options you can apply to shapes.

let me **try**

Open the student data file **wd4-09-SpaNewsletter** and try this skill on your own:

1. Add a **12-Point Star** shape next the *What's New* article title.
2. Save the file as directed by your instructor and close it.

Skill 4.10 Adding WordArt to Documents

Sometimes you'll want to call attention to text you have added to your document. You could format the text by using character effects, or if you want the text to really stand out, use **WordArt**. WordArt Quick Styles are predefined graphic styles you can apply to text. These styles include a combination of color, fills, outlines, and effects.

To add WordArt to a document:

1. Click the **Insert** tab.

2. In the *Text* group, click the **Insert WordArt** button and select a Quick Style from the gallery.

3. Replace the text *Your Text Here* with the text for your document.

After you have added WordArt to your document, you can modify it just as you would any other text. Use the *Font* box and *Font Size* box on the *Home* tab to change the font or font size of WordArt.

FIGURE WD 4.15

tell me **more**

In Word 2010, WordArt was changed to allow a wide range of stylization. In previous versions of Microsoft Word, WordArt came with a predefined set of graphic styles that could be formatted, but on a very limited basis.

let me **try**

Open the student data file **wd4-10-SpaNewsletter** and try this skill on your own:

1. Place the cursor at the top of the document.
2. Add WordArt to the document using the **Gradient Fill–Blue, Accent 1, Reflection** style.
3. Replace the text *Your Text Here* with **The Weekly Wrap.**
4. Save the file as directed by your instructor and close it.

Skill 4.11 Adding an Online Video

Today documents are not only printed and read, but often they are delivered and primarily viewed in an electronic format. A new feature in Word 2013 is the ability to add **online video** to a document. You can use Microsoft's *Bing Video Search* to search for videos online and then add them to your documents.

To add an online video to a document:

1. Click the **Insert** tab.
2. In the *Media* group, click the **Online Video** button.

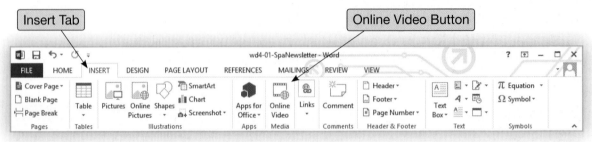

FIGURE WD 4.16

3. The *Insert Video* dialog opens.
4. Type a word describing the video you want to search for in the **Bing Video Search** box and click the **Search** button.

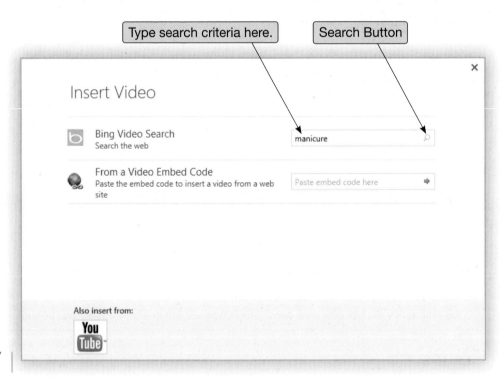

FIGURE WD 4.17

5. Word displays thumbnail results that match the search criteria.
6. Click a thumbnail to select it and click the **Insert** button to add the video to your document.

word 2013   chapter 4 Working with Pictures, Tables, and Charts

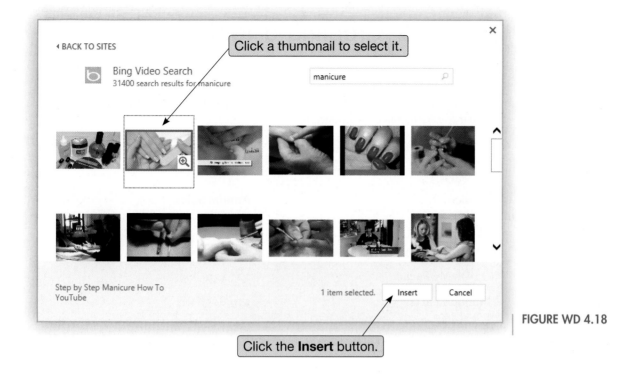

Click a thumbnail to select it.

‹ BACK TO SITES

Bing Video Search
31400 search results for manicure

manicure

Step by Step Manicure How To
YouTube

1 item selected.   Insert   Cancel

Click the **Insert** button.

FIGURE WD 4.18

tips & tricks

To play a video in a document, click the **Play** button. However, not all videos allow you to play the video from the document. If you cannot play the video inside the document, right-click the video and select **Open in Browser** to play the video in your Web browser.

tell me **more**

You can also search for videos to add to documents directly from *YouTube* or embed a video from a Web site by entering a video embed code.

let me try

Open the student data file **wd4-11-SpaProductReport** and try this skill on your own:

1. Place the cursor in the blank line under the first paragraph in the **Basic Mani** section.
2. Open the **Insert Video** dialog.
3. Search for a video about **manicure.**
4. Insert the **Step by Step Manicure How To** video. It is the selected thumbnail in Figure 4.18. *Note:* If you do not see the same thumbnails as in the figure, insert an online video of your choice.
5. Save the file as directed by your instructor and close it.

Skill 4.12 Creating a Table

A **table** helps you organize information for effective display. Tables are organized by **rows**, which display horizontally, and **columns**, which display vertically. The intersection of a row and column is referred to as a **cell**. Tables can be used to display everything from dates in a calendar to sales numbers to product inventory.

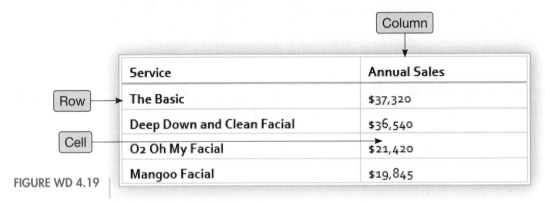

FIGURE WD 4.19

To create a simple table:

1. Click the **Insert** tab.
2. Click the **Table** button.
3. Select the number of cells you want by moving the cursor across and down the squares.
4. When the description at the top of the menu displays the number of rows and columns you want, click the mouse.
5. The table is inserted into your document.

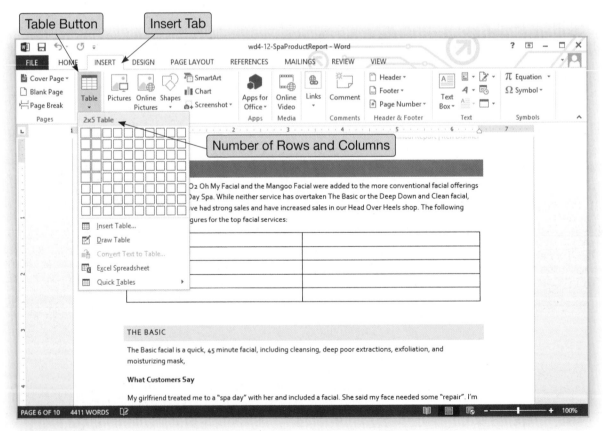

FIGURE WD 4.20

word 2013   chapter 4 Working with Pictures, Tables, and Charts

tips & tricks

Rather than inserting a table and then adding data, you can convert existing text into a table. After selecting the text to be converted, click the **Table** button and click **Insert Table...** The number of rows and columns will automatically be determined by the tabs and paragraphs in the selection.

tell me **more**

Word 2013 comes with a number of Quick Tables building blocks. These templates are preformatted for you and include sample data. To insert a Quick Table, click the **Tables** button, point to **Quick Tables,** and select a building block option from the gallery. After you insert a Quick Table, just replace the sample data with your own.

another **method**

To insert a table, you can also:

1. Click the **Table** button and select **Insert Table...**
2. In the *Insert Table* dialog box, enter the number of rows and columns for your table.
3. Click **OK.**

let me **try**

Open the student data file **wd4-12-SpaProductReport** and try this skill on your own:

1. Navigate to the *FACIALS* section of the document and place the cursor on the blank line under the first paragraph of the section.
2. Insert a table that has **two columns** and **five rows.**
3. Save the file as directed by your instructor and close it.

Skill 4.13 Working with Tables

Once you have inserted a blank table, you will need to enter data. When entering data in a table, it is a good idea to use the first row as a heading row by typing a short description of the content for the column in each cell. After you have labeled each column, continue entering the data into your table.

To enter data in a table:

1. Place the cursor in the cell where you want to enter the data.
2. Type the data just as you would in normal text.
3. Press (Tab ⇆) to move to the next cell and enter more data.
4. When you reach the last cell in the last row of a table, pressing [Tab] on the keyboard will create a new row in the table.
5. Continue pressing (Tab ⇆) until all data are entered.

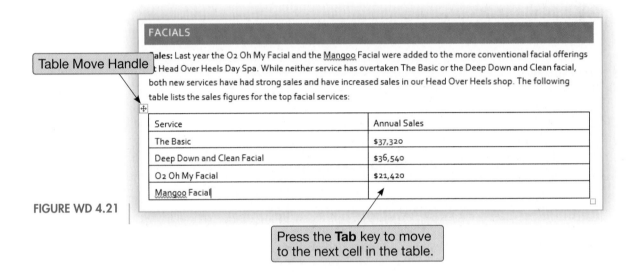

Table Move Handle

FIGURE WD 4.21

Press the **Tab** key to move to the next cell in the table.

After you have entered data in a table, you will most likely want to manipulate all or part of the table. You can select individual rows or columns to work with or the entire table:

❱ To select a row, point to the left side of the row you want to select. When the cursor changes to a white arrow ⇗, press the mouse button. The selected row will appear highlighted.

❱ To select a column, point to the top of the column you want to select. When the cursor changes to a black, down-pointing arrow ↓, press the mouse button. The selected column will appear highlighted.

❱ To select the entire table, click the **table move handle** that appears at the upper left corner of the table when it is active.

tell me **more**

When working with tables, the conventional way to identify a cell is by column and row. Columns are typically referred to by letters and rows by numbers. Thus, the first cell in the third row would be identified as "cell A3" and the third cell in the first row would be identified as "C1."

another **method**

To select parts of a table, you can also:

1. Click the **Table Tools Layout** tab.
2. In the *Table* group, click the **Select** button and select an option.

let me **try**

Open the student data file **wd4-13-SpaProductReport** and try this skill on your own:

1. Navigate to the empty table in the *FACIALS* section (it is located on page 6 of the student data file).
2. Practice selecting a row, a column, and the entire table.
3. Enter the following information in the table. Press the (Tab ⇄) key to move between cells in the table.

SERVICE	ANNUAL SALES
The Basic	$37,320
Deep Down and Clean Facial	$36,540
O2 Oh My Facial	$21,420
Mangoo Facial	$19,845

4. Save the file as directed by your instructor and close it.

Skill 4.14 Inserting Rows and Columns

Once you have created a table, you often find you need more rows or columns. In Word 2013, you can now quickly add rows and columns to tables with **Insert Controls**. Insert Controls appear when you roll your mouse over the left edge of a row or the top edge of a column.

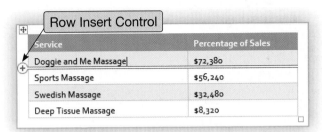

FIGURE WD 4.22

To add a new row using an Insert Control:

1. Roll your mouse along the left side of the table.
2. When the **Insert Control** appears where you want to add the new row, click the **control.**

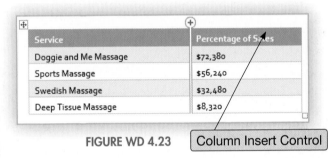

FIGURE WD 4.23 Column Insert Control

To add a new column using an Insert Control:

1. Roll your mouse along the top of the table.
2. When the **Insert Control** appears where you want to add the new column, click the **control.**

tips & tricks

A quick way to insert a new row at the end of a table is to place the cursor in the last cell in the last row and then press the `Tab` key. A new row is automatically added to the table, with your cursor in its first cell.

another method

▶ To insert an additional row and column, you can also click the **Table Tools Layout** tab. In the *Rows & Columns* group, click the **Insert Above** or **Insert Below** buttons to insert a new row. Click the **Insert Left** or **Insert Right** buttons to insert a new column.

▶ You can also insert rows and columns by right-clicking in a cell, pointing to **Insert** and selecting **Insert Rows Above, Insert Rows Below, Insert Columns to the Left,** or **Insert Columns to the Right.**

▶ You can also insert rows and columns by right-clicking in a cell, clicking the **Insert** button on the Mini toolbar, and selecting an option.

let me try

Open the student data file **wd4-14-SpaProductReport** and try this skill on your own:

1. Navigate to the table in the *FACIALS* section.
2. Insert a new row between the first and second row in the table.
3. Insert a new column on the right side of the table.
4. Save the file as directed by your instructor and close it.

Skill 4.15 Deleting Columns, Rows, and Cells

After you have added information to your table, you may find that you no longer want to include everything you added. Even if you delete the text in a table row or column, the empty row or column still remains. To remove the row or column from the table, you must delete the row or column, not just the text. When you delete a row or column from a table, the content along with the table element is removed.

To delete a row or column:

1. Select the row or column you want to delete.
2. The Mini toolbar displays.
3. Click the **Delete** button and select an option.

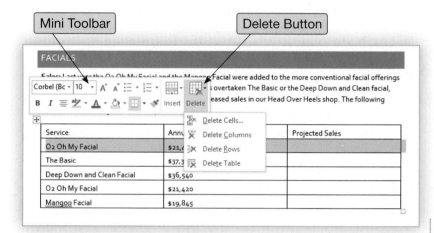

FIGURE WD 4.24

tips & tricks

You can also delete individual cells from a table. When you delete a cell, the *Delete Cells* dialog appears. Here you can choose to shift the cells to the left or up. You can also choose to delete the entire row or column the cell belongs to.

another method

To delete rows and columns you can also:

▸ Select the row or column you want to delete. Right-click in the row or column, and select **Delete Row** or **Delete Column.**

▸ Click in the row or column you want to delete. Click the **Table Tools Layout** tab. In the *Rows & Columns* group, click the **Delete** button and select an option.

let me try

Open the student data file **wd4-15-SpaProductReport** and try this skill on your own:

1. Navigate to the table in the *FACIALS* section.
2. Delete the **second row** in the table.
3. Delete the **Projected Sales** column.
4. Save the file as directed by your instructor and close it.

Skill 4.16 Sizing Tables, Columns, and Rows

When you insert a table, it covers the full width of the page and the columns and rows are evenly spaced. Once you have entered your data, you will probably find the table is larger than it needs to be and the columns and rows need adjusting. You can resize your table using Word's *AutoFit* commands.

To adjust the width and height of cells using the *AutoFit* command:

1. Click in the table you want to resize.
2. Click the **Table Tools Layout** tab.
3. In the *Cell Size* group, click the **AutoFit** button.
4. Select **AutoFit Contents** to resize the cell to fit the text of the table. Select **AutoFit Window** to resize the table to the size of the page.

   Rather than using the *AutoFit* command, you can specify a width and height for table cells from the Ribbon.

To adjust the width and height of cells:

1. Click in the row or column you want to resize.
2. On the *Table Tools Layout* tab, in the *Cell Size* group, adjust the numbers for the **Table Row Height** and **Table Column Width** by clicking the up and down arrows in the control box.

   To resize all the rows in a table so they have the same height, in the *Cell Size* group click the **Distribute Rows** button. Click the **Distribute Columns** to resize all the columns in a table so they have the same width.

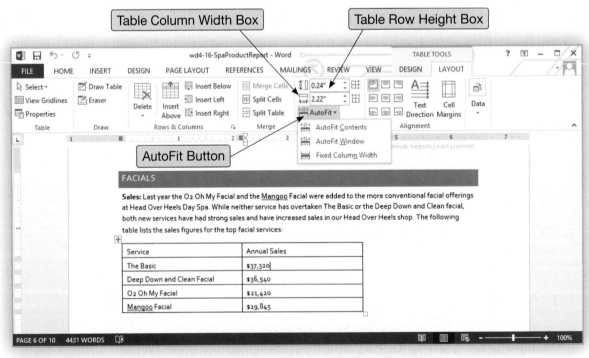

FIGURE WD 4.25

word 2013 chapter 4 Working with Pictures, Tables, and Charts

tips & tricks

Once you have resized a table, you will probably want to position it better on the page. You can do this by using the **table move handle** tool that appears at the top-left corner of the table when the mouse pointer is placed over the table. Click the move handle and drag the table to where you want it.

tell me **more**

Each cell is set up as one line, but if you type more data than will fit in one line, Word will automatically wrap and create another line within the cell, making the row taller. If this happens, all the cells in that row will be affected.

another **method**

To resize a table, you can also:

1. Select the table you want to resize.
2. When the **resize handle** appears at the bottom-right corner of the table, click and drag it until you achieve the desired size. This method can also be used to resize columns and rows.

let me **try**

Open the student data file **wd4-16-SpaProductReport** and try this skill on your own:

1. Navigate to the table in the *FACIALS* section.
2. Use the **AutoFit** command to resize the table so it fits the window.
3. Save the file as directed by your instructor and close it.

Skill 4.17 Merging and Splitting Cells

When you first create a table, it is a grid of rows and columns. But what if you want to display your content across columns or across rows? For instance, if the first row of your table includes the title for the table, then you will probably want to display the title in a single cell that spans all the columns of the table. In this case, you will want to *merge* the cells in the first row into one cell. On the other hand, if you have a cell that contains multiple values, you may want to *split* the cell so it can display each value in a separate row or column. Use the merge cells and split cells commands to customize the layout of tables. Merging cells entails combining multiple cells into one; splitting a cell divides the cell into multiple cells.

To merge cells in a table:

1. Select the cells you want to merge into one.
2. Click the **Table Tools Layout** tab.
3. In the *Merge* group, click the **Merge Cells** button.

To split a cell in a table:

1. Select the cell you want to split.
2. In the *Merge* group, click the **Split Cells** button.
3. In the *Split Cells* dialog box, enter the number of columns and rows.
4. Click **OK** to split the cell.

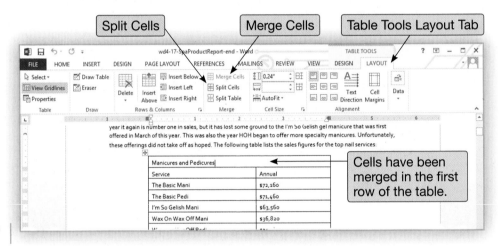

FIGURE WD 4.26

tips & tricks

In addition to splitting cells, you also split a table, creating two tables from one. To split a table into two tables:

1. Place the cursor in the row where you want to split the table.
2. In the *Merge* group, click the **Split Table** button.

another method

▶ To merge cells, you can right-click the selected cells and select **Merge Cells** from the menu.

▶ To split cells, you can right-click a cell and select **Split Cells...** from the menu.

let me try

Open the student data file **wd4-17-SpaProductReport** and try this skill on your own:

1. Navigate to the table in the *MANICURES AND PEDICURES* section.
2. Split the first row of the table into two columns and one row.
3. Merge the cells in the first row of the table.
4. Save the file as directed by your instructor and close it.

word 2013   chapter 4 Working with Pictures, Tables, and Charts

Skill 4.18 Sorting Data in Tables

After you have entered data in a table, you may decide it needs to be displayed in a different order. **Sorting** rearranges the rows in your table by the text in a column or columns. Word allows you to sort data based on the first character of each entry. You can sort in alphabetical or numeric order, in either ascending (A–Z) or descending (Z–A) order.

To sort a column alphabetically:

1. Click the **Table Tools Layout** tab.
2. In the *Data* group, click the **Sort** button.

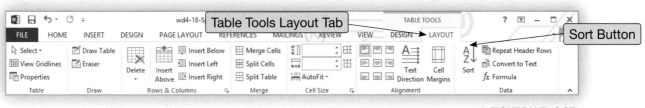

FIGURE WD 4.27

3. The *Sort* dialog box opens.
4. Click the **Sort by** arrow and select a field to sort by.
5. The *Ascending* radio button is selected by default.
6. If your table has a header row that you do not want to include in the sort, select the **Header row** radio button.
7. Click **OK** to sort the text in the table.

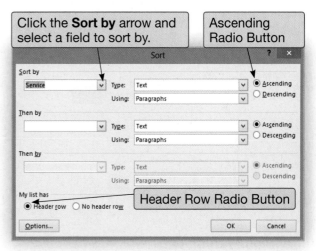

FIGURE WD 4.28

tips & tricks

You can sort by text, number, or date. You can refine the sort by choosing additional fields to sort by:

» If you want to sort the text in reverse order, from Z to A, click the **Descending** radio button.

» Word can sort upper- and lowercase letters differently. Click the **Options...** button in the *Sort* dialog box and then click the **Case sensitive** check box in the *Sort Options* dialog box.

another method

To open the *Sort* dialog box, from the *Home* tab, in the *Paragraph* group, click the **Sort** button.

let me try

Open the student data file **wd4-18-SpaProduct Report** and try this skill on your own:

1. Navigate to the table in the *MANICURES AND PEDICURES* section.
2. Open the **Sort** dialog.
3. Sort the table in descending order based on the content of the **Annual** column. Be sure not to include the header row in the sort.
4. Save the file as directed by your instructor and close it.

Skill 4.19 Applying Table Quick Styles

Just as you can apply complex formatting to paragraphs using Quick Styles for text, you can apply complex formatting to tables using Quick Styles for tables. Using Quick Styles for tables, you can change the text color along with the borders and shading for a table, giving it a professional, sophisticated look without a lot of work.

To apply a Quick Style to a table:

1. Click the **Table Tools Design** tab.
2. In the *Table Styles* group, click the **More** button.
3. Select a Quick Style from the *Quick Styles* gallery.

By default, the Word *Table Styles* gallery displays styles that include header rows, banded rows, and first column layouts. Depending on the information in your table, you may not want to format your table using all these options. If you want to change the options that display in the gallery, check or uncheck the options in the *Table Styles Options* group.

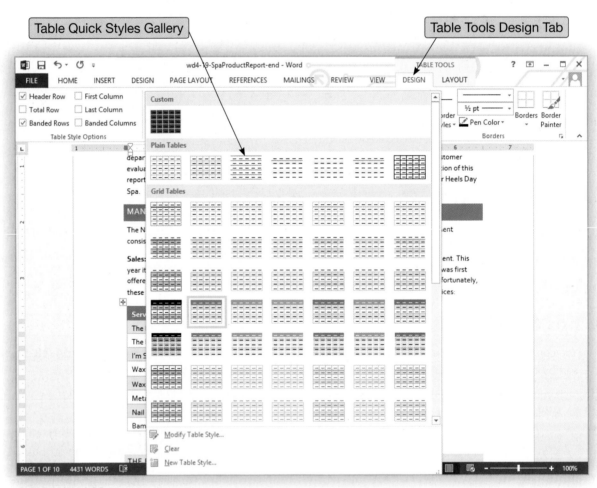

FIGURE WD 4.29

word 2013   chapter 4 Working with Pictures, Tables, and Charts

tips & tricks

To create your own table style, click the **More** button and select **New Table Style...** In the *Create New Style from Formatting* dialog box, you can create a new table style based on an existing table style, changing options such as gridlines and shading to suit your needs. When you save the style, it will appear in the *Table Styles* gallery.

tell me **more**

In addition to applying a Quick Style to a table, you can change the shading, or background color, applied to the table. Adding shading to a table helps it stand out on a page. To apply shading to a table, click the **Shading** button in the *Table Styles* group. A palette of colors displays. Select a color to change the background color for the table.

another **method**

The *Table Styles* group on the Ribbon displays the latest Quick Styles you have used. If you want to apply a recently used Quick Style, you can click the option directly from the Ribbon without opening the *Quick Styles* gallery.

let me **try**

Open the student data file **wd4-19-SpaProductReport** and try this skill on your own:

1. Navigate to the table in the *MANICURES AND PEDICURES* section.
2. Change the *Quick Style* gallery display so formats with **first column** formatting do not display.
3. Apply the **Grid Table 4–Accent 1** Quick Style to the table (it is the second option in the fourth row under *Grid Tables*).
4. Save the file as directed by your instructor and close it.

Skill 4.20 Adding Borders to a Table

When you first create a table, it uses the simple grid style. You can apply a Quick Style to your table to quickly add formatting, but what if you want to further adjust the look of a table after applying the Quick Style? You can choose different shading for your table and add and remove borders to change the look of the entire table or just parts of the table.

To change the borders for a table:

1. Select the table you want to change.

2. Click the **Table Tools Design** tab.

3. In the *Borders* group, click the **Borders** button arrow.

4. Click a border option to apply it to the table.

If your table does not show borders, you can display **gridlines** to give you a visual guide. The gridlines appear as a dotted line on screen but do not print as part of the final document. To display gridlines, click the **Borders** button and select **View Gridlines.**

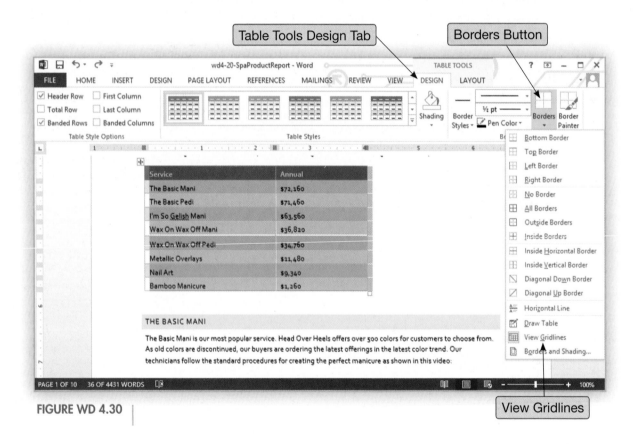

FIGURE WD 4.30

tips & tricks

The **Border Styles** button allows you format specific borders in your table.

1. On the *Table Tools Design* tab, in the *Borders* group, click the **Border** Styles button.
2. Select an option from the gallery.
3. The *Border Painter* becomes active.
4. Click and drag the mouse across the border you want to change to apply the border style.

another method

You can change the borders of a table by clicking the *Home* tab. In the *Paragraph* group, click the arrow next to the *Borders* button and select an option.

You can change borders and shading through the *Borders and Shading* dialog box. To open the *Borders and Shading* dialog box:

❭ From the *Home* tab or from the *Design* tab, click the arrow next to the *Borders* button and select **Borders and Shading...**
❭ Right-click on the table and select **Borders and Shading...** from the menu.

let me try

Open the student data file **wd4-20-SpaProductReport** and try this skill on your own:

1. Select the table in the *MANICURES AND PEDICURES* section.
2. Apply an **outside border** to the table.
3. Save the file as directed by your instructor and close it.

Skill 4.21 Creating a Chart

Charts allow you to take raw data and display them in a visual way. A **chart** takes the values you have entered in a spreadsheet and converts them to graphic representation. In Word, you can create a wide variety of charts, including bar charts, pie charts, column charts, and line charts.

To add a chart to a document:

1. Click the **Insert** tab.
2. In the *Illustrations* group, click the **Add a Chart** button.

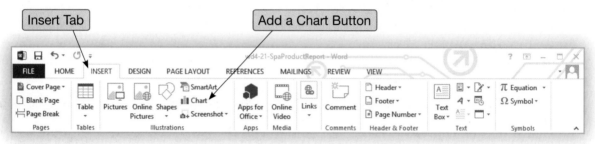

FIGURE WD 4.31

3. In the *Insert Chart* dialog, click a chart type category to display that category in the right pane.
4. Click a chart type in the right pane to select it.
5. Click **OK** to add the chart to the document.

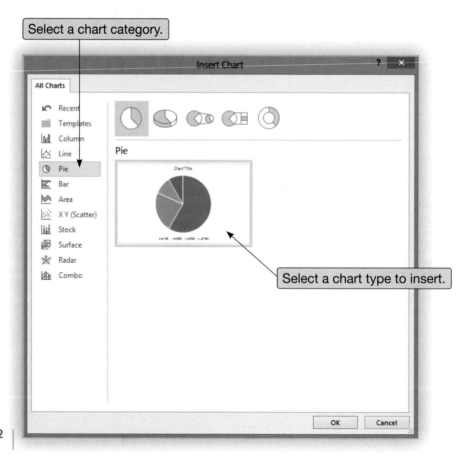

FIGURE WD 4.32

Word automatically opens the *Chart in Microsoft Word* dialog. Think of this dialog as a simplified spreadsheet where you can enter the data for your chart. The dialog opens with sample data entered for you.

1. Replace the sample data with your own data.
2. Click the **Close** button to return to Word to see your finished chart.

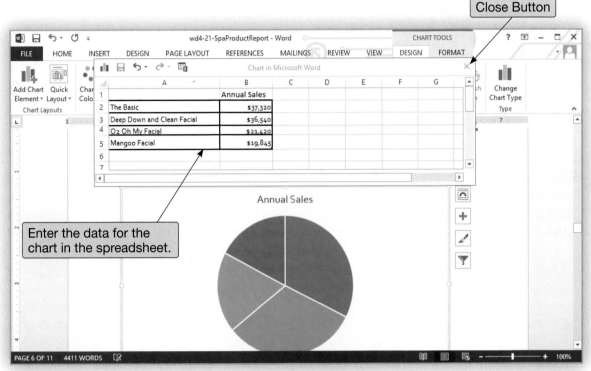

FIGURE WD 4.33

tell me **more**

As you enter data in the *Chart in Microsoft Word* dialog, Word will update the chart as you enter data and move from cell to cell in the spreadsheet.

let me **try**

Open the student data file **wd4-21-SpaProductReport** and try this skill on your own:

1. Navigate to the *FACIALS* section and place your cursor on the empty line.
2. Insert a **pie chart** into the document.
3. Enter the following information for the chart:

	ANNUAL SALES
The Basic	$37,320
Deep Down and Clean Facial	$36,540
O2 Oh My Facial	$21,420
Mangoo Facial	$19,845

4. Close the *Chart in Microsoft Word* dialog.
5. Save the file as directed by your instructor and close it.

Skill 4.22 Modifying a Chart

When you insert a chart, Word displays the chart based on the chart type and the document's theme. But what if you want to change the look of your chart? Word includes a number of chart styles for you to choose from. These styles are a combination of chart layout styles and formatting options.

To change the style of a chart:

1. Select the chart you want to change.

2. Click the **Chart Styles** button on the right side of the chart.

3. Scroll the list of styles. Click a style to apply it to the chart.

To hide and show chart elements, such as the chart title and legend, click the **Chart Elements** button and select and deselect options to show and hide them on the chart.

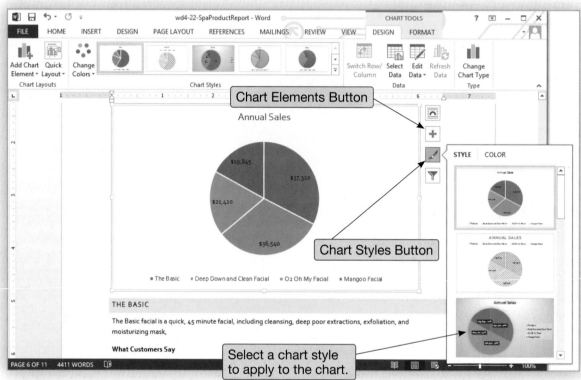

FIGURE WD 4.34

tips & tricks

To change the color of the chart, click the **Color** button in the *Chart Styles* pane. Word displays a number of color sets for you to choose from. These color sets are based on the color theme applied to the document. Select a color set to apply to the chart.

another method

To change the chart style, you can also:

1. Click the **Chart Tools Design** tab.

2. In the *Chart Styles* group, click the style you want to use, or click the **More** button to see all of the chart styles available.

let me try

Open the student data file **wd4-22-SpaProductReport** and try this skill on your own:

1. Navigate to the *FACIALS* section of the document and select the chart.

2. Apply the **Style 3** chart style to the chart.

3. Save the file as directed by your instructor and close it.

Online picture
Clip art
Clips
Resize handle
Layout Options
Alignment guides
Move cursor
Quick Styles
SmartArt
Shape
WordArt

Online Video
Table
Row
Column
Cell
Insert Control
Merge cells
Split cells
Sorting
Gridlines
Chart

concepts review

1. To add clip art to a document, click the _____ button.

   a. Insert Picture

   b. Online Picture

   c. Online Video

   d. Insert Shape

2. To have text wrap around an image, select the image and click the _____ button.

   a. Layout Options

   b. Group

   c. Align

   d. Rotate

3. When you move an image on a page, special green lines called _____ appear, helping you align the image to other elements on the page.

   a. grids

   b. guides

   c. anchors

   d. handles

4. A(n) _____ is a combination of formatting, including color, shadows, and reflections, that you apply to pictures.

   a. Picture Effect

   b. Artistic Effect

   c. Quick Style

   d. Style Set

5. Visual diagrams containing graphic elements with text boxes for you to enter your information in are called _____.

   a. charts

   b. SmartArt

   c. WordArt

   d. tables

6. _____ allows you to quickly add rows and columns to tables.
   a. An Alignment Guide
   b. An Insert Control
   c. A header row
   d. The merge cells command

7. You can add online pictures from _____.
   a. *Office.com*
   b. *Bing Image Search*
   c. your SkyDrive
   d. All of the above

8. To display the content of multiple cells in a single cell that spans several columns, you should _____ the cells
   a. merge
   b. split
   c. insert
   d. autofit

9. Preset drawing objects, such as block arrows and callouts, that you can quickly add to your document are called _____.
   a. clips
   b. shapes
   c. pictures
   d. SmartArt

10. _____ are organized by rows, which display horizontally, and columns, which display vertically.
    a. Charts
    b. Tables
    c. Diagrams
    d. None of the above

projects

skill review 4.1

In this project you will be editing the *WD2013-SkillReview-4-1* document from Suarez Marketing.

Skills needed to complete this project:

- Inserting Online Pictures (Skill 4.1)
- Resizing Pictures (Skill 4.2)
- Changing Picture Layouts (Skill 4.3)
- Moving Pictures (Skill 4.4)
- Inserting SmartArt (Skill 4.8)
- Creating a Table (Skill 4.12)
- Working with Tables (Skill 4.13)
- Inserting Rows and Columns (Skill 4.14)
- Merging and Splitting Cells (Skill 4.17)
- Sizing Tables, Columns, and Rows (Skill 4.16)
- Applying Table Quick Styles (Skill 4.19)
- Adding Borders to a Table (Skill 4.20)
- Inserting a Picture (Skill 4.5)
- Positioning Pictures (Skill 4.6)

1. Open the **WD2013-SkillReview-4-1** document.

2. Save this document as: **[your initials]WD-SkillReview-4-1**

3. Insert an online picture in the document.

   a. Place the cursor in the blank line above the **What Clients are Saying** heading.

   b. Click the **Insert** tab.

   c. In the *Illustrations* group, click the **Online Pictures** button.

   d. In the *Office.com Clip Art* search box, type **customer service** and click the **Search** button.

   e. Find the photograph of the **woman with the cash register.** Click the **image** to select it and click the **Insert** button.

4. Resize a picture.

   a. With the picture selected, on the *Picture Tools Format* tab, in the *Size* group, type **1.5"** in the *Height* box and press ⏎ Enter .

5. Change the layout on a picture.

   a. With the picture selected, click the **Layout Options** button.

   b. Select the **Square** wrapping option.

   c. Click outside the *Layout Options* box to hide it.

6. Move a picture.

   a. Click and drag the picture up and to the right.

   b. Using the guides, place the picture so it is aligned just under the horizontal line in the *Why I Do What I Do* section and aligned with the right side of the text in the document.

7. Insert a *SmartArt* diagram.

   a. Place the cursor in the empty line in the *Suarez marketing process* section.

   b. Click the **Insert** tab.

   c. In the *Illustrations* group, click the **Insert a SmartArt Graphic** button.

   d. Click the **Cycle** category and click the **Segmented Cycle** option. Click **OK.**

   e. In the upper left segment, type `Analyze Needs`.

   f. In the upper right segment, type `Design Project`.

   g. In the lower segment, type `Implement Campaign`.

   h. Click outside the diagram to deselect it.

8. Add a table to the document and enter text into the table.

   a. Place the cursor in the empty line at the end of the document.

   b. Click the **Insert** tab.

   c. In the *Tables* group, click the **Add a Table** button and select a **2 × 1** (two columns and one row) table.

   d. Type the information below into the table. Press **Tab** to move forward from cell to cell. Press **Tab** at the end of a row to insert a new row.

Commitment	To the needs of the client
Communication	Seek first to listen
Trust	Begins with open communication
Integrity	Doing the right thing
Customers	Always come first
Teamwork	Working together for success
Success	Results with integrity
Creativity	Ideas before results
Win-Win	Is always the goal

9. Insert a row.

   a. Place the cursor in the first row of the table.

   b. Click the **Table Tools Layout** tab.

   c. In the *Rows & Columns* group, click the **Insert Rows Above** button.

   d. Type `Suarez Marketing Beliefs`

   e. Apply the following formatting to the text:

      i. Font: **Calibri Light**

      ii. Size: **14 pt**

      iii. Color: **Blue, Accent 5**

10. Merge cells in a table.

    a. Select the first row in the table.

    b. Click the **Table Tools Layout** tab.

    c. In the *Merge* group, click the **Merge Cells** button.

11. Change the height of rows in a table.

    a. Select the table.

    b. On the *Table Tools Layout* tab, in the *Cell Size* group, click the **Height box up arrow** until **0.3"** appears in the box.

12. Apply a Quick Style to the table.

    a. Click the **Table Tools Design** tab.

    b. In *Table Style Options* group, click the **First Column** check box so it is deselected.

    c. In the *Table Styles* group, click the **More** button.

    d. In the *List Tables* section, select the **List Table 2–Accent 5** Quick Style (it is the second to last style in the first row).

13. Apply a border to the table.

    a. On the *Table Tools Design* tab, in the *Borders* group, click the **Borders** button.

    b. Select **Outside Border.**

14. Insert a logo from a location on your computer.

    a. Navigate to the beginning of the document and place the cursor above the name **Maria Suarez.**

    b. Click the **Insert** tab.

    c. In the *Illustrations* group, click the **Pictures** button.

    d. In the *Insert Picture* dialog, browse to your student data file location, select the **Suarez_logo** file, and click the **Insert** button.

15. Position the logo on the page.

    a. On the *Picture Tools Format* tab, in the *Arrange* group, click the **Position** button.

    b. Select the **Position in Top Right with Square Text Wrapping** option (it is the third option in the first row under *With Text Wrapping*).

16. Save and close the document.

skill review 4.2

In this project you will be editing the *WD2013-SkillReview-4-2* document for the Tri-State Book Festival.

Skills needed to complete this project:

- Adding WordArt to Documents (Skill 4.10)
- Changing Picture Layouts (Skill 4.3)
- Inserting a Shape (Skill 4.9)
- Applying Quick Styles to Pictures (Skill 4.7)
- Creating a Chart (Skill 4.21)
- Modifying a Chart (Skill 4.22)
- Working with Tables (Skill 4.13)
- Deleting Columns, Rows, and Cells (Skill 4.15)
- Merging and Splitting Cells (Skill 4.17)

- Inserting Rows and Columns (Skill 4.14)
- Sorting Data in Tables (Skill 4.18)
- Applying Table Quick Styles (Skill 4.19)
- Inserting Online Pictures (Skill 4.1)
- Resizing Pictures (Skill 4.2)
- Moving Pictures (Skill 4.4)

1. Open the **WD2013-SkillReview-4-2** document.

2. Save this document as: **[your initials]WD-SkillReview-4-2**

3. Add WordArt to a document.

   a. Place the cursor at the top of the document.

   b. Click the **Insert** tab.

   c. In the *Text* group, click the **Insert Word Art** button.

   d. Select the **Gradient Fill–Teal, Accent 1, Reflection** WordArt style (it is the second option in the second row of the gallery).

   e. Type **Tri-State Book Festival**.

4. Change the layout of the WordArt.

   a. Click the **Layout Options** button.

   b. Select the **In Line with Text** option.

   c. Click outside the *Layout Options* box to hide it.

5. Insert a shape.

   a. Click the **Insert** tab.

   b. In the *Illustrations* group, click the **Shapes** button and select **Vertical Scroll** option in the *Stars and Banners* section.

   c. The cursor changes to a crosshair cursor.

   d. Click to the right of the WordArt text you added to add the scroll shape (the drawing should be 1.25" in height and 1.13" in width).

   e. If necessary, move the scroll shape so the bottom is aligned with the bottom of the WordArt and it appears within the blue page border.

6. Apply a Quick Style to a picture.

   a. If necessary, select the scroll shape at the top of the document.

   b. On the *Drawing Tools Design* tab, in the *Shape Styles* group, click the **More** button.

   c. In the *Shape Quick Styles* gallery, select **Colored Outline–Blue, Accent 3** (it is the fourth option in the first row).

7. Add a pie chart to the document.

   a. Place the cursor on the empty line below the line *The following chart shows the breakdown of authors by genre:*.

   b. Click the **Insert** tab.

   c. In the *Illustrations* group, click the **Add a Chart** button.

   d. In the *Insert Chart* dialog, click the **Pie** category on the left.

   e. Verify the **Pie** option (the first option) is selected.

   f. Click **OK**.

   g. In the *Chart in Microsoft Word* dialog, change the data in the chart to match Figure WD 4.35.

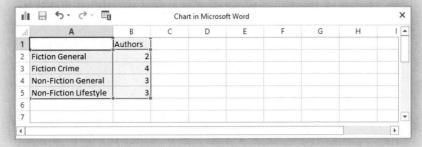

FIGURE WD 4.35

    h. Click the **Close** button in the *Chart in Microsoft Word* dialog.

8. Modify the look of the chart.

    a. Click the **Chart Styles** button.

    b. Scroll the list of chart styles and rest your mouse over each style to see the name of the style. Select the **Style 6** option.

    c. Click outside the chart to deselect it.

9. Delete rows from tables.

    a. Navigate to *AGENDA* section.

    b. In the first table, select the row with the text **Monday October 10.**

    c. Click the **Table Tools Layout** tab.

    d. In the *Rows & Columns* group, click the **Delete** button.

    e. Click **Delete Rows.**

    f. Repeat these steps to delete the first row of the other two tables in this section.

10. Merge cells in a table.

    a. In the *Monday October 10* table, select the **Cocktail reception and dinner cell** and the **two empty cells** to the right.

    b. On the *Table Tools Layout* tab, in the *Merge* group, click the **Merge Cells** button.

11. Insert a row to a table.

    a. In the *Monday October 10* table, place the cursor in the **4:00–5:00 cell.**

    b. Move the cursor to the left until you see the **Insert Row** button above the cell.

    c. Click the **Insert Row** button to add a new blank row.

    d. In the blank cell under *Time,* type `2:00-3:00`

    e. In the blank cell under *The Westfield Theater,* type `Keynote and Welcome`

12. Sort data in a table.

    a. In the *Monday October 10* table, select all the rows except the first row.

    b. On the *Table Tools Layout* tab, in the *Data* group, click the **Sort** button.

    c. Verify the column will sort in ascending order, by the first column, using the text in the cells. Click **OK.**

13. Apply Quick Styles to tables.

    a. Select the **Monday October 10** table.

    b. Click the **Table Tools Design** tab.

    c. In the *Table Styles* group, click the **More** button.

    d. In the *Grid Tables* section, click the **Grid Table 5 Dark–Accent 2** option (it is the third option in the third row under *Grid Tables*).

    e. Apply this table Quick Style to the other two tables in the *AGENDA* section.

FIGURE WD 4.36

14. Insert an online picture.

   a. Place the cursor at the beginning of the first paragraph in the *AUTHORS* section.

   b. Click the **Insert** tab.

   c. In the *Illustrations* group, click the **Online Pictures** button.

   d. In the *Office.com Clip Art* search box, type `stack of books` and click the **Search** button.

   e. Find the photograph of the **spiraling stack of books** (see Figure WD 4.36). **NOTE:** If you do not see the same image as in the figure, insert an online picture of your choice.

   f. Click the **image** to select it and click the **Insert** button.

15. Resize a picture and change the layout.

   a. With the picture selected, on the *Picture Tools Format* tab, in the *Size* group, type **2.5"** in the *Height* box and press ⬅ Enter .

   b. Click the **Layout Options** button.

   c. Select the **Square** option in the *With Text Wrapping* section.

16. Save and close the document.

challenge yourself **4.3**

In this project you will be editing the *WD2013-ChallengeYourself-4-3* document from Greenscapes landscaping company.

Skills needed to complete this project:

- Inserting Online Pictures (Skill 4.1)
- Resizing Pictures (Skill 4.2)
- Changing Picture Layouts (Skill 4.3)
- Moving Pictures (Skill 4.4)
- Inserting SmartArt (Skill 4.8)
- Inserting a Picture (Skill 4.5)
- Positioning Pictures (Skill 4.6)
- Creating a Table (Skill 4.12)
- Working with Tables (Skill 4.13)
- Sorting Data in a Table (Skill 4.18)
- Inserting Rows and Columns (Skill 4.14)
- Merging and Splitting Cells (Skill 4.17)
- Sizing Tables, Columns, and Rows (Skill 4.16)
- Applying Table Quick Styles (Skill 4.19)
- Adding Borders to a Table (Skill 4.20)

FIGURE WD 4.37

1. Open the **WD2013-ChallengeYourself-4-3** document.

2. Save this document as: **[your initials]WD-ChallengeYourself-4-3**

3. Insert an online picture in the document.

   a. Place the cursor on the blank line at the end of the *Our Philosophy* section.

   b. Search for images of a **landscaped garden** on the *Office.com Clip Art* site.

   c. Insert the photograph of the **Landscaped garden and lawn** (see Figure WD 4.37). **NOTE:** If you do not see the same image as in the figure, insert an online picture of your choice.

4. Resize the picture so it is **1.25"** in height.

5. Apply the **Square** layout option to the picture.

6. Move a picture so it is aligned under the *Our Philosophy* heading with the paragraph text displayed to the right. Use the guides so the top of the pictured is aligned with the top of the paragraph text and the left side of the picture is aligned with the left side of the heading text.

7. Insert a *SmartArt* diagram.

    a. Place the cursor in the empty line after the first paragraph in the *Leaf Removal* section.

    b. Insert a **Basic Process** SmartArt diagram.

    c. Enter `Blow and Rake` in the first box.

    d. Enter `Gather and Haul Away` in the second box.

    e. Enter `Compost` in the third box.

8. Insert a logo from a location on your computer.

    a. Navigate to the *Services* section of the document. Place the cursor before the *Lawn Care* heading.

    b. Insert the **greenscapes_logo** picture from you student data file location.

9. Change the position of the logo so it appears in the **top left corner of the page with square wrapping.**

10. Add a table to the document and enter text into the table.

    a. Place the cursor at the end of the document.

    b. Insert a table with the following information:

Lawn Maintenance	Fertilization, Insect and Disease Control	$ 99.00 per treatment
Shrub and Tree Maintenance	Pruning, Fertilization, Insect and Disease Control	$ 125.00 per hour
Leaf Removal	Composting included	$ 25.00 per hour
Lawn Care	Mowing, Edging, Weed-eating	$ 25.00 per service (weekly) $ 18.00 per service (bi-weekly)
All Four Services	15% Customer Discount	
Specialty Services	As Requested	Call for a quote

11. Sort data in the table

    a. Select the first four rows of the table.

    b. Sort the text in the selected row in ascending order based on the first column.

12. Insert a row and merge cells.

    a. Insert a new row above the first row in the table.

    b. Type `Greenscapes' Services and Pricing` in the first cell.

    c. Change the font of the text to be **Calibri, 16 pt.**

    d. Merge the three cells in the first row of the table.

13. Change the height of the first row in the table to be **0.4"** tall.

14. Apply a Quick Style to the table.

    a. Change the table Quick Styles to show styles without the first column formatted.

    b. Apply the **Grid Table 5 Dark–Accent 3** Quick Style to the table (it is the fourth option in the third row of the *Grid Tables* section).

15. Apply a border to the table.

    a. Select the table.

    b. Apply **all borders** to the table.

16. Save and close the document.

challenge yourself **4.4**

In this project you will be editing the *WD2013-ChallengeYourself-4-4* document from the Spring Hills Community.

Skills needed to complete this project:

- Adding WordArt to Documents (Skill 4.10)
- Changing Picture Layouts (Skill 4.3)
- Creating a Chart (Skill 4.21)
- Modifying a Chart (Skill 4.22)
- Working with Tables (Skill 4.13)
- Inserting Rows and Columns (Skill 4.14)
- Deleting Columns, Rows, and Cells (Skill 4.15)
- Sorting Data in Tables (Skill 4.18)
- Applying Table Quick Styles (Skill 4.19)
- Inserting Online Pictures (Skill 4.1)
- Resizing Pictures (Skill 4.2)
- Positioning Pictures (Skill 4.6)
- Applying Quick Styles to Pictures (Skill 4.7)

1. Open the **WD2013-ChallengeYourself-4-4** document.

2. Save this document as: **[your initials]WD-ChallengeYourself-4-4**

3. Add WordArt to a document and change the layout options.

    a. Place the cursor at the top of the document.

    b. Insert WordArt using the **Fill–Green Accent 1, Shadow** style (it is the second option in the first row of the WordArt gallery).

    c. Change the WordArt text to **Spring Hills Community Safety Strategies**.

    d. Change the layout of the WordArt to be in line with the text.

4. Add a chart to the document.

    a. Place the cursor on the blank line after the first paragraph in the *What Electronics Are Being Targeted* section.

    b. Insert a **Clustered Column** chart.

    c. Change the data in the chart to match Figure WD 4.38.

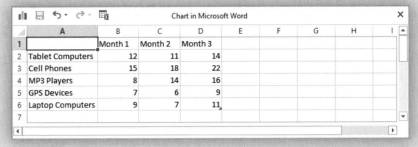

FIGURE WD 4.38

5. Modify the look of the chart.

    a. Apply the **Style 3** Quick Style to the chart.

    b. Hide the **chart title** on the chart.

6. Insert a column to a table.

    a. Place the cursor in the table at the end of the document (in the *Future Safety Modifications* section).

    b. Add a column to the right of the existing column.

7. Insert a row and enter data in a table.

    a. Insert a row above the first row in the table.

    b. In the first cell of the new row, type **Modification**

    c. In the second cell of the new row, type **Status**

    d. Add the status for each modification as shown in Figure WD 4.39.

Modification	Status
New security officer positions	Approved
New security gates	In Progress
Electric security vehicles	Approved
Security card entrance for all garages	In Progress
Increased security cameras	Approved
Reinforcements to perimeter fence	Approved
Weekly security meetings with staff	Approved
Increased security budget	Denied

FIGURE WD 4.39

8. Delete rows from tables.

    a. Select the last row in the table.

    b. Delete the row.

9. Sort data in a table.

    a. Select all the rows in the table except the first row.

    b. Sort the table in ascending order based on the text in column 2.

10. Apply a Quick Styles to tables.

    a. Change the table Quick Styles to show styles without the first column formatted.

    b. Apply the **Plain Table 1** style to the table (it is the second option in the *Plain Tables* section).

FIGURE WD 4.40

11. Insert an online picture.

    a. Place the cursor at the end of the first paragraph in the *Security Staff* section.

    b. Search for images of a **security guard** on the *Office.com Clip Art* site.

    c. Insert the illustrated picture of **Security guard at a gate** (see Figure WD 4.40).
        NOTE: If you do not see the same image as in the figure, insert an online picture of your choice.

12. Resize the picture so the height is **1.2"**.

13. Position the picture using the **Position in Middle Left with Square Text Wrapping** option.

14. Apply the **Center Shadow Rectangle** Quick Style to the picture.

15. Save and close the document.

on your own 4.5

In this project you will be editing the *WD2013-OnYourOwn-4-5* document. This document contains data results for a behavior change project.

Skills needed to complete this project:

- Inserting Online Pictures (Skill 4.1)
- Resizing Pictures (Skill 4.2)
- Changing Picture Layouts (Skill 4.3)
- Moving Pictures (Skill 4.4)
- Applying Quick Styles to Pictures (Skill 4.7)
- Creating a Table (Skill 4.12)
- Working with Tables (Skill 4.13)
- Inserting Rows and Columns (Skill 4.14)
- Merging and Splitting Cells (Skill 4.17)
- Sorting Data in Tables (Skill 4.18)
- Applying Table Quick Styles (Skill 4.19)
- Creating a Chart (Skill 4.21)
- Modifying a Chart (Skill 4.22)

1. Open the **WD2013-OnYourOwn-4-5** document.

2. Save this document as: **[your initials]WD-OnYourOwn-4-5**

3. Search for pictures of students raising hands on *Office.com Clip Art* and insert a picture of your choice.

4. Resize the picture so it fits well in the document.

5. Change the layout options on the picture to wrap with the text.

6. Move the picture so it appears to the right of the first paragraph of the document.

7. Apply a Quick Style of your choice to the picture.

8. Create a new table in the *Observation Phase* section and cut and paste the text from the section into the table. Do not include the Totals in the table. Delete all extra tabs and blank lines that remain after cutting the text.

9. Create a new table in the *Implementation Phase* section and cut and paste the text from the section into the table. Do not include the Totals in the table. Delete all extra tabs and blank lines that remain after cutting the text.

10. Insert a new row to the top of the *Implementation Phase table.* In the second cell of the new row, enter **Raises Hand**. In the third cell of the new row, enter **Does Not Raise Hand**. In the fourth cell of the new row, enter **Percentage**.

11. Insert a new row to the top of the *Observation Phase* table. Cut the text **Observation Phase** and paste it into the first cell of the new table. Merge the cells in the new row.

12. Insert a new row to the top of the *Implementation Phase* table. Cut the text **Implementation Phase** and paste it into the first cell of the new table. Merge the cells in the new row.

13. Sort the data in the *Implementation Phase* table so the dates appear in ascending order.

14. Apply a Quick Style of your choice to the **Observation Phase** table and the **Implementation Phase** table.

15. Create a **pie chart** using the information in the Totals rows in each table. Add the charts below the *Totals* row for each table.

16. Modify the charts so the titles do not appear on the chart.

17. The final document should look similar to Figure WD 4.41 (your document may vary). Save and close the document.

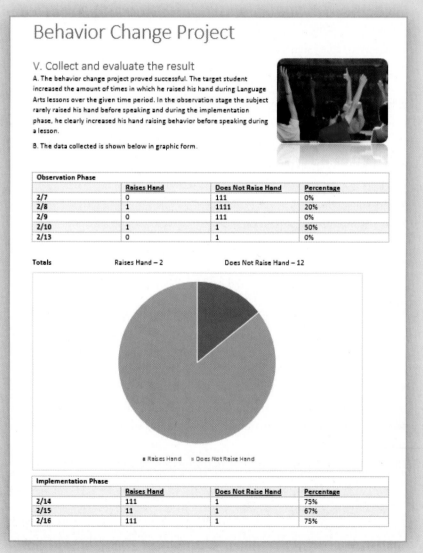

FIGURE WD 4.41

fix it 4.6

In this project you will be correcting the *WD2013-FixIt-4-6* document from Suarez Marketing.

Skills needed to complete this project:

- Positioning Pictures (Skill 4.6)
- Inserting SmartArt (Skill 4.8)
- Resizing Pictures (Skill 4.2)
- Changing Picture Layouts (Skill 4.3)
- Moving Pictures (Skill 4.4)
- Applying Quick Styles to Pictures (Skill 4.7)
- Working with Tables (Skill 4.13)
- Inserting Rows and Columns (Skill 4.14)
- Deleting Columns, Rows, and Cells (Skill 4.15)
- Sizing Tables, Columns, Rows (Skill 4.16)
- Merging and Splitting Cells (Skill 4.17)
- Sorting Data in Tables (Skill 4.18)
- Applying Table Quick Styles (Skill 4.19)
- Adding Borders to a Table (Skill 4.20)

1. Open the **WD2013-FixIt-4-6 document.**
2. Save this document as: **[your initials]WD-FixIt-4-6**
3. Position a picture.
   a. Select the **Suarez Marketing** logo in the middle of the first page.
   b. Position the picture to be in the upper right corner of the page with square wrapping.
4. Insert a *SmartArt* diagram.
   a. Navigate to *The Suarez* Process section.
   b. Place the cursor in the blank line above the bulleted list. Insert a **Segmented Cycle** diagram.
   c. Cut and paste the items from the bulleted list into the segments of the diagram. Remove any extra blank lines.
5. Resize and change the layout of a picture.
   a. Select the large photograph of the woman with a cash register.
   b. Change the size of the picture to be **1.75"** tall and **1.75"** wide.
   c. Change the layout option of the picture to use the **Tight** text wrapping option.
6. Move the picture to right side of the document using guides to align the picture with the right edge of the text. Have the picture display just below the blue horizontal line in the *What I Do What I Do* section.
7. Apply the **Soft Edge Rectangle** Quick Style to the picture (it is the sixth option in the *Picture Quick Styles* gallery).

8. Insert a row in a table.

   a. Navigate to the table at the end of the document.

   b. Insert a new row at the bottom of the table.

   c. Cut and paste the **Win-Win** text into the first cell of the new row.

   d. Cut and paste the **Is always the goal** text into the second cell of the new row.

9. Delete a row in a table.

   a. This table includes a duplicate row of information.

   b. Find the duplicated information and delete one of the rows.

10. Use the **AutoFit** command to resize the table columns to fit the window.

11. **Merge** the two cells in the first row of the table.

12. Sort the table so the first column displays in alphabetical order. Be sure not to include the first row in the sort.

13. Apply the **Grid Table 1 Light–Accent 5** Quick Style to the table (it is the sixth option in the first row in the *Grid Tables* section). Be sure the **First Column Table Style Option** is not part of the design.

14. Apply an **outside border** to the table.

15. Save and close the document.

chapter **5**

Working with Reports, References, and Mailings

In this chapter, you will learn the following skills:

❭ Use Autocorrect

❭ Check for grammar errors

❭ Replace words using the Thesaurus

❭ Use the Tabs dialog and add tab leaders

❭ Insert and update a table of contents, footnotes, and endnotes

❭ Use a report reference style, add citations, and create a bibliography

❭ Mark words in a document to create an index

❭ Display a document in different views

❭ Create a new document from a template

❭ Use mail merge to create mailings

❭ Create envelopes and labels

skills

introduction

In this chapter you will learn the skills to create reports and mailings. First you will learn to use some of Word's valuable tools for writing documents, including AutoCorrect, Grammar check, and the Thesaurus. You will add a number of reference elements to a report, including a table of contents, footnotes, and captions. You will learn about reference styles and add citations and then create a bibliography from citations you have added. You will mark entries and create an index for a document from those entries. You will also learn about the different views in Word and ways you can display your documents. In the second part of this chapter, you will create a new form letter from a template and then create a mail merge from that letter. Finally, you will learn how to create and print envelopes and labels.

Skill 5.1 Using AutoCorrect

While you are typing, Word's **AutoCorrect** feature analyzes each word as it is entered. Each word you type is compared to a list of common misspellings, symbols, and abbreviations. If a match is found, AutoCorrect automatically replaces the text in your document with the matching replacement entry. For example, if you type "teh," AutoCorrect will replace the text with "the."

You can create your own AutoCorrect entries, as well as modify pre-existing ones. Auto-Correct also allows you to check for common capitalization errors. If you find yourself making spelling errors that AutoCorrect does not recognize, you can add your own entries to the AutoCorrect replacement list.

To add a new entry to the AutoCorrect list:

1. Click the **File** tab.
2. Click the **Options** button.
3. In the *Word Options* dialog, click the **Proofing** button.
4. Click the **AutoCorrect Options...** button.

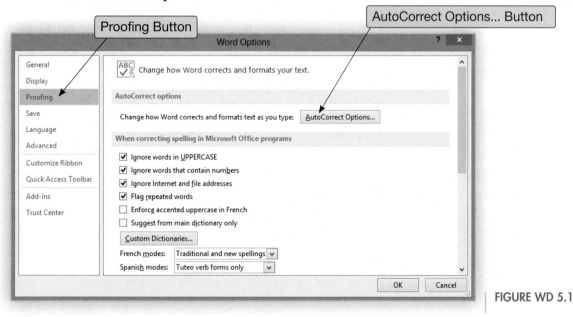

FIGURE WD 5.1

5. Type your commonly made mistake in the *Replace* box.

6. Type the correct spelling in the *With* box.

7. Click **OK** in the *AutoCorrect* dialog.

8. Click **OK** in the *Word Options* dialog.

The next time you type the error, Word will automatically correct it for you.

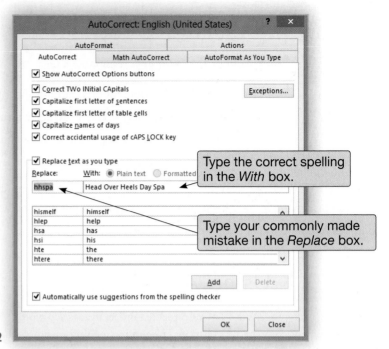

FIGURE WD 5.2

tips & tricks

If you find yourself typing certain long phrases over and over again, you can use the AutoCorrect feature to replace short abbreviations with long strings of text that you don't want to type. For example, you could replace the text *hhspa* with *Head Over Heels Day Spa*. This will not only save you time when typing, but more important, it will ensure accuracy in your documents.

tell me **more**

AutoCorrect does more than just fix spelling errors. From the *AutoCorrect* dialog you can set options to:

❯ Correct accidental use of the Caps Lock key.

❯ Automatically capitalize the first letter in a sentence or the names of days.

❯ Automatically apply character formatting such as bold and italic, and format lists and tables.

Explore the *AutoCorrect* dialog on your own to discover all the options available.

let me **try**

Open the student data file **wd5-01-SpaProductReport** and try this skill on your own:

1. Display Backstage view.

2. Open the **Word Options** dialog.

3. Display the **Proofing** options and open the **AutoCorrect** dialog.

4. Create an AutoCorrect entry to change **hhspa** to **Head Over Heels Day Spa** when typed.

5. Close the **Word Options** dialog.

6. Place the cursor between the words **at** and **The** in the first paragraph of the document.

7. Type **hhpsa.** Be sure to include the period. Notice Word replaces the text with the entry you created.

8. Save the file as directed by your instructor and close it.

Skill 5.2 Checking Grammar

In addition to checking spelling, the *Spelling & Grammar* command can analyze your document for grammar errors. It searches through your document and displays the errors in the order they are found. Spelling errors display in the *Spelling* task pane and grammar errors are displayed in the *Grammar* task pane. Word displays the original word along with potential corrections for you to select or ignore.

To check a document for grammar errors:

1. Click the **Review** tab.
2. In the *Proofing* group, click the **Spelling & Grammar** button.
3. When Word encounters the first grammar error, the error is displayed in the *Grammar* task pane.
4. Review the grammar suggestions to determine which one is correct:
   - Click a suggestion and click the **Change** button to make the correction.
   - Click **Ignore** to skip the grammar error.
5. A message appears to tell you when the spelling and grammar check is complete. Click **OK** to close the *Grammar* task pane and return to the document.

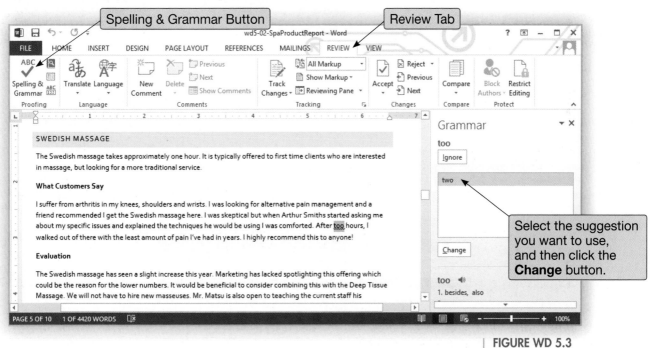

FIGURE WD 5.3

tips & tricks

At the bottom of the task pane, you will see definitions, along with audio pronunciations, of each word to help you make your selection.

another method

To display the *Grammar* task pane, you can also press the F7 key.

let me try

Open the student data file **wd5-02-SpaProductReport** and try this skill on your own:

1. Start the **Spelling & Grammar** check.
2. Correct each grammar error as it is displayed in the task pane.
3. Save the file as directed by your instructor and close it.

Skill 5.3 Using the Thesaurus

When writing documents, you may find you are reusing a certain word over and over again and would like to use a different word that has the same meaning. Microsoft Word's **Thesaurus** tool provides you with a list of synonyms (words with the same meaning) and antonyms (words with the opposite meaning).

To replace a word using the Thesaurus:

1. Place the cursor in the word you want to replace.
2. Click the **Review** tab.
3. In the *Proofing* group, click the **Thesaurus** button.
4. The selected word appears in the *Search for* box of the *Thesaurus* task pane with a list of possible meanings below it. Each possible meaning has a list of synonyms (and, in some cases, antonyms).
5. Point to a synonym (or antonym), and click the arrow that appears to display a menu of options.
6. Click **Insert** on the menu to replace the original word with the one you selected.

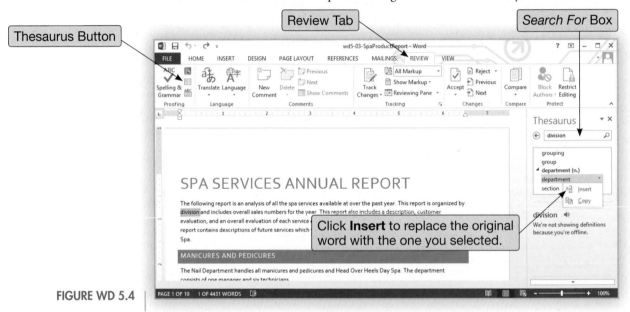

Thesaurus Button   Review Tab   Search For Box

Click **Insert** to replace the original word with the one you selected.

FIGURE WD 5.4

tips & tricks

You can look up and replace words with synonyms without opening the *Thesaurus* task pane. Right-click the word you want to replace, point to **Synonyms.** Word lists a number of possible synonyms on the submenu. Click a synonym to replace the original word with the synonym.

another method

To look up a word using the Thesaurus, you can also:

》 Right-click the word, point to *Synonyms*, and select **Thesaurus...**

》 With the cursor in the word you want to look up, press ⬆ Shift + F7 on the keyboard.

let me try

Open the student data file **wd5-03-SpaProductReport** and try this skill on your own:

1. Select the word **division** in the second sentence of the first paragraph.
2. Using the Thesaurus, replace the word with the synonym **department.**
3. Save the file as directed by your instructor and close it.

word 2013   chapter 5 Working with Reports, References, and Mailings

Skill 5.4 Using the Tabs Dialog

You can quickly add tabs to a document by selecting a tab stop type and clicking on the ruler where you want the tab to appear. Another way to set tabs in your document is through the *Tabs* dialog. From the *Tabs* dialog, you can add new tabs or modify or clear existing tabs.

To set tab stops in the *Tabs* dialog:

1. On the *Home* tab, in the *Paragraph* group, click the **dialog launcher.**
2. In the *Paragraph* dialog box, click the **Tabs...** button.
3. The *Tabs* dialog opens.
4. In the *Tab stop position:* box, type the number of where you want the tab stop to appear.
5. Click a radio button in the *Alignment* section.
6. Click **OK.**

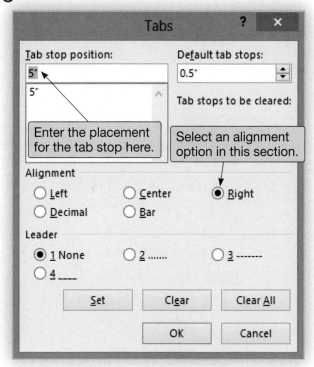

FIGURE WD 5.5

tips & tricks

❯ Click the **Clear All** button to clear all the tabs displayed in the *Tabs* dialog.

❯ To add the tab stop and continue working in the *Tabs* dialog, click the **Set** button instead of **OK.**

another method

To open the *Tabs* dialog, you can double-click a tab stop on the ruler.

let me try

Open the student data file **wd5-04-SpaProductReport** and try this skill on your own:

1. Select the list of services and sales figures in the *Manicures and Pedicures* section.
2. Open the **Paragraph** dialog.
3. Open the **Tabs** dialog.
4. Add a **right tab stop** at **5".**
5. Save the file as directed by your instructor and close it.

Skill 5.5 Adding Tab Leaders

Adding **tab leaders** can make data even easier to read. Tab leaders fill in the space between tabs with solid, dotted, or dashed lines. Using tab leaders helps associate columns of text by leading the reader's eye from left to right.

To add tab leaders:

1. Select the text to which you want to add the leader.
2. On the *Home* tab, in the *Paragraph* group, click the **dialog launcher.**
3. In the *Paragraph* dialog, click the **Tabs...** button.
4. In the *Leader* section of the *Tabs* dialog, select the leader option you want.
5. Click **OK.**

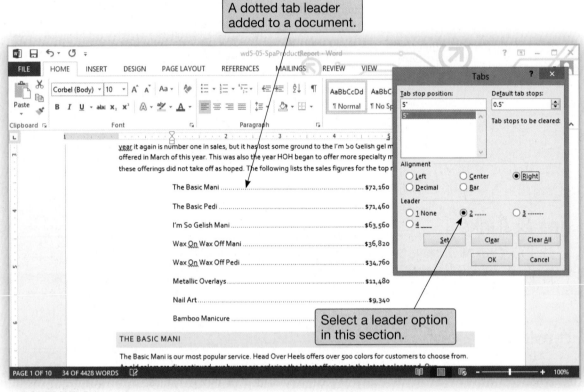

A dotted tab leader added to a document.

Select a leader option in this section.

FIGURE WD 5.6

tips & tricks

When creating a table of contents for your document, use tab leaders to visually link section headings with page numbers.

another method

To open the *Tabs* dialog, you can double-click a tab stop on the ruler.

let me try

Open the student data file **wd5-05-SpaProductReport** and try this skill on your own:

1. Select the list of services and sales figures in the *Manicures and Pedicures* section.
2. Open the **Tabs** dialog.
3. Add a **dotted tab leader** to the text (option **2** in the *Leader* section of the *Tabs* dialog).
4. Save the file as directed by your instructor and close it.

Skill 5.6 Inserting a Table of Contents

If you have a long document with many sections and headings, it is a good idea to include a **table of contents** at the beginning of the document. A table of contents lists the topics and associated page numbers, so your reader can easily locate information. The table of contents is created from heading styles in the document. If you want your document's section titles to display in the table of contents, be sure to apply heading styles to that text.

To insert a table of contents:

1. Verify the insertion point is at the beginning of the document.

2. Click the **References** tab.

3. In the *Table of Contents* group, click the **Table of Contents** button and select an option from the gallery.

4. The table of contents is added to the beginning of the document.

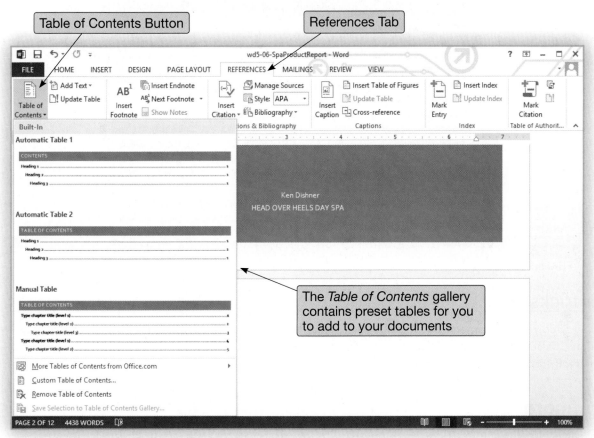

Table of Contents Button

References Tab

The *Table of Contents* gallery contains preset tables for you to add to your documents

FIGURE WD 5.7

skill 5.6   Inserting a Table of Contents

www.mhhe.com/simnet | WD–167

If you make changes to your document after you have inserted a table of contents, you should be sure to update the table of contents to keep the information accurate. To update the table of contents, click the **Update Table** button in the *Table of Contents* group. You can also update the table of contents by clicking on the table of contents and clicking the **Update Table...** button at the top of the control.

To remove a table of contents, click the **Table of Contents** button and select **Remove Table of Contents** at the bottom of the gallery.

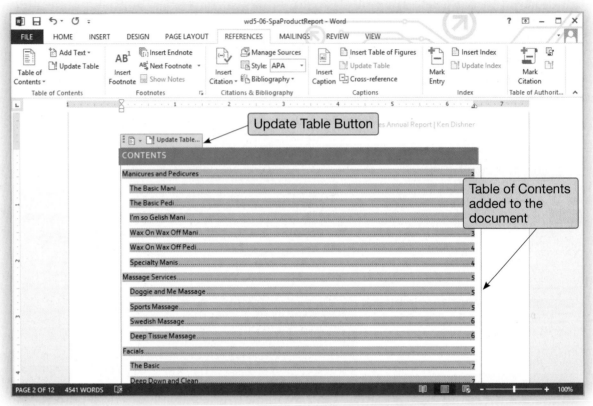

FIGURE WD 5.8

tips & tricks

If you want to add your own customized table of contents, click **Insert Table of Contents...** at the bottom of the gallery. The *Table of Contents* dialog opens. Here you can choose different options for the table of contents, including tab leaders, formats, and page number formatting.

tell me **more**

A table of contents is typically based on heading styles, but you can create a table of contents based on custom styles or from marked entries.

A table of contents is a building block that is added to the document. When you select the building block, extra controls appear at the top, including the *Table of Contents* and the *Update Table...* buttons.

let me try

Open the student data file **wd5-06-SpaProductReport** and try this skill on your own:

1. Place the cursor on the blank page between the cover page and the beginning of the document.
2. Insert a table of contents based on the **Automatic Table 1** format.
3. Save the file as directed by your instructor and close it.

Skill 5.7 Inserting Footnotes and Endnotes

Footnotes and **endnotes** provide your reader with further information on a topic in a document. They are often used for source references. Footnotes and endnotes are composed of two parts: a **reference mark** (a superscript character placed next to the text) and the associated text. Footnotes appear at the bottom of a page, whereas endnotes are placed at the end of the document.

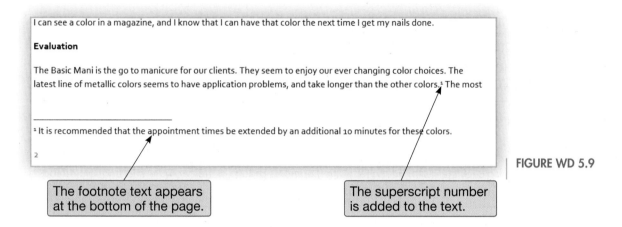

> I can see a color in a magazine, and I know that I can have that color the next time I get my nails done.
>
> **Evaluation**
>
> The Basic Mani is the go to manicure for our clients. They seem to enjoy our ever changing color choices. The latest line of metallic colors seems to have application problems, and take longer than the other colors.[1] The most
>
> _____
>
> [1] It is recommended that the appointment times be extended by an additional 10 minutes for these colors.
>
> 2

The footnote text appears at the bottom of the page.

The superscript number is added to the text.

FIGURE WD 5.9

To insert a footnote:

1. Place your cursor where you want the footnote to appear.
2. Click the **References** tab.
3. In the *Footnotes* group, click the **Insert Footnote** button.
4. The superscript number is added next to the text, and the cursor is moved to the footnote area at the bottom of the page.
5. Type the text for your footnote. When you are finished, return to your document by clicking anywhere in the main document area.

To insert an endnote:

1. Place your cursor where you want the endnote to appear.
2. Click the **References** tab.
3. In the *Footnotes* group, click the **Insert Endnote** button.
4. The superscript number is added next to the text, and the cursor is moved the endnote area at the end of the document.
5. Type the text for your endnote.

Insert Footnote Button   **Insert Endnote Button**   **References Tab**

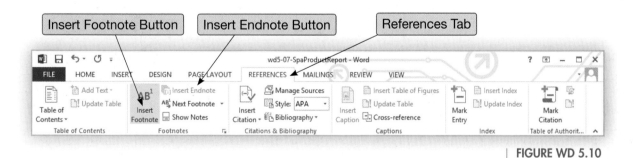

FIGURE WD 5.10

To convert footnotes to endnotes or vice versa, click the **dialog launcher** in the *Footnotes* group. In the *Footnote and Endnote* dialog, click the **Convert...** button, choose an option, and click **OK.**

tips & tricks

Click the **Next Footnote** button to navigate to the next footnote in the document. Click the arrow next to the *Next Footnote* button to display a menu allowing you to navigate to previous footnotes and between endnotes in the document.

To delete a footnote, you must first select the reference mark in the document and press **Delete** on the keyboard. If you select and delete the text of the footnote, the reference mark will remain and the footnote will not be removed from the document.

tell me **more**

Once you have inserted and formatted your first footnote or endnote, Word automatically numbers all subsequent notes in your document for you. If you add a new footnote between two existing footnotes, Word will renumber all the footnotes in the document, keeping them in sequential order.

another **method**

To insert a footnote, you can also click the **dialog launcher** in the *Footnotes* group. In the *Footnote and Endnote* dialog, verify that the **Footnote** radio button is selected and click **Insert.**

let me **try**

Open the student data file **wd5-07-SpaProductReport** and try this skill on your own:

1. Place the cursor at the end of the third sentence in the first paragraph in the *Evaluation* section under *The Basic Mani* (the sentence ending *and take longer than the other colors* on the third page of the document).

2. Add a footnote that reads: `It is recommended that the appointment times be extended by an additional 10 minutes for these colors.`

3. Save the file as directed by your instructor and close it.

Skill 5.8 Adding a Caption

A **caption** is a brief description of an illustration, chart, equation, or table. Captions can appear above or below the image, and typically begin with a label followed by a number and the description of the image. Captions are helpful when referring to images within paragraphs of text (see Figure 1: An example of a caption).

To add a caption to a figure:

1. Select the figure you want to add the caption to.
2. Click the **References** tab.
3. In the *Captions* group, click the **Insert Caption** button.
4. The *Caption* dialog opens.
5. Click the **Label** arrow and select a figure type.
6. Click the **Position** arrow and select where you want the caption to appear.
7. Type any additional text, such as a description of the figure, in the *Caption* box.
8. Click **OK** to close the dialog and add the caption.

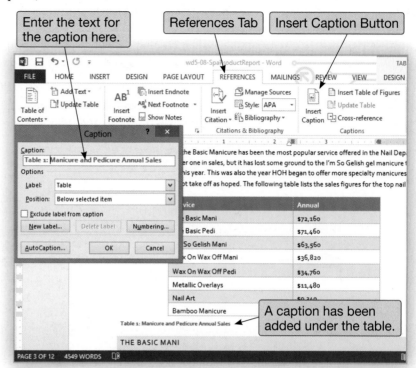

FIGURE WD 5.11

Skill 5.9 Selecting a Reference Style

A **reference style** is a set of rules used to display references in a bibliography. These rules include the order of information, when and how punctuation is used, and the use of character formatting, such as italics and bold. The two most common reference styles in use today are *APA, MLA,* and *Chicago;* however, there are a number of other reference styles you can choose from. It is important that you use the correct reference style for the subject of your document.

When creating a bibliography, it is important to use a consistent reference style for your citations. Word makes this easy by allowing you to set the reference style for the entire document at once.

To change the reference style for a document:

1. Click the **References** tab.

2. In the *Citations & Bibliography* group, click the arrow next to *Style* and select a style from the list.

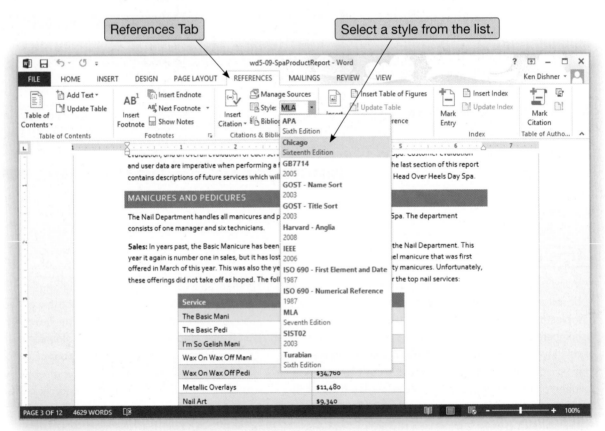

FIGURE WD 5.12

The following table lists the available styles in Word and when they are most commonly used.

STYLE ABBREVIATION	FULL NAME	PURPOSE
APA Sixth Edition	American Psychological Association	Education, psychology, and social sciences
Chicago Sixteenth Edition	The Chicago Manual of Style	Books, magazines, and newspapers
GB7714 2005	NA	Used in China
GOST—Name Sort	Russian State Standard	Used in Russia
GOST—Title Sort	Russian State Standard	Used in Russia
Harvard—Anglia 2008	Harvard reference style	For the specification at Anglia Ruskin University
IEEE 2006	IEEE Citation Reference	Research papers in technical fields
ISO 690—First Element and Date	International Standards Organization	Patents and industry (both print and nonprint works)
ISO 690—Numerical Reference	International Standards Organization	Patents and industry (both print and nonprint works)
MLA Seventh Edition	Modern Language Association	Arts and humanities
SIST02	NA	Used in Asia
Turabian Sixth Edition	Turabian	All subjects (designed for college students)

tips & tricks

When you change the reference style for a document, all citations are automatically updated to use the new style.

tell me more

To see a preview of the source style, click the **Manage Sources** button in the *Citations & Bibliography* group. The preview box at the bottom of the *Manage Sources* dialog shows how the selected reference will appear as a citation and in the bibliography.

let me try

Open the student data file **wd5-09-SpaProductReport** and try this skill on your own:

1. Navigate to the second paragraph of the document. Notice the format of the reference *(Faah)* in the first sentence.
2. Change the reference style for the document to use the **Chicago Sixteenth Edition** style.
3. Notice how the reference has changed to *(Faah 2012)*.
4. Save the file as directed by your instructor and close it.

Skill 5.10 Adding Citations to Documents

When you use materials in a document from other sources, such as a book or a journal article, you need to give credit to the original source material. A **citation** is a reference to such source material. Citations include information such as the author, title, publisher, and the publication date.

To add a citation to a document, you must first create the source:

1. Place the cursor where you want to add the citation.
2. Click the **References** tab.
3. In the *Citations & Bibliography* group, click the **Insert Citation** button and select **Add New Source...**
4. In the *Create Source* dialog, click the arrow next to *Type of Source* and select an option.
5. In the *Author* box, type the name of the author.
6. In the *Title* box, type the title of the book or article.
7. In the *Year* box, type the year the book or article was published.
8. Add other information about the source to the appropriate fields.
9. When you are finished, click **OK** to add the citation to the document.

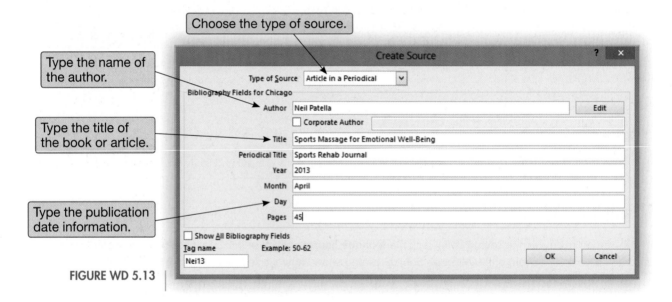

Choose the type of source.

Type the name of the author.

Type the title of the book or article.

Type the publication date information.

FIGURE WD 5.13

After you have added a new source, it appears on the *Insert Citation* menu. To add the same source to another part of the document, click the **Insert Citation** button and select the source for the citation.

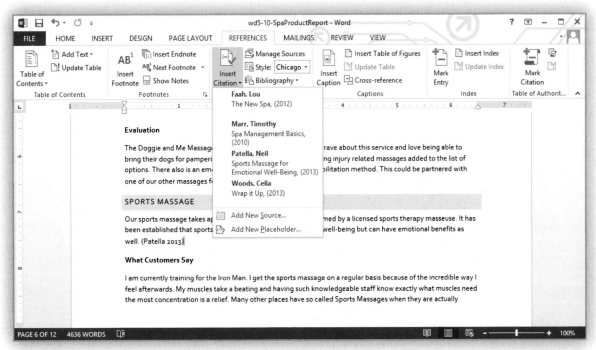

FIGURE WD 5.14

tips & tricks

When you add a citation, the citation appears inside parentheses at the place where you inserted it. A citation includes basic information from the source, including the author, year, title, and pages. A bibliography lists all the citations in a document and includes more of the source information than the citation does.

tell me more

Citations appear in the document as a control. When you click the control, you will see an arrow on the right side. Click the arrow to display a menu for editing the source and the citation. In the *Edit Source* dialog, you can change the information you added when you created the source. In the *Edit Citation* dialog, you can change information specific to the citation, such as page numbers.

let me try

Open the student data file **wd5-10-SpaProductReport** and try this skill on your own:

1. Navigate to the *Sports Massage* section and place the cursor at the end of the first paragraph.

2. Add a new source with the following information:

Type of source	**Article in Periodical**
Author	**Neil Patella**
Title	**Sports Massage for Emotional Well-Being**
Periodical Title	**Sports Rehab Journal**
Year	**2013**
Month	**April**
Pages	**45**

3. Save the file as directed by your instructor and close it.

Skill 5.11 Creating a Bibliography

A **bibliography** is a compiled list of sources you referenced in your document. Typically, bibliographies appear at the end of a document and list all the sources you marked throughout the document. Microsoft Word 2013 comes with a number of prebuilt bibliography building blocks for you to use. When you select one of these building blocks, Word will search the document and compile all the sources from your document and format them according to the style you chose.

To add a bibliography to a document:

1. Place the cursor at the end of the document.

2. Click the **References** tab.

3. In the *Citations & Bibliography* group, click the **Bibliography** button and select one of the bibliography building blocks.

4. The bibliography is added to the end of the document, listing all the sources referenced in the document.

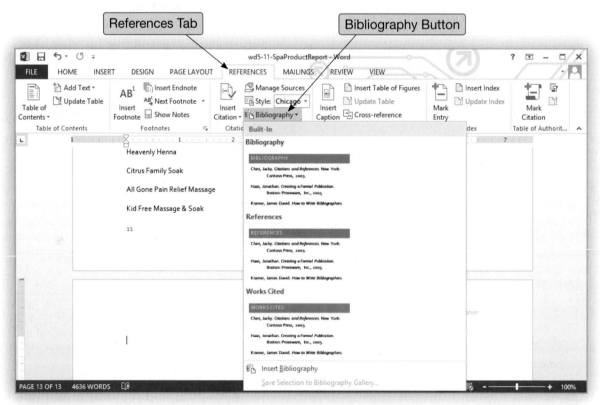

FIGURE WD 5.15

another **method**

To add a simple bibliography, click the **Insert Bibliography** command at the bottom of the *Bibliography* gallery.

let me **try**

Open the student data file **wd5-11-SpaProductReport** and try this skill on your own:

1. Navigate to the end of the document. Place the cursor at the top of the blank page.

2. Add a bibliography using the **References** style.

3. Save the file as directed by your instructor and close it.

Skill 5.12 Marking Entries

When creating long documents, you may want to add an index to the document to help your readers quickly locate specific information. To create an index you must first mark the topics you want to include, and then create the index. When formatting marks are hidden, marked entries look no different from other text in the document. However, when the index is created, Word finds all the marked entries and adds them to the index.

To mark entries:

1. Select the word or phrase you want to add to the index.
2. Click the **References** tab.
3. In the *Index* group, click the **Mark Entry** button.
4. The word or phrase appears in the *Main entry* box.
5. Click the **Mark** button to mark the entry.
6. Click the **Close** button to close the *Mark Index Entry* dialog.

After you mark an entry, Word adds the *XE (Index Entry)* formatting mark to the word and displays all formatting marks in the document, so you can double-check your page layout. However, formatting marks should be hidden before you create and insert the index to make it easier to view your final document.

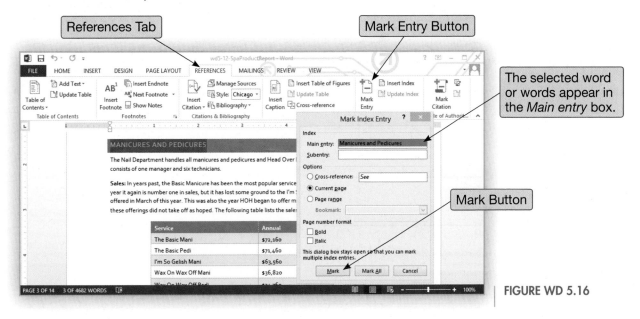

FIGURE WD 5.16

tips & tricks

To add a reference to every instance of a word to the index, click the **Mark All** button in the *Mark Index Entry* dialog.

another method

To open the *Mark Index Entry* dialog, you can also click the **Insert Index** button in the *Index* group. In the *Index* dialog, click the **Mark Entry...** button.

let me try

Open the student data file **wd5-12-SpaProductReport** and try this skill on your own:

1. Select the text **manicures and pedicures** in the first sentence of the *Manicures and Pedicures* section.
2. Mark the text as an entry to use in the index.
3. Save the file as directed by your instructor and close it.

Skill 5.13 Creating an Index

An **index** is a list of topics and associated page numbers that typically appears at the end of a document. Adding an index to your document can help your readers find information quickly.

An index entry can reference a single word, a phrase, or a topic spanning several pages. You can also add cross-references to your index.

To add an index to a document:

1. Place the cursor at the end of the document.
2. Click the **References** button.
3. In the *Index* group, click the **Insert Index** button.
4. The *Index* dialog opens.
5. Click the **Formats** arrow and select a format.
6. Modify the other options until the preview looks the way you want.
7. Click **OK** to insert the index into your document.

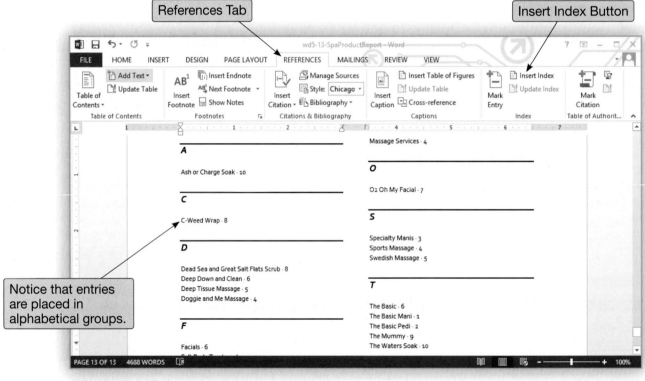

FIGURE WD 5.17

tips & tricks

To add new entries to an index, do not type directly in the index. Instead, mark the entries and then update the index. Any entries typed directly into the index will be deleted when the index is updated. To update an index, first select the index and then click the **Update Index** button in the *Index* group.

tell me **more**

A cross-reference is an index entry that refers to another entry in the index rather than to a page in the document. Cross-references are often used to direct readers from an uncommon entry to a more frequently used one.

let me try

Open the student data file **wd5-13-SpaProductReport** and try this skill on your own:

1. Navigate to the end of the document. Place the cursor at the top of the last page.
2. Insert an index based on the **Modern** format. The entries should display in two columns.
3. Save the file as directed by your instructor and close it.

from the perspective of . . .

GRADUATE STUDENT

When I wrote my first term paper, my professor rejected it informing me that it wasn't formatted correctly and I was using the wrong reference style. I didn't understand. I had typed everything very carefully, but apparently I was supposed to use the APA style and not the MLA style. After that, I started using the reference tools built into Word 2013. Now I can generate a table of contents from headings in my paper, mark entries for my index as I write, and auto-generate the index. Most important, I can set my reference style to use the APA style, add my sources, and create a bibliography in the right style. When I resubmitted my paper, my professor was impressed with how well it was formatted. I got an A!

Skill 5.14 Using Views

By default, Microsoft Word displays documents in Print Layout view, but you can display your documents in a number of other ways. Each view has its own purpose, and considering what you want to do with your document will help determine which view is most appropriate to use.

To switch between different views, click the appropriate icon located in the lower-right corner of the status bar next to the zoom slider.

Read Mode—Use this view when you want to review a document. Read Mode presents the document in an easy-to-read format. In this view, the Ribbon is no longer visible. To navigate between screens, use the navigation buttons on the left and right side of the window.

Print Layout view—Use this view to see how document elements will appear on a printed page. This view will help you edit headers and footers, and adjust margins and layouts.

Web Layout view—Use this view when designing documents that will be viewed on-screen, such as a Web page. Web Layout view displays all backgrounds, drawing objects, and graphics as they will appear on-screen. Unlike Print Layout view, Web Layout view does not show page edges, margins, or headers and footers.

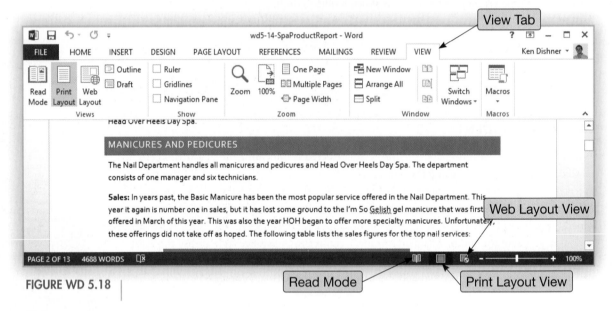

FIGURE WD 5.18

tell me **more**

In previous versions of Word, Outline view and Draft view were accessible from the status bar. In Word 2013, you can now only access these views from the *View* tab:

Outline view—Use this view to check the structure of your document. In Outline view, you can collapse the document's structure to view just the top-level headings or expand the structure to see the document's framework. Outline view is most helpful when you use a different style for each type of heading in your document.

Draft view—Use this simplified layout view when typing and formatting text. Draft view does not display headers and footers, page edges, backgrounds, or drawing objects.

another **method**

To switch views, you also can click the **View** tab and select a view from the *Views* group.

let me **try**

Open the student data file **wd5-14-SpaProduct Report** and try this skill on your own:

1. Switch to **Read Mode.**
2. Switch to **Web Layout** view.
3. Switch back to **Print Layout** view.
4. Close the file.

Skill 5.15 Using Read Mode

Today more and more documents are read on devices such as tablets and smartphones. Word 2013 now includes Read Mode, which is designed for reading documents in electronic format. In Read Mode, documents are displayed as screens rather than pages.

To display a document in Read Mode:

1. Click the **Read Mode** button on the status bar.
2. Click the **Next** button to navigate to the next screen.
3. Click the **Back** button to navigate to the previous screen.

Read Mode comes with specific tools to modify the look of the document as you read. When reading documents electronically, some people prefer a softer screen appearance than black text on a white background, while others prefer reading white text on a black background. Read Mode comes with specific tools to modify the look of the document as you read, including changing the page color.

To change the page color in Read Mode:

1. Click the **View** menu.
2. Point to **Page Color** and select an option:
   - **None**—Displays black text on a white background
   - **Sepia**—Displays black text on a sepia tone background
   - **Inverse**—Displays white text on a black background

FIGURE WD 5.19

tell me **more**

If you resize the Read Mode window, the text will automatically resize to fit the window. If you make the window smaller, you will notice the number of screens to display increases. If you make the window larger, the number of screens to display decreases.

another **method**

To navigate through pages of a document in Read Mode, you can also use the horizontal scrollbar along the bottom of the window.

let me **try**

Open the student data file **wd5-15-SpaProductReport** and try this skill on your own:

1. Switch to **Read Mode.**
2. Change the color of the page to **Sepia.**
3. Navigate to the next screen in the document.
4. Navigate to the previous screen in the document.
5. Save the file as directed by your instructor and close it.

Skill 5.16 Creating a New Document Using a Template

A **template** is a document with predefined settings that you can use as a pattern to create a new file of your own. Using a template makes creating a fully formatted and designed new file easy, saving you time and effort. There are templates available for letters, memos, résumés, newsletters, and almost any other type of document you can imagine.

To create a new document from a template:

1. Click the **File** tab to open Backstage view.
2. Click **New.** Word 2013 includes a variety of templates that are copied to your computer when you install the application. These templates are always available from the *New* page. Additional templates that you download are also displayed on the *New* page, so your screen may look different from the one in Figure WD 5.20.
3. Click each template preview picture for a brief description of the template.
4. When you find the template you want to use, click the **Create** button.
5. A new document opens, prepopulated with all of the template elements.

FIGURE WD 5.20

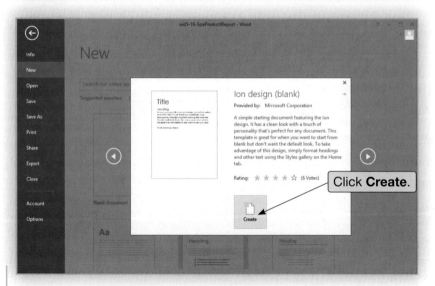

FIGURE WD 5.21

You can search for more document templates online. (You must have an active Internet connection.)

1. Near the top of the *New* page, in the *Search online templates* box, type a keyword or phrase that describes the template you want.

2. Click the **Start searching** button (the magnifying glass image at the end of the *Search online templates* box).

3. The search results display previews of the templates that match the keyword or phrase you entered. To further narrow the results, click one of the categories listed in the *Filter by* pane at the right side of the window. Notice that each category lists the number of templates available.

4. When you find the template you want, click it to display the larger preview with detailed information about the template, and then click **Create.**

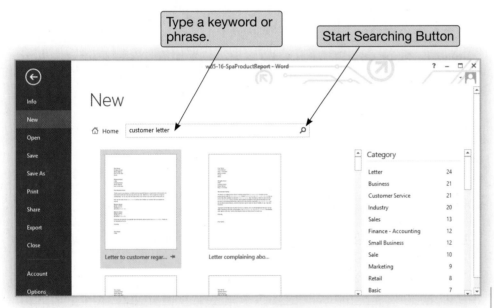

FIGURE WD 5.22

tell me **more**

Some templates include fully formed documents with sample text for you to replace with your own information. Other templates are empty shells based on a certain design. The template includes the proper styles applied to document elements to help you get started in creating well formatted documents using proper desktop publishing rules.

let me **try**

Open the student data file **wd5-16-Document1** and try this skill on your own:

1. Display the **New** page in Backstage.
2. Search for a template of a **new customer letter.**
3. Create a new document based on the **Thank you letter to new customer** template.
4. Save the new file as directed by your instructor and close it. Close the original file you opened but do not save it.

Skill 5.17 Starting a Mail Merge

Suppose you have a letter you want to send out to 20 recipients, but you want each person's name to appear on the letter, giving it a more personal touch. You could write the letter and save 20 versions—one for each recipient—but this is time-consuming and cumbersome. In Word, you can take a list of names and addresses and merge them with a standard document, creating a personalized document for each name on your list. This process is called a **mail merge**.

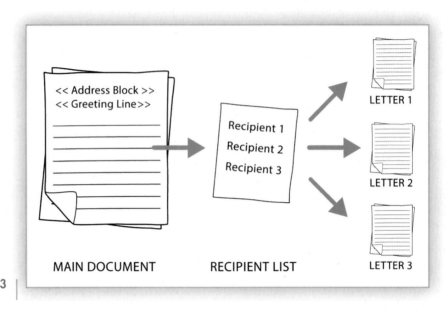

FIGURE WD 5.23

Before you create a mail merge, you first select a main document type. To set up the main document:

1. Click the **Mailings** tab.

2. In the *Start Mail Merge* group, click the **Start Mail Merge** button and select **Letters.**

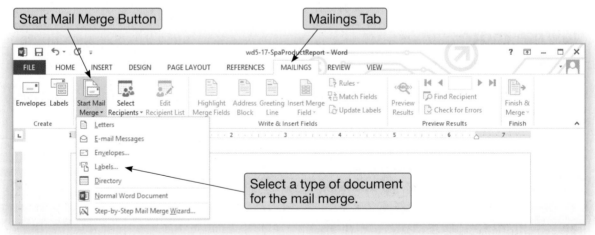

FIGURE WD 5.24

tips & tricks

Use mail merge to automatically create labels, envelopes, directories, and e-mails, as well as form letters.

tell me **more**

You can also create a mail merge using the *Mail Merge Wizard*, which will take you through creating the mail merge step by step. To display the *Mail Merge Wizard*, click the **Start Mail Merge** button and select **Step by Step Mail Merge Wizard...**

let me **try**

Open the student data file **wd5-17-CustomerLetter** and try this skill on your own:

1. Start a new mail merge for a **letter.**
2. Keep this file open for working on the next skill.

from the perspective of . . .

PAROLE OFFICER

I have several form letters that I use to send to my clients when they have a parole violation or have missed a court mandated appointment. Often times, I am sending several letters out to clients at the same time, so I use mail merge to make the process go faster. I keep all my clients' information in an Access database that I use to create the recipients list. I can select which clients to add to the merge and then add the address block and greeting line to the form letter. I print all the letters at once, send them out, and I am done—until the next violation occurs.

Skill 5.18 Selecting Recipients

The **recipients list** for the mail merge is a table of names and address for the people you want to include in the merge. You can import recipients from an existing Access database or Word document, or you can enter the recipients' information in manually.

To select recipients for the mail merge:

1. Click the **Mailings** tab.
2. In the *Start Mail Merge* group, click the **Select Recipients** button.
3. Select **Use an Existing List...**
4. In the *Select Data Source* dialog, select a data source and click **Open.**

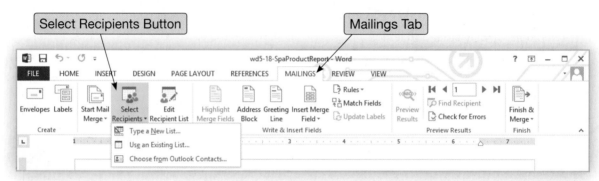

FIGURE WD 5.25

To enter recipients for the mail merge manually:

1. In the *Start Mail Merge* group, click the **Select Recipients** button and select **Type a New List...**
2. In the *New Address List* dialog, enter the information for the recipient in the appropriate boxes.
3. Click the **New Entry** button to add another recipient.
4. Continue adding all the recipients for the mail merge. When you are done, click **OK** to create the list of recipients.

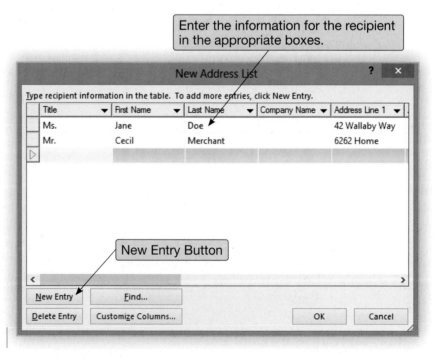

FIGURE WD 5.26

Once you have added a list of recipients, you can then edit the recipients list, making any changes to information that may be incorrect.

To edit the recipients list:

1. On the *Mailings* tab, in the *Start Mail Merge* group, click the **Edit Recipient List** button.

2. Click in any field to change the information for the recipients.

3. Click the checkmark next to a name to deselect it and exclude the recipient from the mail merge.

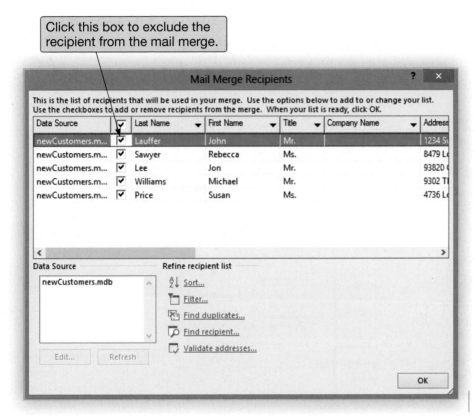

FIGURE WD 5.27

tell me **more**

When you enter contacts manually, Word creates an Access database from the information you entered. The database is then stored on your hard drive in the *My Data Sources* folder in the *My Documents* folder for your user account.

another **method**

You can also add recipients from your Outlook contacts list.

let me **try**

With the document from the previous skill still open, try this skill on your own:

1. Add a list of recipients to the mail merge based on an existing list.

2. Select the **newCustomers** database as the source for the list of recipients. You will find the database in the location where you downloaded your student data files for this book.

3. Keep this file open for working on the next skill.

Skill 5.19 Adding an Address Block

The main document of a mail merge contains the text and merge fields, which appear on every version of the merged document. **Merge fields** are placeholders that insert specific data from the recipients list you created. If you are writing business letters, you can add an **address block** merge field where the address for the recipient should appear. An address block will display the name and address of the recipient in the standard business letter format.

To add an address block merge field:

1. Click in the document where you want the merge field to appear.
2. On the *Mailings* tab, in the *Write & Insert Fields* group, click the **Address Block** button.
3. In the **Insert Address Block** dialog, make any changes to the display and click **OK.**

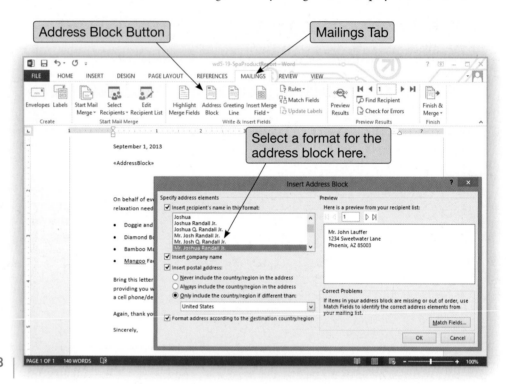

Address Block Button

Mailings Tab

Select a format for the address block here.

FIGURE WD 5.28

tips & tricks

The *Insert Address Block* dialog includes a preview of how the merge fields will display in the document. Click the **Next** and **Previous** buttons to navigate through the list of recipients to see how each one will display before finalizing your choices.

tell me **more**

The three basic types of merge fields are:

Address Block—Inserts a merge field with the name and address of the recipient.

Greeting Line—Inserts a field with a greeting and the recipient's name.

Merge Fields—Allows you to insert merge fields based on your data source, such as first names, last names, addresses, phone numbers, and e-mail addresses.

let me **try**

With the document from the previous skill still open, try this skill on your own:

1. Place the cursor on the first blank line under the date.

2. Insert an address block using the following format: **Mr. Josh Randall Jr.**

3. Keep this file open for working on the next skill.

word 2013 chapter 5 Working with Reports, References, and Mailings

Skill 5.20 Adding a Greeting Line

When writing a letter, you should always open with a **greeting line** personally addressing the reader by name. This is where creating a mail merge can save you a lot of time and effort. When you add a greeting line to a mail merge, you choose the format for the greeting line. Then, Word inserts each name in the recipients list into the greeting line, creating personalized letters without having to create each one individually.

To add a greeting line merge field:

1. Click in the document where you want the merge field to appear.
2. On the *Mailings* tab, in the *Write & Insert Fields* group, click the **Greeting Line** button.
3. In the *Insert Greeting Line* dialog, make any changes to the display and click **OK**.

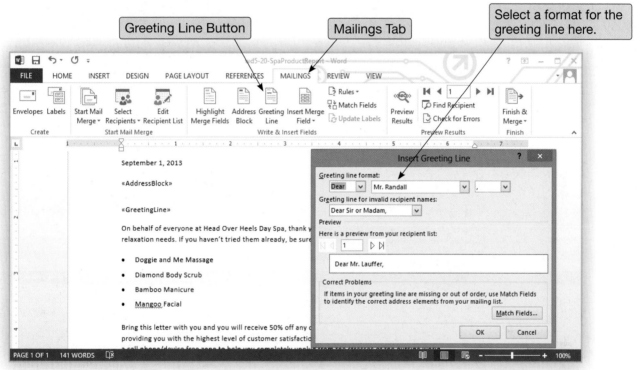

FIGURE WD 5.29

tips & tricks

The *Insert Greeting Line* dialog includes a preview of how the merge fields will display in the document. Click the **Next** and **Previous** buttons to navigate through the list of recipients to see how each one will display before finalizing your choices.

tell me **more**

To add individual merge fields:

1. Click in the document where you want the merge field to appear.
2. Click the **Insert Merge Field** button and select an option to insert.

let me try

With the document from the previous skill still open, try this skill on your own:

1. Place the cursor on the blank line under the address block.
2. Insert a greeting line based on the following format: **Dear Mr. Randall:**
3. Keep this file open for working on the next skill.

Skill 5.21 Previewing and Finishing the Merge

Before you complete the mail merge and print your documents, it is a good idea to review each document created in the merge.

To preview the mail merge:

1. On the *Mailings* tab, in the *Preview Results* group, click the **Preview Results** button.
2. Click the **Next Record** and **Previous Record** buttons to navigate among different documents.

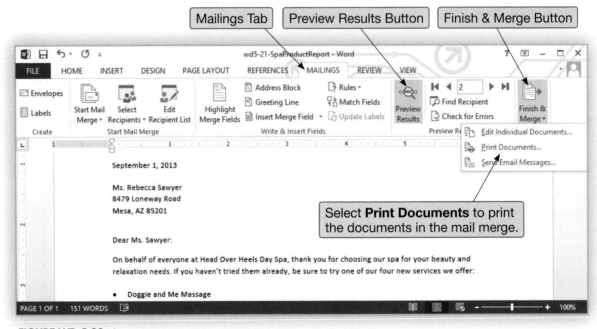

FIGURE WD 5.30

FIGURE WD 5.31

After you have previewed the mail merge, the last step is to finish the merge by printing the documents.

To print the documents in the mail merge:

1. On the *Mailings* tab, in the *Finish* group, click the **Finish & Merge** button and select **Print Documents...**
2. In the *Merge to Printer* dialog, verify the **All** radio button is selected to print all the documents in the merge.
3. Click **OK.**

tips & tricks

Before you finish the merge, click the **Check for Errors** button to review your documents for errors.

tell me **more**

If you want to modify letters individually, click **Edit individual letters...** Then, in the *Merge to New Document* dialog, select the records you want to change and click **OK.** Word opens a new document based on the selected records. Make any changes you want, and then print or save the document just as you would any other file.

If you want to send the document via e-mail, click **Send E-mail Messages...** Enter the subject line and mail format. Select the recipients you want to send the document to and click **OK.**

let me **try**

With the document from the previous skill still open, try this skill on your own:

1. Preview the mail merge.

2. Navigate through each letter to see how it will display.

3. Print all the letters in the mail merge. **NOTE:** If you are using this in class or in your school's computer lab, check with your instructor about printing permissions before completing this step.

4. Save the file as directed by your instructor and close it.

Skill 5.22 Creating Envelopes

With Word you can create an envelope and print it without leaving the document you are working on. Word's preset formats take care of the measuring and layout for you.

To create and print an envelope:

1. Click the **Mailings** tab.
2. In the *Create* group, click the **Envelopes** button.

FIGURE WD 5.32

3. Type the address of the person you are sending the document to in the *Delivery address* text box.
4. Type your address in the *Return address* text box.
5. Click the **Print** button in the *Envelopes and Labels* dialog.

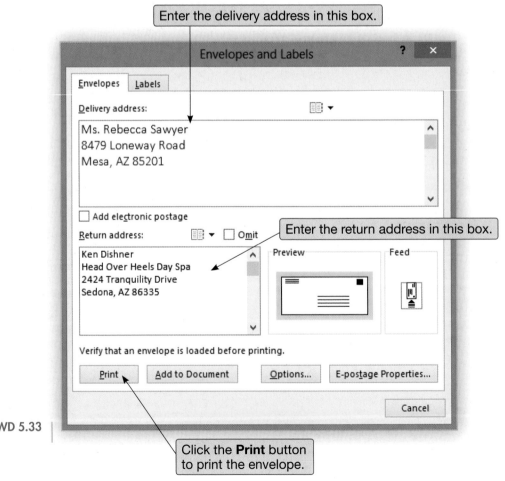

FIGURE WD 5.33

tips & tricks

By default, Word selects a standard envelope size. If your envelope is a different size, you can change the size of the envelope through the *Envelope Options* dialog. In the *Envelopes and Labels* dialog, click the **Options...** button. The *Envelop Options* dialog opens. Click the **Envelope size** arrow and select an envelope size. Click **OK** in the *Envelope Options* dialog.

tell me more

When you open the *Envelopes and Labels* dialog, Word searches your document for an address. If it finds what looks like an address, it will copy it directly into the dialog for you. Of course, you can always change this if it's not what you need.

another method

To open the *Envelopes and Labels* dialog, you can also click the **Labels** button, and then click the **Envelopes** tab to create an envelope.

let me try

Open the student data file **wd5-22-Document1** and try this skill on your own:

1. Open the *Envelopes and Labels* dialog.
2. Add the following delivery address:

   Ms. Rebecca Sawyer

   8479 Loneway Road

   Mesa, AZ 85201
3. Add the following return address:

   Ken Dishner

   Head Over Heels Day Spa

   2424 Tranquility Drive

   Sedona, AZ 86335
4. Send the envelope to the printer. **NOTE:** If you are using this in class or in your school's computer lab, check with your instructor about printing permissions before completing this step.
5. Save the file as directed by your instructor and close it.

Skill 5.23 Creating Labels

Rather than trying to create a document of labels with the correct margin and label size, you can use Word's preset label formats. Before creating your labels, first check the packaging for the manufacturer name and the product name or number.

To create labels:

1. Click the **Mailings** tab.
2. In the *Create* group, click the **Labels** button.

FIGURE WD 5.34

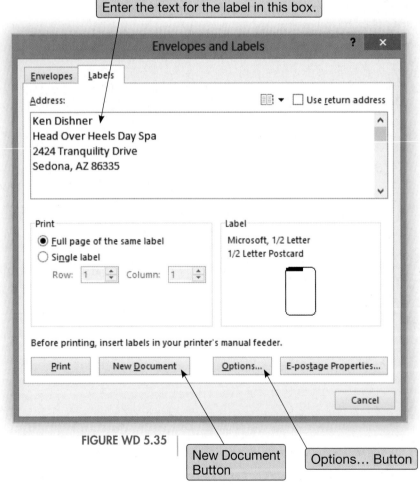

FIGURE WD 5.35

3. The type text for the label in the *Address* box.
4. Click the **Options...** button.
5. Click the **Label vendors** arrow and find the name of the company that made the labels you want to use.
6. Scroll the list of product numbers until you find the one that matches your labels.
7. Click **OK** in the *Label Options* dialog.
8. Click the **New Document** button.

Word creates the document as a table with the proper margins and spacing between cells. The cells in the table are prepopulated with the text you entered in the *Address* box in the *Envelopes and Labels* dialog.

word 2013   chapter 5 Working with Reports, References, and Mailings

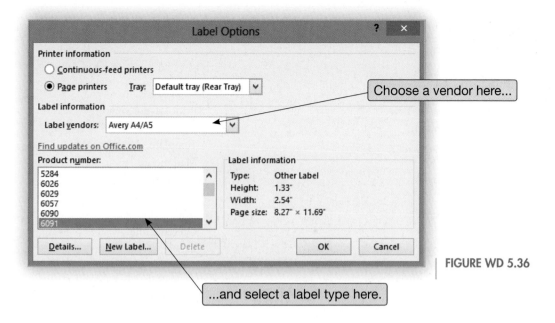

Choose a vendor here...

...and select a label type here.

FIGURE WD 5.36

tips & tricks

If you need to create a page of labels with different text, leave the *Address* box empty, choose the label type, and create the document. Word will create a document of empty labels. Click in each cell and type the text for the labels you want to create.

tell me **more**

You can choose to print a full page of the same label or a single label. Use the full page option if you are printing return address labels that you will need several of. Use the single label option for creating individual labels, such as labels for file folders.

another **method**

To open the *Envelopes and Labels* dialog, you can also click the **Envelopes** button, and then click the **Labels** tab to create a label.

let me **try**

Open the student data file **wd5-23-Document1** and try this skill on your own:

1. Open the *Envelopes and Labels* dialog.
2. Add the following return address:

   Ken Dishner

   Head Over Heels Day Spa

   2424 Tranquility Drive

   Sedona, AZ 86335

3. Open the *Label Options* dialog and select the vendor **Avery A4/A5** and the product number **3651**.
4. Create a new document of labels.
5. Save the file as directed by your instructor and close it.

key terms

AutoCorrect	Index
Thesaurus	Read Mode
Tab leaders	Print Layout view
Table of contents	Web Layout view
Footnotes	Template
Endnotes	Mail merge
Reference mark	Recipients list
Caption	Merge fields
Reference style	Address block
Citation	Greeting line
Bibliography	Labels

concepts review

1. A _____ fills in the space between tabs with solid, dotted, or dashed lines.

   a. border

   b. tab leader

   c. tab marker

   d. none of the above

2. When creating a mail merge, you can add recipients _____.

   a. by typing them in manually

   b. by importing them from an Access database

   c. by importing them from Outlook

   d. all of the above

3. To look up a synonym for a word use the _____.

   a. grammar check

   b. Thesaurus

   c. Dictionary

   d. translate tool

4. When you add a table of contents to a document, the entries created are based on _____.

   a. marked entries

   b. headings

   c. custom styles

   d. all of the above

5. You can add a caption for a _____.

   a. figure

   b. table

   c. neither a nor b

   d. both a and b

6. A _____ appears at the bottom of a page and is composed of two parts: a reference mark (a superscript character placed next to the text) and the associated text.

   a. footnote

   b. endnote

   c. index

   d. citation

7. To view documents optimally on an electronic device, such as a tablet, you should use _____.

   a. Read Mode

   b. Print Layout view

   c. Web Layout view

   d. Draft view

8. A _____ is a set of rules used to display references in a bibliography.

   a. source

   b. reference style

   c. template

   d. citation

9. If you often mistype a word, use Word's _____ to automatically replace the misspelling with the correct spelling as you type.

   a. find and replace commands

   b. spelling check

   c. grammar check

   d. AutoCorrect

10. _____ are placeholders that insert specific data for recipients you added to a mail merge.

   a. Merge fields

   b. Labels

   c. Recipients lists

   d. all of the above

projects

skill review 5.1

In this project you will be working on a research paper about alternate assessments for students.

Skills needed to complete this project:

- Checking Grammar (Skill 5.2)
- Using the Thesaurus (Skill 5.3)
- Using the Tabs Dialog (Skill 5.4)
- Adding Tab Leaders (Skill 5.5)
- Inserting a Table of Contents (Skill 5.6)
- Inserting Footnotes and Endnotes (Skill 5.7)
- Selecting a Reference Style (Skill 5.9)
- Adding Citations to Documents (Skill 5.10)
- Creating a Bibliography (Skill 5.11)
- Marking Entries (Skill 5.12)
- Creating an Index (Skill 5.13)
- Using Views (Skill 5.14)

1. Open the **WD2013-SkillReview-5-1** document.
2. Save this document as: **[your initials]WD-SkillReview-5-1**
3. Check for grammar errors in the document.
   a. Click the **Review** tab.
   b. In the *Proofing* group, click the **Spelling & Grammar** button.
   c. The first grammar error found should be **a** instead of **an.** Click the **Change** button in the *Grammar* task pane to fix the error.
   d. The second and third grammar errors found indicate **Behind** should not be capitalized. Click the **Ignore** button to keep the capitalization the same for both instances found.
   e. If Word finds a spelling error on the name **Kettler,** click the **Ignore All** button to keep the spelling of this name throughout the document.
4. Use the Thesaurus to look up synonyms of a word.
   a. Navigate to the beginning of the document.
   b. In the first paragraph under *Introduction,* select the word **pick** in the second sentence.
   c. On the *Review* tab, in the *Proofing* group, click the **Thesaurus** button.
   d. Scroll the list of synonyms, in the *select (v.)* section, point to **choose** and click the **arrow.**
   e. Click **Insert** on the menu.

5. Add an AutoCorrect entry and type the text to see the correction.

   a. Click the **File** tab.

   b. Click **Options.**

   c. In the *Word Options* dialog, click **Proofing.**

   d. Click the **AutoCorrect Options...** button.

   e. In the *Replace* box, type `accomodations`. In the *With* box, type `accommodations`.

   f. Click the **Add** button.

   g. Click **OK** in the *AutoCorrect* dialog. Click **OK** in the *Word Options* dialog.

   h. Place the cursor between the words **of** and **that** in the first sentence of the first paragraph of the document.

   i. Type `accomodations.` Notice Word replaces the misspelled word with the correct spelling you added.

6. Add a new tab through the *Tabs* dialog.

   a. Place the cursor at the beginning of the first paragraph of the document.

   b. Click the **Home** tab.

   c. In the *Paragraph* group, click the **dialog launcher.**

   d. In the *Paragraph* dialog, click the **Tabs...** button.

   e. In the *Tab stop position* box, type `0.5"`.

   f. Verify the alignment of the tab is set to Left and there is no tab leader. Click the **Set** button.

   g. Click **OK** in the *Tabs* dialog.

   h. Press the [Tab] key to indent the paragraph by 0.5".

7. Insert a table of contents.

   a. Place the cursor before the **Introduction** heading.

   b. Click the **Page Layout** tab.

   c. In the *Page Setup* group, click the **Breaks** button and select **Page.**

   d. Place the cursor on the empty line on the newly inserted page.

   e. Click the **References** tab.

   f. In the *Table of Contents* group, click the **Table of Contents** button and select **Automatic Table 2.**

8. Insert a footnote.

   a. Navigate to the *No Child Left Behind* section of the document. Place the cursor after the word **state** in the first sentence.

   b. On the *References* tab, in the *Footnotes* group, click the **Insert Footnote** button.

   c. Type the following text for the footnote: `For this paper the Ohio state standards are employed.`

9. Add a new source and insert a citation.

   a. Navigate to the *Modified Achievement Standards* section. Place the cursor before the period in the second sentence of the last paragraph of the section. This is the sentence ending with *scheduling, presentation format or response format.*

   b. On the *References* tab, in the *Citations & Bibliography* group, click the **Insert Citation** button and select **Add New Source.**

c. In the *Create Source* dialog, select **Journal Article** as the type of source. Enter `Pamela Johnson` as the author. Enter `The Benefits of Administration of Alternate Assessments` as the title. Enter `New Horizons` as the journal name. Enter `2012` for the year.

d. Click **OK** to create the source.

e. Navigate to the *Who Will Benefit* section. Place the cursor before the last period at the end of the second paragraph in the section. This is the sentence ending with *validity of the alternate assessment.*

f. On the *References* tab, in the *Citations & Bibliography* group, click the **Insert Citation** button and select the **Johnson, Pamela** citation.

10. Change the reference style for the document.

a. On the *References* tab, in the *Citations & Bibliography* group, click the **Style** arrow.

b. Select **APA Sixth Edition.**

11. Add a bibliography to the document.

a. Place the cursor at the end of the document.

b. Click the **Page Layout** tab.

c. In the *Page Setup* group, click the **Breaks** button and select **Page.**

d. Click the **References** tab.

e. In the *Citations &Bibliography* group, click the **Bibliography** button and select **References.**

12. Mark and entry for the index.

a. Navigate to the *No Child Left Behind* section. Select **No Child Left Behind Act (NCLB)** in the first sentence of the first paragraph.

b. On the *References* tab, in the *Index* group, click the **Mark Entry** button.

c. In the *Mark Index Entry* dialog, click the **Mark** button.

d. Click the **Close** button.

e. Click the **Home** tab.

f. In the *Paragraph* group, click the **Show/Hide** button to hide formatting marks in the document.

13. Create an index for the document.

a. Navigate to the end of the document and place the cursor on the empty line under the *References* section.

b. Click the **Page Layout** tab.

c. In the *Page Setup* group, click the **Breaks** button and select **Page.**

d. Click the **References** tab.

e. In the *Index* group, click the **Insert Index** button.

f. Click the **Formats** arrow and select **Modern.**

g. Click **OK** to add the index.

14. Display the document in different views.

a. Navigate to the beginning of the document.

b. On the status bar, click the **Read Mode** button.

c. Click **View,** point to **Page Color,** and select **Sepia.**

d. Click the **Next** button to advance to the next page in the document.

e. Navigate through the document using the **Back** and **Next** buttons.

f. On the status bar, click the **Print Layout** button to return to *Print Layout* view.

15. Save and close the document.

In this project you will be creating a mail merge based on a template.

Skills needed to complete this project:

- Creating a New Document Using a Template (Skill 5.16)
- Using the Thesaurus (Skill 5.3)
- Starting a Mail Merge (Skill 5.17)
- Selecting Recipients (Skill 5.18)
- Adding an Address Block (Skill 5.19)
- Adding a Greeting Line (Skill 5.20)
- Previewing and Finishing the Merge (Skill 5.21)

1. Open the **WD2013-SkillReview-5-2** document.
2. Create a new document from a template.
   a. Click the **File** tab.
   b. Click **New.**
   c. In the *Search for online templates* box, type `letter to new client`. Click the **Start searching** button.
   d. Click the **Introductory letter to new client** template. NOTE: You may see two templates with this description. Choose the letter with the following description: *Welcome a new client to your company with this letter template, which encloses information about your services and provides account and contact information.*
   e. Click the **Create** button to create the new document based on the template.
3. Save this document as: `[your initials]WD-SkillReview-5-2`
4. Remove information from the document.
   a. Select the recipient address block (*[Recipient Name], [Title], [Company Name], [Steen Address], [City, ST Zip Code].* Press the [Delete] key to remove the text.
   b. Delete the **Dear [Recipient Name]:** line.
   c. Delete the last two sentences in the second paragraph (beginning with **Your account manager,**).
5. Insert your own text into the document.
   a. In the first sentence of the first paragraph, delete the [**Company Name**] control. Type `Suarez Marketing`.
   b. In the first sentence of the first paragraph, delete the [**business type**] control. Type `marketing`.
   c. In the last sentence of the third paragraph, delete the [**Company Name**] control. Type `Suarez Marketing`.
   d. Delete the [**Your Name**] control in the salutation. Type `Maria Suarez`.
   e. Delete the [**Title**] control. Type `President`.
   f. Select the company address block at the top of the document. Delete the **Your Name** control and the **Company Name** control. Enter the following information in the company address block at the top of the document:

      `Maria Suarez`

      `Suarez Marketing`

      `1212 Main St.`

      `St. Louis MO 63144`
   g. Click the **Date** control and select today's date.

6. Use the **Thesaurus** to look up synonyms of a word.

    a. In the first paragraph, select the word **choosing** in the first sentence.

    b. On the *Review* tab, in the *Proofing* group, click the **Thesaurus** button.

    c. In the list of synonyms, point to **selecting** and click the **arrow.**

    d. Click **Insert** on the menu.

7. Start a new mail merge.

    a. Click the **Mailings** tab.

    b. Click the **Start Mail Merge** button and select **Letters.**

8. Add recipients to the mail merge.

    a. On the *Mailings* tab, in the *Start Mail Merge* group, click the **Select Recipients** button and select **Use an Existing List...**

    b. Browse to your student data file location, select the **Clients** file, and click the **Open** button.

    c. In the *Select Table* dialog, select the **Clients** table and click **OK.**

9. Add an address block to the document.

    a. Place the cursor after the zip code in the company address block and press **[Enter] twice.**

    b. On the *Mailings* tab, in the *Write & Insert Fields* group, click the **Address Block** button.

    c. In the *Insert recipient's name in this format* box, select the **Josh Randall Jr.** format. Click **OK.**

10. Add a greeting line to the document.

    a. Place the cursor at the beginning of the first paragraph and press `← Enter`. Place the cursor on the empty line.

    b. On the *Mailings* tab, in the *Write & Insert Fields* group, click the **Greeting Line** button.

    c. In the *Insert Greeting Line* dialog, click the arrow next to the punctuation under *Greeting line format* and select the **colon (:).** Click **OK.**

11. Preview the merged documents.

    a. On the *Mailings* tab, in the *Preview Results* group, click the **Preview Results** button.

    b. In the *Preview Results* group, click the **Next Record** button to advance through the letters in the mail merge.

12. Print the merged documents.

    a. On the *Mailings* tab, in the *Finish* group, click the **Finish & Merge** button and select **Print Documents...**

    b. Verify the **All** radio button is selected. Click **OK.**

    c. The *Print* dialog opens. Click **OK** to print all the letters in the merge. If you do not want to print the merge, click **Cancel. NOTE:** If you are using this in class or in your school's computer lab, check with your instructor about printing permissions before completing this step.

13. Save and close the document. Close but do not save the original blank document.

In this project you will be adding working on a safety report from the Spring Hills Community.

Skills needed to complete this project:

- Using AutoCorrect (Skill 5.1)
- Checking Grammar (Skill 5.2)
- Using the Thesaurus (Skill 5.3)
- Adding a Caption (Skill 5.8)
- Using the Tabs Dialog (Skill 5.4)
- Adding Tab Leaders (Skill 5.5)
- Inserting a Table of Contents (Skill 5.6)
- Inserting Footnotes and Endnotes (Skill 5.7)
- Marking Entries (Skill 5.12)
- Creating an Index (Skill 5.13)
- Using Views (Skill 5.14)
- Using Read Mode (Skill 5.15)

1. Open the **WD2013-ChallengeYourself-5-3** document.
2. Save this document as: **[your initials]WD-ChallengeYourself-5-3**
3. Add an AutoCorrect entry and type the text to see the correction.
   a. Create an AutoCorrect entry that will change the letters **ghc** to **Green Hills Community** when typed.
   b. Place the cursor between the words **the** and **Outside** on the second line in the first paragraph of the document. Type **ghc**. (Be sure to include the period after the letters). Notice Word changes the text to the entry you just created.
4. Using Word's grammar check, check the documents for any grammar errors and correct the errors that are found. Ignore any spelling errors that appear on names.
5. Use the Thesaurus to look up synonyms of a word.
   a. Select the word **community** in the second sentence of the first paragraph *(Outside our gated community)*.
   b. Use the Thesaurus to replace the word **community** with the synonym **neighborhood.**
6. Add a caption to a chart.
   a. Select the chart on page 2.
   b. Add a caption that reads **Figure 1: Top 5 Targeted Electronics**. Have the figure appear below the chart.
7. Add a new tab through the *Tabs* dialog.
   a. Select the list of full-time officers at the bottom of page 3.
   b. Using the *Tabs* dialog, add a **right tab** and the **5"** mark. Include a **dotted tab leader** (option 2).
   c. For each item in the bulleted list, place the cursor between the name and the number of years. Remove the space and press [Tab].
   d. Repeat these steps for the list of part-time officers.

8. Insert a table of contents.

   a. Place the cursor before the document title **Spring Hills Community Safety Strategies** (at the top of the second page).

   b. Add a table of contents based on the **Automatic Table 1** style.

9. Insert a footnote.

   a. Place the cursor at the end of the heading **Basic Tips for Staying Safe.**

   b. Insert a footnote that reads: `Adapted from Dwight Hill's safety presentation.`

10. Mark and entry for the index.

    a. Select the text **top five targeted electronics** at the end of the first paragraph in the *What Electronics Are Being Targeted* section.

    b. Mark the text for use in an index. Close the *Mark Index Entry* dialog.

    c. Hide the formatting marks when you are done.

11. Create an index for the document.

    a. Navigate to the end of the document and add a page break. If necessary, remove the bullet style from the blank line at the top of the new page.

    b. Insert an index based on the **Bulleted** format. Have the index display in one column.

12. Display the document in different views.

    a. Switch to **Read Mode.**

    b. Navigate through the document.

    c. Switch back to **Print Layout** view.

13. Save and close the document.

challenge yourself 5.4

In this project you will be working on a letter for a mail merge from the Greenscapes landscaping company.

Skills needed to complete this project:

- Using AutoCorrect (Skill 5.1)
- Checking Grammar (Skill 5.2)
- Using the Thesaurus (Skill 5.3)
- Using the Tabs Dialog (Skill 5.4)
- Using Views (Skill 5.14)
- Using Read Mode (Skill 5.15)
- Starting a Mail Merge (Skill 5.17)
- Selecting Recipients (Skill 5.18)
- Adding an Address Block (Skill 5.19)
- Adding a Greeting Line (Skill 5.20)
- Previewing and Finishing the Merge (Skill 5.21)

1. Open the **WD2013-ChallengeYourself-5-4** document.

2. Save this document as: `[your initials]WD-ChallengeYourself-5-4`

3. Add an AutoCorrect entry and type the text to see the correction.

   a. Create an AutoCorrect entry that will change the letter **gsc** to **Greenscapes** when typed.

   b. Place the cursor between the words **at** and **thank** on the first line in the first paragraph of the document. Type **gsc,** (Be sure to include the comma after the letters). Notice Word changes the text to the entry you just created.

4. Using Word's grammar check, check the documents for any grammar errors and correct the errors that are found. Ignore any spelling errors.

5. Use the Thesaurus to look up synonyms of a word.

   a. Select the word **picking** in the first sentence of the first paragraph (*for picking us for your lawn care needs.*).

   b. Use the Thesaurus to replace the word **picking** with the synonym **choosing.**

6. Switch views.

   a. Switch to **Read Mode** to review the document.

   b. Switch back to **Print Layout** view.

7. Start a new mail merge for creating letters.

8. Add recipients to the mail merge.

   a. Add recipients to the mail merge based on an existing list.

   b. Browse to your student data file location, and open the **Customers** file as the recipients source.

   c. In the *Select Table* dialog, select the **Customers** table from the database.

9. Add an address block to the document.

   a. Place the cursor on the first empty line under the date.

   b. Add an **address block** to the letter based on the **Mr. Josh Randall Jr.** format.

10. Add a greeting line to the document.

    a. Place the cursor on the empty line under the address block.

    b. Add a greeting line to the letter. Have the field follow the this format:
    Dear Mr. Randall:

11. Preview the merged documents reviewing how each will appear when printed.

12. Print the merged documents.

13. Save and close the document.

on your own 5.5

In this project you will be creating a mail merge letter to job applicants who did not meet the required qualifications.

Skills needed to complete this project:

- Creating a New Document Using a Template (Skill 5.16)
- Using AutoCorrect (Skill 5.1)
- Checking Grammar (Skill 5.2)
- Using the Thesaurus (Skill 5.3)
- Using the Tabs Dialog (Skill 5.4)
- Using Views (Skill 5.14)
- Using Read Mode (Skill 5.15)

- Creating a New Document Using a Template (Skill 5.16)
- Starting a Mail Merge (Skill 5.17)
- Selecting Recipients (Skill 5.18)
- Adding an Address Block (Skill 5.19)
- Adding a Greeting Line (Skill 5.20)
- Previewing and Finishing the Merge (Skill 5.21)
- Creating Envelopes (Skill 5.22)
- Creating Labels (Skill 5.23)

1. Open the **WD2013-OnYourOwn-5-5** document.
2. Search for **template letters about job candidates.** Create a new document based on a template of your choice.
3. Save this document as: **[your initials]WD-OnYourOwn-5-5**
4. Add your own information and remove any information in the template you do not want to use.
5. If the template includes an address block and/or a greeting line, delete those elements from the document.
6. Create an AutoCorrect entry for a word you frequently mistype. If possible, try adding the word to the document by typing the short entry you entered.
7. Using Word's grammar check, check the documents for any grammar errors and correct any errors that are found.
8. Use the Thesaurus to look up a word and replace it with a synonym.
9. Switch to **Read Mode** and read through the document. Switch back to **Print Layout** view.
10. Start a new mail merge for creating letters.
11. Use the *New Address List* dialog to add recipients to the mail merge. Create a list of fictitious job candidates including names and addresses.
12. Add an address block using a format of your choice to the document.
13. Add a greeting line using a format of your choice to the document.
14. Preview the merged documents reviewing how each will appear when printed.
15. Print the merged documents.
16. Save and close the document.

fix it 5.6

In this project you will be working on a paper about behavior modification.

Skills needed to complete this project:
- Using AutoCorrect (Skill 5.1)
- Checking Grammar (Skill 5.2)
- Using the Thesaurus (Skill 5.3)
- Using the Tabs Dialog (Skill 5.4)
- Adding Tab Leaders (Skill 5.5)
- Inserting a Table of Contents (Skill 5.6)
- Inserting Footnotes and Endnotes (Skill 5.7)

- Adding a Caption (Skill 5.8)
- Selecting a Reference Style (Skill 5.9)
- Adding Citations to Documents (Skill 5.10)
- Creating a Bibliography (Skill 5.11)
- Marking Entries (Skill 5.12)
- Creating an Index (Skill 5.13)
- Using Views (Skill 5.14)
- Using Read Mode (Skill 5.15)

1. Open the **WD2013-FixIt-5-6** document.

2. Save this document as: `[your initials]WD-FixIt-5-6`

3. Add an AutoCorrect entry to change the word **behaviour** to **behavior** when typed.

4. Using Word's grammar check, check the documents for any grammar errors and correct the errors that are found.

5. Use the Thesaurus to look up synonyms of a word.

   a. In the fourth sentence of the first paragraph, select the word **first** (*in their first home*).

   b. Using the Thesaurus, replace the word with the synonym **original.**

6. Add new tabs through the *Tabs* dialog.

   a. Navigate to the *V. Collect and evaluate the result* section.

   b. Turn on formatting marks to view the tabs in the section.

   c. Select the all the data in the *Observation Phase* section (from *2/7* to *86%*)

   d. Using the *Tabs* dialog, place a left tab stop at **1"**. Place a center tab stop at **3.5"**. Place a right tab stop at **5".**

   e. Apply a dotted tab leader to each of the tab stops.

   f. Repeat these steps for the data in the *Implementation Phase* section.

   g. Turn off formatting marks.

7. Navigate to the *I. Identify Target Behavior* section of the document and insert a table of contents based on the **Automatic Table 1** format.

8. Add a footnote after the first sentence in the document that reads: `To protect the identity of the student, I will use the pseudonym Andrew.`

9. Mark and entry for the index.

   a. Navigate to *paragraph B* in the *I. Identify Target Behavior* section of the document.

   b. Select **Language Arts classroom** in the first sentence of the paragraph.

   c. Mark the text for use as an entry in the index.

   d. Hide the formatting marks

10. Add a new blank page to the end of the document and insert an index based on the **Modern** format. Have the entries display in a single column.

11. Display the document in Read Mode to read through the document for accuracy.

12. Save and close the document.

chapter **6**

Exploring Advanced Document Features

In this chapter, you will learn the following skills:

- Adjust character spacing
- Create and modify styles
- Create an AutoText entry
- Apply columns and insert a column break
- Adjust paragraph settings
- Insert a horizontal line and add borders and shading to paragraphs
- Customize lists
- Set automatic hyphenation
- Add a drop cap and a text box
- Link content from another application using the *Paste Special* command
- Customize the behavior of features in Word

Skill **6.1** Applying Other Character Effects

Skill **6.2** Using Character Spacing

Skill **6.3** Working with the Styles Task Pane

Skill **6.4** Creating a New Style

Skill **6.5** Modifying a Style

Skill **6.6** Renaming Styles

Skill **6.7** Creating AutoText Entries

Skill **6.8** Inserting Symbols

Skill **6.9** Applying Columns

Skill **6.10** Inserting a Column Break

Skill **6.11** Changing Line Spacing Using the Paragraph Dialog

Skill **6.12** Adjusting Spacing Before and After Paragraphs

Skill **6.13** Setting First Line and Hanging Indents

Skill **6.14** Adding a Horizontal Line

Skill **6.15** Adding Borders and Shading to Paragraphs

Skill **6.16** Creating Custom Bulleted Lists

Skill **6.17** Creating Multilevel Lists

Skill **6.18** Customizing Multilevel Lists

Skill **6.19** Using Automatic Hyphenation

Skill **6.20** Adding a Drop Cap to a Paragraph

Skill **6.21** Adding a Quote Text Box

Skill **6.22** Using Paste Special

Skill **6.23** Customizing Word

skills

introduction

This chapter provides you with skills for creating sophisticated documents. First, you will work with character formatting and then move on to creating and modifying styles. You will learn how to create AutoText entries and add symbols to documents. You will learn advanced document formatting techniques including applying columns and adjusting paragraph formatting. You will also learn how to customize lists including bulleted and multilevel lists. Desktop publishing features, including drop caps and text boxes, are covered here. Finally, you will learn how to paste linked data from other applications into your Word documents.

Skill 6.1 Applying Other Character Effects

Character effects are formatting styles that are applied to individual characters or words rather than paragraphs. You probably use bold, italic, and underline character effects often, but there are other character effects that you can apply to text to emphasize parts of your document.

Some of these character effects can be applied by clicking a button in the *Font* group on the *Home* tab:

Strikethrough—Draws a horizontal line through the text. Strikethrough can be used to show text from a document that is no longer relevant.

Subscript—Draws a small character below the bottom of the text. Subscripts are often used in mathematical equations and chemical formulas, such as H_2O.

Superscript—Draws a small character above the top of the text. Superscript are often used for numbers and mathematical equations, such as $E = mc^2$.

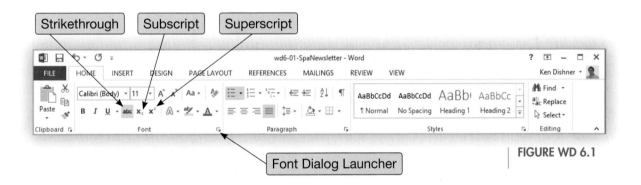

FIGURE WD 6.1

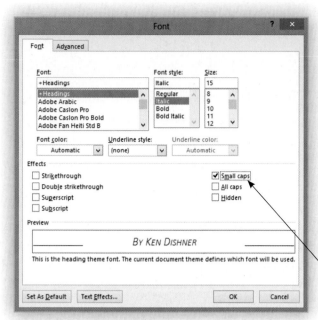

The *Font* dialog contains other character formatting options not available from the *Font* group. These effects include Shadow, Outline, and Small Caps among others.

To apply character formatting from the *Font* dialog:

1. Select the text to be changed.
2. On the *Home* tab, in the *Font* group, click the **dialog launcher** in the lower right corner of the group.
3. In the *Font* dialog, in the *Effects* section, click a checkmark next to the character effect you want to apply to the text.
4. Click **OK** to apply the formatting to the text.

Select a character effect in the *Effects* section.

FIGURE WD 6.2

tips & tricks

The *Preview* area of the *Font* dialog displays how the selected text will appear with the formatting applied.

tell me **more**

When character formatting has been applied to text, the button on the Ribbon appears highlighted (with a blue background). Click the button again to remove the formatting.

another method

To open the *Font* dialog, you can also press (Ctrl) + (D) on the keyboard.

To apply the **subscript** character formatting, you can also press (Ctrl) + (=) on the keyboard.

To apply the **superscript** character formatting, you can also press (Ctrl) + (Shift) + (=) on the keyboard.

let me try

Open the student data file **wd6-01-SpaNewsletter** and try this skill on your own:

1. Select the **Bamboo Manicure** bullet point on the second page of the newsletter. Be sure to select all the text for the bullet point.
2. Apply the strikethrough character effect to the selected text.
3. On page 1 of the newsletter, select the text **By Ken Dishner** under the *What's New* article title.
4. Open the **Font** dialog.
5. Apply the **small caps** character formatting to the text.
6. If you will be moving on to the next skill in this chapter, leave the document open to continue working. If not, save the file as directed by your instructor and close it.

Skill 6.2 Using Character Spacing

Character spacing gives you more control over the appearance of the text in your document. By expanding the spacing between characters, you can give your text a more open feel. By condensing the spacing between characters, you can fit text into a smaller space.

To change the spacing between characters:

1. Select the text you want to change.
2. On the *Home* tab, in the *Font* group, click the **dialog launcher** 🔲 .
3. Click the **Advanced** tab.
4. From the *Spacing* list, select **Expanded** or **Condensed.**
5. Enter a value for the spacing in the *By* box.
6. The *Preview* area displays an example of what your text will look like.
7. Click **OK** in the dialog to apply the changes.

Clicking the **Advanced** tab in the *Font* dialog gives you the following options:

❯ **Scaling**—Allows you to resize the selected text, making it either larger or smaller.

❯ **Spacing**—Alters the spacing between all selected letters by the same amount.

❯ **Positioning**—Raises or lowers the selection in relation to the baseline.

❯ **Kerning**—The amount of space between certain characters to create the appearance of even spacing.

Click the *Spacing* arrow and select an option.

Enter a value for the spacing in the *By* box.

Preview Area

FIGURE WD 6.3

tips & tricks

Click the **Set as Default** button to change the default font style in the Normal template to the selected font formatting.

another method

To open the *Font* dialog, you can also press Ctrl + D on the keyboard.

let me try

If you do not have the data file from the previous skill open, open the student data file **wd6-02-SpaNewsletter** and try this skill on your own:

1. Select the **What's New** article title.
2. Open the **Font** dialog to change character spacing for the selected text.
3. Change the font spacing to be expanded by **3** points.
4. If you will be moving on to the next skill in this chapter, leave the document open to continue working. If not, save the file as directed by your instructor and close it.

Skill 6.3 Working with the Styles Task Pane

The **Styles task pane** lists all the text styles available in a document. You can apply styles to text from the *Styles* task pane, as well as create new styles and modify existing styles.

To apply a style from the *Styles* task pane:

1. On the *Home* tab, in the *Styles* group, click the **dialog launcher** .
2. The *Styles* task pane appears.
3. Click a style in the task pane to apply that style to the selected text.

FIGURE WD 6.4

Styles Dialog Launcher

There are five basic style types you can apply from the *Styles* task pane:

Paragraph—Formatting applied to the entire paragraph (such as line spacing and alignment).

Character—Formatting applied to the text characters only (such as font, font size, and font color).

Linked (paragraph and character)—Formatting applied as paragraph or character styles (such as headings). If a paragraph is selected, the paragraph style of the linked style is applied. If only part of a paragraph is selected (such as a word or phrase), the character style is applied and the paragraph style is not affected.

Table—Formatting applied to tables (such as borders and shading).

List—Formatting applied to lists (such as bullet or numbering format).

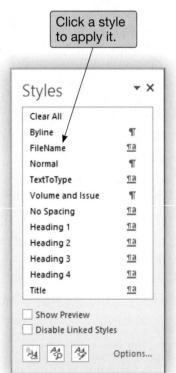

Click a style to apply it.

FIGURE WD 6.5

tips & tricks

Click the **Show Preview** check box, to change the style names in the list from plain text to formatted text that shows how text will appear when the style is applied to it.

tell me **more**

When you open the *Styles* task pane, each style is listed with an icon next to the name, indicating the type of style for each item in the task pane.

let me try

If you do not have the data file from the previous skill open, open the student data file **wd6-03-SpaNewsletter** and try this skill on your own:

1. Select the text **By Stone Rivers** under the *Four New Services* article title.
2. Open the **Styles** task pane.
3. From the *Styles* task pane, apply the **Byline** style to the selected text.
4. If you will be moving on to the next skill in this chapter, leave the document open to continue working. If not, save the file as directed by your instructor and close it.

Skill 6.4 Creating a New Style

Text styles include all the formatting applied to the text. This formatting includes paragraph styles, including alignment and line spacing, and character styles, such as font and font color. Word comes with a number of built-in styles for you to use, but what if you want to save and reuse your own custom styles? You can save your own your own styles based on text that you have formatted.

To create a new style based on formatting:

1. Select the text you want to base the new style on.
2. On the *Home* tab, in the *Styles* group, click the **More** button to display the *Styles* gallery.
3. At the bottom of the gallery, click **Create a Style.**

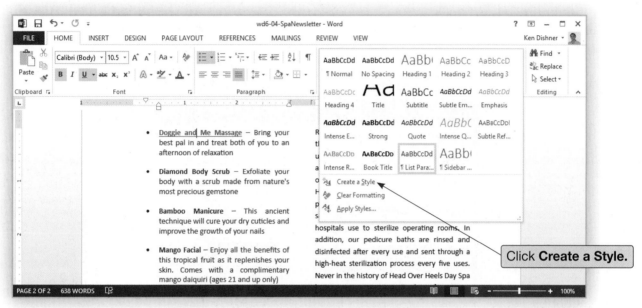

FIGURE WD 6.6

4. The *Create New Style from Formatting* dialog opens.
5. Type the name for the new style in the *Name* box.
6. Click **OK** to create the new style.

FIGURE WD 6.7

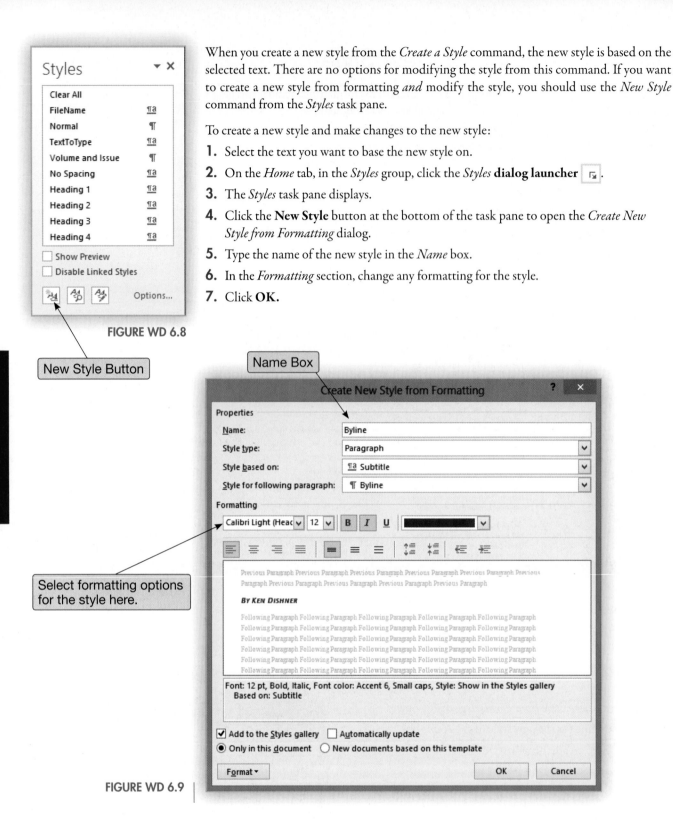

When you create a new style from the *Create a Style* command, the new style is based on the selected text. There are no options for modifying the style from this command. If you want to create a new style from formatting *and* modify the style, you should use the *New Style* command from the *Styles* task pane.

To create a new style and make changes to the new style:

1. Select the text you want to base the new style on.
2. On the *Home* tab, in the *Styles* group, click the *Styles* **dialog launcher** ⌐.
3. The *Styles* task pane displays.
4. Click the **New Style** button at the bottom of the task pane to open the *Create New Style from Formatting* dialog.
5. Type the name of the new style in the *Name* box.
6. In the *Formatting* section, change any formatting for the style.
7. Click **OK.**

FIGURE WD 6.8

New Style Button

Name Box

Create New Style from Formatting

Properties

Name: Byline

Style type: Paragraph

Style based on: ¶a Subtitle

Style for following paragraph: ¶ Byline

Formatting

Calibri Light (Head 12 **B** *I* U

Previous Paragraph Previous Paragraph Previous Paragraph Previous Paragraph Previous Paragraph Previous Paragraph Previous Paragraph Previous Paragraph Previous Paragraph Previous Paragraph

BY KEN DISHNER

Following Paragraph Following Paragraph

Font: 12 pt, Bold, Italic, Font color: Accent 6, Small caps, Style: Show in the Styles gallery
Based on: Subtitle

☑ Add to the Styles gallery   ☐ Automatically update
● Only in this document   ○ New documents based on this template

Format ▾   OK   Cancel

Select formatting options for the style here.

FIGURE WD 6.9

When you create a new style using either method, the new style appears in the task pane and in the *Styles* gallery. To apply the new style to text, select the text to apply the new style to and click the style name in the gallery or the task pane.

tips & tricks

In the *Create New Style from Formatting* dialog, click the **Format** button to open additional dialogs to further modify the style. These include the *Font, Paragraph, Tabs, Borders and Shading, Language, Frame, Numbering and Bullets, Customize Keyboard,* and *Format Text Effects* dialogs.

another method

To create a new style and make changes to the new style you can also:

1. Select the text you want to base the new style on.
2. On the *Home* tab, in the *Styles* group, click the **More** button to display the *Styles* gallery.
3. At the bottom of the gallery, click **Create a Style.**
4. In the dialog, click the **Modify...** button.
5. Make the changes in the *Create New Style from Formatting* dialog and click **OK.**

let me try

If you do not have the data file from the previous skill open, open the student data file **wd6-04-SpaNewsletter** and try this skill on your own:

1. Select the text **Doggie and Me Massage** on the second page of the newsletter. It is the green underlined text in the bulleted list.
2. Display the *Styles* gallery and select **Create a Style.**
3. Name the style **Bulleted item** and save the new style.
4. Apply the new style to the other bolded text in the bulleted list.
5. Select the text **Head Over Heels Spa** under *The Weekly Wrap* newsletter title.
6. Open the **Styles** task pane.
7. Click the **New Style** button.
8. Create a new **Paragraph** style named **Head Over Heels** from the selected text. Change the font to **Myriad Pro** or a font of your choice.
9. If you will be moving on to the next skill in this chapter, leave the document open to continue working. If not, save the file as directed by your instructor and close it.

Skill 6.5 Modifying a Style

When you apply the same formatting style to text throughout a document, you can be assured that all the text has the same formatting applied. But what if you decide that you want to change the look of a style throughout a document? There are two methods you can choose from: modifying the style or updating the style based on the formatting applied to selected text.

To modify a style:

1. On the *Home* tab, in the *Styles* group, right-click the style you want to change in the *Styles* gallery.
2. Select **Modify...** from the shortcut menu.
3. The *Modify Style* dialog opens.
4. In the *Formatting* section, select the formatting you want to apply to the style.
5. Click **OK.**

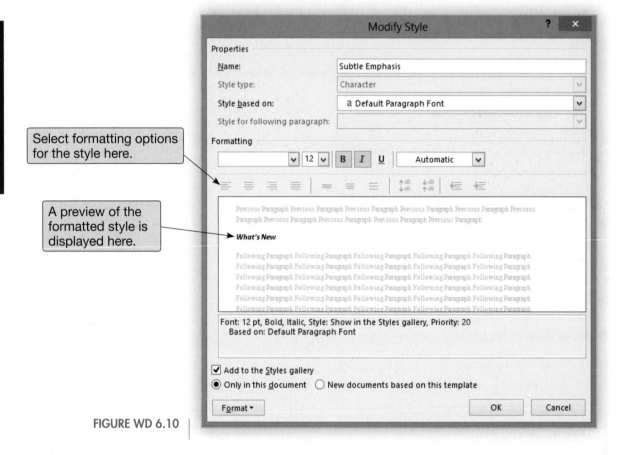

FIGURE WD 6.10

If you have text that already contains the formatting want to change the style to, you can update the style to match the formatting of selected text.

To update a style to match the formatting of selected text:

1. Select the text or place the cursor in the text with the formatting you want for the updated style.
2. On the *Home* tab, in the *Styles* group, right-click the style you want to change in the *Styles* gallery.
3. Select **Update [name of style] to Match Selection** from the shortcut menu.

Right-click the style . . .

. . . and select the update to match command.

FIGURE WD 6.11

tips & tricks

If you do not see the style you want to modify in the collapsed *Styles* gallery on the Ribbon, click the **More** button to view the entire gallery.

tell me more

Whether you modify or update a style, the new style formatting will be applied to any text in the document with that style applied.

another method

You can also modify a style from the *Styles* task pane:

1. On the *Home* tab, in the *Styles* group, click the **dialog launcher.**
2. In the *Styles* task pane, point to the style you want to change. Click the arrow that appears.
3. Select either the **Update [name of style] to Match Selection** or the **Modify...** command from the menu.

let me try

If you do not have the data file from the previous skill open, open the student data file **wd6-05-SpaNewsletter** and try this skill on your own:

1. Place the cursor in the **What's New** title on the first page of the newsletter.
2. Open the *Modify Style* dialog to change the **Subtle Emphasis** style.
3. Change the style to use **12 pt** font size and **bold** character formatting.
4. Update the **Heading 1** style to match the formatting of the current text.
5. If you will be moving on to the next skill in this chapter, leave the document open to continue working. If not, save the file as directed by your instructor and close it.

Skill 6.6 Renaming Styles

The Word 2013 *Normal* template includes a standard set of styles with default style names. These style names describe the part of the document the style is applied to. For example, the *Normal* style is typically applied to paragraph text in a document, while the *Title* style is used for title text on a cover page. The *Heading 1, Heading 2,* and *Heading 3* styles are used for heading styles throughout the document. You can keep these default names, or you can rename a style to something more meaningful to you.

To rename a style:

1. On the *Home* tab, in the *Styles* group, right-click the style in the *Styles* gallery.

2. Select **Rename...** from the shortcut menu.

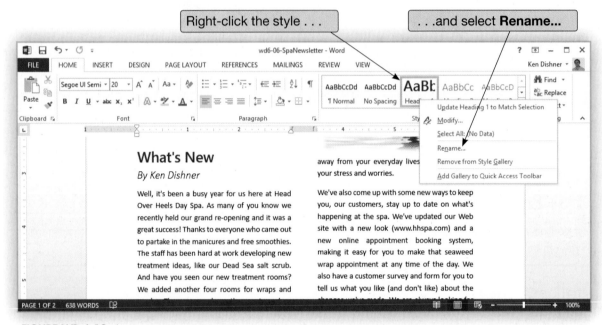

FIGURE WD 6.12

FIGURE WD 6.13

3. In the *Rename Style* dialog, type the new name of the style and click **OK.**

tips & tricks

If you do not see the style you want to modify in the collapsed *Styles* gallery on the Ribbon, click the **More** button to view the entire gallery.

tell me **more**

When you change the name of a style, the new style name only appears in the document that was open when you changed the style. If you create a new document, it will not include the new style name.

another **method**

You can change the name of a style from the *Modify Style* dialog. Type the new name in the *Name* box, and click **OK**.

let me **try**

If you do not have the data file from the previous skill open, open the student data file **wd6-06-SpaNewsletter** and try this skill on your own:

1. Open the *Rename Style* dialog to rename the **Heading 1** style.
2. Rename the style **Article Title.**
3. If you will be moving on to the next skill in this chapter, leave the document open to continue working. If not, save the file as directed by your instructor and close it.

from the perspective of . . .

MARKETING MANAGER

When creating marketing materials to send out to customers and potential customers, I always try to create a cohesive visual identity for our brand. In the past, I applied formatting to a part of a document and then used *Format Painter* to copy that formatting to other parts of the document. But I found that if I changed the formatting, I would have to go in and copy the formatting again. This was too much work! Now I use styles to apply formatting to my documents. I create my styles and then apply them to all the other parts of the document. The best part is that if I decide to change that style, all I have to do is modify the style one time and all the other text is updated automatically for me.

Skill 6.7 Creating AutoText Entries

If you are using a snippet of formatted text in your documents over and over again, you may want to save the text as an **AutoText** entry. AutoText entries are pieces of reusable content that are stored as building blocks. AutoText entries include not only the text of the entry but any formatting that has been applied.

To create an AutoText entry:

1. Select the text you want to save as an AutoText entry.
2. Click the **Insert** tab.

Insert Tab

Explore Quick Parts Button

Select **Save Selection to AutoText Gallery.**

Point to AutoText

FIGURE WD 6.14

3. In the *Text* group, click the **Explore Quick Parts** button.
4. Point to **AutoText** and select **Save Selection to AutoText Gallery.**
5. The *Create New Building Block* dialog opens.
6. Type the name for the entry in the *Name* box.
7. Click **OK**.

To add the custom AutoText to your document, click the **Explore Quick Parts** button, point to **AutoText,** and select the AutoText entry you added.

Type the name for the AutoText entry here.

AutoText gallery is selected.

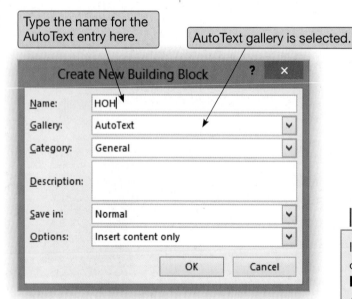

FIGURE WD 6.15

let me **try**

If you do not have the data file from the previous skill open, open the student data file **wd6-07-SpaNews-letter** and try this skill on your own:

1. Select the text **Head Over Heels Spa** on the first page of the newsletter. This text can be found under the title *The Weekly Wrap.*
2. Save the text as an AutoText entry with the name **HOH.**
3. If you will be moving on to the next skill in this chapter, leave the document open to continue working. If not, save the file as directed by your instructor and close it.

tips & tricks

To delete an AutoText entry, click the **Explore Quick Parts** button and select **Building Block Organizer...** Select the building block you want to delete and click the **Delete** button.

Skill 6.8 Inserting Symbols

A **symbol** is a special text character that is inserted into a document rather than typed on the keyboard. Symbols include special characters, such as copyright and trademark signs, mathematical operators, and foreign currency symbols.

Some of the more common symbols include:

©	Copyright sign
®	Registered sign
™	Trademark sign
€	Euro sign
£	Pound sign
¥	Yen sign

To insert a symbol:

1. Click the **Insert** tab.
2. In the *Symbols* group, click the **Symbol** button and select an option from the gallery.

The most recently used symbols appear in the *Symbols* gallery. To view additional symbols to insert, click **More Symbols...** at the bottom of the gallery. In the *Symbol* dialog, you can choose to insert special characters or to insert symbols that are part of a font set.

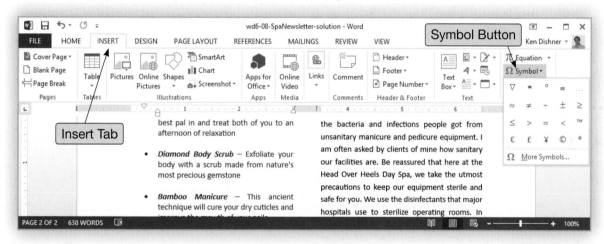

FIGURE WD 6.16

tips & tricks

The *Symbol, Wingdings, and Webdings* font sets include a variety of pictographs for you to add to your documents.

tell me **more**

Word comes with a number of predefined mathematical equations you can add to documents. To add a mathematical equation to a document, click the **Insert** tab. In the *Symbols* group, click the **Equation** button and select an option.

another **method**

Some symbols can be inserted by typing a combination of keystrokes on the keyboard. For example, typing (c) will automatically be changed to the copyright sign symbol (©), and typing a colon, a hyphen, and a closed parenthesis will be replaced by a smiley face (☺).

let me **try**

If you do not have the data file from the previous skill open, open the student data file **wd6-08-SpaNewsletter** and try this skill on your own:

1. Place the cursor after the words **Mangoo Facial** in the bulleted list on the second page of the newsletter.
2. Add the **registered sign** symbol after the words **Mangoo Facial.**
3. Save the file as directed by your instructor and close it.

Skill 6.9 Applying Columns

Newsletter pages are often laid out in **columns.** The text of these pages continues from the bottom of one column to the top of the next column. Word comes with a number of preset column options, making it easy to create columns of text in a document.

To apply columns to text:

1. Click the **Page Layout** tab.
2. In the *Page Setup* group, click the **Columns** button and select an option. Selecting **One, Two,** or **Three** will create evenly spaced columns. Choosing **Left** or **Right** will create a two-column layout with one column narrower than the other.

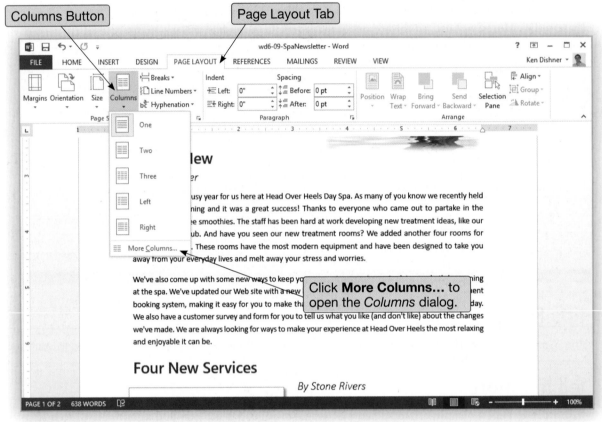

FIGURE WD 6.17

The *Columns* dialog gives you more control when creating columns in a document. In the *Columns* dialog, you cannot only set the number of columns, but also control the width of columns and spacing between columns. You can use the *Columns* dialog to apply columns to text or to modify existing columns in a document.

word 2013   Exploring Advanced Document Features

To modify columns using the *Columns* dialog:

1. On the *Page Layout* tab, in the *Page Setup* group, click the **Columns** button and select **More Columns....**

2. The *Columns* dialog opens.

3. In the *Presets* area, click the number of columns you want to apply to the document.

4. Click the up and down arrows under *Spacing* to increase and decrease the amount of space that appears between the columns.

5. Click **OK** to apply the column settings.

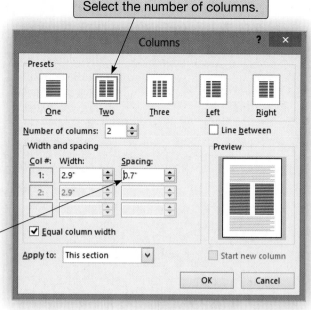

Select the number of columns.

Enter the amount of space to appear between columns.

FIGURE WD 6.18

tips & tricks

If you know you want your document to appear in column format, set the columns before you enter the document text. When you type the text for your document, it will automatically be formatted in columns.

tell me **more**

When the *Equal column width* check box is selected, Word will automatically create columns of equal width. If you want your columns to be different widths, uncheck this option and set the width for each column in the *Width* boxes.

another **method**

To change the spacing between columns, you can also type a value in the *Spacing* box in the *Columns* dialog.

let me try

Open the student data file **wd6-09-SpaNewsletter** and try this skill on your own:

1. Press Ctrl + A to select the entire document.

2. Format the document so the text appears in two columns.

3. Modify the spacing between the documents to be **0.7".**

4. If you will be moving on to the next skill in this chapter, leave the document open to continue working. If not, save the file as directed by your instructor and close it.

Skill 6.10 Inserting a Column Break

After you have added columns to your document, you may find that the text does not break across the columns exactly as you would like. In this case, you can add a column break where you want the bottom of the column to be. A **column break** marks where one column ends and moves the following text to the top of the next column.

To insert a column break:

1. Place the cursor before the text you want to appear at the top of the next column.

2. Click the **Page Layout** tab.

3. In the *Page Setup* group, click the **Breaks** button and select **Column.**

A column break is added. The text following the break now appears at the top of the next column.

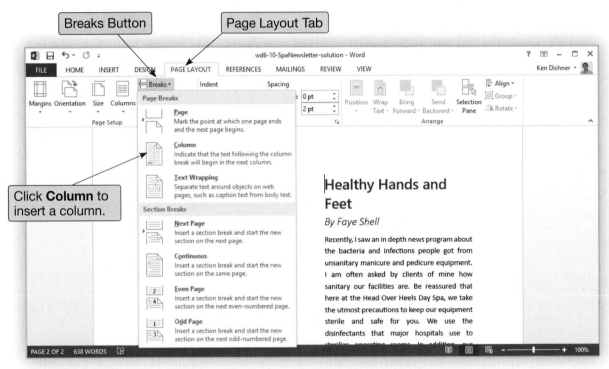

FIGURE WD 6.19

tips & tricks

❱ To view column breaks in a document, click the **Show/Hide** button in the *Paragraph* group on the *Home* tab.

❱ If you are displaying a list of items across multiple columns, use column breaks to create columns that contain same number of items.

another method

To insert a column break, you can also press Ctrl + Shift + Enter.

let me try

If you do not have the data file from the previous skill open, open the student data file **wd6-10-SpaNewsletter** and try this skill on your own:

1. Place the cursor before the article heading **Healthy Hands and Feet.** This is the heading at the bottom of the first column on page 2.

2. Insert a column break.

3. Save the file as directed by your instructor and close it.

word 2013   Exploring Advanced Document Features

Skill 6.11 Changing Line Spacing Using the Paragraph Dialog

From the Ribbon you can change the line spacing in a document using one of Word's preset options—single spacing, 1.5 line spacing, double spacing, etc. But what if you need a little more or a little less white space between lines than these options offer? You can also adjust line spacing from the *Paragraph* dialog.

To change line spacing from the *Paragraph* dialog:

1. Place the cursor in the paragraph you want to change.
2. On the *Home* tab, in the *Paragraph* group, click the **dialog launcher** .
3. The *Paragraph* dialog opens.
4. In the *Spacing* section, click the **Line Spacing** arrow and select **Multiple.**
5. Type a value for the line spacing in the *At* box.
6. Click **OK** to apply the changes.

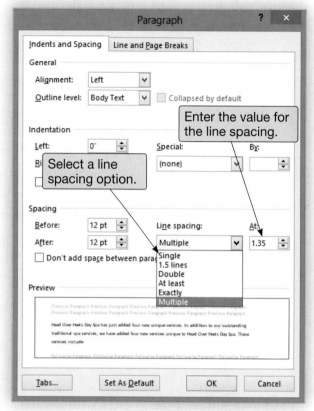

FIGURE WD 6.20

tell me **more**

When you select *Multiple*, Word multiplies the line height by the number in the *At* box to determine the spacing between lines. For the *At least* and *Exact* options, the value entered in the *At* box equals the exact number of points for the spacing between lines.

another **method**

To open the *Paragraph* dialog, you can also right-click the text and select **Paragraph...** from the shortcut menu.

To adjust the value in the *At* box, you can also click the up and down arrows. The value will be adjusted in .5 increments.

let me **try**

Open the student data file **wd6-11-FourNewServices** and try this skill on your own:

1. Place the cursor in the first paragraph in the letter. This is the paragraph beginning with *Head Over Heels has just added.*
2. Change the spacing for the paragraph to **1.25** lines.
3. If you will be moving on to the next skill in this chapter, leave the document open to continue working. If not, save the file as directed by your instructor and close it.

Skill 6.12 Adjusting Spacing Before and After Paragraphs

The default spacing after paragraphs in Word is 8 pt. This creates an evenly spaced document with some spacing between paragraphs to make it easier to tell when one paragraph ends and another begins. Sometimes you will want to increase the amount of space after paragraphs or add space above the paragraph in addition to below the paragraph. You could use the *Add Space Before* and *Add Space After* commands from the *Line Spacing* button in the *Paragraph* group, but those commands do not give you much control over the amount of space that is added. If you want to set an exact point amount for the white space that appears before or after a paragraph, you should use the *Before* and *After* controls in the *Paragraph* group on the *Page Layout* tab.

To adjust the amount of white space that appears above and below paragraphs:

1. Place the cursor in the paragraph you want to change.

2. Click the **Page Layout** tab.

3. In the *Paragraph* group, click the up and down arrows next to the *Before* box to adjust the spacing above the paragraph.

4. Click the up and down arrows next to the *After* box to adjust the spacing below the paragraph.

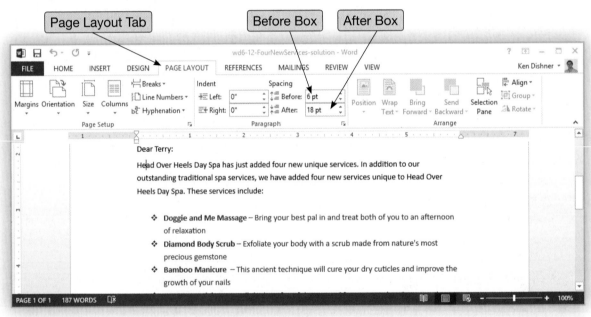

FIGURE WD 6.21

tips & tricks

When you click the up and down arrows, the value for the spacing adjusts by 6 pts. You can also type a value in the box to apply more precise spacing.

another method

You can also adjust the spacing before and after paragraphs from the *Paragraph* dialog:

1. On the *Home* tab, in the *Paragraph* group, click the **dialog launcher** .
2. The *Paragraph* dialog opens.
3. In the *Spacing* section, click the arrows next to the *Before* and *After* boxes to adjust the spacing.
4. Click **OK** to apply the changes.

let me try

If you do not have the data file from the previous skill open, open the student data file **wd6-12-FourNewServices** and try this skill on your own:

1. Place the cursor in the first paragraph in the letter. This is the paragraph beginning with *Head Over Heels has just added.*
2. Change the spacing before the paragraph to **6 pt** and the spacing after the paragraph to **18 pt.**
3. Save the file as directed by your instructor and close it.

from the perspective of . . .

ADMINISTRATIVE ASSISTANT

When I first started my job, I thought I really knew Word. All I had to do was write up letters and memos and get my boss to sign off on them before sending them out. Well, the first time I presented my boss with a memo to review, I thought I was going to be fired! It turns out she's a real stickler when it comes to formatting paragraphs. I always hit return to get enough space between paragraphs and to get the memo to fit on one page, but my boss informed me that the proper way to do it is to add spacing between paragraphs. She explained when someone else works on my documents those extra line spaces can really mess things up. In the end, I really learned a lot about how to properly format professional documents, and now everything I send out meets with her approval.

Skill 6.13 Setting First Line and Hanging Indents

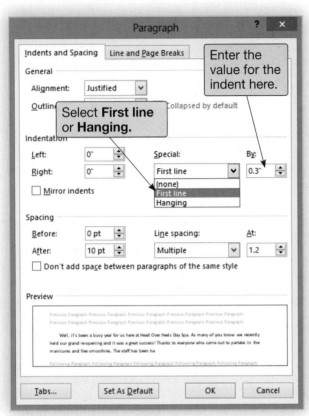

FIGURE WD 6.22

The indent commands indent all lines in a paragraph the same amount. If you want only the first line of a paragraph to be indented and the remainder of the paragraph to be left aligned, then use a **first line indent**. If you want the first line of a paragraph to be left aligned and the remainder of the paragraph to be indented, use a **hanging indent**. In the *Format Paragraph* dialog you can set options for first line indents and hanging indents.

To set first line or hanging indents:

1. Place the cursor in the paragraph you want to change.
2. On the *Home* tab, in the *Paragraph* group, click the **dialog launcher** .
3. In the *Indentation* section, click the **Special** arrow and select an option.
4. Click the up and down arrows next to the *By* box to adjust the amount for the indent.

tips & tricks

Use the *Left* and *Right* boxes in the *Indentation* section of the *Paragraph* dialog to increase the indents on either side of the paragraph. Increasing both indents by the same amount will center the paragraph and set it off visually from the other paragraphs in the document.

tell me **more**

Hanging indents are typically used in bibliographies and in some lists to set off the information. Hanging indents should not be used in body paragraphs of a document.

another **method**

To open the *Paragraph* dialog, you can also:

) Right-click the paragraph and select **Paragraph...**

) Click the **Page Layout** tab. In the *Paragraph* group, click the **dialog launcher.**

let me **try**

Open the student data file **wd6-13-SpaNewsletter** and try this skill on your own:

1. Place the cursor in the first paragraph of the *What's New* article. This is the paragraph beginning with *Well, it's been.*
2. Open the **Paragraph** dialog.
3. Set a first line indent at **0.3".**
4. Save the file as directed by your instructor and close it.

word 2013   Exploring Advanced Document Features

Skill 6.14 Adding a Horizontal Line

When you work with long documents, you may find that you want to separate one piece of content from the surrounding text but not create a new heading or section in the document. A **horizontal line** is a decorative element you can insert into a document. Use a horizontal line to add a visual divider to separate a part of a document without changing the underlying content structure.

To add a horizontal line to a document:

1. Place the cursor where you want the line to appear.
2. On the *Home* tab, in the *Paragraph* group, click the **Borders** button and select **Horizontal Line.**

FIGURE WD 6.23

tell me **more**

A horizontal line is not the same as a bottom border applied to a paragraph. Horizontal lines are more graphic in nature, typically incorporating illustration elements.

let me **try**

Open the student data file **wd6-14-SpaNewsletter** and try this skill on your own:

1. Place the cursor after the **Ken Dishner** byline in the *What's New* article.
2. Add a horizontal line.
3. Save the file as directed by your instructor and close it.

Skill 6.15 Adding Borders and Shading to Paragraphs

Just as you can add borders and shading to a table, you can also add borders and shading to paragraphs in your documents. When you add a border or shading to a paragraph, the paragraph will stand out to your readers, placing extra emphasis on the content in the formatted paragraph.

To add shading to a paragraph:

1. Place the cursor in the paragraph you want to add the shading to.
2. On the *Home* tab, in the *Paragraph* group, click the **Shading** button.
3. Click a color in the color palette to apply the shading.

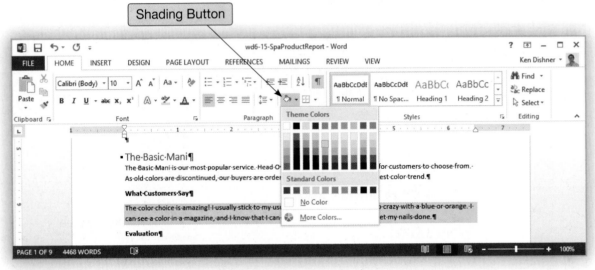

FIGURE WD 6.24

To add a border to a paragraph:

1. Place the cursor in the paragraph you want to add the border to.
2. On the *Home* tab, in the *Paragraph* group, click the **Borders** button.
3. Select **Borders and Shading...** to open the *Borders and Shading* dialog.

FIGURE WD 6.25

word 2013   Exploring Advanced Document Features

4. Select an option for the border under *Setting*.
5. Click an option in the *Style* box.
6. Click the **Color** arrow and select a color for the border.
7. Click the **Width** arrow and select a width for the border.
8. A preview of the border appear in the *Preview* area.
9. Click **OK** to apply your changes.

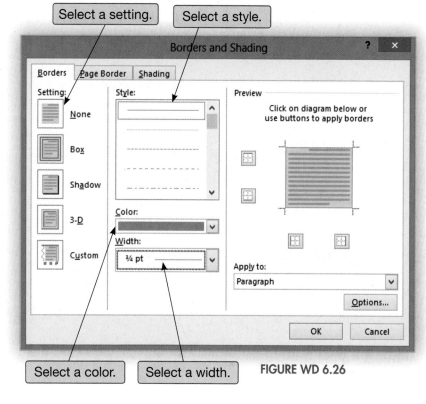

FIGURE WD 6.26

tips & tricks

When you select an option under *Setting* in the *Borders and Shading* dialog, Word applies the border on the top, bottom, left side, and right side of the paragraph. The *Preview* area includes a button for each part of the border. Click a button to turn a part of the border on or off. The *Preview* area will display the changes as you make them.

another method

You can also apply shading to a paragraph through the *Borders and Shading* dialog. Click the **Shading** tab. Click the **Fill** button arrow and select a color from the color palette. Click **OK** to apply the shading to the paragraph. Notice when you click the **Shading** button on the Ribbon, the new shading color you applied is highlighted in the palette.

let me try

Open the student data file **wd6-15-SpaProductReport** and try this skill on your own:

1. Place the cursor in the paragraph under the **What Customers Say** heading in the *The Basic Mani* section.
2. Add shading to the paragraph using the **Blue, Accent 1, Lighter 60%** color (the fifth color in the third row under *Theme Colors*).
3. Open the **Borders and Shading** dialog.
4. Apply a box border to the paragraph. It should use the **solid line style** (the first option), the **Blue Accent 1** color (the fifth color in the first row under *Theme Colors*), and be **1 pt** thick.
5. Save the file as directed by your instructor and close it.

Skill 6.16 Creating Custom Bulleted Lists

Word comes with a number of bullet styles for you to use in bulleted lists. But what if you want to use a different image for a bullet? The *Symbol, Wingdings,* and *Webdings* font sets contain a wide variety of pictographs you can use as bullets in lists.

To create a custom bulleted list using a symbol:

1. Place the cursor in the bulleted list you want to change.
2. On the *Home* tab, in the *Paragraph* group, click the **Bullets** button.
3. Select **Define New Bullet...**

Borders Button

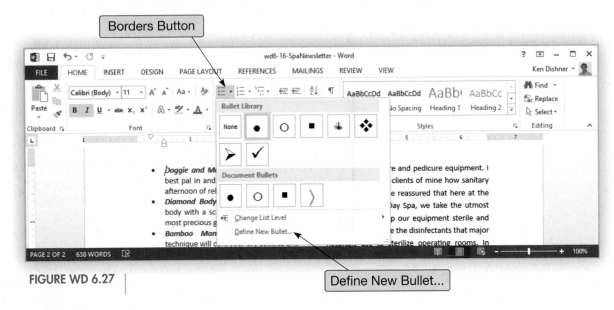

FIGURE WD 6.27

Define New Bullet...

Symbol... Button

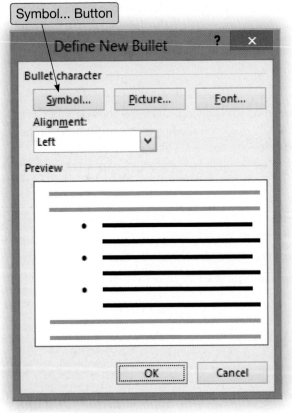

FIGURE WD 6.28

4. The *Define New Bullet* dialog opens.
5. Click the **Symbol...** button.
6. The *Symbol* dialog opens with the *Symbol* font selected. Click the **Font** arrow and select a font.
7. Click a square on the grid to select the symbol.
8. Click **OK** in the *Symbol* dialog to apply the symbol as the bullet.
9. Click **OK** in the *Define New Bullet* dialog to apply the new bullet.

word 2013   Exploring Advanced Document Features

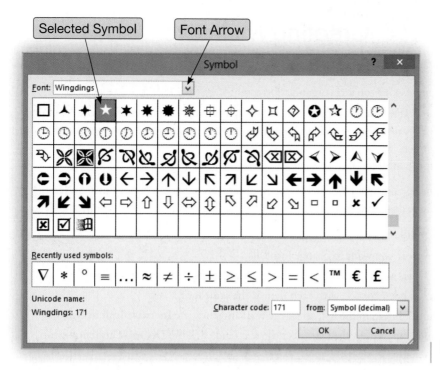

Selected Symbol

Font Arrow

FIGURE WD 6.29

tips & tricks

If you have a picture on your computer you want to use as the bullet symbol, click the **Picture...** button to open the *Insert Picture* dialog. Select the picture you want to use as the bullet and click **OK.**

tell me **more**

When you open the *Symbol* dialog, the most recently used symbols appear at the bottom of the dialog.

another **method**

To open the *Define New Bullet* dialog, you can also right-click the text you want to change. On the Mini toolbar, click the **Bullets** button and select **Define New Bullet...**

let me **try**

Open the student data file **wd6-16-SpaNewsletter** and try this skill on your own:

1. Place the cursor in the bulleted list at the top of the second page of the newsletter.
2. Open the **Define New Bullet** dialog.
3. Open the **Symbol** dialog.
4. Apply the **Wingdings 171** symbol as the bullet (it is the five-point star).
5. Save the file as directed by your instructor and close it.

skill 6.16   Creating Custom Bulleted Lists

Skill 6.17 Creating Multilevel Lists

A **multilevel list** divides your content into several levels of organization.

1. For example, your top level organization might start with 1.
   a. The next level appears indented, and the numbering scheme restarts at the beginning.
2. When you return to the first outline level, the numbering scheme picks up with the next number.
   a. But the sublevels restart each time.

A multilevel numbered list can have up to nine levels of organization. The numbering for sublevels can be displayed in a variety of formats, available from the *Multilevel List* gallery.

To create a multilevel list:

1. Select the text you want to change into a list.
2. On the *Home* tab, in the *Paragraph* group, click the **Multilevel List** button.
3. The list has been created with each item at the same level.
4. To demote an item in the list, select the text, and click the **Increase Indent** button.
5. To promote an item in the list, select the text, and click the **Decrease Indent** button.

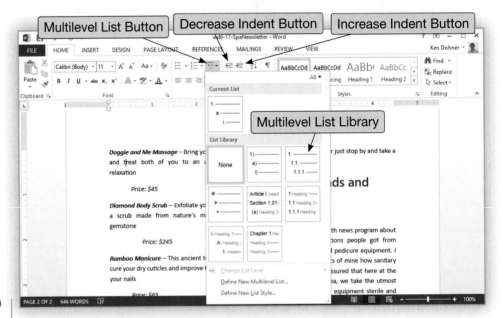

FIGURE WD 6.30

tell me **more**

Some multilevel lists show headings, which are based on predefined styles. Heading 1 text is placed at the topmost level of the list, followed by Heading 2 text, followed by Heading 3, etc.

another **method**

To change the level of an item in the list, you can also place the cursor in the item you want to change. Click the **Multilevel List** button. Point to **Change List Level** and select an option.

let me **try**

Open the student data file **wd6-17-SpaNewsletter** and try this skill on your own:

1. Select the four services at the top of the second page of the newsletter (from *Doggie and Me Massage* to *Price: $75*).
2. Convert the selected text to a multilevel list using the bulleted list style.
3. Promote the **Price** item under *Diamond Body Scrub* by one level.
4. Save the file as directed by your instructor and close it.

word 2013   Exploring Advanced Document Features

Skill 6.18 Customizing Multilevel Lists

Word comes with a number of predesigned multi-level list styles. These styles include common formats for creating multilevel lists. You may find that one of the predesigned styles is close to what you need but not quite. You can apply a style to the list and then modify the look for any level within the list.

To create a custom multilevel list format:

1. Place the cursor in the list you want to change.

2. On the *Home* tab, in the *Paragraph* group, click the **Multilevel List** button.

3. Click **Define New Multilevel List...** at the bottom of the *Multilevel List* gallery.

4. In the *Define new Multilevel list* dialog, click the level you want to modify.

5. Click the **Number style for this level** drop-down arrow and select a style to apply to the level.

6. Click **OK** to apply your changes.

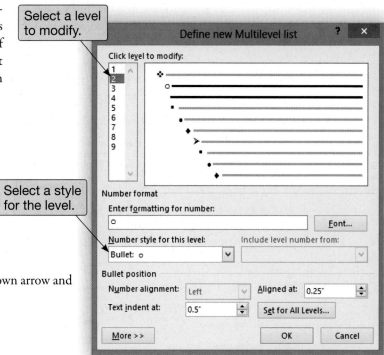

FIGURE WD 6.31

tips & tricks

If you know you do not want to use one the preset multilevel lists in the *List Library*, you can select **Define New Multilevel List...** and create the customized list from the *Define new Multilevel list* dialog without applying a multilevel list style first.

let me try

Open the student data file **wd6-18-SpaNewsletter** and try this skill on your own:

1. Place the cursor in the multilevel list at the top of the second page of the newsletter.

2. Open the *Define new Multilevel list* dialog.

3. Change the **second level** in the multilevel list to use the open circle bullet.

4. Save the file as directed by your instructor and close it.

Skill 6.19 Using Automatic Hyphenation

When you come to the end of a line, word wrap automatically moves the cursor to the next line and places the next word you type at the beginning of the next line. This can leave the right side of a document looking ragged and uneven, or if a paragraph is justified, it can leave awkward space between words. One way to avoid this unsightly formatting is to allow Word to automatically hyphenate words for you. When **automatic hyphenation** is enabled, Word will add hyphens to words at the end of a line instead of placing the whole word on the following line.

To enable automatic hyphenation:

1. Click the **Page Layout** tab.
2. In the *Page Setup* group, click the **Hyphenation** button and select **Automatic.**
3. To turn automatic hyphenation off, click the **Hyphenation** button and select **None.**

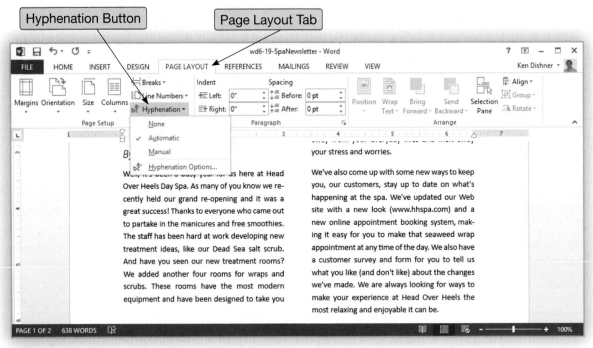

FIGURE WD 6.32

tips & tricks

With automatic hyphenation, Word chooses where to break the word across lines. If you want to choose where to hyphenate a word yourself, select **Manual** from the *Hyphenation* menu.

tell me **more**

The *Hyphenation* dialog allows you to control the number of consecutive hyphens in a document as well as set a zone that will control the length of space allowed at the end of a line.

let me **try**

Open the student data file **wd6-19-SpaNewsletter** and try this skill on your own:

1. Enable automatic hyphenation for the document.
2. Disable automatic hyphenation for the document.
3. Save the file as directed by your instructor and close it.

word 2013   Exploring Advanced Document Features

Skill 6.20 Adding a Drop Cap to a Paragraph

In some documents, you may notice that the first letter of a paragraph is larger and lower than the rest of the text. This is called a **drop cap.** Drop caps are often used in such layouts as brochures and newsletters to add visual interest and to draw the reader's attention to the text.

There are two basic styles of drop caps:

Dropped style—The *Dropped* style places the drop cap in front of the number of specified lines of text (three by default). In the *Dropped* style, the remaining paragraph text wraps under the drop cap so the drop cap and the text of the paragraph are left-aligned.

In Margin style—The *In Margin* style places the drop cap in the margin of the paragraph in front of the number of specified lines of text. With the *In Margin* style, the remaining paragraph text is left-aligned with the first lines of the paragraph, not the drop cap.

To add a drop cap to a paragraph:

1. Click in the paragraph where you want to add the drop cap.
2. Click the **Insert** tab.
3. In the *Text* group, click the **Drop Cap** button and select an option—**Dropped** or **In Margin.**

FIGURE WD 6.33

tips & tricks

) You can modify the look of your drop cap by clicking **Drop Cap Options...** on the menu. In the *Drop Cap* dialog, you can change the type of drop cap, the font used, how tall the drop cap is, and how far the drop cap is from the paragraph text.
) To clear the drop cap, click **None** on the menu.

another method

You can also apply a drop cap from the *Drop Cap* dialog. Click the **Drop Cap** button and select **Drop Cap Options...** to open the dialog. Select a drop cap option and click **OK.**

let me try

Open the student data file **wd6-20-SpaNewsletter** and try this skill on your own:

1. Add a **Dropped** style drop cap to the first paragraph of the newsletter.
2. Save the file as directed by your instructor and close it.

Skill 6.21 Adding a Quote Text Box

A **pull quote** is a piece of text from your document that is "pulled" out and displayed as a graphic element on the page. Pull quotes can add visual interest to your document and give your readers a quick snapshot of its content.

A **sidebar** is a block of information separate from the main document. Sidebars are typically aligned along one side of the page or along the top or bottom of the page. They usually contain information related to the main document, but not found in the document. Unlike pull quotes, sidebars are usually anchored along one side of the page and extend for the length or width of the page.

To add a pull quote or a sidebar to your document:

1. Click the **Insert** tab.
2. In the *Text* group, click the **Text Box** button and select an option from the gallery.
3. Type your text in the box.

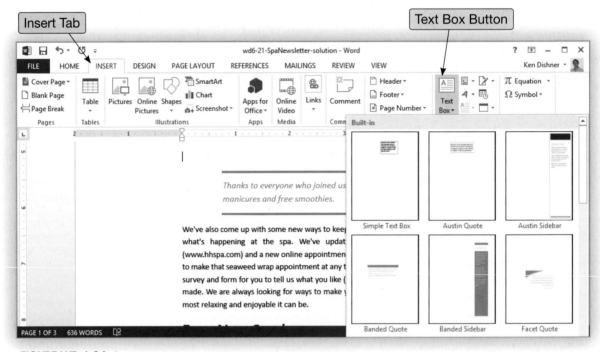

FIGURE WD 6.34

tips & tricks

To modify a pull quote or sidebar, click the **Format** tab under *Text Box Tools*. Here you can control text box styles, shadow effects, the size of the quote box, and the placement of the text box.

another method

You can also add a pull quote or sidebar through the *Building Blocks Organizer*.

let me try

Open the student data file **wd6-21-SpaNewsletter** and try this skill on your own:

1. Place the cursor on the blank line between the first and second paragraph in the *What's New* article.
2. Add the **Austin Quote** text box to the document.
3. Add the text **Thanks to everyone who joined us for manicures and free smoothies.** to the text box.
4. Save the file as directed by your instructor and close it.

Skill 6.22 Using Paste Special

Using the **Paste Special** command, an object from another Office application (for example, an Excel spreadsheet) can be inserted into a Word document. When pasting source material from another program, you have two choices:

Linked objects—Linked data are stored in the source file. Information in a linked object is updated if the source file is edited. Double-click the linked object to open the source file.

Embedded objects—Once pasted into your Word document, embedded objects do not change if you modify the source file. Double-click the embedded object to edit it within the Word document.

To use the *Paste Special* command:

1. Copy the object you want to paste.
2. On the *Home* tab, in the *Clipboard* group, click the **Paste** button arrow and select **Paste Special.**
3. If you want to paste the material as a linked object, click the **Paste link** radio button.
4. Select a format for pasting the object in the *As* box.
5. Click **OK.**

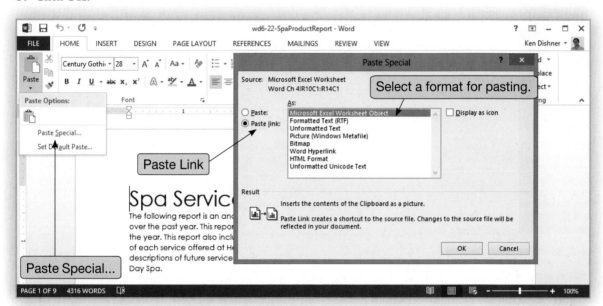

FIGURE WD 6.35

tips & tricks

Information in a linked object is updated every time you open the document. To update an object manually, right-click the object and select **Update Link.**

tell me **more**

The *Paste Special* options available vary depending on the type of source material. Some objects may only be available to paste as an embedded object, not a linked object.

let me **try**

Open the student data file **wd6-22-SpaProductReport** and try this skill on your own:

1. Open the **Services_2014** Excel document.
2. Select the data in the table on the **Manicures and Pedicures** worksheet (from cell A1 to cell B9). Copy the data to the *Clipboard*.
3. Navigate to the **wd6-22-SpaProductReport** file and place the cursor in the empty line above the heading *The Basic Mani*.
4. Open the **Paste Special** dialog.
5. Paste the item as a **linked object** in the Microsoft Excel format.
6. Save the file as directed by your instructor and close it.

Skill 6.23 Customizing Word

When first installed, every version of Word has the same features enabled. However, you can enable and disable some of the user interface features, including the Mini toolbar, Live Preview, and ScreenTips, through the *Word Options* dialog. When you change a user interface option, the behavior for that feature will be affected until you change the behavior again, even if you exit Word and reopen it again.

1. Click the **File** tab to open Backstage view.
2. Click **Options.**

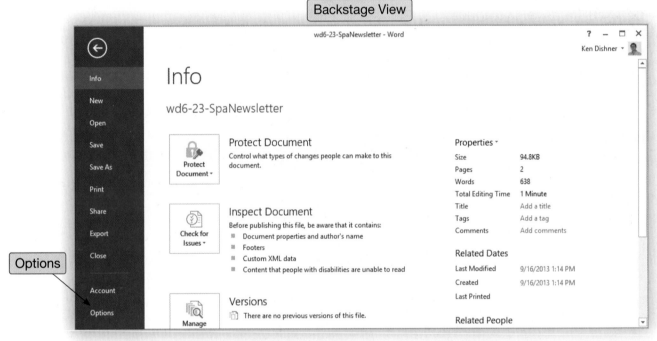

FIGURE WD 6.36

3. Verify you are on the *General* tab of the *Word Options* dialog. In the *User Interface options* section, make the changes you want, and then click **OK** to save your changes.

   a. Check or uncheck **Show Mini toolbar on selection** to control whether or not the Mini toolbar appears when you hover over selected text. (This does not affect the appearance of the Mini toolbar when you right-click.)

   b. Check or uncheck **Enable Live Preview** to turn the Live Preview feature on or off.

   c. Make a selection from the ScreenTip style list:
   - *Show feature descriptions in ScreenTips* displays Enhanced ScreenTips when they are available.
   - *Don't show feature descriptions in ScreenTips* hides Enhanced ScreenTips. The ScreenTip will still include the keyboard shortcut if there is one available.
   - *Don't show ScreenTips* hides ScreenTips altogether, so if you hold your mouse over a button on the Ribbon, nothing will appear.

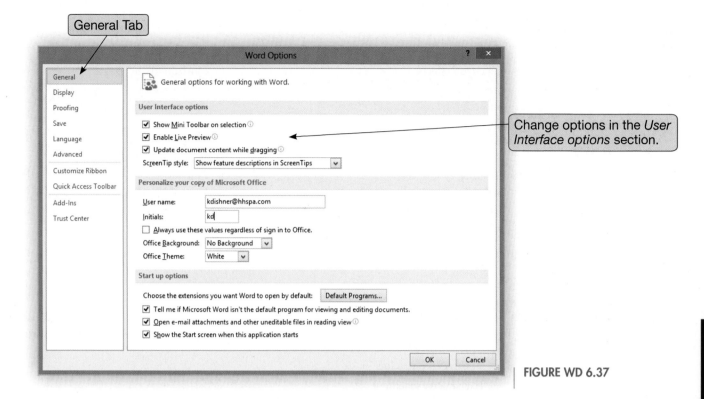

General Tab

Change options in the *User Interface options* section.

FIGURE WD 6.37

tell me **more**

The *Word Options* dialog also allows you to control features such as AutoCorrect, displaying formatting marks, and autosaving the document while you work.

let me **try**

Open the student data file **wd6-23-SpaNewsletter** and try this skill on your own:

1. Open the **Word Options** dialog.
2. Hide the Mini toolbar on selection.
3. Disable Live Preview.
4. Change the display of ScreenTips so Enhanced ScreenTips are not displayed but a ScreenTip still displays when the mouse is resting over a button.
5. Close the **Word Options** dialog and apply the changes.
6. If directed by your instructor, open the **Word Option** dialog again and change the options back to the original settings.
7. Close the file.

key terms

Character effects
Strikethrough
Subscript
Superscript
Character spacing
Styles task pane
AutoText
Symbol
Columns
Column break
First line indent
Hanging indent

Horizontal line
Multilevel list
Automatic hyphenation
Drop cap
Dropped style drop cap
In Margin style drop cap
Pull quote
Sidebar
Paste Special
Linked objects
Embedded objects

concepts review

1. To add spacing between characters in a word, you should increase the _____.
   a. paragraph spacing
   b. character spacing
   c. line spacing
   d. kerning

2. The _____ lists all the text styles available in a document.
   a. Styles task pane
   b. Styles gallery
   c. Themes gallery
   d. Font dialog

3. _____ are pieces of reusable content that are stored as building blocks.
   a. AutoText entries
   b. Styles
   c. Symbols
   d. Drop caps

4. Some symbols can be added to documents by typing a combination of characters.
   a. True
   b. False

5. A _____ marks where one column ends and moves the following text to the top of the next column.
   a. page break
   b. section break
   c. column break
   d. continuous break

6. A _____ indents the first line of a paragraph with the remainder of the paragraph left aligned
   a. hanging indent
   b. first line indent
   c. beginning indent
   d. mirrored indent

7. An example of a symbol font set is
   a. Webdings.
   b. Wingdings.
   c. Both a and b
   d. Neither a nor b

8. In the *Dropped* style drop cap, the remaining paragraph text wraps under the drop cap so the drop cap and the text of the paragraph are left-aligned.
   a. True
   b. False

9. A(n) _____ is a piece of text from your document that is "pulled" out and displayed as a graphic element on the page.
   a. AutoText
   b. pull quote
   c. sidebar
   d. None of the above

10. Information in an embedded object is updated if the source file is edited.
    a. True
    b. False

projects

Data files for projects can be found on
www.mhhe.com/office2013skills

skill review 6.1

In this project, you will be formatting a brochure from Suarez Marketing.

Skills needed to complete this project:

- Applying Other Character Effects (Skill 6.1)
- Using Character Spacing (Skill 6.2)
- Creating a New Style (Skill 6.4)
- Working with the Styles Task Pane (Skill 6.3)
- Adding a Horizontal Line (Skill 6.14)
- Setting First Line and Hanging Indents (Skill 6.13)
- Changing Line Spacing Using the Paragraph Dialog (Skill 6.11)
- Adding Borders and Shading to Paragraphs (Skill 6.15)
- Adjusting Spacing Before and After Paragraphs (Skill 6.12)
- Creating Custom Bulleted Lists (Skill 6.16)

1. Open the start file **WD2013-SkillReview-6-1** and resave the file as:

    `[your initials]WD-SkillReview-6-1`

2. If the document opens in Protected View, click the **Enable Editing** button in the Message Bar at the top of the document so you can modify the document.

3. Appl y a character effect and adjust character spacing.

    a. Select the heading **Mission Statement.**

    b. On the *Home* tab, in the *Font* group, click the **dialog launcher** to open the *Font* dialog.

    c. Select **All caps.**

    d. Click the **Advanced** tab.

    e. Click the **Spacing** arrow and select **Expanded.**

    f. Type **2** in the *By* box and click **OK.**

4. Save a new style and apply it to other text in the document.

    a. On the *Home* tab, in the *Styles* group, click the **More** button.

    b. Click **Create a Style.**

    c. In the *Create New Style from Formatting* dialog, enter **Brochure Heading** as the name of the style. Click **OK.**

    d. Place the cursor in the **Experience** heading.

    e. Click the **Brochure Heading** style in the *Styles* task pane.

    f. Use these steps to apply the *Brochure Heading* to the other headings in the document (*Why I Do What I Do, What Clients Are Saying, Professional Credentials, The Suarez Marketing Process,* and *The Suarez Marketing Belief System*).

word 2013   Exploring Advanced Document Features

5. Add a horizontal line.

    a. Place the cursor in the blank line above *Mission Statement.*

    b. On the *Home* tab, in the *Paragraph* group, click the **Borders** button and select **Horizontal Line.**

6. Set a first line indent.

    a. Click in the paragraph under *Mission Statement.*

    b. On the *Home* tab, in the *Paragraph* group, click the **dialog launcher** to open the *Paragraph* dialog.

    c. In the *Indentation* section, click the **Special** arrow and select **First line.**

    d. Click the **By** down arrow two times so the box reads **0.3".**

    e. Click in the paragraph under *Experience.* Repeat the above steps to set a first line indent at **0.3"** for the paragraph.

    f. Click **OK.**

7. Adjust line spacing using the *Paragraph* dialog.

    a. Select the numbered list on the first page of the brochure (under *Why I Do What I Do*).

    b. On the *Home* tab, in the *Paragraph* group, click the **dialog launcher** to open the *Paragraph* dialog.

    c. In the *Line Spacing* section, type **1.1** in the *At* box and click **OK.**

8. Add shading and a border to a paragraph.

    a. Place the cursor in the first quote in the *What Clients Are Saying* section.

    b. On the *Home* tab, in the *Paragraph* group, click the **Shading** button and select **Blue-Gray, Text 2, Lighter 80%.**

    c. In the *Paragraph* group, click the **Borders** button and select **Borders and Shading...**

    d. In the *Borders and Shading* dialog, click **Box** under *Setting.* Use the solid line style. Change the color to **Blue-Gray, Text 2** and have the width set at **½ pt.**

9. Add space before and after a paragraph.

    a. Select the two lines of text under **Professional Credentials.**

    b. Click the **Page Layout** tab.

    c. In the *Paragraph* group, click the up arrow to the right of the **Before** box one time so the box reads **6 pt.**

    d. In the *Paragraph* group, click the up arrow to the right of the **Before** box two times so the box reads **12 pt.**

10. Create a custom bulleted list.

    a. Place the cursor in the bulleted list at the end of the document.

    b. On the *Home* tab, in the *Paragraph* group, click the **Bullets** button and select **Define New Bullet.**

    c. In the *Define New Bullet* dialog, click the **Symbol** button.

    d. In the *Symbol* dialog, click the **Font** arrow and select **Wingdings.**

    e. Scroll to the bottom of the font set and select the open box with the checkmark (Wingdings 254). Click **OK** in the *Symbol* dialog.

    f. Click **OK** in the *Define New Bullet* dialog.

11. Save and close the document.

skill review 6.2

In this project, you will be formatting the agenda for the Tri-State Book Festival.

Skills needed to complete this project:

- Using Automatic Hyphenation (Skill 6.19)
- Adjusting Spacing Before and After Paragraphs (Skill 6.12)
- Inserting Symbols (Skill 6.8)
- Adding a Drop Cap to a Paragraph (Skill 6.20)
- Using Paste Special (Skill 6.22)
- Setting First Line and Hanging Indents (Skill 6.13)
- Creating Multilevel Lists (Skill 6.17)
- Customizing Multilevel Lists (Skill 6.18)
- Changing Line Spacing Using the Paragraph Dialog (Skill 6.11)
- Adding Borders and Shading to Paragraphs (Skill 6.15)
- Renaming Styles (Skill 6.6)
- Modifying a Style (Skill 6.5)
- Applying Columns (Skill 6.9)
- Inserting a Column Break (Skill 6.10)

1. Open the start file **WD2013-SkillReview-6-2** and resave the file as:

   `[your initials]WD-SkillReview-6-2`

2. If the document opens in Protected View, enable editing so you can make changes to the document.

3. Turn off automatic hyphenation.

   a. Click the **Page Layout** tab.

   b. In the *Page Setup* group, click the **Hyphenation** button and select **None.**

4. Adjust spacing before and after paragraphs.

   a. Place the cursor in the first paragraph of the document.

   b. On the *Page Layout* tab, in the *Paragraph* group, type **5** in the *Before* box and press Enter.

   c. Type **10** in the *After* box and press Enter.

5. Insert a symbol.

   a. Place the cursor after the word **Festival** in the first sentence of the first paragraph of the document.

   b. Click the **Insert** tab.

   c. In the *Symbols* group, click the **Symbol** button and select the **registered sign** (®). **NOTE:** If you do not see the registered sign in the *Symbol* gallery, click **More Symbols...** in the *Symbol* dialog, and find the registered sign on the *Special Characters* tab.

6. Add a drop cap to a paragraph.

   a. With the cursor in the first paragraph of the document, click the **Insert** tab.

   b. In the *Text* group, click the **Drop Cap** button and select **Dropped.**

   c. Click the **Drop Cap** button again and select **Drop Cap Options...**

   d. Next to *Lines to Drop* click the down arrow one time so **2** appears in the box.

   e. Click **OK.**

7. Add linked content using the *Paste Special* command.

   a. Launch **Microsoft Excel 2013.**

   b. Open the **Tri-State Authors** Excel workbook from you student data file location.

   c. Select the chart on the **Authors** tab.

   d. On the *Home* tab, in the *Clipboard* group, click the **Copy** button.

   e. Return to the **Tri-State Book Festival** document you were working on.

   f. Place the cursor in the blank line on the first page of the document under *The following chart shows the breakdown of authors by genre.*

   g. On the *Home* tab, in the *Clipboard* group, click the **Paste** button arrow and select **Paste Special…**

   h. Click the **Paste link** radio button.

   i. Select **Microsoft Excel Chart Object** and click **OK.**

   j. Return to the **Tri-State Authors** workbook.

   k. Change the value in **cell B2** to **2.**

   l. Save and close the workbook.

   m. Return to the **Tri-State Book Festival** document you were working on.

   n. Right-click the chart you inserted and select **Update Link.**

8. Set a first line indent.

   a. Place the cursor in the paragraph under the chart (the one beginning with *Admission for the festival*).

   b. On the *Home* tab, in the *Paragraph* group, click the **dialog launcher.**

   c. In the *Indentation* section, click the **Special** arrow and select **First line.**

   d. Click the **By** down arrow one time so the box reads **0.4".**

   e. Click **OK.**

9. Apply and modify a multilevel list.

   a. Select the 11 lines of text before the *Agenda* heading (from *Full Admission* (*3 days*) to *Healthy Cooking Demonstration* (*$10*)).

   b. On the *Home* tab, in the *Paragraph* group, click the **Multilevel List** button and select the bulleted multilevel list style.

   c. Click in the **Price: $35** line. In the *Paragraph* group, click the **Decrease Indent** button one time, so the bullet changes from the square bullet to the arrow bullet.

   d. Change the other items with the square bullet to the arrow bullet using the **Decrease Indent** command.

   e. Click the **Multilevel List** button and select **Define New Multilevel List…**

   f. If necessary, select the second level of the list. Click the **Number style for this level** arrow and select the **open circle** bullet style.

   g. Click **OK.**

10. Change line spacing using the *Paragraph* dialog.

   a. Select the multilevel list you created.

   b. On the *Home* tab, in the *Paragraph* group, click the **dialog launcher.**

   c. Click the **Line Spacing** arrow and select **Multiple.**

   d. Type **1.8** in the *At* box.

   e. Click **OK.**

11. Add a border to a paragraph.

    a. Place the cursor in the last paragraph of the **Agenda** section (beginning with *The Exhibit floor*).

    b. On the *Home* tab, in the *Paragraph* group, click the **Borders** button and select **Borders and Shading...**

    c. Select **Box** under *Setting*.

    d. Select the **third** option under *Style*.

    e. Click the **Color** arrow and select **Dark Purple, Text 2** (it is the fourth option in the first row under *Theme Colors*).

    f. Click the **Width** arrow and select **1 pt.**

    g. Click **OK.**

12. Rename a style.

    a. Navigate to the **Authors** section of the document.

    b. On the *Home* tab, in the *Styles* group, click the **More** button to display the *Styles* gallery.

    c. Right-click the **Autho Name** and select **Rename...**

    d. In the *Rename Style* dialog, type **Author Name.**

    e. Click **OK.**

13. Modify a style.

    a. Right-click the **Author Name** style and select **Modify...**

    b. In the *Formatting* section, click the **Bold** button.

    c. Click the **Color** arrow and select **Dark Purple, Text 2, Darker 50%** (it is the fourth option in the last row under *Theme Colors*).

    d. Click **OK.**

14. Apply columns and insert a column break.

    a. Select the list of authors including the *Non-Fiction* and *Fiction* headings (from *Non-Fiction* to *Featured work: A Detailed Man*).

    b. Click the **Page Layout** tab.

    c. In the *Page Setup* group, click the **Columns** button and select **Two.**

    d. Place the cursor at the beginning of the **Fiction** heading.

    e. On the *Page Layout* tab, in the *Page Setup* group, click the **Breaks** button.

    f. Select **Column Break.**

15. Save and close the document.

challenge yourself 6.3

In this project, you will be formatting the services document for the Greenscapes landscaping company.

Skills needed to complete this project:

- Changing Line Spacing Using the Paragraph Dialog (Skill 6.11)
- Adding a Horizontal Line (Skill 6.14)
- Adding Borders and Shading to Paragraphs (Skill 6.15)
- Adjusting Spacing Before and After Paragraphs (Skill 6.12)

- Applying Other Character Effects (Skill 6.1)
- Using Character Spacing (Skill 6.2)
- Creating a New Style (Skill 6.4)
- Working with the Styles Task Pane (Skill 6.3)
- Modifying a Style (Skill 6.5)
- Creating Custom Bulleted Lists (Skill 6.16)
- Setting First Line and Hanging Indents (Skill 6.13)
- Inserting Symbols (Skill 6.8)
- Using Automatic Hyphenation (Skill 6.19)

1. Open the start file **WD2013-ChallengeYourself-6-3** and resave the file as:
   `[your initials]WD-ChallengeYourself-6-3`

2. If the document opens in Protected View, enable editing so you can make changes to the document.

3. Change line spacing from the *Paragraph* dialog.
   a. Select all the text in the document by pressing `Ctrl` + `A`.
   b. Open the *Paragraph* dialog, and change the line spacing to be **1.3"**.

4. Add a horizontal line.
   a. Place the cursor in the blank line above the first paragraph.
   b. Insert a **horizontal line.**

5. Add shading to a paragraph.
   a. Place the cursor in the first paragraph of the document.
   b. Add shading to the paragraph using the **Light Green** color (it is the fifth option under *Standard Colors*).

6. Adjust spacing before and after a paragraph.
   a. Place the cursor in the **Services** heading.
   b. Adjust the spacing before the paragraph to be **24 pt.**
   c. Adjust the spacing after the paragraph to be **0 pt.**

7. Apply character effects and change character spacing.
   a. Select the heading **Our Philosophy.**
   b. Apply the **small caps** character formatting to the text.
   c. Change the character spacing to be expanded by **1.5 pt.**

8. Create a new style based on formatting.
   a. Verify the **Our Philosophy** heading is still selected.
   b. Create a new style named **Section Headings.**
   c. Change the style to use the **Orange, Accent 6, Darker 25%** color (it is the last option in the fifth row under *Theme Colors*).

9. Apply styles from the *Styles* task pane.
   a. Display the *Styles* task pane.
   b. Apply the **Section Headings** style to the **Services** and **Pricing** headings.

10. Modify the **Heading 2** style by changing the font to **Myriad Pro** and by removing the **bold** formatting.

11. Create a custom bulleted list.
    a. Place the cursor in the bulleted list in the **Lawn Maintenance** section.
    b. Change the bullet to use the **Wingdings 203 symbol** (✄).

12. Apply a hanging indent at **0.6"** to each of the items in the *Specialty Services* section (*Koi ponds, Water landscapes, Nature paths, Chicken coops,* and *Compost silos*).

13. Insert a symbol.

   a. Place the cursor after **CompSilos** in the last item in the *Specialty Services* section.

   b. Insert a **trademark sign** (™).

14. Turn off automatic hyphenation for the document.

15. Save and close the document.

challenge yourself 6.4

In this project, you will be modifying the safety report for the Spring Hills Community.

Skills needed to complete this project:

- Using Automatic Hyphenation (Skill 6.19)
- Changing Line Spacing Using the Paragraph Dialog (Skill 6.11)
- Using Character Spacing (Skill 6.2)
- Setting First Line and Hanging Indents (Skill 6.13)
- Creating Custom Bulleted Lists (Skill 6.16)
- Using Paste Special (Skill 6.22)
- Adjusting Spacing Before and After Paragraphs (Skill 6.12)
- Adding Borders and Shading to Paragraphs (Skill 6.15)
- Renaming Styles (Skill 6.6)
- Modifying a Style (Skill 6.5)
- Applying Columns (Skill 6.9)
- Inserting a Column Break (Skill 6.10)

1. Open the start file **WD2013-ChallengeYourself-6-4** and resave the file as:

   [your initials]WD-ChallengeYourself-6-4

2. If the document opens in Protected View, enable editing so you can make changes to the document.

3. Enable automatic hyphenation for the document.

4. Change line spacing using the *Paragraph* dialog.

   a. Press Ctrl + A to select the entire document.

   b. Using the *Paragraph* dialog, change the line spacing for the document to **1.4** lines.

5. Change character spacing on the title of the document to be expanded by **2 pt.**

6. Apply a first line indent at **0.3"** to the first paragraph under each of the main headings in the document (*Tips for Staying Safe, What Electronics Are Being Targeted, Our Safety Vision, Security Staff,* and *Future Safety Modifications*). Do not add a first line indent to the bulleted list in the *Basic Tips for Staying Safe* section.

7. Use custom bullets in a bulleted list.

   a. Place the cursor in the bulleted list in the *Basic Tips for Staying Safe* section.

   b. Apply the symbol **Wingdings 254** as the bullet for the list (it is an open box with a checkmark).

8. Add linked content using the *Paste Special* command.

   a. Launch **Microsoft Excel 2013** and open the **Theft by Category Data** Excel workbook from you student data file location.

b. Copy the chart on the **Thefts** tab to the *Clipboard*.

c. Return to the **Spring Hills Community Safety Strategies** document you were working on.

d. Place the cursor in the empty line above the *Our Safety Vision* heading.

e. Open the **Paste Special** dialog and paste the chart as a linked **Microsoft Excel Chart Object.**

f. Return to the **Theft by Category Data** workbook.

g. Change the value in **cell D2** to **25.** Change the value in **cell D3** to **19.** Change the value in **cell D4** to **12.**

h. Save and close the workbook.

i. Return to the **Spring Hills Community Safety Strategies** document you were working on.

j. Update the chart you inserted.

9. In the *Managers* section, add **6 pt** spacing after each manager's name.

10. Add shading to a paragraph.

   a. Select the paragraph above the *Security Staff* heading.

   b. Apply the **Lime, Accent 2** shading to the paragraph (it is the seventh option in the first row under *Theme Colors*).

11. Rename the **Heading 1** style to **Sections.**

12. Remove the underline character effect from the **Sections** heading and change the heading to **Dark Green, Text 2** color (it is the fourth option in the first row under *Theme Colors*).

13. Apply columns and insert a column break.

   a. Select all the text in the *Full-Time Officers* section and the *Part-Time Officers* section.

   b. Arrange the text in two columns.

   c. Add a column break at the beginning of the *Part-Time Officers* heading.

14. Save and close the document.

on your own 6.5

In this project, you will be modifying the *Behavior Change Project* report.

Skills needed to complete this project:

- Using Character Spacing (Skill 6.2)
- Adding a Horizontal Line (Skill 6.14)
- Changing Line Spacing Using the Paragraph Dialog (Skill 6.11)
- Adjusting Spacing Before and After Paragraphs (Skill 6.12)
- Setting First Line and Hanging Indents (Skill 6.13)
- Adding a Drop Cap to a Paragraph (Skill 6.20)
- Adding Borders and Shading to Paragraphs (Skill 6.15)
- Using Paste Special (Skill 6.22)
- Modifying a Style (Skill 6.5)
- Creating a New Style (Skill 6.4)
- Working with the Styles Task Pane (Skill 6.3)

1. Open the start file **WD2013-OnYourOwn-6-5** and resave the file as:

   `[your initials]WD-OnYourOwn-6-5`

2. If the document opens in Protected View, click the **Enable Editing** button in the Message Bar at the top of the document so you can modify the document.

3. Adjust the character spacing to Expanded on the title of the document.

4. Add a horizontal line under the title of the document.

5. Increase the line spacing of the first paragraph using the *Paragraph* dialog.

6. Increase the spacing after the first paragraph to 24.

7. Apply a first line indent to the first paragraph.

8. Add a drop cap to the first paragraph.

9. Add shading to the paragraph above the first table of data (the paragraph beginning with *The data collected*).

10. Open the **Behavior Change Data.xlsx** file from your student data location. Paste the two charts from the workbook as linked objects into the blank lines in the appropriate section of the document.

11. Change the color of the **Heading 1** style to a color of your choice.

12. Apply a color of your choice to the text **Observation Phase** in the first row of the first table. Create a new style based on the formatted text named **Phase Name.** Apply the **Phase Name** style to the text in the first row of the second table (*Implementation Phase*).

13. Save and close the document.

fix it 6.6

In this project, you will be fixing a brochure from Suarez Marketing.

Skills needed to complete this project:

- Working with the Styles Task Pane (Skill 6.3)
- Using Character Spacing (Skill 6.2)
- Adding a Horizontal Line (Skill 6.14)
- Renaming Styles (Skill 6.6)
- Modifying a Style (Skill 6.5)
- Creating a New Style (Skill 6.4)
- Changing Line Spacing Using the Paragraph Dialog (Skill 6.11)
- Adding Borders and Shading to Paragraphs (Skill 6.15)
- Setting First Line and Hanging Indents (Skill 6.13)
- Adjusting Spacing Before and After Paragraphs (Skill 6.12)
- Applying Columns (Skill 6.9)
- Inserting a Column Break (Skill 6.10)
- Adding a Quote Text Box (Skill 6.21)
- Creating Custom Bulleted Lists (Skill 6.16)
- Using Automatic Hyphenation (Skill 6.19)

1. Open the start file **WD2013-FixIt-6-6** and resave the file as:

   `[your initials]WD-FixIt-6-6`

2. If the document opens in Protected View, click the **Enable Editing** button in the Message Bar at the top of the document so you can modify the document.

3. Apply the **Title** style to the title of the document (*Online Learning Plan*).

4. Adjust the character spacing on the title so it is expanded by **1.5 pt.**

5. Add a horizontal line under the title.

6. Rename the **Sectionns** style to **Sections.**

7. Modify the **Sections** heading to use **Blue-Gray, Accent 1** color (it is the fifth option in the first row under *Theme Colors*).

8. Create a new style named `Subsections` based on the formatting applied to the text **Online Learning Offerings and Programs** on page 2 of the document.

9. Apply the **Subsections** style to the other bolded lines of text in the *Where are we now with Online Learning?* section.

10. Change the line spacing of the first paragraph to be **1.08** lines.

11. Apply shading to the first paragraph using the **Dark Purple, Text 2, Lighter 80%** color (it is the fourth option in the second row under *Theme Colors*).

12. Set a first line indent on the first paragraph set to **0.3".**

13. Fix the spacing after the **Online Course** paragraph to match the other paragraphs in the section.

14. Apply a two column layout to the four course types in the *Definition of Online Learning Modes* section.

15. Add a column break so *Television or tele-web course* appears at the top of the second column.

16. Place the cursor at the end of the *Online Learning Offerings and Programs* subsection heading. Insert a pull quote using the **Austin Quote** text box that reads **Fairlawn Community College has over 800 fully online course sections.**

17. Change the numbered list at the end of the document to a bulleted list using the **Wingdings 224** symbol (it is a right-pointing arrow).

18. Turn off automatic hyphenation.

19. Save and close the document.

chapter **7**

Working with Long Documents and Creating Forms

In this chapter, you will learn the following skills:

❭ Navigate long documents

❭ Apply section breaks, keep paragraphs together, and manage orphans and widows

❭ Use Outline view

❭ Add sections and change page orientation

❭ Create a table of figures and modify a table of contents

❭ Apply different odd and even headers

❭ Add fields to documents

❭ Create and modify a form

skills

introduction

This chapter provides you with the skills for working with long documents and creating forms. First you will learn a number of ways to quickly navigate through a document including using the *Navigation* pane, Word's *Go To* feature, and bookmarks. Next, you will learn ways to manage the display of paragraphs and other document features such as footnotes, headers, and the table of contents. Finally, you will learn to create a form, including adding and modifying controls and protecting the form.

Skill 7.1 Navigating Long Documents

The **Navigation pane** has three tabs. The first tab displays all the headings in your document, like an outline. The second tab displays a thumbnail of each page of a document. The third tab allows you to search for text in a document.

To use the *Navigation* pane:

1. Click the **View** tab.
2. In the *Show* group, click the **Navigation Pane** check box.

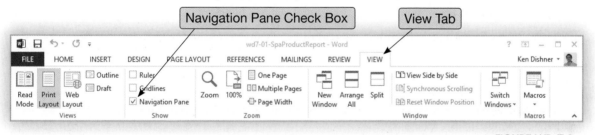

FIGURE WD 7.1

3. The *Headings* tab displays all the headings in the document. Click a heading on the first tab of the *Navigation* pane to jump to that part of the document.
4. Click the **Pages** tab to display thumbnails of each page in the document.
5. Scroll the pages and click a thumbnail to navigate to that page in the document.

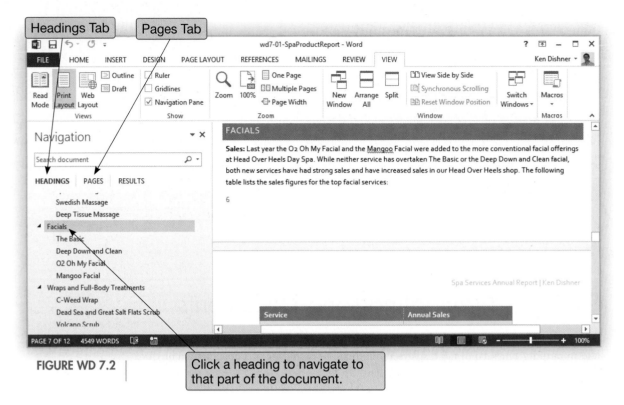

Headings Tab

Pages Tab

Click a heading to navigate to that part of the document.

FIGURE WD 7.2

tips & tricks

▶ To close the *Navigation* pane, click the **X** in the upper-right corner of the pane.

▶ If a heading has subheadings associated with it, the heading will appear with a triangle to the left of the name. Click the triangle to hide or show any subheadings associated with the heading.

▶ To show just the Heading 1 items in the *Navigation* pane, right-click the *Navigation* pane and select **Collapse All**.

tell me **more**

The first tab of the *Navigation* pane displays the hierarchy of headings, with *Heading 1* text being at the top and any associated subheadings listed below it. In order for headings to appear in this list, they must be formatted using a heading style.

another **method**

To display the *Navigation* pane, you can also press ⌃Ctrl + F on the keyboard. Using this method will open the *Navigation* pane with the *Results* tab displayed.

let me **try**

Open the student data file **wd7-01-SpaProductReport** and try this skill on your own:

1. Display the *Navigation* pane.
2. Using the *Navigation* pane, navigate to the **Facials** section of the document.
3. Display the **Pages** tab in the *Navigation* pane.
4. Using the *Navigation* pane, navigate to the seventh page in the document.
5. If you will be moving on to the next skill in this chapter, leave the document open to continue working. If not, close the file.

Skill 7.2 Using Go To

The **Go To** command allows you to quickly "jump" to any part of a document. You can choose to navigate to a specific page, section, or line number. You can also navigate to a specific bookmark you inserted or comments made by a reviewer.

To use the *Go To* command to navigate to a page:

1. On the *Home* tab, in the *Editing* group, click the **Find** button arrow and select **Go To...**
2. The *Find and Replace* dialog opens with the *Go To* tab selected.

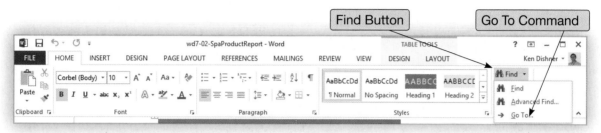

FIGURE WD 7.3

3. In the *Go to what* box, verify *Page* is selected.
4. In the *Enter page number* box, enter the page number to navigate to and click **Go To.**

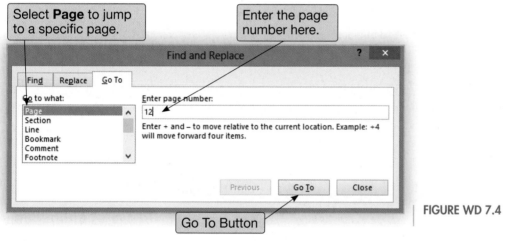

FIGURE WD 7.4

tell me **more**

You can use the *Go To* command to navigate to specific objects in a document, such as a table, graphic, or equation.

another **method**

To open the *Find and Replace* dialog with *Go To* tab displayed, you can also press Ctrl + G on the keyboard.

let me try

If you do not have the data file from the previous skill open, open the student data file **wd7-02-SpaProductReport** and try this skill on your own:

1. Open the **Find and Replace** dialog with the *Go To* tab displayed.
2. Navigate to **page 12** of the document.
3. If you will be moving on to the next skill in this chapter, leave the document open to continue working. If not, close the file.

Skill 7.3 Adding Bookmarks

If you are working with a long document, you may want to mark certain places in the document to come back to at a later time. A **bookmark** is an invisible marker that allows you to quickly navigate back to a specific location in a document.

To add a bookmark to a document:

1. Place the cursor where you want to add the bookmark.
2. Click the **Insert** tab.
3. In the *Links* group, click the **Bookmark** button.

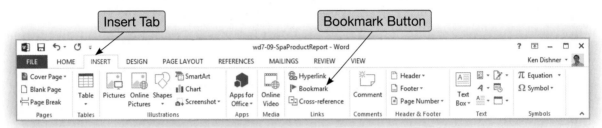

FIGURE WD 7.5

4. Type the name of the bookmark in the *Bookmark name* box.
5. Click the **Add** button.

To navigate to a bookmark:

1. On the *Insert* tab, in the *Links* group, click the **Bookmark** button.
2. In the *Bookmark* dialog, select the name of the bookmark you want to navigate to and click the **Go To** button.

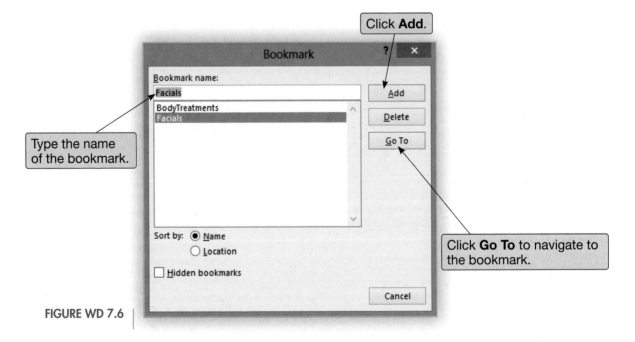

FIGURE WD 7.6

tips & tricks

To delete a bookmark, select the name of the bookmark in the *Bookmark* dialog, and click the **Delete** button.

tell me more

You cannot include spaces in bookmark names. If you want to include multiple words as the name of the bookmark, you should type the name without the spaces and capitalize each word in the name. For example, if you want to add a bookmark to the analysis section about a company, you could name the bookmark "CompanyAnalysis."

another method

You can also navigate to a bookmark from the *Go To* tab in the *Find and Replace* dialog.

let me try

If you do not have the data file from the previous skill open, open the student data file **wd7-03-SpaProductReport** and try this skill on your own:

1. Place the cursor in the **Facials** heading.
2. Open the **Bookmark** dialog.
3. Add a new bookmark to the *Facials* heading named **Facials**.
4. Open the **Bookmark** dialog again.
5. Navigate to the **BodyTreatments** bookmark.
6. Close the **Bookmark** dialog.
7. If you will be moving on to the next skill in this chapter, leave the document open to continue working. If not, save the file as directed by your instructor and close it.

from the perspective of . . .

MASTER'S CANDIDATE

My thesis is over one hundred pages long. When I started working on it, I would scroll through the document looking for the part I wanted to work on. Then I discovered Word's *Navigation* pane. Since I formatted my thesis using heading styles, I can display the *Navigation* pane and quickly navigate to the part I want to work on. I have also added bookmarks to the parts that don't display in the *Navigation* pane. Now I can quickly and easily get to any part of my document without scrolling through the whole thing.

Skill 7.4 Adding Cross-References

If you are working with a long document, you may have content in one part of the document that relates to content in another part of the document. A **cross-reference** is a link you add to a document that directs the reader to another part of the document for more or related information. By default Word inserts cross-references as hyperlinks so your readers can use them to navigate to the related information.

To add a cross-reference:

1. Click the **Insert** tab.
2. In the *Links* group, click the **Cross-reference** button.

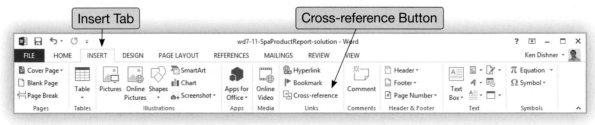

Insert Tab

Cross-reference Button

FIGURE WD 7.7

3. In the *Cross-reference* dialog, click the **Reference type** arrow and select the type of object you want to link to.
4. Click the **Insert reference to** arrow, and select how the reference should appear.
5. In the *For which* box, select the object you want to link to.
6. Click the **Insert** button.
7. The cross-reference is added to the document.

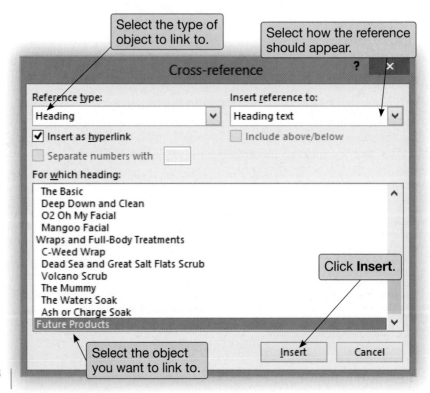

Select the type of object to link to.

Select how the reference should appear.

Click **Insert**.

Select the object you want to link to.

FIGURE WD 7.8

Cross-references often begin with directions to the reader, such as "See" or "Go to." When Word inserts the cross-reference, it will only insert the name of the cross-reference. You must type the directions to the reader for yourself. For example, if you want your cross-reference to read "See the Financial Statistics section" and the heading for the section is "Financial Statistics," you must type *See the* and then insert the cross-reference, and then type *section*. Only the words *Financial Statistics* will be linked as the cross-reference.

tips & tricks

» Press (Ctrl) and click the cross-reference text to navigate to the linked location.

» You can choose to have the cross-reference display the exact text of what you are linking to, or a location in the document, such as a page number or the words "above" or "below."

tell me **more**

You can link to a number of types of objects using a cross-reference. These objects include numbered items in lists, headings, bookmarks, footnotes, endnotes, equations, figures, and tables.

another **method**

To open the *Cross-reference* dialog, you can also click the **References** tab. In the *Captions* group, click the **Cross-reference** button.

let me **try**

If you do not have the data file from the previous skill open, open the student data file **wd7-4-SpaProductReport** and try this skill on your own:

1. Place the cursor in the space after the word (*see* near the end of the first paragraph under *Facials*). Be sure to place the cursor after the space and before the closing parenthesis.

2. Open the **Cross-reference** dialog.

3. Add a cross-reference to the **Future Products** heading text.

4. Close the **Cross-reference** dialog.

5. If you will be moving on to the next skill in this chapter, leave the document open to continue working. If not, save the file as directed by your instructor and close it.

Skill 7.5 Replacing with Special Characters

The *Replace* feature in Word allows you to quickly replace text within a document. In addition to replacing text, you can also replace using special characters. These **special characters** include commonly used characters that are not readily available by typing on the keyboard, such as an em dash or en dash. Other special characters are only visible when the *Show/Hide Formatting* feature is active, such as column breaks, tabs, and nonbreaking spaces.

To replace text with special characters:

1. On the *Home* tab, in the *Editing* group, click the **Replace** button.
2. Type the word or phrase you want to change in the *Find what* box.
3. Place the cursor in the **Replace with** box.
4. Click the **More >>** button to display the expanded *Find and Replace* dialog.
5. Click the **Special** button and select a special character to use in the replace.
6. Click **Replace** to replace just that one instance of the text.
7. Click **Replace All** to replace all instances of the word or phrase.
8. Word displays a message telling you how many replacements it made. Click **OK** in the message that appears.
9. To close the *Find and Replace* dialog, click the **Cancel** button.

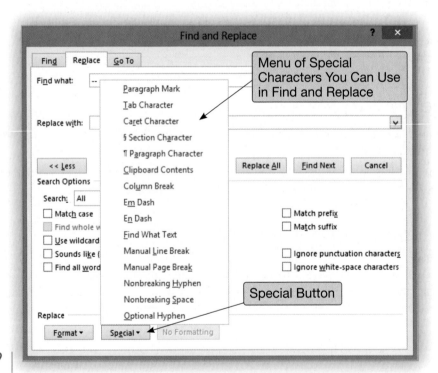

FIGURE WD 7.9

tell me **more**

From the *Format* button in the expanded *Find and Replace* dialog, you can quickly replace formatting throughout the document.

another **method**

When you select a special character, Word inserts the carat symbol (^) followed by a letter into the currently selected box. You can type the key combination in the box rather than selecting the special character from the *Special* menu. To type the carat symbol, press Shift + 6 on the keyboard. The following table lists some of the more common key combinations you can use:

SPECIAL CHARACTER	KEY COMBINATION
Paragraph Mark	^p
Tab Character	^t
Column Break	^n
Em Dash	^+
En Dash	^=
Nonbreaking Space	^s
Section Break	^b

let me **try**

If you do not have the data file from the previous skill open, open the student data file **wd7-05-SpaProductReport** and try this skill on your own:

1. If necessary, move to the beginning of the document. Open the **Find and Replace** dialog with the *Replace* tab displayed.

2. Use the **Replace All** command to replace all instances of two hyphens (--) with an **em dash.**

3. If you will be moving on to the next skill in this chapter, leave the document open to continue working. If not, save the file as directed by your instructor and close it.

Skill 7.6 Keeping Paragraphs Together

Sometimes you will want to be sure information in your document is displayed on the same page and not broken across two pages. You can adjust the settings of a paragraph so the text of the paragraph will never break across a page by using the **Keep with next** command. You can also modify a paragraph so that it will always appear on the same page as the following paragraph by using the **Keep lines together** command.

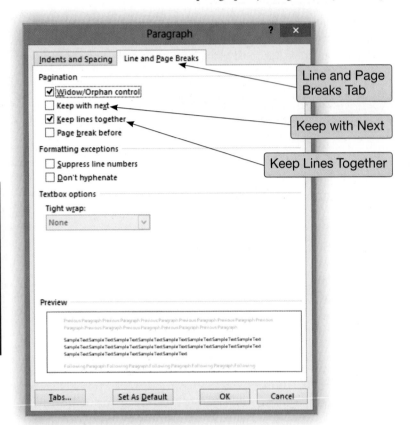

FIGURE WD 7.10

To adjust how paragraph text breaks across a page:

1. Place the cursor anywhere in the paragraph you want to change.
2. On the *Home* tab, in the *Paragraph* group, click the **dialog launcher** .
3. In the *Paragraph* dialog, click the **Line and Page Breaks** tab.
4. Under *Pagination,* select **Keep lines together** to prevent the paragraph from breaking across the page.
5. Select **Keep with next** to force the paragraph to print on the same page as the following paragraph.
6. Click **OK**.

tips & tricks

To always force a paragraph to a new page regardless of where it appears on a page, on the *Line and Page Breaks* tab, click the **Page break before** check box.

another method

To open the *Paragraph* dialog, you can also right-click the paragraph you want to change and select **Paragraph...** from the menu.

let me try

If you do not have the data file from the previous skill open, open the student data file **wd7-06-SpaProductReport** and try this skill on your own:

1. Place the cursor in the paragraph at the bottom of page 11.
2. Change the option so the paragraph will not break across the page.
3. Place the cursor in the **What customers say** heading at the bottom of page 10.
4. Change the option so the heading will always be on the same page as the following paragraph.
5. If you will be moving on to the next skill in this chapter, leave the document open to continue working. If not, save the file as directed by your instructor and close it.

Skill 7.7 Managing Orphans and Widows

An **orphan** is the first line of a paragraph that prints at the bottom of a page by itself. A **widow** is the last line of a paragraph that prints at the top of a page by itself. Widows and orphans can be distracting and can make your document look unprofessional.

To prevent widows and orphans in a document:

1. Place the cursor anywhere in the paragraph you want to change.
2. On the *Home* tab, in the *Paragraph* group, click the **dialog launcher** ,
3. In the *Paragraph* dialog, click the **Line and Page Breaks** tab.
4. Under *Pagination*, select the **Widow/Orphan control** check box.
5. Click **OK**.

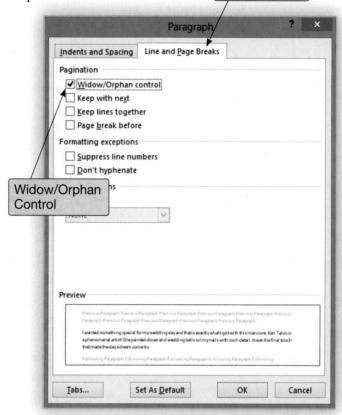

FIGURE WD 7.11

tell me **more**

When you first create a document, widow and orphan control is active by default.

let me **try**

If you do not have the data file from the previous skill open, open the student data file **wd7-07-SpaProductReport** and try this skill on your own:

1. Place the cursor in the line at the top of page 8.
2. Turn on **Widow/Orphan control** for the paragraph.
3. If you will be moving on to the next skill in this chapter, leave the document open to continue working. If not, save the file as directed by your instructor and close it.

Skill 7.8 Using Outline View

If you are creating a long document, it is more than likely that the document will be divided into multiple parts designated by heading styles. One way to organize the headings in your document is to use **Outline view**. In Outline view, you can add your main topics for a document and then insert subtopics as needed. Once you have created your outline, you can switch back to Print Layout view to type the main text of your document, or you can choose to continue working in Outline view.

To switch to Outline view:

1. Click the **View** tab.
2. In the *Views* group, click the **Outline** button.

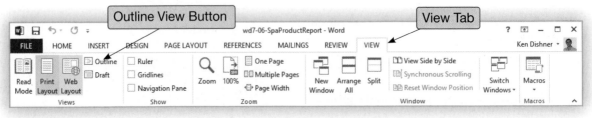

FIGURE WD 7.12

To change the level of a topic in Outline view:

1. Select the topic you want to change.
2. Click the **Promote** button to move the topic up one heading level.
3. Click the **Demote** button to move the topic down one heading level.
4. Use the **Move Up** and **Move Down** buttons to reorder topics in Outline view.
5. Use the **Expand** and **Collapse** buttons to display and hide subtopics in Outline view.
6. Click the **Close Outline View** button to return to Print Layout view.

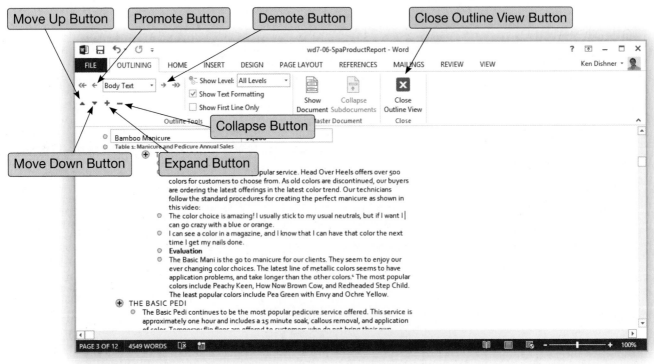

FIGURE WD 7.13

word 2013   chapter 7 Working with Long Documents and Creating Forms

tell me **more**

❯ In Outline view, a minus sign next to a topic indicates there are no subtopics associated with that topic. A plus sign indicates that a topic includes the subtopics listed directly below it.

❯ Each level in Outline view will use the corresponding heading style from the style template. For example, Level 1 topics will use the *Heading 1* style, Level 2 topics will use the *Heading 2* style, and so on.

another **method**

❯ To demote an item, you can also press (Tab) on the keyboard.

❯ To expand and collapse a heading, you can also double click on the **plus sign** next to the heading.

let me **try**

If you do not have the data file from the previous skill open, open the student data file **wd7-08-SpaProductReport** and try this skill on your own:

1. Navigate to page 3 of the document. Switch to **Outline** view.
2. Place the cursor in **The Basic Mani** heading and promote the heading one level.
3. Place the cursor on the next line (**What Customers Say**) and move the item down so it is under the paragraph beginning with *The Basic Mani is our most popular.*
4. Place the cursor back in **The Basic Mani** heading and hide the subtopics.
5. Close Outline view.
6. If you will be moving on to the next skill in this chapter, leave the document open to continue working. If not, save the file as directed by your instructor and close it.

Skill 7.9 Adding Sections to Documents

If you have a part of a document that has a wide table or figure, it may not fit on the printed page with normal margins. You don't want to change the margins for the entire document to the *Narrow* setting in order to fit one table, so what do you do? A **section** is a designated part of a document that can be formatted separately from the rest of the document. You can add the large table in its own section that is set to have narrow margins and then keep the remaining document with the original settings.

To add a section to a document:

1. Click the **Page Layout** tab.
2. In the *Page Setup* group, click the **Breaks** button.
3. In the *Section Breaks* section:
   - Click **Next Page** to insert a new section and a hard page break.
   - Click **Continuous** to insert a new section without adding a page break.

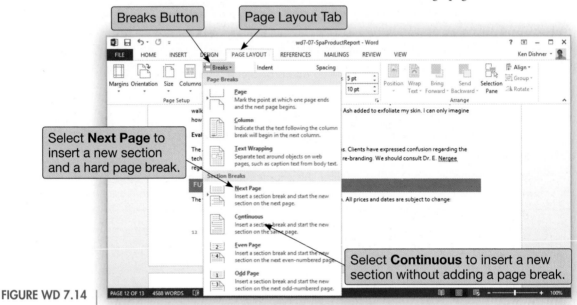

FIGURE WD 7.14

tips & tricks

To delete a section, switch to Draft view. Here all the section breaks are displayed. Select a section break and press the (Delete) key on the keyboard to delete a section. When you delete a section, the content from the section takes on the formatting from the preceding section.

tell me **more**

There are two other section breaks you can add to documents:

Even Page—Starts the new section on the next even-numbered page in the document.

Odd Page—Starts the new section on the next odd-numbered page in the document.

let me try

If you do not have the data file from the previous skill open, open the student data file **wd7-09-SpaProductReport** and try this skill on your own:

1. Place the cursor at the end of the paragraph before the **Future Products** heading (the paragraph ending with *technology explanation*).
2. Add a section break that will move the *Future Products* section to a new page.
3. If you will be moving on to the next skill in this chapter, leave the document open to continue working. If not, save the file as directed by your instructor and close it.

Skill 7.10 Changing Page Orientation

The default page orientation for Word documents is **portrait**. This means the height of the page is greater than the width (like a portrait hanging on a wall). Portrait works well if you are writing documents such as papers or letters. But what if you have a table that is wider than the standard page? **Landscape** orientation turns the page on its side so the width of the page is greater than the height.

To change the orientation of a document:

1. Click the **Page Layout** tab.
2. In the *Page Setup* group, click the **Orientation** button and select **Portrait** or **Landscape.**

FIGURE WD 7.15

tips & tricks

If you have divided your document using section breaks, selecting an orientation will only affect the section you are in. To change the orientation for the entire document, click the **dialog launcher** in the *Page Setup* group to open the *Page Setup* dialog. Click the orientation you want for the section, and then click the **Apply to** arrow and select **Whole Document**.

another method

You can also change the orientation for a document in the *Page Setup* dialog. To open the *Page Setup* dialog, click the **dialog launcher** in the *Page Setup* group.

let me try

If you do not have the data file from the previous skill open, open the student data file **wd7-10-SpaProductReport** and try this skill on your own:

1. Place the cursor in the **Future Products** section at the end of the document.
2. Change the orientation for the section to **Landscape.**
3. If you will be moving on to the next skill in this chapter, leave the document open to continue working. If not, save the file as directed by your instructor and close it.

Skill 7.11 Customizing Footnotes and Endnotes

When you insert a footnote, they are numbered consecutively using the 1, 2, 3 format. Endnotes are numbered using lowercase roman numerals (i, ii, iii). You may decide that you want to use letters or symbols instead of the default numbering format for footnotes and endnotes in your document. You can customize the format of footnotes and endnotes through the *Footnote and Endnote* dialog.

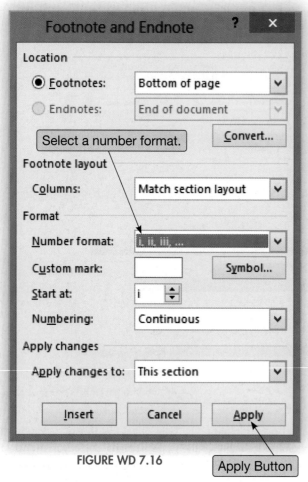

FIGURE WD 7.16

To customize the format of footnotes and endnotes:

1. Place the cursor in the footnote or endnote you want to change.
2. Click the **References** tab.
3. In the *Footnotes* group, click the **dialog launcher** ⬚.
4. The *Footnote and Endnote* dialog opens.
5. In the *Format* section, click the **Number format** drop-down arrow and select a format.
6. Click the **Apply** button to apply the changes and close the dialog.

tips & tricks

You can add your own custom marks by using symbols. Click the **Symbol...** button next to *Custom mark* and select a symbol to use from the *Symbol* dialog.

tell me more

Footnotes and endnotes can be numbered consecutively throughout the entire document, for each section within the document, or on each page. If you choose to number the footnotes for a section or page, when the next section or page begins, the numbering will start over again.

let me try

If you do not have the data file from the previous skill open, open the student data file **wd7-11-SpaProductReport** and try this skill on your own:

1. Place the cursor in the footnote at the bottom of page 4.
2. Open the **Footnote and Endnote** dialog.
3. Change the footnote format to use lowercase roman numerals.
4. If you will be moving on to the next skill in this chapter, leave the document open to continue working. If not, save the file as directed by your instructor and close it.

Skill 7.12 Creating a Table of Figures

A **table of figures** lists all the illustrations, graphs, tables, charts, equations, and pictures in a document, along with their associated page numbers. Adding a table of figures to your documents gives your readers a quick reference to find illustrations, tables, and equations that you considered important enough to warrant adding captions to.

To insert a table of figures:

1. Place your cursor where you want to insert the table of figures.
2. Click the **References** tab.
3. In the *Captions* group, click the **Insert Table of Figures** button.

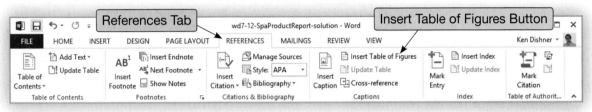

FIGURE WD 7.17

4. In the *Table of Figures* dialog, click the **Formats** arrow and select a format.
5. Modify the other options until the preview looks the way you want.
6. Click **OK** to insert the table of figures into your document.

A table of figures displays the page number of the caption associated with the figure; therefore, in order for a figure to be included in the table of figures, it must have a caption. To add a caption to a figure, click the **References** tab. In the *Captions* group, click the **Insert Caption** button. In the *Caption* dialog, type the text for the caption in the *Caption* box and select a type of label. Click **OK** to add the caption to the figure.

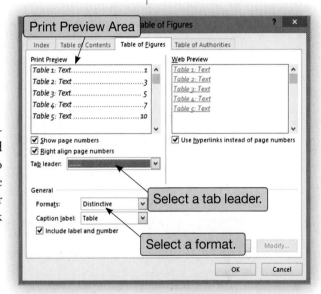

FIGURE WD 7.18

tips & tricks

If you change any captions in your document, be sure to update the table of figures. To update the table of figures, click in the table of figures to select it, and click the **Update Table** button in the *Captions* group on the *References* tab.

let me try

If you do not have the data file from the previous skill open, open the student data file **wd7-12-SpaProductReport** and try this skill on your own:

1. Navigate to the end of the document and place the cursor in the blank line under the **Figures** heading.
2. Open the **Table of Figures** dialog.
3. Apply the **Distinctive** format to the table of figures and change the tab leader to a dotted line.
4. Change the caption label to **Table** and add the table of figures to the document.
5. If you will be moving on to the next skill in this chapter, leave the document open to continue working. If not, save the file as directed by your instructor and close it.

Skill 7.13 Modifying a Table of Contents

When you insert a table of contents using one of Word's built-in styles, you may find that you want to change the look of the table of contents. From the *Table of Contents* dialog, you can change the look of a table of contents for a document including changing the format, the tab leader style, and then number of levels displayed.

To modify a table of contents:

1. Click the **References** tab.
2. In the *Table of Contents* group, click the **Table of Contents** button.
3. Select **Custom Table of Contents...**
4. In the *Table of Contents* dialog, a preview of the table of contents appears in the *Print Preview* area.

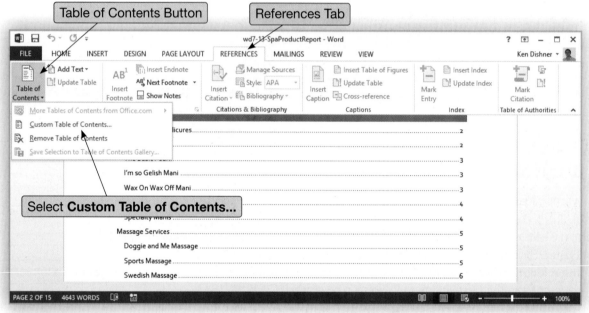

FIGURE WD 7.19

5. Click the **Tab leader** drop-down arrow and select a style for the tab leader that appears between the heading title and the page number.
6. In the *General* section, click the **Formats** drop-down arrow and select a format for the table of contents.
7. As you make changes, the *Print Preview* area updates with the selections you made.
8. Click **OK.**
9. A message box appears asking if you want to replace the table of contents. Click **Yes** to apply the changes you made in the *Table of Contents* dialog.

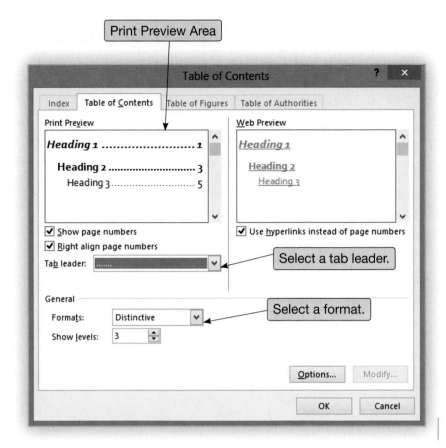

Print Preview Area

Select a tab leader.

Select a format.

FIGURE WD 7.20

tips & tricks

By default, the table of contents shows three heading levels. This means that it will include all Heading 1, Heading 2, and Heading 3 titles in the document. To change the number of headings displayed in the table of contents, click the up and down arrows next to *Show levels* in the *General* section.

let me try

If you do not have the data file from the previous skill open, open the student data file **wd7-13-SpaProductReport** and try this skill on your own:

1. Navigate to the table of contents for the document.
2. Open the **Table of Contents** dialog.
3. Apply the **Distinctive** format to the table of contents and change the tab leader to a **dotted line.**
4. If you will be moving on to the next skill in this chapter, leave the document open to continue working. If not, save the file as directed by your instructor and close it.

Skill 7.14 Insert Different Odd and Even Headers and Footers

When working with long documents, you may want to have one page display a particular header or footer and the opposite page display a different header or footer. For example, you might have the company name on the odd numbered pages and the page numbers on the even numbered pages.

To display a different header or footer on odd and even pages:

1. Double-click the header or footer of the document.
2. Click the **Header & Footer Tools Design** tab.
3. In the *Options* group, click the **Different Odd & Even Pages** check box.

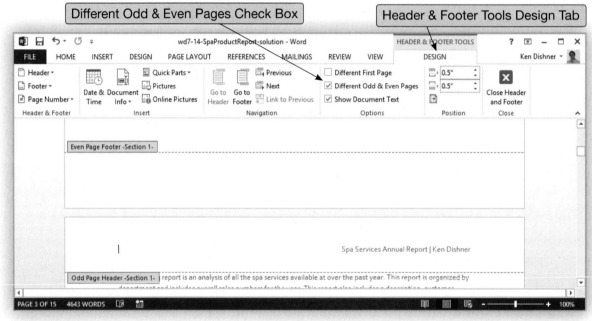

FIGURE WD 7.21

another **method**

To activate the header and display the *Header & Footer Tools Design* tab, you can also:

❱ Click the **Insert** tab. In the *Header & Footer* group, click the **Header** button and select **Edit Header.**
❱ Right-click the header area and select **Edit Header.**

let me **try**

If you do not have the data file from the previous skill open, open the student data file **wd7-14-SpaProductReport** and try this skill on your own:

1. Navigate to the top of page 4 and make the header active.
2. Change the header so it will be different on odd and even pages.
3. Close the header.
4. If you will be moving on to the next skill in this chapter, leave the document open to continue working. If not, save the file as directed by your instructor and close it.

Skill 7.15 Adding a Header or Footer to the Gallery

Word comes with a number of prebuilt headers and footers for you to add to your documents. But what if you have your own custom header, such as a company logo, or footer, such as a legal disclaimer? You can create headers and footers from parts of a document and add them to the *Header* gallery or the *Footer* gallery. After you add a new header or footer to the gallery, it will be available to all documents you create from that point forward.

To add a header to the gallery:

1. Select the text and/or graphics you want as the header.
2. Click the **Insert** tab.
3. In the *Header & Footer* group, click the **Header** button and select **Save Selection to Header Gallery...**
4. Enter a meaningful name for the header in the *Name* box, and click **OK**.

To add a footer to the gallery, follow the same steps as above, but instead of clicking the **Header** button, click the **Footer** button and select **Save Selection to Footer Gallery...**

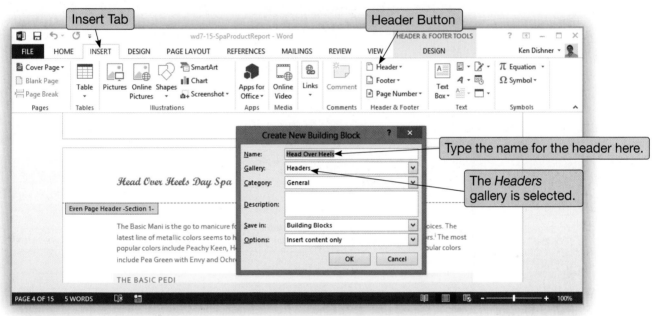

| FIGURE WD 7.22

tips & tricks

To delete a custom header or footer you added, open the **Building Blocks Organizer**. Select the header or footer you created, and click the **Delete** button.

tell me more

When you add a custom header or footer to the gallery, the text is saved as a building block and can be accessed through the *Building Blocks Organizer*.

let me try

If you do not have the data file from the previous skill open, open the student data file **wd7-15-SpaProductReport** and try this skill on your own:

1. Select the text **Head Over Heels Day Spa** at the top of page 3.
2. Save the text to the *Header* gallery.
3. Name the new building block **Head Over Heels Day Spa.**
4. If you will be moving on to the next skill in this chapter, leave the document open to continue working. If not, save the file as directed by your instructor and close it.

Skill 7.16 Using Fields in Documents

When you add page numbers to documents or you insert a table of contents from one of Word's built-in building blocks, Word is actually inserting fields into the document. A **field** is a placeholder for content that might change in a document. Word inserts fields for you when you add certain content to your document, such as building blocks. In some cases, you may want to manually add a field to your document, such as adding the number of pages in a document to the page number or inserting the date the document was created.

To add a field to a document:

1. Place the cursor where you want to add the field.
2. Click the **Insert** tab.
3. In the *Text* group, click the **Explore Quick Parts** button and select **Field...**
4. In the *Field* dialog, select a field in the *Field names* box.
5. Under *Field properties,* select a format for the field if available.
6. Click **OK** to insert the field and close the dialog.

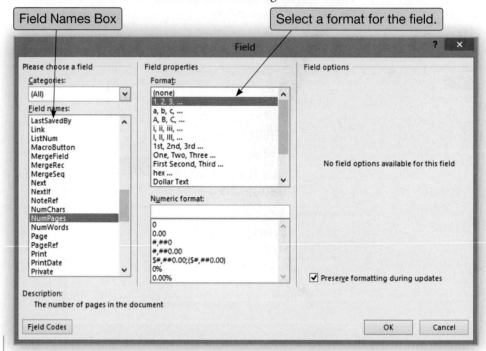

FIGURE WD 7.23

tips & tricks

In Word 2013, most fields are available from pre-built content controls. It is easier to insert the field through one of these controls than from the *Field* dialog.

another method

If you have the header or footer of the document active, you can also add a field by clicking the **Explore Quick Parts** button in the *Insert* group on the *Header & Footer Tools Design* tab.

let me try

If you do not have the data file from the previous skill open, open the student data file **wd7-16-SpaProductReport** and try this skill on your own:

1. Activate the footer on page 3 and type **of** after the page number. Be sure to have a space before and after the word.
2. Open the **Field** dialog.
3. Add the **NumPages** field with the **1, 2, 3** format.
4. Save the file as directed by your instructor and close it.

Skill 7.17 Designing a Simple Form

A **form** is a document or part of a document that a reader can interact with. The first step in designing a form is to display the *Developer* tab on the Ribbon.

To display the *Developer* tab:

1. Click the **File** tab and select **Options.**

FIGURE WD 7.24

2. In the *Word Options* dialog, click **Customize Ribbon.**
3. Under *Customize the Ribbon,* click the **Developer** check box so a checkmark appears in the box.
4. Click **OK** to close the *Word Options* dialog and display the *Developer* tab.

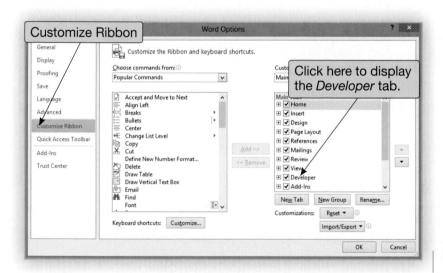

FIGURE WD 7.25

Forms include controls that can be clicked by the reader or interacted with by the reader to provide information. These controls include check boxes, drop-down lists, date pickers, and text boxes.

The following table lists the common controls you can add to forms:

ICON	NAME	DESCRIPTION
Aa	Rich Text Content Control	Inserts a text content control that includes formatting.
Aa	Plain Text Content Control	Inserts a text content control that does not include formatting.
	Picture Content Control	Inserts a picture control where pictures can be added to the form.
	Building Block Gallery Control	Allows users to select a specific block of text that has been saved as a building block.
✓	Check Box Content Control	Inserts a check box control that can be toggled between selected and not selected.
	Combo Box Content Control	Inserts a list control where users can select from options that are set or type their own answers.
	Drop-Down List Content Control	Inserts a list control where users cans select for a set of options.
	Date Picker Content Control	Inserts a control where users can select a date from a calendar interface.

To add controls to a form:

1. Place the cursor in the document where you want to add the control.
2. Click the **Developer** tab.
3. In the *Controls* group, click the **Design Mode** button.
4. Click a control to add to the form.

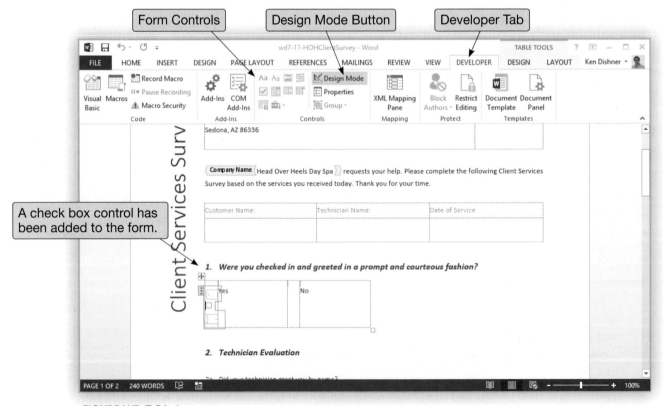

FIGURE WD 7.26

tips & tricks

After you have added controls, click the **Design Mode** button again to exit *Design Mode.* You can then test the controls to see how they will behave for your users.

tell me **more**

In past versions of Word, controls in forms were ActiveX controls. You can insert these controls from the **Legacy Tools** button in the *Controls* group .

let me **try**

Open the student data file **wd7-17-HOHClientSurvey** and try this skill on your own:

1. Open the **Word Options** dialog box.
2. Display the **Developer** tab.
3. Switch to **Design Mode.**
4. Add a check box control in the table cell to the left of the word **Yes** under the first question.
5. Add another check box control to the table cell to the left of the word **No** under the first question.
6. If you will be moving on to the next skill in this chapter, leave the document open to continue working. If not, save the file as directed by your instructor and close it.

from the perspective of . . .

PHYSICAL THERAPIST

Many of our patients have mobility issues with their hands and arms. We used to have patients fill out patient evaluation forms by hand, but sometimes we couldn't read the handwriting! Now we have form that can be filled out on a tablet. Patients answer the questions by tapping or selecting answers, and when something requires a short answer, we can read the answers.

Skill 7.18 Modifying Control Properties in a Form

Some controls, such as check boxes, text boxes, and date pickers, can be added to a form with no further modification required. Other controls, such as drop-down lists and combo boxes require you to add options for your reader to select.

To add options to a control:

1. Verify you are in *Design Mode*.

2. Select the control you want to modify.

3. On the *Developer* tab, in the *Controls* group, click the **Properties** button.

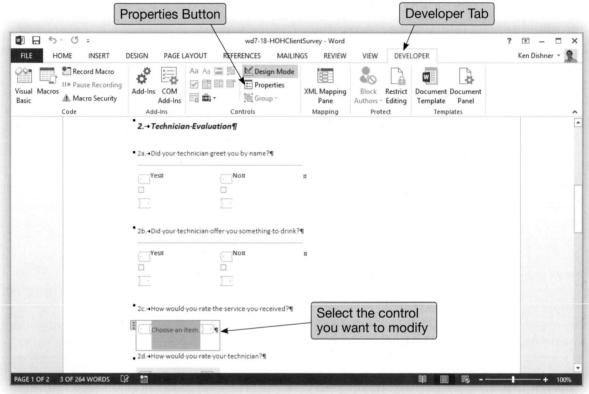

FIGURE WD 7.27

4. Click the **Add...** button.

5. The *Add Choice* dialog opens.

6. Type the text you want to display in the control in the *Display Name* box.

7. Click **OK.**

8. Continue adding choices for the control.

9. When you are done, click **OK** in the *Content Control Properties* dialog.

10. Click the **Design Mode** button to exit *Design Mode* and test the control.

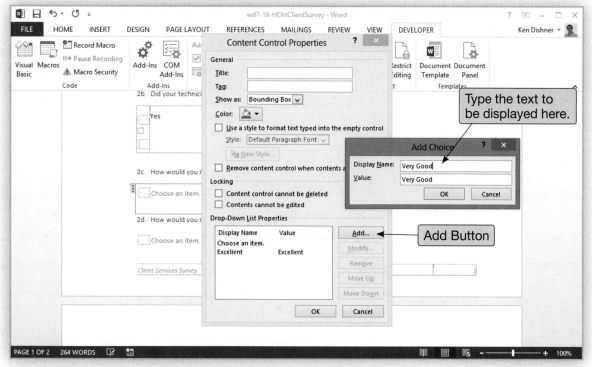

FIGURE WD 7.28

tips & tricks

After adding items to list, you can reorder the items by clicking the **Move Up** and **Move Down** buttons.

tell me **more**

From the *Content Control Properties* dialog, you can lock controls so they cannot be deleted or edited.

let me **try**

If you do not have the data file from the previous skill open, open the student data file **wd7-18-HOHClientSurvey** and try this skill on your own:

1. Verify you are in *Design Mode*. Place your cursor in the first drop-down list content control under the second question (item **2c**).

2. Open the **Content Control Properties** dialog.

3. Add a new item for the drop-down list.

4. Add the text **Excellent** as the display text.

5. Add the following items to the drop-down list: **Very good, Good, Unsatisfactory.**

6. When you are done, exit *Design Mode* and test the control.

7. If you will be moving on to the next skill in this chapter, leave the document open to continue working. If not, save the file as directed by your instructor and close it.

Skill 7.19 Protecting a Form

Once you have created your form, you will want to protect the form to only allow others to fill in the form and not modify any other part of the form. From the *Restrict Editing* task pane, you can change the permissions on a document to only allow others to interact with form controls. This will prevent readers from changing other parts of the document such as text or images.

To protect a form:

1. Click the **Developer** tab.
2. In the *Protect* group, click the **Restrict Editing** button.
3. The *Restrict Editing* task pane displays.
4. Under *Editing restrictions,* click the **Allow only this type of editing in the document** check box.
5. Click the drop-down arrow and select **Filling in forms.**
6. In the *Start enforcement* section, click the **Yes, Start Enforcing Protection** button.

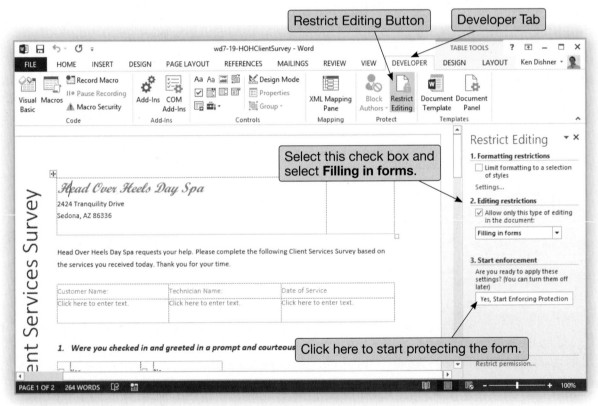

FIGURE WD 7.29

7. You can add a password that will be required to be entered to stop protecting the form. In the *Start Enforcing Protection* dialog, type a password in the *Enter new password (optional)* box.

8. Type the password again in the *Reenter password to confirm* box.

9. Click **OK** to start protecting the form.

FIGURE WD 7.30

tell me **more**

When a form is protected, the *Stop protection* button displays in the task pane. Click this button to stop protecting the form. If you have added a password to the form, you will be asked to enter the password in order to stop protection.

another **method**

To display the *Restrict Editing* task pane, you can also:

1. Click the **File** tab.
2. In Backstage view, on the *Info* page, click the **Protect Document** button.
3. Select **Restricting Editing.**

let me **try**

If you do not have the data file from the previous skill open, open the student data file **wd7-19-HOHClientSurvey** and try this skill on your own:

1. Display the **Restrict Editing** task pane.
2. Start enforcing protection on the document so users will only be able to fill in the form and not modify other parts of the document.
3. Add the password **hoh135** to the form and start protecting it.
4. Save the file as directed by your instructor and close it.

key terms

Navigation pane
Go To
Bookmark
Cross-reference
Special characters
Keep with next
Keep lines together
Orphan

Widow
Outline view
Section
Portrait
Landscape
Table of figures
Field
Form

concepts review

1. The *Navigation* pane's *Pages* tab allows you to quickly jump to headings in your document.

   a. True

   b. False

2. To prevent a paragraph from breaking across a page use the _____ command.

   a. Widow/Orphan control

   b. Keep with next

   c. Keep lines together

   d. Page break before

3. A(n) _____ is a designated part of a document that can be formatted separately from the rest of the document.

   a. page

   b. section

   c. outline

   d. heading

4. When a document is formatted in landscape orientation, the height of the page is greater than the width.

   a. True

   b. False

5. A _____ is a link you add to a document that directs the reader to another part of the document for more or related information.

   a. footnote

   b. bookmark

   c. cross-reference

   d. index

6. A _____ lists all the illustrations, graphs, charts, equations, and pictures in a document, along with their associated page numbers.

   a. table of figures

   b. table of contents

   c. table of authorities

   d. index

7. You can set a document header to display a company name on odd numbered pages and the document title on even numbered pages.
   a. True
   b. False

8. A _____ is a placeholder for content that might change in a document.
   a. style
   b. field
   c. text box
   d. building block

9. To create a form, you must first display the _____ tab.
   a. Design
   b. Insert
   c. Page Layout
   d. Developer

10. A _____ content control allows your readers to select from a list of options you provide.
   a. check box
   b. combo box
   c. rich text
   d. date picker

Data files for projects can be found on
www.mhhe.com/office2013skills

projects

skill review 7.1

In this project you will be working on research paper about alternate assessments for students.

Skills needed to complete this project:

- Managing Orphans and Widows (Skill 7.7)
- Using Go To (Skill 7.2)
- Adding Bookmarks (Skill 7.3)
- Navigating Long Documents (Skill 7.1)
- Adding Cross-References (Skill 7.4)
- Adding Sections to Documents (Skill 7.9)
- Using Outline View (Skill 7.8)
- Keeping Paragraphs Together (Skill 7.6)
- Customizing Footnotes and Endnotes (Skill 7.11)
- Modifying a Table of Contents (Skill 7.13)
- Using Fields in Documents (Skill 7.16)

1. Open the start file **WD2013-SkillReview-7-1** and resave the file as:
   `[your initials]WD-SkillReview-7-1`

2. If the document opens in Protected View, click the **Enable Editing** button in the Message Bar at the top of the document so you can modify the document.

3. Manage widows and orphans.

   a. Press `Ctrl` + `A` to select the entire document.

   b. On the *Home* tab, in the *Paragraph* group, click the **dialog launcher.**

   c. Click the **Line and Page Breaks** tab.

   d. Click the **Widow/Orphan control** check box to select it.

   e. Click **OK**.

4. Navigate to a page using *Go To*.

   a. On the *Home* tab, in the *Editing* group, click the **Find** button arrow and select **Go To**.

   b. Verify **Page** is selected in the *Go to what* box. Type **5** in the *Enter page number* box.

   c. Click **Go To...**

   d. Click **Close** to close the *Find and Replace* dialog.

5. Add a bookmark.

   a. Place the cursor in the Student Eligibility heading.

   b. Click the **Insert** tab.

   c. In the *Links* group, click the **Bookmark** button.

   d. Type `StudentEligibility` in the *Bookmark name* box.

   e. Click **Add**.

6. Navigate to a heading using the *Navigation* pane.

   a. Click the **View** tab.

   b. In the *Show* group, click the **Navigation Pane** check box to display the *Navigation* pane if it is not already open.

   c. Click the **What is an Alternative Assessment** heading.

7. Add a cross-reference.

   a. Place the cursor before the second closing parenthesis in the first paragraph (after **See**). Be sure the cursor is placed after the space.

   b. Click the **Insert** tab.

   c. In the *Links* group, click the **Cross-reference** button.

   d. In the *Cross-reference* dialog, click the **Reference type** arrow and select **Heading.**

   e. In the *For which heading* box, click **Modified Achievement Standards.**

   f. Click **Insert.**

   g. Click **Close** to close the *Cross-reference* dialog.

8. Add a section break to the document.

   a. Place the cursor at the end of the **Conclusion** section (after **world of education**).

   b. Click the **Page Layout** tab.

   c. In the *Page Setup* group, click the **Breaks** button and select **Next Page** under *Section Breaks.*

9. Navigate using a bookmark and use Outline view.

   a. Click the **Insert** tab.

   b. In the *Links* group, click the **Bookmark** button.

   c. Verify the **StudentEligibility** bookmark is selected.

    d. Click **Go To.**

    e. Click **Close** to close the *Bookmark* dialog.

    f. Click the **View** tab.

    g. In the *Views* group, click the **Outline** button.

    h. In the *Outline Tools* group, click the **Promote** button.

    i. Click the **Close Outline View** button.

10. Prevent a paragraph from breaking across a page.

    a. Place the cursor in the paragraph at the bottom of page 3.

    b. On the *Home* tab, in the *Paragraph* group, click the **dialog launcher.**

    c. If necessary, click the **Line and Page Breaks** tab.

    d. Click the **Keep lines together** check box to select it.

    e. Click **OK.**

11. Change the format of footnotes.

    a. Click the **References** tab.

    b. In the *Footnotes* group, click the **dialog launcher.**

    c. Click the **Number format** drop-down arrow and select the **A, B, C** format.

    d. Click **Apply.**

12. Customize the table of contents.

    a. Navigate to the table of contents for the document.

    b. If necessary, click the **References** tab.

    c. In the *Table of Contents* group, click the **Table of Contents** button and select **Custom Table of Contents...**

    d. Click the **Formats** arrow and select **Fancy.**

    e. Click the **Tab leader** arrow and select the **solid line** tab leader (the fourth option on the menu).

    f. Click **OK.**

    g. Click **Yes** in the message box.

13. Add a field.

    a. Double-click the header area at the top of page 2.

    b. Place the cursor after the page number and type **a space,** the word **of**, and another **space.**

    c. Click the **Insert** tab.

    d. In the *Text* group, click the **Explore Quick Parts** button and select **Field...**

    e. Scroll the *Field names* box and select **NumPages.**

    f. Select the **1, 2, 3** format and click **OK.**

    g. On the *Header & Footer Tools Design* tab, click the **Close Header and Footer** button.

14. Save and close the document.

skill review 7.2

In this project, you will modifying a form for the Tri-State Book Festival.

Skills needed to complete this project:

- Managing Orphans and Widows (Skill 7.7)
- Adding Bookmarks (Skill 7.3)

- Navigating Long Documents (Skill 7.1)
- Using Go To (Skill 7.2)
- Replacing with Special Characters (Skill 7.5)
- Using Fields in Documents (Skill 7.16)
- Designing a Simple Form (Skill 7.17)
- Modifying Control Properties in a Form (Skill 7.18)
- Protecting a Form (Skill 7.19)

1. Open the start file **WD2013-SkillReview-7-2** and resave the file as:
   `[your initials]WD-SkillReview-7-2`

2. If the document opens in Protected View, enable editing so you can make changes to the document.

3. Manage widows and orphans.

   a. Press (Ctrl) + (A) to select the entire document.

   b. On the *Home* tab, in the *Paragraph* group, click the **dialog launcher.**

   c. Click the **Line and Page Breaks** tab.

   d. Select the **Widow/Orphan control** check box.

   e. Click **OK.**

4. Add a bookmark.

   a. Navigate to line **Barrett Baker at:** on page 2.

   b. Click the **Insert** tab.

   c. In the *Links* group, click the **Bookmark** button.

   d. In the *Bookmark name* box, type: `ContactInfo`

   e. Click **Add.**

5. Use the *Navigation* pane to navigate a document.

   a. Click the **View** tab.

   b. In the *Show* group, click the **Navigation Pane** check box.

   c. On the *Headings* tab of the *Navigation* pane, click the **Fiction Writers Association of the Tri-State Region** heading.

6. Use the *Go To* command to navigate to a bookmark.

   a. On the *Home* tab, in the *Editing* group, click the **Find** button arrow and select **Go To...,**

   b. In the *Go to what* box, select **Bookmark.**

   c. The *ContactInfo* bookmark displays in the *Enter bookmark name* box.

   d. Click **Go To.**

   e. Click the **Close** button to close the *Find and Replace* dialog.

7. Replace using special characters.

   a. Navigate to the beginning of the document.

   b. On the *Home* tab, in the *Editing* group, click the **Replace** button.

   c. Type a hyphen (-) in the *Find what* box.

   d. Place the cursor in the **Replace with** box.

   e. Click the **More >>** button.

   f. Click the **Special** button and select **En Dash.**

g. Click the **Find Next** button three times so the hyphen in the first instance of **October 10–12** is selected.

h. Click **Replace.**

i. Click the **Find Next** button once so the hyphen in the second instance of **October 10–12** is selected.

j. Click **Replace.**

k. Click **Close** in the *Find and Replace* dialog to close the dialog.

8. Add a number of pages field.

a. Double-click the footer area at the bottom of page 1.

b. Place the cursor after the word **of.**

c. Click the **Insert** tab.

d. In the *Text* group, click the **Explore Quick Parts** button and select **Field...**

e. Scroll the *Field names* box and select **NumPages.**

f. Select the **1, 2, 3** format and click **OK.**

g. On the *Header & Footer Tools Design* tab, click the **Close Header and Footer** button.

9. Display the *Developer* tab.

a. Click the **File** tab.

b. Click **Options.**

c. Click the **Customize Ribbon** button.

d. In the *Customize the Ribbon* box, click the **Developer** check box if it is not already checked.

e. Click **OK.**

10. Add controls to a form.

a. Place the cursor at the end of the **Name:** line on page one.

b. On the *Developer* tab, in the *Controls* group, click the **Design Mode** button.

c. In the *Controls* group, click the **Rich Text Content Control** button.

d. Add another rich text content control at the end of the next line (the *Agency:* line).

e. Place the cursor at the beginning of the first line under **Agency name:** (beginning with *No, I won't be able to...*). The cursor should be before the space at the beginning of the line.

f. On the *Developer* tab, in the *Controls* tab, click the **Check Box Content Control.**

g. Add another check box control to the beginning of the next line (beginning with *Yes, I plan to attend...*).

11. Add options for drop-down lists.

a. Select the drop-down list content control under the **Please reserve the following type of room for me:** line.

b. On the *Developer* tab, in the *Controls* group, click the **Properties** button.

c. Click the **Add...** button.

d. In the *Display Name* box, type **King.** Click **OK.**

e. Add the following items to the list:

`Two Doubles`

`Mini-Suite`

f. Click **OK** in the *Content Control Properties* dialog.

12. Protect a form.

    a. On the *Developer* tab, in the *Protect* group, click the **Restrict Editing** button.

    b. Click the **Allow only this type of editing in the document** check box.

    c. Click the drop-down arrow and select **Filling in forms.**

    d. Click the **Yes, Start Enforcing Protection** button.

    e. In the **Enter new password (optional)** box, type: `tsb123`

    f. In the **Reenter password to confirm** box, type: `tsb123`

    g. Click **OK.**

13. Save and close the document.

challenge yourself **7.3**

In this project you will be working on research paper about the efficacy of acupuncture in the treatment of lower back pain.

Skills needed to complete this project:

- Navigating Long Documents (Skill 7.1)
- Keeping Paragraphs Together (Skill 7.6)
- Adding Bookmarks (Skill 7.3)
- Replacing with Special Characters (Skill 7.5)
- Using Go To (Skill 7.2)
- Adding Cross-References (Skill 7.4)
- Adding Sections to Documents (Skill 7.9)
- Using Outline View (Skill 7.8)
- Modifying a Table of Contents (Skill 7.13)
- Customizing Footnotes and Endnotes (Skill 7.11)
- Using Fields in Documents (Skill 7.16)

1. Open the start file **WD2013-ChallengeYourself-7-3** and resave the file as: `[your initials]WD-ChallengeYourself-7-3`

2. If the document opens in Protected View, enable editing so you can make changes to the document.

3. Use the *Navigation* pane to navigate to the **Conclusion** heading.

4. Modify the paragraph settings for the **Conclusion** heading so it will always appear on the same page as the following paragraph.

5. Add a bookmark to the beginning of the **Works Cited** heading. Name the bookmark `WorksCited`.

6. Replace all instances of a hyphen with the **nonbreaking hyphen** special character.

7. Use the *Go To* command to navigate to the first page of the document.

8. Add a cross-reference that links to the **Acupuncture v. Massage Therapy** heading. Place the cross-reference between the words **the** and **section** in the second to last sentence in the *Introduction* paragraph. The cross-reference should look like this: (**see the Acupuncture v. Massage Therapy section**).

9. Open the **Bookmark** dialog and navigate to the **WorksCited** bookmark.

10. Add a section break before the **Works Cited** heading that will move the content to a new page.

11. Switch to **Outline** view and promote the **Works Cited** heading up one level. When you are done, close Outline view.

12. Navigate to the table of contents for the document. Modify the table of contents to use the **Distinctive** format.

13. Customize the format for the footnotes in the document to use the uppercase letters (A, B, C...) format (under the *Number format* menu in the *Footnote and Endnote* dialog).

14. Add the **number of pages field** after the word **of** in the footer of the document. Use the **1, 2, 3** format. Be sure to include a space before the field.

15. Save and close the document.

challenge yourself 7.4

In this project you will be working on a safety initiative document for the Spring Hills Community. You will be modifying the document as well as adding form controls.

Skills needed to complete this project:
- Keeping Paragraphs Together (Skill 7.6)
- Replacing with Special Characters (Skill 7.5)
- Navigating Long Documents (Skill 7.1)
- Adding Bookmarks (Skill 7.3)
- Using Go To (Skill 7.2)
- Adding Cross-References (Skill 7.4)
- Using Outline View (Skill 7.8)
- Adding Sections to Documents (Skill 7.9)
- Creating a Table of Figures (Skill 7.12)
- Modifying a Table of Contents (Skill 7.13)
- Customizing Footnotes and Endnotes (Skill 7.11)
- Changing Page Orientation (Skill 7.10)
- Designing a Simple Form (Skill 7.17)
- Protecting a Form (Skill 7.19)

1. Open the start file **WD2013-ChallengeYourself-7-4** and resave the file as:
   `[your initials]WD-ChallengeYourself-7-4`

2. If the document opens in Protected View, enable editing so you can make changes to the document.

3. Navigate to the bottom of page 3. Change the paragraph settings for the last two lines on the page so they appear with the following paragraph.

4. Replace all hyphens (-) in the document with **nonbreaking hyphens.**

5. Use the *Navigation* pane to navigate to the **Safety Assessment** heading.

6. Add a bookmark to the beginning of the **Safety Assessment** heading. Name the bookmark `SafetyAssessment`.

7. Use the *Go To* command to navigate to the third page in the document.

8. Place the cursor before the closing parenthesis in the first paragraph under **Our Safety Vision** (after the word **See**).

9. Add a cross-reference to the **Full-Time Officers** heading. Change the reference for the cross-reference to **Above/below.** Close Outline view when you are done.

10. Switch to **Outline** view and promote the **Full-Time Officers** heading and the **Part-Time Officers** heading one level (so they are Level 2).

11. Place the cursor at the beginning of the **Safety Assessment** heading. Insert a **continuous section break.**

12. Place the cursor before the **Figures** heading. Insert a **next page section break.**

13. Insert a table of figures under the **Figures** heading. Use the **Classic** style with a **dotted** tab leader.

14. Navigate to page 2 of the document.

15. Update the table of contents to use the **Classic** style with a **dotted** tab leader.

16. Update the footnotes for the document to use the **i, ii, iii** format.

17. Use the bookmark you created to navigate to the **Safety Assessment** section. Change the orientation for the section to **landscape.**

18. Add a **check box content control** to each of the blank cells before each option in the table in the **Safety Assessment** section.

19. Change the protection on the document so readers will only be able to fill in the form and not change other parts of the document. Add `spring358` as the password to unlock the protection.

20. Save and close the document.

on your own 7.5

In this project, you will be creating a personal task form for your class.

Skills needed to complete this project:
- Keeping Paragraphs Together (Skill 7.6)
- Adding Sections to Documents (Skill 7.9)
- Changing Page Orientation (Skill 7.10)
- Using Outline View (Skill 7.8)
- Using Fields in Documents (Skill 7.16)
- Designing a Simple Form (Skill 7.17)
- Modifying Control Properties in a Form (Skill 7.18)
- Protecting a Form (Skill 7.19)

1. Open the start file **WD2013-OnYourOwn-7-5** and resave the file as: `[your initials]WD-OnYourOwn-7-5`

2. If the document opens in Protected View, click the **Enable Editing** button in the Message Bar at the top of the document so you can modify the document.

3. Personalize the information at the top of the document with your course name, instructor name, and class time.

4. Adjust the paragraph settings so the *Course Milestones* heading and text appears on the same page as the table.

5. Add a continuous section break before the *Course Milestones* section.

6. Change the page orientation for the *Course Milestones* section so the entire table is visible.

7. Use Outline view to promote the *Projects and Assignments* heading and the *Course Milestones* heading up one level.

8. Add the number of pages field to the page number in the footer.

9. Add a footnote to the *Projects and Assignments* paragraph and customize that footnote to use a format of your choice. If you do not know how to add a footnote, see skill 5.7 Inserting Footnotes and Endnotes in Chapter 5).

10. Add appropriate form controls to each element of each table. Use rich text content controls, check box content controls, date picker content controls, and drop-down list controls.

11. Protect the document so others will only be able to fill in the form and not modify the rest of the document.

12. Save and close the document.

fix it 7.6

In this project you will be fixing a paper on behavior modification.

Skills needed to complete this project:

- Adding Sections to Documents (Skill 7.9)
- Changing Page Orientation (Skill 7.10)
- Navigating Long Documents (Skill 7.1)
- Adding Cross-References (Skill 7.4)
- Keeping Paragraphs Together (Skill 7.6)
- Customizing Footnotes and Endnotes (Skill 7.11)
- Modifying a Table of Contents (Skill 7.13)
- Replacing with Special Characters (Skill 7.5)
- Creating a Table of Figures (Skill 7.12)
- Using Fields in Documents (Skill 7.16)

1. Open the start file **WD2013-FixIt-7-6** and resave the file as:

   `[your initials]WD-FixIt-7-6`

2. If the document opens in Protected View, click the **Enable Editing** button in the Message Bar at the top of the document so you can modify the document.

3. The tables on page 5 do not fit on the page in portrait orientation. Fix this by doing the following:

   a. Add a section break that will place the **Collect and evaluate the result** section on a new page.

   b. Change the orientation for the section to **landscape.**

4. There is a missing cross-reference in the file. Navigate to the **Collect and chart baseline data** heading and add a cross-reference to the **Collect and evaluate the result** heading after the word **See** at the end of the last paragraph in the section. Be sure to insert the reference to the heading text.

5. Navigate to the bottom of page 3. Paragraph A.2 breaks across two pages. Fix this by changing the paragraph settings so the entire paragraph appears on the same page.

6. The footnotes in the document use symbols rather than numbers. Fix this by changing the footnote format from symbols to the **1, 2, 3** number format.

7. Modify the table of contents to use the **Distinctive** format with a **dotted** tab leader.

8. There are some places where hyphenated words break across two lines. Fix this by replacing all hyphens with **nonbreaking hyphens.**

9. There is no table of figures in the document. Fix this by adding a table of figures to the end of the document (under the *Figures* heading). Use the **Distinctive** format with a **dotted** tab leader.

10. The footer is missing the save date. First, navigate to the bottom of page 2. Fix the footer by clicking the right side of the active footer area and adding a **SaveDate field.** Use the **MMMM d, yyyy** date format (so the date looks similar to this *January 1, 2014*).

11. Save and close the document.

chapter 8

Exploring Advanced Tables, Charts, and Graphics

In this chapter, you will learn the following skills:

- Convert text to a table
- Add formulas to a table
- Format table borders and margins
- Customize a chart
- Change the look of SmartArt
- Enhance graphics by applying artistic effects, correcting, and changing the color
- Remove the background from an image
- Crop an image
- Reset pictures
- Align and group pictures
- Format and add text to a shape
- Compress pictures
- Insert a screenshot

Skill **8.1** Defining a Header Row in a Table

Skill **8.2** Converting Text to a Table

Skill **8.3** Adding Formulas and Functions to Tables

Skill **8.4** Using Table Border Painter

Skill **8.5** Adjusting Cell Margins

Skill **8.6** Inserting a Quick Table

Skill **8.7** Customizing Charts

Skill **8.8** Modifying SmartArt

Skill **8.9** Applying Artistic Effects to Pictures

Skill **8.10** Correcting Pictures

Skill **8.11** Changing the Color of Pictures

Skill **8.12** Removing the Background from Pictures

Skill **8.13** Resetting Pictures

Skill **8.14** Cropping Graphics

Skill **8.15** Aligning Images

Skill **8.16** Grouping Images

Skill **8.17** Formatting a Shape

Skill **8.18** Adding Text to a Shape

Skill **8.19** Changing Pictures

Skill **8.20** Compressing Pictures

Skill **8.21** Inserting a Screenshot

skills

introduction

In Chapter 4, you were introduced to tables and graphics and how they can enhance the appearance and readability of a document. We carry this a bit further in this chapter, in which you will learn more advanced skills for working with tables, including converting text into tables, using formulas in tables, and creating new table styles. Additionally, you will learn how to format charts and SmartArt diagrams. You will learn how to use some of the more advanced graphic tools available in Word, including applying artistic effects and removing the background from pictures. Other advanced graphic skills, such as cropping images and grouping images, are covered in this chapter giving you the foundation to create graphic-rich, professional-looking documents.

Skill 8.1 Defining a Header Row in a Table

When you apply a table Quick Style, you can choose from formats that include banded rows, first columns, or a header row. A **header row** is the first row in a table and contains headings for each column in the table. Think of the header row as the top anchor for a table. If you have a long table that breaks across a page, you will want the header row to repeat on the top of the next page.

To set header rows to repeat across pages:

1. Place your cursor in the first row of the table.
2. Click the **Table Tools Layout** tab.
3. In the *Data* group, click the **Repeat Header Rows** button.

To turn off the *Repeat Header Rows* feature, click the **Repeat Header Rows** button again.

FIGURE WD 8.1

tips & tricks

You can assign more than one row to repeat at the top of the page. Select all the rows you want to repeat at the top of each page, and click the **Repeat Header Rows** button. Now when the table breaks across a page, all the rows you selected will appear at the top of the table.

tell me **more**

You must to begin your selection with the first row of the table. If your cursor is in a later row in the table, the *Repeat Header Rows* button will not be active.

let me try

Open the student data file **wd8-01-SpaProductReport** and try this skill on your own:

1. Place the cursor in the first row of the table in the *Sales Summary* section (at the bottom of page 10).
2. Change the table so the heading row will repeat at the top of the next page.
3. If you will be moving on to the next skill in this chapter, leave the document open to continue working. If not, save the file as directed by your instructor and close it.

Skill 8.2 Converting Text to a Table

Sometimes information displayed in a table can be more easily understood. If you have a list of names, addresses, and phone numbers, it makes sense to create a table with three columns to present your information. But what if you have already entered information in paragraph format? Microsoft Word allows you to convert text from paragraphs into a table.

To convert text to a table:

1. Select the text you want to convert to a table.
2. Click the **Insert** tab.
3. Click the **Table** button and select **Convert Text to Table...**

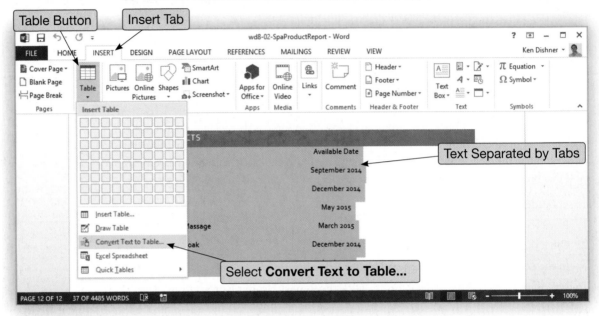

FIGURE WD 8.2

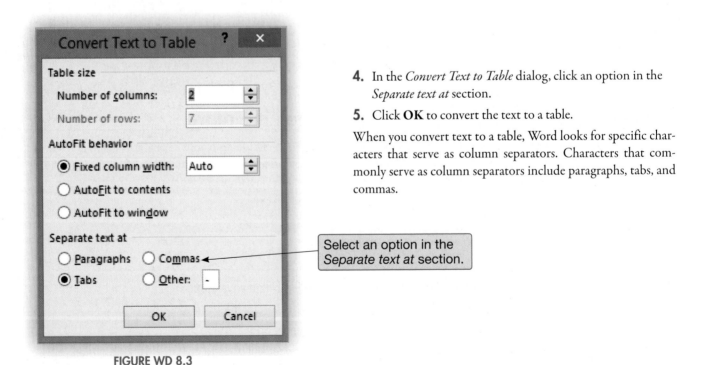

4. In the *Convert Text to Table* dialog, click an option in the *Separate text at* section.
5. Click **OK** to convert the text to a table.

When you convert text to a table, Word looks for specific characters that serve as column separators. Characters that commonly serve as column separators include paragraphs, tabs, and commas.

FIGURE WD 8.3

Just as you can convert text into a table, you can also convert a table back into text:

1. Select the table you want to convert.
2. Click the **Table Tools Layout** tab.
3. In the *Data* group, click the **Convert to Text** button.
4. Select an option to separate the text with.
5. Click **OK.**

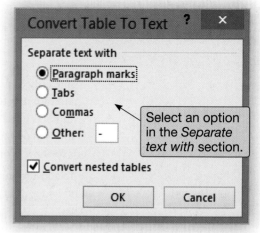

FIGURE WD 8.4

tell me **more**

You can use almost any character to mark where you want to separate your columns of text. Type the character in the *Other* box. The number of columns will change to display the number of columns created based on the character you entered. If the number of columns appears to be correct, click **OK** to create the table.

let me **try**

If you do not have the data file from the previous skill open, open the student data file **wd8-02-SpaProductReport** and try this skill on your own:

1. Select the seven lines of text under the *Future Products* heading on page 12.
2. Open the **Convert Text to Table** dialog.
3. Convert the text to a table with the text separated at tabs.
4. Navigate to the bottom of page 1 and select the table.
5. Convert the table to text separated by paragraph marks.
6. If you will be moving on to the next skill in this chapter, leave the document open to continue working. If not, save the file as directed by your instructor and close it.

Skill 8.3 Adding Formulas and Functions to Tables

Spreadsheet programs like Microsoft Excel use **formulas** to perform calculations. You can add formulas to a table in Word to perform similar calculations, such as adding a column of numbers or calculating the average of a set of numbers. A formula begins with an equals sign and contains arguments, operators, and functions. The easiest way to add a formula to a table is to allow Word to create a default formula based on the data in your table.

To add a formula to a table using Word's default formula:

1. Place your cursor in the cell where you want to insert the formula.
2. Click the **Table Tools Layout** tab.
3. In the *Data* group, click the **Formula** button.

FIGURE WD 8.5

4. Word displays a default formula based on the data in the table in the *Formula* box.
5. Click **OK** to add the formula to the table.

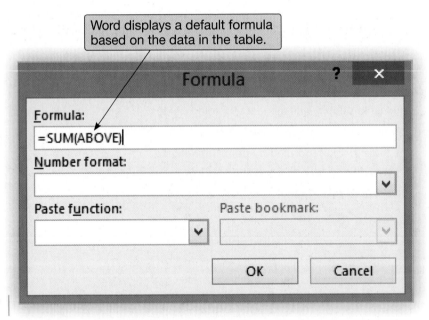

FIGURE WD 8.6

The default formula in Word will calculate all the cells in the table either above, below, to the right, or to the left of the active cell. You can also specify a range of cells to calculate within the table. A **cell range** is identified by the address of the cell in the upper left corner of the range, followed by a colon, and then the address of the cell in the lower right corner of the range. The **cell address** is the cell's column and row position. Rows are identified by numbers and columns are identified by letters. The cell address format is the column letter followed by the row number. For example, the cell address of the third cell in the second column of the table is B3.

To enter a formula using a function and cell range:

1. In the *Formula* box, delete the formula, leaving the equals sign.
2. Click the **Paste function** arrow.
3. Select a function.
4. Enter the arguments (cells you want to calculate) between the parentheses.

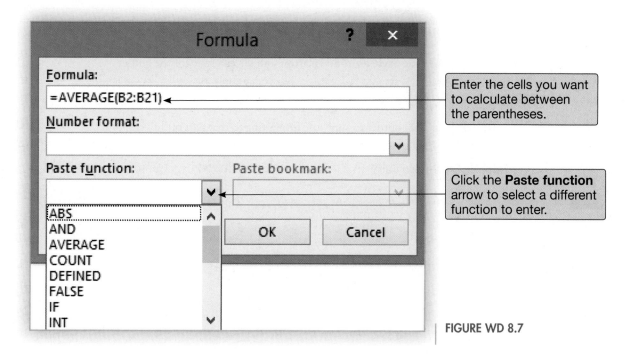

FIGURE WD 8.7

tell me **more**

Functions are preprogrammed shortcuts for calculating complex equations (like the average of a group of numbers). Word includes 18 predefined functions you can use to perform calculations. Some common functions include:

❯ **SUM**—Totals the values in the column or row.
❯ **AVERAGE**—Calculates the average of the values in the column or row.
❯ **MAX**—Displays the largest value in the column or row.
❯ **MIN**—Displays the smallest value in the column or row.

let me **try**

If you do not have the data file from the previous skill open, open the student data file **wd8-03-SpaProductReport** and try this skill on your own:

1. Place the cursor in the empty cell in the second to last row of the table in the *Sales Summary* section (at the bottom of page 11).
2. Open the **Formula** dialog to add a formula to the cell.
3. Enter a formula that will sum the values from the table cells above the selected cell.
4. Place the cursor in the empty cell in the last row of the table.
5. Open the **Formula** dialog.
6. Enter a formula that will calculate the average of cells **B2:B21.**
7. If you will be moving on to the next skill in this chapter, leave the document open to continue working. If not, save the file as directed by your instructor and close it.

Skill 8.4 Using Table Border Painter

The **Border Painter** feature in Word allows you to quickly apply stylized borders to tables. Instead of opening the *Borders and Shading* dialog to create a custom border, you can activate the *Border Painter* and set the line style, width, and color from commands on the Ribbon.

To apply table borders using the *Border Painter:*

1. With the cursor in the table, click the **Table Tools Design** tab.
2. In the *Borders* group, click the **Border Painter** button to activate it.
3. Click the **Line Style** drop-down arrow and select a style for the border.
4. Click the **Line Weight** drop-down arrow and select a thickness for the border.
5. Click the **Pen Color** drop-down arrow and select a color for the border.
6. Click on a cell border to apply the formatting to that part of the cell border.

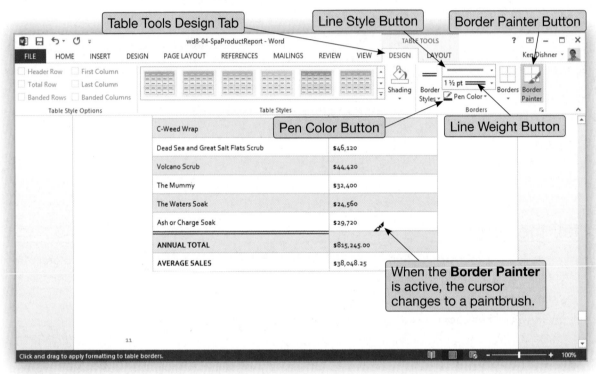

FIGURE WD 8.8

tips & tricks

Click the **Border Styles** button in the *Borders* group to choose from a number of predesigned borders. These borders are based on the document's theme colors and include single and double line border options.

another method

You can also click and drag along the table's borders to apply the formatting.

word 2013   chapter 8 Exploring Advanced Tables, Charts, and Graphics

let me try

If you do not have the data file from the previous skill open, open the student data file **wd8-04-SpaProductReport** and try this skill on your own:

1. Place the cursor the **Annual Total** cell near the bottom of the table on page 11.
2. Activate the **Border Painter** feature.
3. Change the line style of the border to the **double line** option (it is the eighth option on the menu).
4. Change the line weight to **1½pt.**
5. Change the pen color to **Blue-Gray, Text 2.**
6. Click the top border of the **Annual Total** cell to apply the border style.
7. Click the top border of the cell to the right to apply the border style (the cell with the value $815,245.00).
8. Press **Esc** to exit the *Border Painter.*
9. If you will be moving on to the next skill in this chapter, leave the document open to continue working. If not, save the file as directed by your instructor and close it.

from the perspective of . . .

LIBRARIAN

I don't really know how to use a lot of software applications, so I use Word for everything! When I need to pull together numbers, I just type them in a Word document and then convert them to a table. I use Word's formula feature to make all my calculations for me. When planning special events, I create a flyer and insert pictures of the library I have taken myself. I use Word's artistic effects and coloring features to really make the images pop. If I need to tweak an image I can remove the background or crop the image right from inside Word. No going to any other program for me!

Skill 8.5 Adjusting Cell Margins

Just as you can adjust the margins on a page, adding white space to the top, bottom, left side, and right side, you can also adjust the margins on cells within a table. The *Table Options* dialog allows you to quickly change the cell margins for the entire table at once.

To adjust the cell margins for a table:

1. Place the cursor in the table you want to change.

2. Click the **Table Tools Layout** tab.

3. In the *Alignment* group, click the **Cell Margins** button to open the *Table Options* dialog.

FIGURE WD 8.9

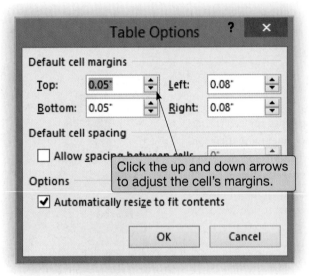

FIGURE WD 8.10

4. In the *Default cell margin* section, click the up and down arrows to increase and decrease the margins for the table's cells.

5. Click **OK** to apply your changes.

tips & tricks

To change the margin of an individual cell, place the cursor in the cell you want to change. On the *Table Tools Layout* tab, in the *Cell Size* group, click the **dialog launcher**. The *Table Properties* dialog opens with the *Cell* tab displayed. Click the **Options...** button to open the *Cell Options* dialog. Uncheck the **Same as the whole table** option under *Cell margins*. Make adjustments to the cell's margins using the up and down arrows. Click **OK** to change the margins for the current cell.

another method

To open the *Table Options* dialog, you can click the **Table Tools Layout** tab. In the *Table* group, click the **Properties** button to open the *Table Properties* dialog. On the *Table* tab in the dialog, click the **Options...** button.

let me try

If you do not have the data file from the previous skill open, open the student data file **wd8-05-SpaProductReport** and try this skill on your own:

1. Place the cursor in the table in the *Manicures and Pedicures* section (on page 1).

2. Open the **Table Options** dialog.

3. Change the top and bottom cell margins for the table to **0.05"**.

4. If you will be moving on to the next skill in this chapter, leave the document open to continue working. If not, save the file as directed by your instructor and close it.

Skill 8.6 Inserting a Quick Table

Word comes with a number of **Quick Table** building blocks. These templates are preformatted for you and include sample data that you can replace with your own data.

To insert a Quick Table:

1. Place the cursor where you want to insert the Quick Table.
2. Click the **Insert** tab.
3. In the *Tables* group, click the **Table** button.
4. Point to **Quick Tables** and select an option from the gallery.

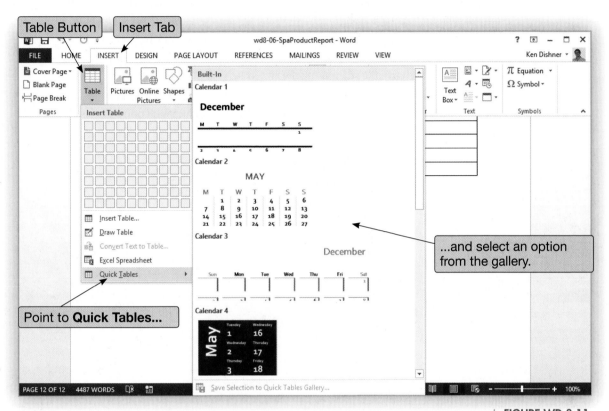

FIGURE WD 8.11

tips & tricks

If you have a table template that you use often, you can save the table to the *Quick Tables* gallery. First, select the table you want to save. Click the **Table** button, point to **Quick Tables,** and select **Save selection to Quick Tables Gallery...** In the *Create New Building Block* dialog, enter a name for the Quick Table and click **OK.**

another method

You can also insert Quick Tables from the *Building Block Organizer*. On the *Insert* tab, in the *Text* group, click the **Quick Parts** button and select **Building Block Organizer...** Scroll the list of building blocks, select a table building block, and click the **Insert** button.

let me try

If you do not have the data file from the previous skill open, open the student data file **wd8-06-SpaProductReport** and try this skill on your own:

1. Place the cursor at the end of the document.
2. Insert the **Calendar 1** Quick Table.
3. Save the file as directed by your instructor and close it.

Skill 8.7 Customizing Charts

All charts include common chart elements which you can adjust to change the display of your charts. The common elements include:

> **Plot area**—The area where the data series are plotted.

> **Chart area**—The area that encompasses the entire chart including the plot area and optional layout elements, such as the title and legend.

> **Chart title**—A text box above or overlaying the chart.

> **Legend**—Tells you which data point or data series is represented by each color in the chart.

> **Data labels**—Display data values for each visual element of the chart (such as the column, bar, pie slice, or line depending on the type of chart in the document).

> **Axes**—The horizontal and vertical grid the data is plotted against. The y axis goes from top to bottom and the x axis goes from left to right. All charts, except pie charts and doughnut charts, plot data along the two axes.

Word includes a number of Quick Layout options for charts. These Quick Layouts include a combination of chart elements which you can apply to charts with one command.

To apply a Quick Layout to a chart:

1. Click an empty area of the chart area to select the chart.

2. Click the **Chart Tools Design** tab.

3. In the *Chart Layouts* group, click the **Quick Layout** button and select an option.

FIGURE WD 8.12

After you have applied a Quick Layout, you may find that your chart appears too cluttered. You can show and chart elements, making the chart easier to read.

To show or hide chart elements:

1. Click an empty area of the chart area to select the chart.

2. Click the **Chart Elements** button that appears near the upper right corner of the chart.

3. Click the check boxes to show or hide chart elements.

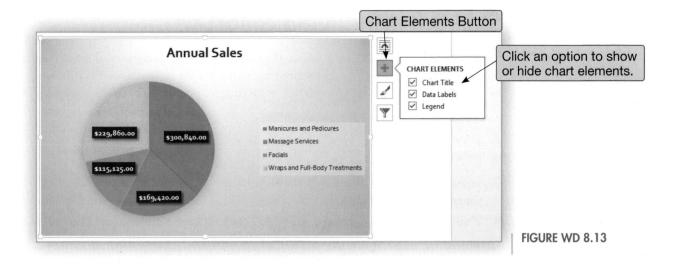

FIGURE WD 8.13

tips & tricks

To change the chart title, click the box to select it and edit the text directly in the text box.

tell me more

When a chart is selected, two contextual tabs are available: the *Chart Tools Design* tab and the *Chart Tools Format* tab. The *Chart Tools Design* tab gives you access to commands for working with the design elements for the chart including the color, style, and data. The *Chart Tools Formatting* tab allows you to apply formatting to parts of the chart. On the *Chart Tools Formatting* tab, in the *Current Selection* group, the *Chart Elements* box displays the name of the chart element that is currently selected. This can be helpful if you need to ensure that you have selected the chart area, plot area, or another chart element to be formatted.

another method

You can hide or show chart elements and control their appearance and position from the *Chart Tools Design* tab. In the *Chart Layouts* group, click the **Add Chart Elements** button, point to the chart element you want and click an option.

let me try

Open the student data file **wd8-07-SpaProductReport** and try this skill on your own:

1. Select the chart in the *Annual Sales* section of the document (on page 12).
2. Apply the **Layout 6** Quick Layout to the chart.
3. Hide the **data labels** for the chart.
4. Save the file as directed by your instructor and close it.

Skill 8.8 Modifying SmartArt

When you add SmartArt to a document, the diagram uses a default style and the default colors pulled from the document's theme. You can modify the look of SmartArt diagrams by changing the style of the diagram as well as selecting from a number of color variations.

To change the style and colors of SmartArt:

1. Select the SmartArt you want to change.

2. Click the **SmartArt Tools Design** tab.

3. In the *SmartArt Styles* gallery, click the **More** button to display the gallery. Click a style to apply to the diagram.

4. Click the **Change Colors** button and select a color variation to apply to the diagram.

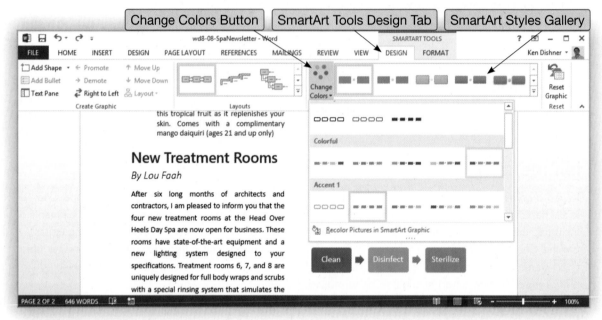

FIGURE WD 8.14

tell me **more**

There are variety of SmartArt styles from which to choose. These styles include a combination of outlines and effects (such as gradients and bevels) that you can apply with a single command.

another **method**

To change the color and style of SmartArt, you can also right-click the diagram and click a button on the Mini toolbar.

let me **try**

Open the student data file **wd8-08-SpaNewsletter** and try this skill on your own:

1. Select the SmartArt diagram on the second page of the newsletter.
2. Apply the **Intense Effect** SmartArt style to the diagram. It is the fifth option in the gallery.
3. Apply the **Colorful Range–Accent Colors 5 to 6** color variation to the diagram.
4. Save the file as directed by your instructor and close it.

Skill 8.9 Applying Artistic Effects to Pictures

Word comes with a number of commands for working with pictures and graphics. These commands allow you to modify pictures using tools that in the past were only available through image editing applications. The **Artistic Effects** command applies a graphic filter to an image. These filters mimic a wide variety of artistic tools, including paint strokes, pencil strokes, watercolors, mosaics, blurs, and glows.

To apply an artistic effect to a picture:

1. Select the image to which you want to apply the artistic effect.
2. Click the **Picture Tools Format** tab.
3. In the *Adjust* group, click the **Artistic Effects** button.
4. Select an option from the gallery to apply it to the picture.

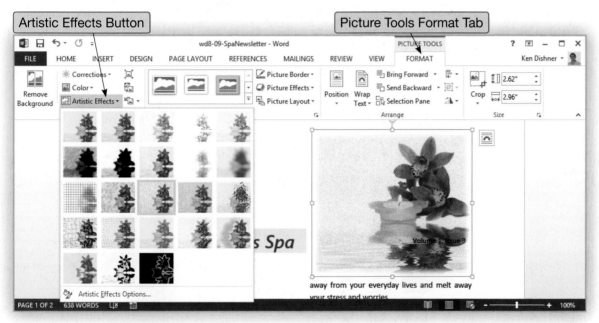

FIGURE WD 8.15

tips & tricks

If you have Live Preview enabled, when you roll your mouse over an option in the gallery, the effect is previewed on the selected image.

let me try

Open the student data file **wd8-09-SpaNewsletter** and try this skill on your own:

1. Select the picture of the flower and candle at the top of the first page.
2. Apply the **Film Grain** artistic effect to the picture (it is the third option in the third row in the *Artistic Effects* gallery).
3. If you will be moving on to the next skill in this chapter, leave the document open to continue working. If not, save the file as directed by your instructor and close it.

Skill 8.10 Correcting Pictures

After you have added a picture to a document, you may find that it does not appear quite the way you want. It may appear too dark or too light, or it could appear slightly blurry. You can correct problems in pictures from the *Picture Tools Format* tab.

To correct a picture:

1. Select the image you want to modify.
2. Click the **Picture Tools Format** tab.
3. In the *Adjust* group, click the **Corrections** button.
4. The gallery displays how the selected image will appear with the correction applied.
5. Select an option from the gallery to make the change.

When you make corrections, you are changing the following properties for a picture:

❱ **Brightness**—Makes the overall picture darker or lighter

❱ **Contrast**—Changes the range of color intensity within the picture. A picture with high contrast will have bolder colors, while a picture with lower contrast will have more muted colors.

❱ **Softness**—Removes hard edges, giving the picture a smoother feel

❱ **Sharpness**—Removes any blurriness, giving the picture a crisper feel

FIGURE WD 8.16

tell me **more**

If the picture you want to change is a drawing, you can adjust the brightness and contrast. If the picture you want to change is a photograph, you can adjust the sharpness of the image in addition to the brightness and contrast.

let me try

If you do not have the data file from the previous skill open, open the student data file **wd8-10-SpaNewsletter** and try this skill on your own:

1. Select the picture of the flower and candle at the top of the first page.
2. Change the picture so it is sharpened by **50%**.
3. Change the picture to have **+20% Brightness** and **−20% Contrast.**
4. If you will be moving on to the next skill in this chapter, leave the document open to continue working. If not, save the file as directed by your instructor and close it.

Skill 8.11 Changing the Color of Pictures

Another graphic effect you can apply to a picture in Word is to recolor the image. When you **recolor** an image, Word takes the image and applies a color overlay. All colors are removed from the image and replaced with shades of one color. The resulting effect is as if you were looking at the image through colored glass.

To color a picture:

1. Select the image you want to color.
2. Click the **Picture Tools Format** tab.
3. In the *Adjust* group, click the **Color** button.
4. The gallery displays how the selected image will appear with the color applied.
5. Select an option from the gallery to apply it to the picture. Point to *More Variations* at the bottom of the gallery to choose from other colors in the document's color theme.

In addition to recoloring a picture, you can change the saturation and color tone of the picture. Adjusting the saturation will change the color intensity of the picture. Adjusting the color tone will give the picture a warmer or cooler appearance by adjusting the picture's temperature.

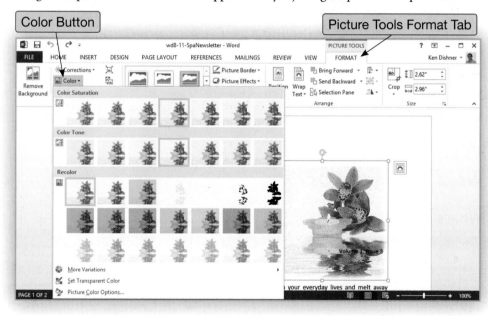

FIGURE WD 8.17

tips & tricks

You can choose to make any color in the picture transparent. Click **Set Transparent Color** at the bottom of the gallery. Click any part of the image that has the color you want to make transparent. Word makes all matching areas of the image transparent.

let me try

If you do not have the data file from the previous skill open, open the student data file **wd8-11-SpaNewsletter** and try this skill on your own:

1. Select the picture of the flower and candle at the top of the first page.
2. Recolor the picture using the **Blue, Accent color 5 Dark** option.
3. If you will be moving on to the next skill in this chapter, leave the document open to continue working. If not, save the file as directed by your instructor and close it.

Skill 8.12 Removing the Background from Pictures

One way to modify a picture is to remove its **background**. When you remove the background from a picture, Word analyzes the picture and calculates which areas are parts of the background. Word then marks the background areas for removal. The resulting effect is as if you had traced the main part of the picture and then erased the background, leaving you with an outline of the picture.

To remove the background from a picture:

1. Select the image from which you want to remove the background.
2. Click the **Picture Tools Format** tab.
3. In the *Adjust* group, click the **Remove Background** button.

FIGURE WD 8.18

4. The *Background Removal* tab displays.
5. Adjust the marked area until the image appears as you want it.
6. Click the **Keep Changes** button to remove the background from the image.

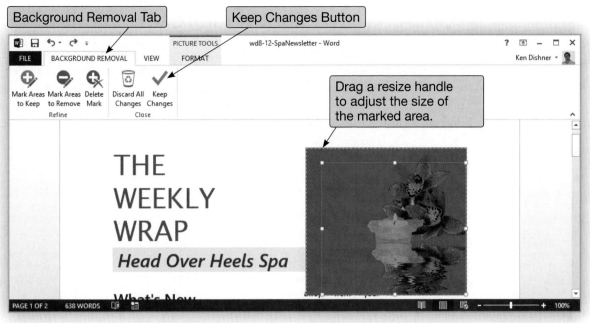

Background Removal Tab

Keep Changes Button

Drag a resize handle to adjust the size of the marked area.

FIGURE WD 8.19

tips & tricks

Click the **Discard All Changes** button to close the *Background Removal* tab and not change the picture.

tell me **more**

You can modify the area marked for removal from the *Refine* group on the *Background Removal* tab:

) **Mark Areas to Keep**—Allows you to draw lines indicating areas not to delete when the background is removed.

) **Mark Areas to Remove**—Allows you to draw lines indicating areas to delete when the background is removed.

) **Delete Mark**—Removes lines you have added marking areas to keep or remove.

another **method**

To accept the changes, you can also:

) Click outside the picture.

) Press **Enter** on the keyboard.

let me **try**

If you do not have the data file from the previous skill open, open the student data file **wd8-12-SpaNewsletter** and try this skill on your own:

1. Select the picture of the flower and candle at the top of the first page.

2. Remove the background from the image.

3. Adjust the area to be kept to include the entire flower. You can do this by dragging the lower right resize handle to the lower right corner of the image and then dragging one of the top resize handles to the top of the image.

4. If you will be moving on to the next skill in this chapter, leave the document open to continue working. If not, save the file as directed by your instructor and close it.

Skill 8.13 Resetting Pictures

If you have made several changes to an image and decide you do not want to keep the changes you made, you could use the *Undo* command to revert the picture to its original state. But what if you have made other changes that you do not want undone? The **Reset Picture** command removes all formatting applied to the picture, reverting the picture to its original state before any formatting was applied.

To reset a picture:

1. Click the **Picture Tools Format** tab.

2. In the *Adjust* group, click the **Reset Picture** button.

3. Any Word formatting you added to the picture is removed.

FIGURE WD 8.20

tips & tricks

Clicking the *Reset Picture* button does not revert the image to the original size. If you want to remove the formatting and change the picture back to the size it was when you first added it to the document, click the arrow next to *Reset Picture* and select **Reset Picture & Size.**

another method

To reset a picture, removing any formatting you added, you can also click the **Reset Picture** button arrow and select **Reset Picture.**

let me try

If you do not have the data file from the previous skill open, open the student data file **wd8-13-SpaNewsletter** and try this skill on your own:

1. Select the picture of the flower and candle at the top of the first page.

2. Use the **Reset Picture** command to remove the formatting that was applied to the picture.

3. If you will be moving on to the next skill in this chapter, leave the document open to continue working. If not, save the file as directed by your instructor and close it.

word 2013   chapter 8 Exploring Advanced Tables, Charts, and Graphics

Skill 8.14 Cropping Graphics

When you add an image to a document, you may only want to show part of the image. You could edit the picture in an image editing application, or you could use the **Crop** tool in Word to trim the picture.

To crop a picture:

1. Select the image you want to crop.

2. Click the **Picture Tools Format** tab.

3. In the *Size* group, click the **Crop** button.

4. Word displays black lines around the edges of the image. These are cropping handles.

5. Point to a cropping handle. When the cursor changes to one of the crop cursors, click and drag toward the center of the image.

6. Press **Enter** to accept the changes.

FIGURE WD 8.21

Notice that the size of the objects in the image does not change. When you crop an image, you are removing part of the image, hiding it from sight. If you want to restore part of an image, use the *Crop* tool to expand the cropped area, and the previously hidden area will be visible. If you know you will not need to restore the image in the future, you can remove the cropped areas of pictures by compressing the images in your document.

another method

To crop an image you can also right-click an image and click the **Crop** button on the Mini toolbar.

let me try

If you do not have the data file from the previous skill open, open the student data file **wd8-14-SpaNewsletter** and try this skill on your own:

1. Select the picture of the flower and candle at the top of the first page.

2. Crop the image from the left side so the empty space to the left of the candle is removed (see Figure WD 8.21).

3. If you will be moving on to the next skill in this chapter, leave the document open to continue working. If not, save the file as directed by your instructor and close it.

Skill 8.15 Aligning Images

When adding images to a document, it is important to place the images so they will have the most impact on the reader. Any graphics that appear in a straight line should be aligned to ensure that they are precisely placed.

To align images:

1. Select the picture or pictures you want to align. Click the **Picture Tools Format** tab.
2. In the *Arrange* group, click the **Align** button and select an option:

   - The **Align Left, Align Center,** and **Align Right** commands align graphics along an invisible vertical line.
   - The **Align Top, Align Middle,** and **Align Bottom** commands align graphics along an invisible horizontal line.

FIGURE WD 8.22

tips & tricks

From the *Align* menu, you can choose what to align your image with. Choose **Align to Page** to align the image with the edges of the page. Choose **Align to Margin** to align the image with the margins you have set. If you have multiple images selected, you can choose **Align Selected Objects** to align the images relative to each other.

tell me **more**

These steps cover aligning images, such as photographs that have been inserted. These steps also apply to formatting drawing objects, and the same commands can be accessed from the *Drawing Tools Format* tab.

let me **try**

If you do not have the data file from the previous skill open, open the student data file **wd8-15-SpaNewsletter** and try this skill on your own:

1. Select the image of the hands on the second page of the newsletter (see Figure WD 8.22).
2. Use the align command to align the image along the right side of the margin.
3. If you will be moving on to the next skill in this chapter, leave the document open to continue working. If not, save the file as directed by your instructor and close it.

Skill 8.16 Grouping Images

When working with images, you may find that you have multiple images that you want to treat as a single image. You can select multiple images and **group** them together, thus turning multiple images into one image that you can easily modify.

To group images:

1. Select the images you want to group as one object.
2. Click the **Picture Tools Format** tab.
3. In the *Arrange* group, click the **Group** button and select **Group.**
4. To ungroup images, click the **Group** button and select **Ungroup.**

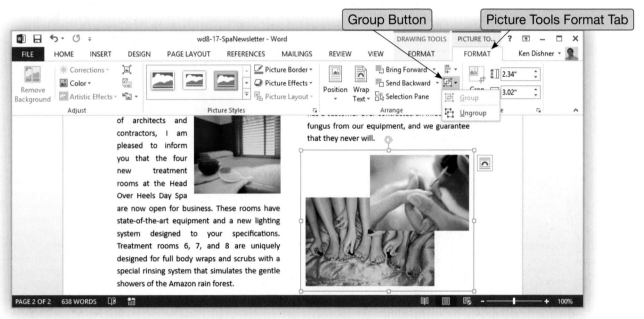

FIGURE WD 8.23

tell me **more**

These steps cover grouping pictures, such as photographs that have been inserted. These steps also apply to formatting drawing objects, and the same commands can be accessed from the *Drawing Tools Format* tab.

another **method**

To group and ungroup images, you can also right-click the selected image or images, point to **Group,** and select an option.

let me **try**

If you do not have the data file from the previous skill open, open the student data file **wd8-16-SpaNewsletter** and try this skill on your own:

1. Select the two images under the *Healthy Hands and Feet* article on page 2 of the newsletter.
2. Group the images so they will be a single object.
3. Ungroup the images.
4. If you will be moving on to the next skill in this chapter, leave the document open to continue working. If not, save the file as directed by your instructor and close it.

Skill 8.17 Formatting a Shape

When you insert a shape to a document, Word applies the default Quick Style for the document's theme to the shape. To adjust the formatting of the shape you can choose a new Quick Style from the *Shapes Styles* gallery.

To apply a Quick Style to a shape:

1. Select the shape you want to change.
2. Click the **Drawing Tools Format** tab.
3. In the *Shape Styles* group, click a Quick Style in the collapsed gallery on the Ribbon.
4. If the Quick Style you want to use does not appear on the Ribbon, click the **More** button to display the gallery and click a Quick Style in the gallery to apply it to the shape.

FIGURE WD 8.24

You can further adjust the look of a shape by changing the following:

❯ **Shape fill**—The color that fills the object. You can choose a solid color from the color palette or fill the color with a gradient or texture.

❯ **Shape outline**—The line that surrounds the shape. You can further adjust the outline of shapes by changing the color, width, and style of the outline.

❯ **Shape effects**—Graphic effects you can apply to shapes including drop shadows, reflections, glows, and bevels.

FIGURE WD 8.25

To further adjust the formatting of a shape:

1. Select the shape you want to change.
2. Click the **Drawing Tools Format** tab.
3. To change the fill of a shape, in the *Shape Styles* group, click the **Shape Fill** button and select an option from the color palette.
4. To change the outline of a shape:
   a. In the *Shape Styles* group, click the **Shape Outline** button.
   b. Select an option from the color palette to change the color of the outline.
   c. Point to **Weight** and select a thickness option for the outline.
   d. Point to **Dashes** and select a dash style for the outline.
5. To apply a shape effect, in the *Shape Styles* group, click the **Shape Effects** button, point to a shape effect, and select an option.

tips & tricks

Point to **Presets** on the *Shape Effects* menu to display a gallery of shape effects that include a combination of drop shadows, reflections, glows, and bevels.

another method

> To change the Quick Style of a shape, you can also right-click the shape and click the **Styles** button on the Mini toolbar.
> To change the fill of a shape, you can also right-click the shape and click the **Fill** button on the Mini toolbar.
> To change the outline of a shape, you can also right-click the shape and click the **Outline** button on the Mini toolbar.

let me try

If you do not have the data file from the previous skill open, open the student data file **wd8-17-SpaNewsletter** and try this skill on your own:

1. Select the blue shape next to the *Four New Services* article on page 1.
2. Apply the **Color Fill–Orange, Accent 2** Quick Style to the shape.
3. Change the shape fill color to **Gold, Accent 4.**
4. Change the shape outline to **1 ½ points** with the **Orange, Accent 2** color.
5. Apply the **Offset Diagonal Bottom Right** drop shadow shape effect (it is the first option in the *Outer* section).
6. If you will be moving on to the next skill in this chapter, leave the document open to continue working. If not, save the file as directed by your instructor and close it.

Skill 8.18 Adding Text to a Shape

One way to bring attention to text in a document is to include it as part of a shape. A shape will draw your audience's focus to whatever text you add to it. When you add a shape to a document, the shape behaves as a text box. All you need to do to add text to the shape is begin typing. You can also go back and add text to shapes that you previously added to a document.

To add text to an existing shape:

1. Select the shape to which you want to add text.

2. Type the text you want to add to the shape.

3. Click outside the shape.

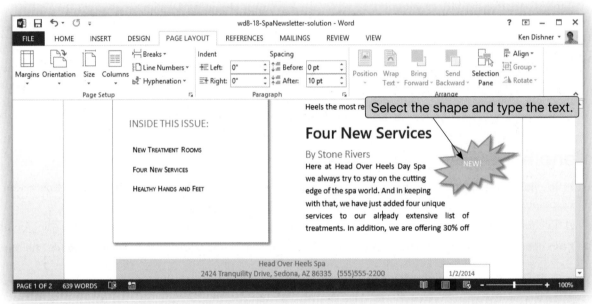

FIGURE WD 8.26

tell me **more**

Just as with any text, you can add complex formatting to the text you add to a shape. You can apply bold, italic, and other character formatting to the shape's text. You can also change the font size and color.

another **method**

To add text to a shape, right-click the shape and select **Add Text.** The cursor appears in the shape ready for you to add your text.

let me **try**

If you do not have the data file from the previous skill open, open the student data file **wd8-18-SpaNewsletter** and try this skill on your own:

1. Select the shape next to the *Four New Services* article on page 1.

2. Add the text **NEW!** to the shape. Click outside the shape when you are done.

3. If you will be moving on to the next skill in this chapter, leave the document open to continue working. If not, save the file as directed by your instructor and close it.

word 2013   chapter 8 Exploring Advanced Tables, Charts, and Graphics

Skill 8.19 Changing Pictures

When you have added a picture to a document, you may find that you want to use a different picture. You could delete the current picture and then insert the new one, or an easier way is to use the **Change Picture** command. When you use the *Change Picture* command, Word replaces the current image with an image you select.

To change a picture:

1. Select the picture you want to change.

2. Click the **Picture Tools Format** tab.

3. In the *Adjust* group, click the **Change Picture** button.

FIGURE WD 8.27

4. In the *Insert Pictures* dialog, click the **Browse** link next to *From a file*.

FIGURE WD 8.28

5. Navigate to the location of the file you want to insert.
6. Click the image to insert and click the **Insert** button.

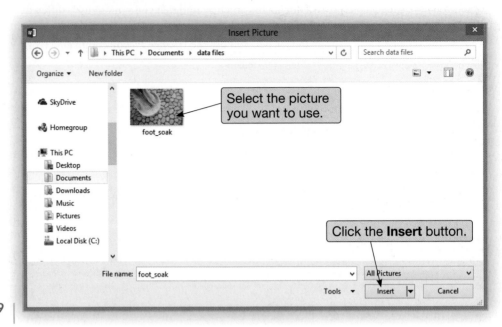

FIGURE WD 8.29

tips & tricks

You can also change out a picture for an online image from Word's Clip Art collection. Type a keyword or keywords in the Office.com *Clip Art* box in the *Insert Pictures* dialog and click the **Search** button. Click a thumbnail in the gallery of results and click the **Insert** button.

tell me **more**

You can choose a picture from a number of locations including your computer's hard drive, the Office.com Clip Art collection, a Bing search on the Internet, or from your SkyDrive account.

another **method**

To change a picture, you can also right-click the picture you want to change and select **Change Picture...** from the shortcut menu.

let me **try**

If you do not have the data file from the previous skill open, open the student data file **wd8-19-SpaNewsletter** and try this skill on your own:

1. Select the picture of the feet on the second page of the newsletter.
2. Select the **Change Picture** command.
3. Browse for a file on your computer.
4. Navigate to the location where you saved the data files for this book.
5. Insert the **foot_soak** picture.
6. If you will be moving on to the next skill in this chapter, leave the document open to continue working. If not, save the file as directed by your instructor and close it.

Skill 8.20 Compressing Pictures

The more images you add to a document, the larger the document's file size will become. Before sending a document to others, a good practice is to reduce the file size as much as possible. One way to reduce the file size of documents is to compress large pictures in the document.

To compress pictures:

1. Select a picture in the document and click the **Picture Tools Format** tab.

FIGURE WD 8.30

2. In the *Adjust* group, click the **Compress Pictures** button.
3. Notice the *Apply only to this picture* and the *Delete cropped areas of pictures* check boxes are selected by default. To compress all the pictures in the document, deselect the **Apply only to this picture** check box.
4. Click **OK** in the *Compress Pictures* dialog.

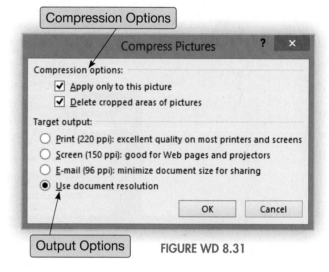

FIGURE WD 8.31

tips & tricks

If the *Delete cropped areas of pictures* check box is selected, all cropped areas of the picture will be removed when you compress the picture. Only check this option if you have cropped images and know you will not need to restore the images in the future.

tell me **more**

The *Target output* allows you to control how much the picture is compressed—the higher the resolution, the less compression of the image. The lower the resolution, the more the image will be compressed, resulting in a smaller file size but potentially lesser quality images.

let me try

If you do not have the data file from the previous skill open, open the student data file **wd8-20-SpaNewsletter** and try this skill on your own:

1. Compress all the pictures in the document. Delete all the cropped areas of the pictures and use the document's resolution.
2. Save the file as directed by your instructor and close it.

Skill 8.21 Inserting a Screenshot

A **screenshot** captures the image on the computer screen (such as an application's interface or a Web page) and creates an image that can then be used just as any other drawing or picture. In the past, you had to use another application to create the screenshot and then insert the image through Word. Now you can use the *Insert Screenshot* command to capture and insert screenshots into documents all from within the Word interface.

To add a screenshot to a document:

1. Open the file or navigate to the Web page you want to take a screenshot of. Do not minimize the window.
2. In your Word document, place the cursor where you want to insert the screenshot.
3. Click the **Insert** tab.
4. In the *Illustrations* group, click the **Screenshot** button.
5. The *Available Windows* section displays a thumbnail image of each of the currently open windows.
6. Click a thumbnail to add the screenshot of that window to the document.

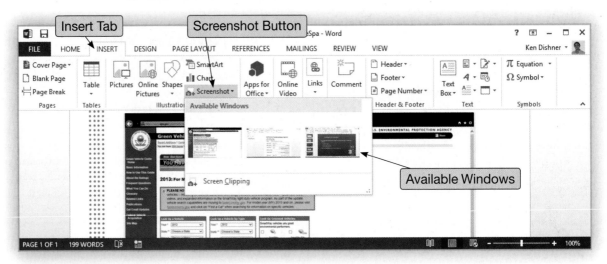

FIGURE WD 8.32

tips & tricks

The *Screenshot* gallery displays thumbnails of all the currently open windows. But what if you want to take a screenshot of only part of a window? You can use the *Screen Clipping* tool take a screenshot of any part of the computer screen.

tell me **more**

If you insert a screenshot from a Web page, Word displays a message box asking if you want to automatically hyperlink the inserted image to the Web site.

let me try

Open the student data file **wd8-21-MobileSpa** and try this skill on your own:

1. Open a browser window and navigate to http://www.epa.gov/greenvehicles
2. Place you cursor in the blank line under the last paragraph.
3. Insert a screenshot of the browser window you opened.
4. Save the file as directed by your instructor and close it.

key terms

Header row
Formulas
Cell range
Cell address
Functions
Border Painter
Quick Table
Plot area
Chart area
Chart title
Legend
Data labels
Axes
Artistic Effects

Brightness
Contrast
Softness
Sharpness
Recolor
Background
Reset Picture
Crop
Group
Shape fill
Shape outline
Shape effects
Change Picture
Screenshot

concepts review

1. A _____ is the first row in a table.

   a. total row

   b. banded row

   c. header row

   d. margin row

2. The _____ feature in Word allows you to quickly apply stylized borders to tables.

   a. Border Painter

   b. Borders and Shading

   c. Format Painter

   d. Outline

3. A formula begins with an equals sign.

   a. True

   b. False

4. Which of the following is an example of a chart element?

   a. Legend

   b. Title

   c. Data label

   d. All of the above

5. Which of the following mimics a wide variety of artistic tools, including paint strokes, pencil strokes, watercolors, mosaics, blurs, and glows?

   a. Color command

   b. Artistic Effects command

   c. Corrections command

   d. All of the above

6. Use the _____ command to trim part of picture, hiding it from view.
   a. Group
   b. Align
   c. Crop
   d. Compress Pictures

7. Which command aligns an image along an invisible horizontal line?
   a. Align Left
   b. Align Center
   c. Align Top
   d. None of the above

8. The _____ command turns multiple objects into a single object.
   a. Group
   b. Merge
   c. Combine
   d. Crop

9. When you compress pictures in a document, you must compress all the pictures in the document.
   a. True
   b. False

10. Use the _____ command to insert an image of another open window on your computer.
    a. Insert Picture
    b. Screenshot
    c. Online Pictures
    d. None of the above

In this project, you will be modifying a customer letter for GreenScapes landscaping company. You will modifying a SmartArt diagram and chart, creating and working with a table, changing the look of the logo, and modifying a shape.

Skills needed to complete this project:

- Modifying SmartArt (Skill 8.8)
- Converting Text to a Table (Skill 8.2)
- Adding Formulas and Functions to Tables (Skill 8.3)
- Adjusting Cell Margins (Skill 8.5)
- Customizing Charts (Skill 8.7)
- Changing the Color of Pictures (Skill 8.11)
- Correcting Pictures (Skill 8.10)
- Aligning Images (Skill 8.15)
- Formatting a Shape (Skill 8.17)
- Adding Text to a Shape (Skill 8.18)

1. Open the start file **WD2013-SkillReview-8-1** and resave the file as:

   `[your initials]WD-SkillReview-8-1`

2. If the document opens in Protected View, click the **Enable Editing** button in the Message Bar at the top of the document so you can modify the document.

3. Modify a SmartArt diagram.

   a. Click the block list SmartArt diagram near the top of the letter.

   b. Click the **SmartArt Tools Design** tab.

   c. In the *SmartArt Styles* group, click the **Subtle Effect** style. It is the third option in the gallery.

   d. In the *SmartArt Styles* group, click the **Change Colors** button and select the **Colored Fill–Accent 6** option. It is the second option in the last row of the gallery.

4. Convert text to a table.

   a. Select the text from *Lawn Care* to *TBD*.

   b. Click the **Insert** tab.

   c. In the *Tables* group, click the **Table** button and select **Convert Text to Table...**

   d. The *Convert Text to Table* dialog opens.

   e. In the *AutoFit behavior* section, select **AutoFit to contents**.

   f. In the *Separate text at* section, click **Tabs**.

   g. Click **OK.**

5. Add a formula to the table.

   a. Place the insertion point in the third column of the fourth row.

   b. If necessary, click the **Table Tools Layout** tab.

   c. In the *Data* group, click the **Formula** button.

   d. In the *Formula box*, type `=SUM(ABOVE)*.85.`

   e. Click **OK.**

   f. You should see *$121.13* per month as the sum.

6. Adjust the margins in the table.

   a. On the *Table Tools Layout* tab, in the *Alignment* group, click the **Cell Margins** button.

   b. In the *Default cell margin* section, click the **Top** up arrow two times so the box reads *0.02"*. Click the **Bottom** up arrow two times so the box reads *0.02"*.

   c. Click **OK.**

7. Customize a chart.

   a. Click an empty area of the chart area to select the chart.

   b. Click the **Chart Tools Design** tab.

   c. In the *Chart Layouts* group, click the **Quick Layout** button and select **Layout 11.**

   d. Click the **Chart Elements** button on the right side of the chart.

   e. Click **Data Labels** to display the values on the chart.

8. Color an image.

   a. Select the **GreenScapes logo** at the top of the page.

   b. Click the **Picture Tools Format** tab.

   c. In the *Adjust* group, click the **Color** button.

   d. Select **Green, Accent color 6 Light.** It is the last option in the last row of the gallery.

9. Adjust the brightness and contrast of an image.

   a. With the logo still selected, on the *Picture Tools Format* tab, in the *Adjust* group, click the **Corrections** button.

   b. Select the **Brightness: +20% Contrast: −40%** option. It is the fourth option in the first row under *Brightness/Contrast.*

10. Align an image.

    a. Select the rounded rectangle shape at the bottom of the page.

    b. Click the **Drawing Tools Format** tab.

    c. In the *Arrange* group, click the **Align** button.

    d. Verify *Align to Margin* is selected and click the **Align Right** option.

11. Format a shape.

    a. With the rounded rectangle still selected, on the *Drawing Tools Format* tab, in the *Shape Styles* group, click the **Shape Fill** button and select **Green, Accent 6.** It is the last option in the first row under *Theme Colors.*

    b. In the *Shape Styles* group, click the **Shape Outline** button and select **Green, Accent 6, Lighter 40%.** It is the last option in the fourth row under *Theme Colors.*

    c. In the *Shape Styles* group, click the **Shape Outline** button again. Point to **Weight** and select **3 pt.**

12. Add text to a shape.

    a. With the rounded rectangle still selected, type **Call us for a free estimate!**

    b. Press (Enter) and type **(702) 555-1045**

    c. Click outside the shape to deselect it.

13. Save and close the document.

In this project, you will be modifying a document about the Tri-State Book Festival. You will be working with images, customizing a chart, and adjusting a table.

Skills needed to complete this project:

- Formatting a Shape (Skill 8.17)
- Adding Text to a Shape (Skill 8.18)
- Customizing Charts (Skill 8.7)
- Aligning Images (Skill 8.15)
- Cropping Graphics (Skill 8.14)
- Defining a Header Row in a Table (Skill 8.1)
- Using Table Border Painter (Skill 8.4)
- Adjusting Cell Margins (Skill 8.5)
- Removing the Background from Pictures (Skill 8.12)
- Resetting Pictures (Skill 8.13)
- Applying Artistic Effects to Pictures (Skill 8.9)
- Correcting Pictures (Skill 8.10)
- Compressing Pictures (Skill 8.20)

1. **Open the start file WD2013-SkillReview-8-2** and resave the file as:

    `[your initials]WD-SkillReview-8-2`

2. If the document opens in Protected View, click the **Enable Editing** button in the Message Bar at the top of the document so you can modify the document.

3. Format a shape.

    a. Select the scroll shape at the top of the document.

    b. Click the **Drawing Tools Format** tab.

    c. In the *Shape Styles* group, click the **Shape Fill** button and select **Gray 50%, Accent 6, Lighter 80%.** It is the last option in the second row under *Theme Colors.*

    d. In the *Shape Styles* group, click the **Shape Outline** button and select **Blue, Accent 3, Darker 50%.** It is the seventh option in the last row under *Theme Colors.*

    e. In the *Shape Styles* group, click the **Shape Outline** button again. Point to **Weight** and select **1 pt.**

4. Add text to a shape.

    a. With the scroll shape still selected, type `October 10-12`

    b. Click outside the shape to deselect it.

5. Customize a chart.

    a. Click an empty area of the chart area to select the chart.

    b. Click the **Chart Tools Design** tab.

    c. In the *Chart Layouts* group, click the **Quick Layout** button and select **Layout 3.**

    d. Click the **Chart Elements** button on the right side of the chart.

    e. Click **Chart Title** to display the values on the chart.

6. Align an image.

    a. Select the picture of the stack of books at the beginning of the document.

    b. Click the **Picture Tools Format** tab.

    c. In the *Arrange* group, click the **Align** button.

    d. Verify *Align to Margin* is selected and click the **Align Left** option.

7. Crop an image.

   a. With the picture of the books still selected, on the *Picture Tools Format* tab, in the *Size* group, click the **Crop** button.

   b. Click and drag the top crop handle down so the picture is cropped right above the open book (see Figure WD 8.33). Click outside the image to accept the cropped image.

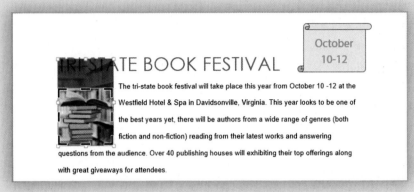

FIGURE WD 8.33

8. Set a header row in a table.

   a. Place the cursor in the first row of the table under the *Tuesday October 11* heading.

   b. Click the **Table Tools Layout** tab.

   c. In the *Data* group, click the **Repeat Header Rows** button.

9. Apply a border using the *Border Painter*.

   a. Place the cursor in the last row of the table under the *Wednesday October 12* heading.

   b. Click the **Table Tools Design** tab.

   c. In the *Borders* group, click the **Border Painter** button.

   d. If necessary, change the line style of the border to the **double line** option (it is the eighth option on the menu).

   e. If necessary, change the line weight to ½ **pt.**

   f. If necessary, change the pen color to **Blue, Accent 3.** It is the seventh color in the first row under *Theme Colors*.

   g. Click and drag across the top border of the last row of the table to apply the border using the *Border Painter*.

10. Adjust cell margins.

    a. With the cursor in the table under the *Wednesday October 12* heading, click the **Table Tools Layout** tab.

    b. In the *Alignment* group, click the **Cell Margins** button.

    c. In the *Default cell margin* section, click the **Bottom** up arrow until the box reads *0.2"*.

    d. Click **OK.**

11. Remove the background from a picture.

    a. Select the picture of the stack of books under the *Authors* heading on page 4.

    b. Click the **Picture Tools Format** tab.

    c. In the *Adjust* group, click the **Remove Background** button.

    d. On the *Background Removal* tab, in the *Close* group, click the **Keep Changes** button.

12. Reset a picture.

    a. Verify the picture of the stack of books is still selected.

    b. On the *Picture Tools Format* tab, in the *Adjust* group, click the **Reset Picture** button.

13. Apply an artistic effect to a picture.

    a. Verify the picture of the stack of books is still selected.

    b. On the *Picture Tools Format* tab, in the *Adjust* group, click the **Artistic Effects** button.

    c. Click the **Plastic Wrap** option. It is the last option in the fourth row of the gallery.

14. Change the brightness and contrast of a picture.

    a. Verify the picture of the stack of books is still selected.

    b. On the *Picture Tools Format* tab, in the *Adjust* group, click the **Corrections** button.

    c. Click the **Brightness: +20% Contrast: −20%** option. It is the fourth option in the second row under *Brightness/Contrast*.

15. Compress the pictures in the document.

    a. Verify the picture of the stack of books is still selected.

    b. On the *Picture Tools Format* tab, in the *Adjust* group, click the **Compress Pictures** button.

    c. In the *Compress Pictures* dialog box, click the **Apply only to this picture** check box (if necessary) to remove the check mark.

    d. Verify the **Delete cropped areas of pictures** check box is selected.

    e. Use the document's resolution and click **OK**.

16. Save and close the document.

challenge yourself 8.3

In this project, you will be modifying the look of an admissions memo. You will be adjusting the look of a photograph as well as converting text into a table and then adding a formula to that table. Skills needed to complete this project:

- Applying Artistic Effects to Pictures (Skill 8.9)
- Resetting Pictures (Skill 8.13)
- Changing the Color of Pictures (Skill 8.11)
- Correcting Pictures (Skill 8.10)
- Removing the Background from Pictures (Skill 8.12)
- Aligning Images (Skill 8.15)
- Converting Text to a Table (Skill 8.2)
- Adding Formulas and Functions to Tables (Skill 8.3)
- Using Table Border Painter (Skill 8.4)
- Adjusting Cell Margins (Skill 8.5)
- Customizing Charts (Skill 8.7)

1. Open the start file **WD2013-ChallengeYourself-8-3** and resave the file as:

    `[your initials]WD-ChallengeYourself-8-3`

2. If the document opens in Protected View, enable editing so you can make changes to the document.

3. Apply an artistic effect and then reset the picture.

    a. Select the picture at the top of the page.

    b. Apply the **Light Screen** artistic effect to the picture (it is the first option in the third row of the gallery).

    c. Use the **Reset Picture** command to return the picture to its original state.

4. Change the look of a picture.

    a. With the picture at the top of the page still selected, color the image using the **Orange, Accent color 2 Dark** option.

    b. Adjust the image to be **20% brighter** and with **40% less contrast.**

    c. Remove the sky from the image using the **Remove Background** command.

    d. Align the image along the right margin of the page.

5. Convert text to a table.

    a. Select the text starting with *Undergraduate Head Count* and ending with *15,772.*

    b. Convert the text to a table. Choose **Auto** for the fixed column width. Choose **Tabs** for separating the text.

6. Merge cells and add a new row.

    a. Merge the first row cells.

    b. Add a row to the bottom of the table.

    c. In the first column of the last row, type `Percent Female`

7. Add a formula to a table.

    a. In the second column of the last row, use a formula to determine the percentage of female student enrolled in the College of Education. *Hint:* You need to divide the 1,678 female students into the SUM(Above) and then multiply by 100. Your formula should look like this **=B4/SUM(Above)*100.** Do not forget to set the number format to **0%.**

    b. Repeat the above step for the third column for the university.

8. Use the *Border Painter*.

    a. Activate the *Border Painter* and change the settings to use the double line border (the eighth option in the gallery), **½ pt** line weight, and **Black, Text 1, Lighter 50%** pen color.

    b. Apply the border to the top border of the last row of the table.

9. Change the top and bottom cell margins on the table to be **0.01".**

10. Modify the chart.

    a. Select the chart and apply the **Layout 3** Quick Layout to the chart.

    b. Display the chart title and the data labels on the chart.

11. Save and close the document.

challenge yourself 8.4

In this project you will be working on the results section of a behavior project report. You will be working with images, converting text to a table, adding formulas to a table, and changing the look of a chart and SmartArt diagram.

Skills needed to complete this project:

- Correcting Pictures (Skill 8.10)
- Cropping Graphics (Skill 8.14)
- Aligning Images (Skill 8.15)

- Grouping Images (Skill 8.16)
- Changing the Color of Pictures (Skill 8.11)
- Compressing Pictures (Skill 8.20)
- Converting Text to a Table (Skill 8.2)
- Defining a Header Row in a Table (Skill 8.1)
- Adding Formulas and Functions to Tables (Skill 8.3)
- Adjusting Cell Margins (Skill 8.5)
- Customizing Charts (Skill 8.7)
- Modifying SmartArt (Skill 8.8)

1. Open the start file **WD2013-ChallengeYourself-8-4** and resave the file as:
   `[your initials]WD-ChallengeYourself-8-4`

2. If the document opens in Protected View, enable editing so you can make changes to the document.

3. Correct and crop and image.
   a. Select the picture showing the back of the students' heads at the top of the document.
   b. Adjust the picture to have **+20% brightness** and **+20% contrast.**
   c. Crop the right side of the picture so the boy in the green shirt does not appear in the picture (see Figure WD 8.34).

FIGURE WD 8.34

4. Group, color, and align images.
   a. Group the two pictures at the top of the first page so they are one object.
   b. Apply the **Sepia color** to the grouped pictures.
   c. Align the grouped pictures to the page's right margin.

5. Compress all the pictures in the document using the document's resolution and permanently remove any cropped areas.

6. Convert text to tables.
   a. In the *Observation Phase* section, select the seven rows of data under the heading and convert the text to a table using the tab character as the separator.
   b. In the *Implementation Phase* section, select the eight rows of data under the heading and convert the text to a table using the tab character as the separator.

7. Repeat the header row for the table in the *Implementation Phase* section.

8. Add formulas to tables.
   a. In the *Observation Phase* section, place the cursor in the second cell in the last row of the table. Add a formula that will sum the values from the cells above the current cell.
   b. Repeat this step for the third cell in the last row.
   c. Place the cursor in the last cell in the last row of the table.
   d. Using a cell reference, enter a formula to determine the percentage of the total number of times the student raised his hand. The result should use the **0%** number format. *Hint:* You need to divide the total of the *Raises Hand* column (cell B7) by SUM(LEFT) and then multiply by 100. Your formula should look like this =**B7/SUM(LEFT)*100**.
   e. Repeat Steps a–c for the table in the *Implementation Phase* section. *Hint:* The cell reference for the total of the *Raises Hand* column in this table is **B8**.

9. Adjust the top cell margin for both tables to be **0.03"**.

10. Apply a Quick Layout to a chart and adjust the display.
    a. Apply the **Layout 2** Quick Layout to the chart in the *Observation Phase* section.
    b. Hide the chart title.
    c. Repeat Steps a–b for the chart in the *Implementation Phase*.
11. Modify a SmartArt diagram.
    a. Select the SmartArt diagram at the end of the document.
    b. Apply the **Moderate Effect** SmartArt style to the diagram.
    c. Apply the **Colorful–Accent Colors** palette to the diagram.
12. Save and close the document.

on your own 8.5

In this project you will be working on a memo from the Trade Winds Food company. You will be adjusting the look of a picture and the display of a chart. You will be converting text to a table and adjusting margins and borders.

Skills needed to complete this project:
- Removing the Background from Pictures (Skill 8.12)
- Applying Artistic Effects to Pictures (Skill 8.9)
- Correcting Pictures (Skill 8.10)
- Changing the Color of Pictures (Skill 8.11)
- Aligning Images (Skill 8.15)
- Resetting Pictures (Skill 8.13)
- Compressing Pictures (Skill 8.20)
- Customizing Charts (Skill 8.7)
- Converting Text to a Table (Skill 8.2)
- Adjusting Cell Margins (Skill 8.5)
- Using Table Border Painter (Skill 8.4)

1. Open the start file **WD2013-OnYourOwn-8-5** and resave the file as:
   `[your initials]WD-OnYourOwn-8-5`
2. If the document opens in Protected View, click the **Enable Editing** button in the Message Bar at the top of the document so you can modify the document.
3. Remove the **aqua** background from the picture at the top of the document.
4. Apply an artistic effect that gives the picture the appearance of having been painted or drawn.
5. Adjust the brightness and contrast on the picture.
6. Change the alignment of the picture to be aligned with the left side of the paragraph text.
7. At any point, use the **Reset Picture** command to reset the picture and then repeat Steps 3–7 to adjust the look of the picture.
8. Compress all the pictures in the document using a resolution of your choice.
9. Apply a Quick Layout of your choice to the chart in the document. Hide and show chart elements as necessary.
10. Convert text into a table starting with *Price* to *$101.50*. Use an appropriate character as the separator for the data.
11. Adjust the cell margins in the table to add spacing to the top and bottom of each cell.
12. Use the *Border Painter* to apply a colorful border to the outside borders of the table.
13. Save and close the document.

WD–332 | www.mhhe.com/simnet

word 2013 chapter 8 Exploring Advanced Tables, Charts, and Graphics

In this project you will be fixing a safety report for the Spring Hills Community. You will be improving the look of a SmartArt diagram, fixing the display of a chart, resetting and formatting a picture, converting text to a table, adding a formula to a table, and adjusting the look of tables.

Skills needed to complete this project:

- Modifying SmartArt (Skill 8.8)
- Customizing Charts (Skill 8.7)
- Resetting Pictures (Skill 8.13)
- Removing the Background from Pictures (Skill 8.12)
- Changing the Color of Pictures (Skill 8.11)
- Correcting Pictures (Skill 8.10)
- Aligning Images (Skill 8.15)
- Cropping Graphics (Skill 8.14)
- Converting Text to a Table (Skill 8.2)
- Adding Formulas and Functions to Tables (Skill 8.3)
- Using Table Border Painter (Skill 8.4)
- Adjusting Cell Margins (Skill 8.5)

1. Open the start file **WD2013-FixIt-8-6** and resave the file as:

    `[your initials]WD-FixIt-8-6`

2. If the document opens in Protected View, click the **Enable Editing** button in the Message Bar at the top of the document so you can modify the document.

3. Change the style of the SmartArt diagram on page 1 to use the **Simple Fill** style.

4. Apply the **Color Fill–Accent 1** colors to the SmartArt diagram.

5. Hide the chart title and the axis title on the chart at the top of page 2.

6. Reset the picture at the top of page 3 to its original settings.

7. Remove the background from the picture so just the officer shows.

8. Color the image using the **Dark Green, Text color 2 Dark** option.

9. Adjust the brightness on the picture to **+20%** and the contrast to **+40%**.

10. Align the picture with the top margin of the page.

11. Crop the picture from the bottom so the picture ends right below the officer's hands.

12. In the *Full-Time Officers* section, select the text from *Employee Name* to *Total*. Be sure to include the space after *Total*. Convert the text to a table using tabs to separate the text.

13. Add a formula to the empty cell in the last row of the table that will add up all the numbers in the cells above.

14. Use the *Border Painter* to apply a double line border using the **Green, Accent 1** pen color and the **½ pt** line weight to the top border of the last row of the table.

15. Repeat Steps 9–11 for the information in the *Part-Time Officers* section.

16. Adjust the top and bottom cell margins for the table in the *Future Safety Modifications* section to be **0.05"**.

17. Save and close the document.

chapter 9

Working with Macros and Finalizing the Document

skills

introduction

This chapter provides you with the skills to share and review documents as well as to automate tasks using macros. First, you will review, comment, and make changes to a document and then accept or reject changes made by reviewers. You will learn about macros, including recording, running, and editing a macro. You will share your documents with others, including exporting as a PDF and sharing documents via OneDrive. Finally, you will learn to ensure that your document is compatible with other versions of Word, how to protect a document by adding a password, and how to mark a document as final.

Skill 9.1 Using Track Changes

The **Track Changes** feature in Word marks any changes made to a document by reviewers. Such changes include any deletions, insertions, or formatting. Word displays some changes directly in the document and other changes in balloons displayed in the margin. When the *Track Changes* feature is active, the *Track Changes* button appears in its active state.

To track changes to a document:

1. Click the **Review** tab.
2. In the *Tracking* group, click the **Track Changes** button.
3. When changes are made to the document, they display either in-line (for insertions and deletions) or in the margin (for comments and formatting changes).
4. Click the **Track Changes** button again to turn the feature off.

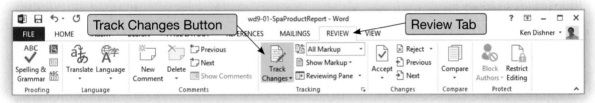

FIGURE WD 9.1

tell me **more**

The **Reviewing pane** displays all the changes in a document. It shows a summary of the revisions in a document, including the number of insertions, deletions, moves, formatting changes, and comments. To display the *Reviewing* pane, click the **Reviewing Pane** button in the *Tracking* group on the *Review* tab.

another **method**

To turn on the *Track Changes* feature, you can also click the bottom half of the **Track Changes** button and select *Track Changes* from the menu.

let me **try**

Open the student data file **wd9-01-SpaProductReport** and try this skill on your own:

1. Turn on the **Track Changes** feature.
2. Select the text *Basic Mani* in the first sentence of the first paragraph in *The Basic Mani* section at the bottom of page 1.
3. Italicize the text.
4. Turn off the **Track Changes** feature.
5. If you will be moving on to the next skill in this chapter, leave the document open to continue working. If not, save the file as directed by your instructor and close it.

Skill 9.2 Adding Comments

A **comment** is a note you add to a document that is not meant to be a part of the document. When you add a comment, it appears in the margin of the document. Comments are useful when you are reviewing a document and want to add messages about changes or errors.

To insert a comment:

1. Place the cursor where you want to add the comment.
2. Click the **Review** tab.
3. In the *Comments* group, click the **New Comment** button.
4. The comment balloon appears in the margin of the document. The cursor appears in the comment.
5. Type your comment.
6. Click outside the balloon to deselect the comment and continue working.

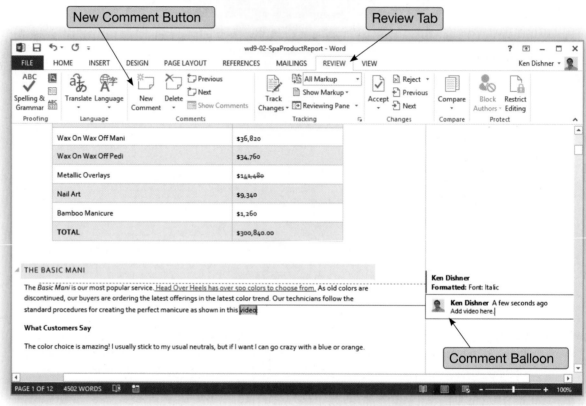

FIGURE WD 9.2

To delete a comment, select the comment you want to delete. In the *Comments* group on the *Review* tab, click the **Delete Comment** button.

If your document has multiple comments, click the **Next Comment** and **Previous Comment** buttons to move between comments in a document.

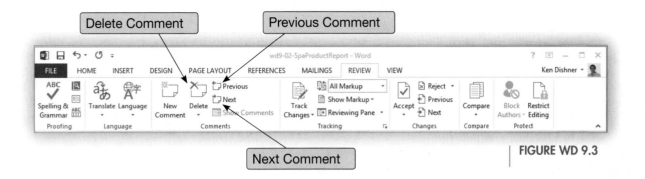

FIGURE WD 9.3

tips & tricks

You can reply to a comment. Click the comment balloon, and then click the icon in the upper right corner of the comment. Another comment appears inside the original comment. Type your reply and click outside.

another method

To add a comment, you can also right-click the area you want to add a comment to and select **New Comment** from the shortcut menu.

let me try

If you do not have the data file from the previous skill open, open the student data file **wd9-02-SpaProductReport** and try this skill on your own:

1. Place the cursor at the end of the first paragraph in *The Basic Mani* section.
2. Add a new comment.
3. Type **Insert video here** and click outside the comment to deselect it.
4. Navigate to the next comment in the document.
5. Navigate back two comments so you are on the first comment in the document.
6. Delete the comment.
7. If you will be moving on to the next skill in this chapter, leave the document open to continue working. If not, save the file as directed by your instructor and close it.

Skill 9.3 Accepting and Rejecting Changes in a Document

When you send a document for review with *Track Changes* on, the document you receive will show all the changes made by reviewers. To finalize the document, you need to accept or reject each change suggested.

There are a number of ways you can accept and reject changes:

Accept or Reject Change and Move to Next—Accepts or rejects the change and automatically moves to the next change in the document.

Accept or Reject Change—Accepts or rejects the change and does not move to the next change in the document.

Accept or Reject All Changes Shown—Accepts or rejects only the currently displayed changes.

Accept or Reject All Changes in Document—Accepts or rejects both visible and hidden changes in the document.

To accept or reject changes in a document:

1. Click the **Review** tab.

2. In the *Changes* group, click the **Next Change** button to navigate to the first change in the document.

3. To accept the selected change and move to the next change, click the **Accept and Move to Next** button.

4. To reject the selected change and move on to the next change, click the **Reject and Move to Next** button.

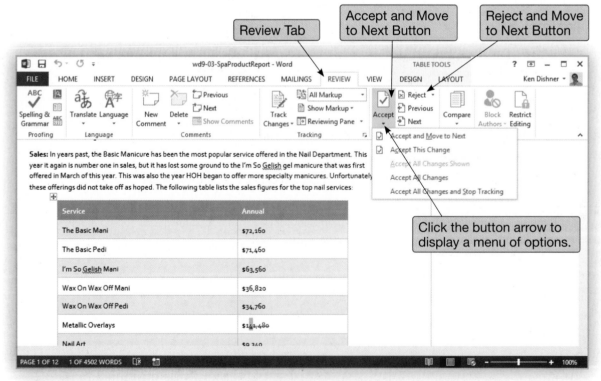

FIGURE WD 9.4

tips & tricks

To navigate between changes in a document, click the **Previous Change** and **Next Change** buttons.

tell me **more**

If you have sent the document to multiple reviewers, each reviewer's comments and changes will be displayed in a specific color. To see which reviewer is represented by which color, in the *Tracking* group, click the **Show Markup** button and point to **Reviewers.** Each reviewer is listed in the menu by color. If a checkmark appears next to the reviewer's name, that reviewer's comments and changes are visible. If there is no check mark next to the reviewer's name, that reviewer's comments and changes have been hidden. Click a reviewer's name on the menu to hide or show comments and changes from that reviewer.

another **method**

❭ To accept a change and automatically move to the next change, you can click the **Accept and Move to Next** button arrow and select the **Accept and Move to Next** command from the menu.

❭ To reject a change and automatically move to the next change, you can click the **Reject and Move to Next** button arrow and select the **Reject and Move to Next** command from the menu.

let me **try**

If you do not have the data file from the previous skill open, open the student data file **wd9-03-SpaProductReport** and try this skill on your own:

1. Place the cursor at the beginning of the document.
2. Move to the first change in the document.
3. The first change found is the insertion of the text **4.** Accept the insertion and move to the next change.
4. The next change found is the deletion of the text, **480.** Reject the deletion and move to the next change.
5. The next change is the formatting on the text **The Basic Mani.** Reject the formatting change and move to the next change.
6. The next change is the insertion of the text **Head Over Heels has over 500 colors to choose from.** Accept the insertion.
7. If you will be moving on to the next skill in this chapter, leave the document open to continue working. If not, save the file as directed by your instructor and close it.

Skill 9.4 Hiding and Showing Changes in a Document

When you activate the *Track Changes* feature in Word, all changes are displayed by default. This includes any comments, deletions, insertions, or formatting changes. Word displays some changes directly in the document and other changes in balloons displayed in the margin. If your document has gone through some major revisions, it may be difficult to differentiate between all the tracked changes. You can show and hide the various changes from the *Tracking* group on the *Review* tab.

To show and hide the different types of tracked changes in a document:

1. Click the **Review** tab.

2. In the *Tracking* group, click the **Show Markup** button.

3. If a change type appears with a checkmark next to it, then it is currently displayed in the document. If a change type appears without a check mark next to it, then it is currently hidden in the document.

4. Click an option on the menu to hide that type of change in the document.

5. Click the same option again to display the hidden changes.

From the *Show Markup* button, you can show or hide comments, ink notations, insertions and deletions, and formatting changes.

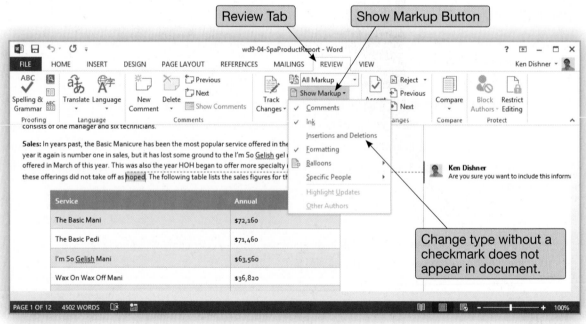

FIGURE WD 9.5

The *Display for Review* menu allows you to display the document in a number of states, including the final version with simplified markup for changes, the final version with all markup for the changes, the final version no markup for changes, and the original document without any markup.

To change the display of tracked changes in a document:

1. On the *Review* tab, in the *Tracking* group, click the **Display for Review** drop-down arrow.
2. Select a display option.

FIGURE WD 9.6

tips & tricks

▸ You can choose to review all changes by all reviewers or specify the type of changes you want to review and by which reviewer. To modify which reviewer's comments are displayed, click the **Show Markup** button in the *Tracking* group, point to **Specific People,** and select the reviewer(s) you want.

▸ You can choose to have all revisions display in balloons or all revisions display in-line. By default revisions are displayed in-line and comments and formatting changes are displayed in balloons. To change the display, click the **Show Markup** button in the *Tracking* group, point to **Balloons,** and select an option.

let me try

If you do not have the data file from the previous skill open, open the student data file **wd9-04-SpaProductReport** and try this skill on your own:

1. Navigate to the top of page 3 where you can see the tracked change.
2. Hide **insertions and deletions** in the document.
3. Show **insertions and deletions** again.
4. Change the track changes option to show **no markup** in the document.
5. Change the track changes option to show **simple markup** in the document.
6. If you will be moving on to the next skill in this chapter, leave the document open to continue working. If not, save the file as directed by your instructor and close it.

Skill 9.5 Locking Track Changes

When you send your documents out for review with *Track Changes* on, you may want to prevent your reviewers from turning the feature off. This will ensure that any changes made by reviewers will be marked and gives you the ability to review and then accept or reject all changes made to the document. Use the **Lock Tracking** feature to add a password to a document that will be required to be entered in order to disable *Track Changes*.

To lock *Track Changes*:

1. Click the **Review** tab.
2. In the *Tracking* group, click the bottom half of the **Track Changes** button.
3. Select **Lock Tracking.**

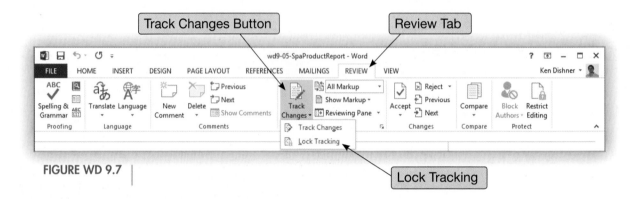

FIGURE WD 9.7

FIGURE WD 9.8

4. In the *Lock Tracking* dialog, type a password that will be required to be entered to unlock *Track Changes* in the *Enter Password (optional)* box.
5. Retype the password in the *Reenter to confirm* box.
6. Click **OK.**

> Type a password that will need to be entered to unlock track changes.

To unlock *Track Changes*:

1. In the *Tracking* group, click the bottom half of the **Track Changes** button again and select **Lock Tracking.**
2. In the *Unlock Tracking* dialog, type the password in the *Password* box.
3. Click **OK.**

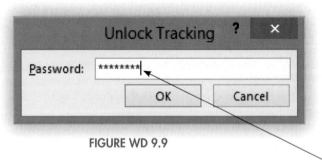

FIGURE WD 9.9

> Type the password to unlock *Track Changes*.

tips & tricks

tell me **more**

Adding a password for locking track changes is not a security feature. It only unlocks the ability to accept and reject changes and turn the *Track Changes* feature off. It does not require a password for your users to open and modify the document. However, any changes made to the document will be tracked.

let me try

If you do not have the data file from the previous skill open, open the student data file **wd9-05-SpaProductReport** and try this skill on your own:

1. Lock tracking in the document so readers will not be able to turn off *Track Changes*.
2. Add the password **HOH1234** as the password.
3. Unlock the tracking in the document using the password **HOH1234** to unlock tracked changes.
4. Save the file as directed by your instructor and close it.

from the perspective of . . .

MEDIA ASSISTANT

In my job, I have to proofread with several other employees. Thanks to *Track Changes,* I can share a file with several colleagues, review their input, and decide which changes I want to accept or reject. I can even add a password preventing others from accidentally turning the feature off. The result is a document worth reading!

Skill 9.6 Combining Documents

If you send your document out to multiple reviewers, you will want to take the changes and combine them into a single document. Word's **Combine** feature allows you to combine two documents into a single document. When you combine two documents, the differences between the two documents are displayed as tracked changes. You can continue combining versions of the same document by different reviewers into the original document. When you are finished, you will have one document with changes from multiple reviewers.

To combine documents into a single document:

1. Click the **Review** tab.

2. In the *Compare* group, click the **Compare** button and select **Combine...** from the menu.

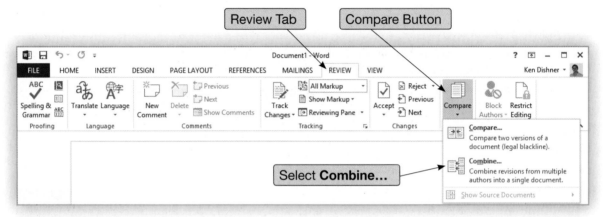

FIGURE WD 9.10

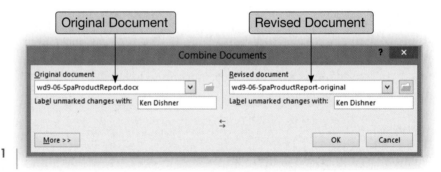

FIGURE WD 9.11

3. In the *Combine Documents* dialog, click the **Original document** drop-down arrow, and select a document.

4. Click the **Revised document** drop-down arrow, and select another version of the document.

5. Click **OK**.

6. Word creates a third document with the differences marked as tracked changes.

7. Repeat these steps to continue combining versions of the same document.

Point to the **Show Source Documents** option on the *Compare* menu to select which documents to display along with the new document—the original, the revised, both versions, or none of the documents.

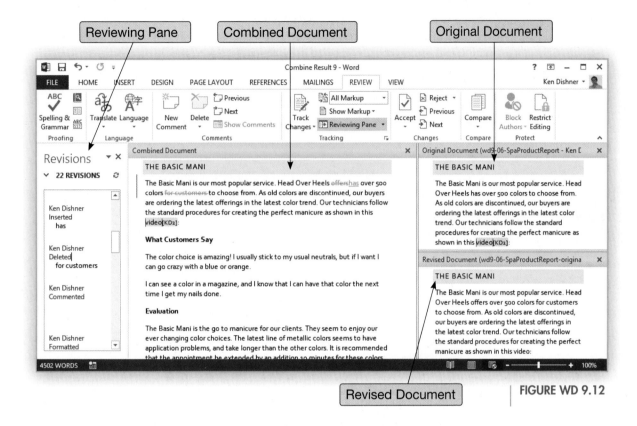

FIGURE WD 9.12

tips & tricks

If the documents you are looking for do not appear in the drop-down list, click the **Open** button next to the drop-down arrow. In the *Open* dialog, navigate to the file you want to use and click **Open.**

let me try

Try this skill on your own:

1. Open the **Combine Documents** dialog.
2. Combine the **wd9-06-SpaProductReport** and the **wd9-06-SpaProductReport-original** documents. If you do not see the documents listed in the drop-down list in the dialog, click the **Open** button and browse to your student data files location.
3. Save the file as directed by your instructor and close it.

Skill 9.7 Comparing Documents

When you are working on multiple versions of the same document, you may not be able to easily find subtle differences between two versions. Word's **Compare** feature allows you to take two documents and create a single document displaying the differences between the two. Word displays the differences as tracked changes which you can then accept or reject to create a final version of the compared documents.

To create a new document that displays the changes between two documents:

1. Click the **Review** tab.
2. In the *Compare* group, click the **Compare** button and select **Compare...** from the menu.

FIGURE WD 9.13

3. In the *Compare Documents* dialog, click the **Original document** drop-down arrow and select a document.
4. Click the **Revised document** drop-down arrow and select another version of the document.
5. Click **OK.**

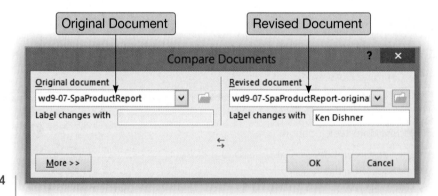

FIGURE WD 9.14

6. Word creates a third document with the differences marked as tracked changes.
7. Accept or reject any changes and save the document.

Point to the **Show Source Documents** option on the *Compare* menu to select which documents to display along with the new document—the original, the revised, both versions, or none of the documents.

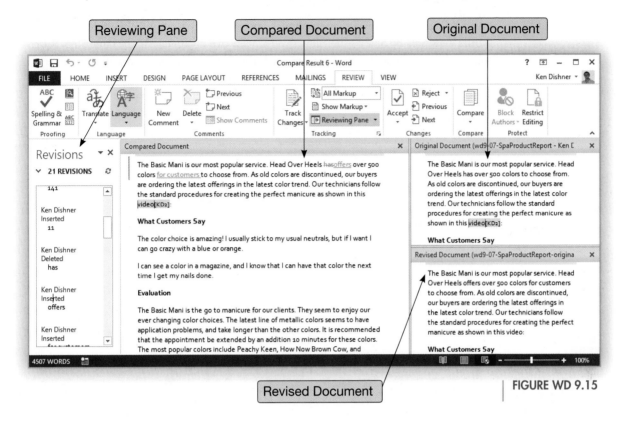

FIGURE WD 9.15

tips & tricks

If the documents you are looking for do not appear in the drop-down list, click the **Open** button next to the drop-down arrow. In the *Open* dialog, navigate to the file you want to use and click **Open.**

tell me **more**

The *Compare* feature is also referred to as *legal blackline*. Use this feature if you want to compare two documents and display the changes between them in a third document. When you compare documents, you are doing just that, comparing the documents. You are not changing the documents themselves.

let me **try**

Try this skill on your own:

1. Open the **Compare Documents** dialog.
2. Compare the **wd9-07-SpaProductReport** document with the **wd9-07-SpaProductReport-original** document. If you do not see the documents listed in the drop-down list in the dialog, click the **Open** button and browse to your student data files location.
3. Save the file as directed by your instructor and close it.

Skill 9.8 Viewing Documents Side by Side

If you have two documents that are similar, you may want to compare them to each other. Word's **View Side by Side** feature allows you to view two documents at the same time. When you view the documents, the **Synchronous Scrolling** feature is on by default. This feature allows you to scroll both documents at once. If you scroll the active document, the other document will scroll at the same time, allowing you to carefully compare documents.

To view two documents side by side:

1. Open the documents you want to view side by side and click the **View** tab.
2. In the *Window* group, click the **View Side by Side** button.
3. The two documents are displayed next to each other. Scroll the active window to scroll both documents at once.
4. Click the **Synchronous Scrolling** button to turn the feature off and scroll each document separately.
5. Click the **View Side by Side** button again to turn this feature off.

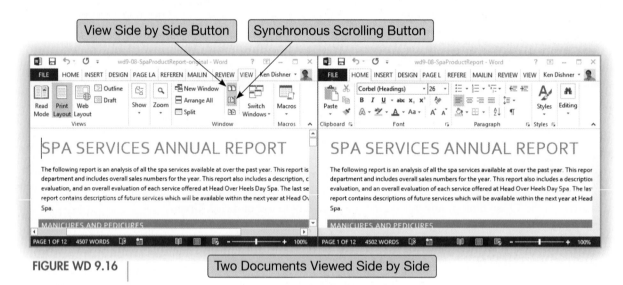

FIGURE WD 9.16 | Two Documents Viewed Side by Side

tips & tricks

When you click the *View Side by Side* button, both documents may not display equally on-screen. Click the **Reset Window Position** button to reset the windows so they share the screen equally.

tell me **more**

If you have more than two documents open, the *Compare Side by Side* dialog will open when you click the **View Side by Side** button. Select a document in the dialog to compare with the current document and click **OK.**

let me try

Open the student data file **wd9-08-SpaProductReport** and try this skill on your own:

1. Open the **wd9-08-SpaProductReport-original** file.
2. View the two open documents side by side.
3. Turn off the **synchronous scrolling** feature.
4. Close both documents.

word 2013   chapter 9 Working with Macros and Finalizing the Document

Skill 9.9 Recording a Macro

A **macro** is a custom set of programming commands written in the **Visual Basic for Applications (VBA)** language. Macros are often used to simplify repetitive tasks, saving you time and effort. Instead of performing the same set of actions over and over, you can just run the macro.

There are two ways to create a macro. If you are familiar with the VBA programming language, you can open the Visual Basic Editor and write the programming code to instruct Word to perform each task in the macro. The easier way to create a macro is to record it. When you record a macro, you complete all the actions you want the macro to perform, and Word converts your keystrokes and mouse clicks to VBA code.

To record a macro:

1. On the *View* tab, in the *Macros* group, click the **Macros** button arrow, and select **Record Macro.**

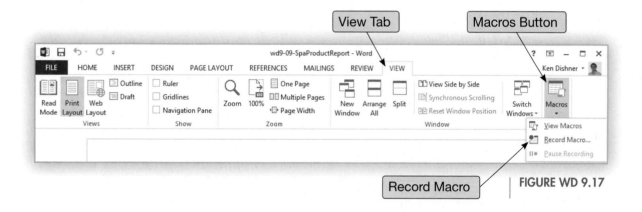

View Tab   Macros Button

Record Macro   **FIGURE WD 9.17**

Macro Name   Keyboard Button

2. In the *Record Macro* dialog, enter a name for the macro in the *Macro name* box.

3. Click the **Store macro in** drop-down arrow and select where to store the macro. In the current document or a template.

4. In the *Description* box, enter a description of the tasks the macro will perform and the circumstances under which the macro should be used.

5. Click the **Keyboard** button to create a keyboard shortcut for the macro.

Description

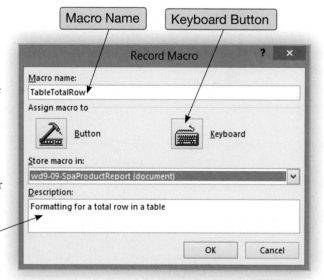

FIGURE WD 9.18

6. In the *Customize Keyboard* dialog, type the keystroke combination for the macro in the *Press new shortcut key* box.

7. Click **Assign** to assign the keyboard shortcut.

8. Click **Close** to begin recording the macro.

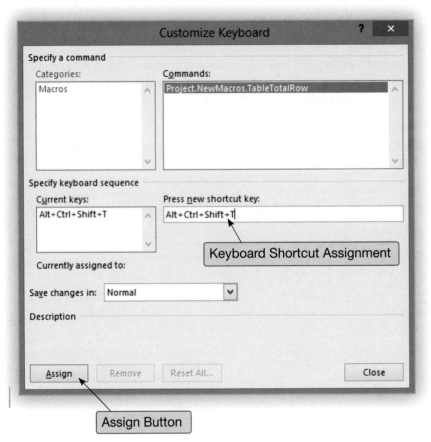

FIGURE WD 9.19

9. The cursor changes to an image of a cassette with an arrow. Word is now recording your typing and mouse clicks to create the macro. Perform all the actions you want the macro to perform. If you make minor mistakes, you can correct them in the VBA code later.

10. When you are finished, click the **Macros** button arrow again and select **Stop Recording.**

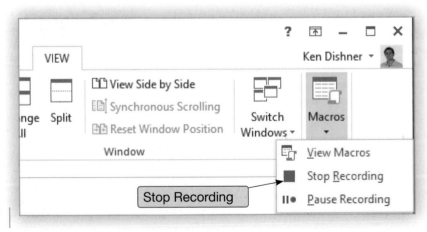

FIGURE WD 9.20

Macros can only be saved in **macro-enabled documents.** If you record a macro in a regular document, when you close the file, Word will display a message stating that the document contains a VB project that cannot be saved in a macro-free document. To save the macro with the document:

1. Click **No** in the message box.
2. The *Save As* dialog opens. Expand the **Save as type** list and select **Word Macro-Enabled Document (*.docm).**
3. Click **Save.**

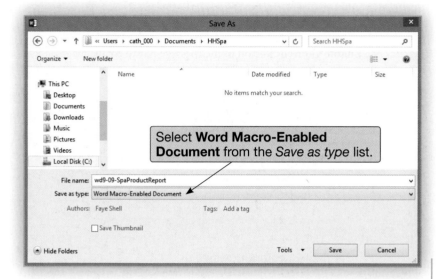

Select **Word Macro-Enabled Document** from the *Save as type* list.

FIGURE WD 9.21

tips & tricks

You can also assign a macro to a button. In the *Record Macro* dialog, click the **Button** button to open the *Word Options* dialog. From here you can assign a button to the Quick Access toolbar that will run the macro when clicked.

tell me **more**

Many keyboard shortcuts are assigned to common Word commands. When you enter a key combination in the *Customize Keyboard* dialog, Word displays *Unassigned* if the key combination is not currently assigned to a command.

let me try

Open the student data file **wd9-09-SpaProductReport** and try this skill on your own:

1. Select the last row in the table in the *Manicures and Pedicures* section.
2. Open the **Record Macro** dialog.
3. Name the macro `TableTotalRow` and store the macro in the current document.
4. Add the description `Formatting for a total row in a table` and open the **Customize Keyboard** dialog.
5. Assign **Alt + Ctrl + Shift + T** as the shortcut key and close the dialog to begin recording the macro.
6. On the *Home* tab, in the *Font* group, click the dialog launcher to open the **Font** dialog. Apply the **Bold Italic** font style to the text.
7. In the *Borders* group, click the **Borders** button arrow and select **Borders and Shading...** to open the *Borders and Shading* dialog.
8. Apply a top border to the row using the **double line** style, **Blue-Gray, Text 2** color (the fourth option in the first row under *Theme Colors*), and **3/4 pt** width.
9. Stop recording the macro.
10. Save the file as a macro-enabled document with the name **wd9-09-SpaProductReport-solution.docm.**
11. If you will be moving on to the next skill in this chapter, leave the document open to continue working. If not, save the file as directed by your instructor and close it.

Skill 9.10 Running a Macro

Macros are only available in macro-enabled documents. A document that can include macros has the file extension **.docm** (macro-enabled templates use the file extension **.dotm**). The document file icon also includes a special icon that looks like this 📄.

When you open a document that contains macros, the Message Bar appears below the Ribbon with the security warning that macros have been disabled. You must click the **Enable Content** button before running a macro.

To run a macro:

1. If necessary, click the **Enable Content** button in the Message Bar to enable macros in the current document.

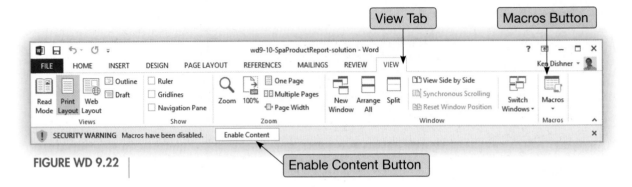

FIGURE WD 9.22

2. On the *View* tab, in the *Macros* group, click the top half of the **Macros** button to open the *Macro* dialog.

3. In the *Macro* dialog, click the name of the macro you want to run. Notice that a description of the purpose of the macro appears near the bottom of the dialog.

4. Click the **Run** button.

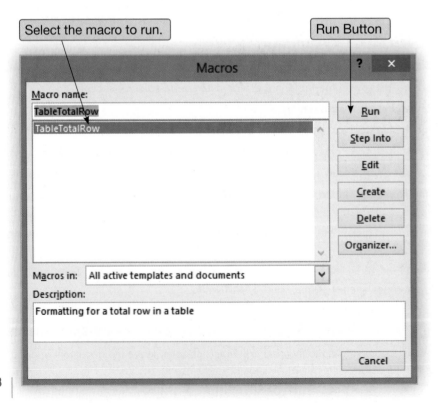

FIGURE WD 9.23

word 2013   chapter 9 Working with Macros and Finalizing the Document

tips & tricks

You can run a macro stored in any active template or open document, not just the document you are working on. By default, the *Macro* dialog displays available macros from all active templates and open documents. When the macro is from another document, the document name will precede the macro name in the *Macro* dialog. To see only the macros contained within a specific document, either expand the *Macros in* list and select the document file name from the list or select **This document** to see only macros in the current document.

tell me **more**

When you run a macro, Word repeats the actions completed when the macro was recorded. This may or may not have the result you intended. For example, if you clicked the **Bold** button to bold text when recording the macro, the macro will repeat the action of clicking the **Bold** button. However, clicking the **Bold** button does not apply formatting but rather toggles the bold character effect on and off. If your text already included bold formatting, running the macro will remove the bold formatting, not apply it to the text.

another **method**

To open the *Macros* dialog, you can also click the **Macros** button arrow and then click **View Macros.**

let me **try**

If you do not have the data file from the previous skill open, open the student data file **wd9-10-SpaProductReport.docm** and try this skill on your own:

1. If necessary, enable the macros in the document.
2. Navigate to the **Massage Services** section and select the last row in the table.
3. Open the **Macros** dialog.
4. Run the **TableTotalRow** macro.
5. If you will be moving on to the next skill in this chapter, leave the document open to continue working. If not, save the file as directed by your instructor and close it.

Skill 9.11 Editing a Macro Using VBA

If you need to make a simple change to a macro, there is no need to rerecord it. Instead, you can edit the underlying VBA code in the **Visual Basic Editor (VBE)**. You do not need to be a programming expert to work in the VBE, but there are a few basics you should know first.

> The Visual Basic Editor is a separate program that runs in its own window.

> Each Word file has its own set of VBA code called a project. Projects are listed in the VBE **Project Explorer** window.

> Projects are made up of **modules** and **objects** that contain groups of code called **procedures**. Procedures in objects are intended for use in that object only. Procedures in modules are usually available to any open Word document. The code for each macro is stored in its own procedure within a module (not an object). A single module may contain the procedures for multiple macros.

> Procedures that perform actions but do not return a value are called subroutines. The code for a subroutine procedure begins with the word *Sub* followed by the name of procedure (or macro) and a set of empty parentheses:

```
Sub TableTotalRow()
```

> Every programming instruction in a procedure begins on a new line. This makes it easy to find the specific instruction you want to edit.

> The last line in a subroutine tells Word that the procedure is finished and to stop executing code:

```
End Sub
```

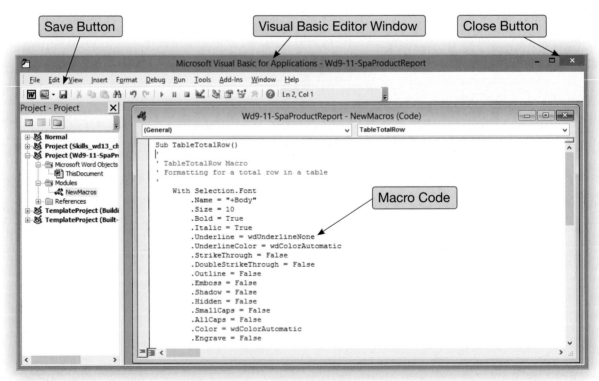

FIGURE WD 9.24

To edit a macro:

1. On the *View* tab, in the *Macros* group, click the top half of the **Macros** button to open the *Macro* dialog.

2. Select the macro you want to edit and then click the **Edit** button.

3. The Visual Basic Editor opens in a new window with the macro code displayed in the code window. Make the changes you want in the code.

4. When you are finished with your changes, click the **Save** button in the VBE toolbar, and then close the VBE window and return to Word.

FIGURE WD 9.25

tips & tricks

To delete a macro, select the macro you want to delete and click the **Delete** button in the *Macros* dialog.

tell me **more**

The *Properties* window in the Visual Basic Editor lists the properties for the selected object or module. You can close the *Properties* window by clicking the **X** next to the *Properties* window title.

let me try

If you do not have the data file from the previous skill open, open the student data file **wd9-11-SpaProductReport.docm** and try this skill on your own:

1. If necessary, enable the macros in the document.
2. Open the **Macros** dialog.
3. Edit the **TableTotalRow** macro.
4. The text should not be italicized. Under *With Selection.Font* find the line *.Italic = True.* Change **True** to **False.**
5. Save the macro and close the Visual Basic Editor window.
6. Select the total row in the table in the *Manicures and Pedicures* section.
7. Run the **TableTotalRow** macro.
8. Run the macro for the total row in the table in each of the following sections: *Massage Services, Facials,* and *Wraps and Full-Body Treatments.*
9. Save the file as directed by your instructor and close it.

Skill 9.12 Exporting a Document as a PDF

If you want to send a document out for others to read and print, but are not sure if your readers are able to open Word documents, you should send it as a PDF. **PDF** stands for *portable document file,* which is Adobe's custom format for displaying forms and documents in a Web browser. When you save a file in PDF format, all your formatting (including fonts, images, and styles) is preserved. PDF files can be read by any computer with Adobe Reader installed, but they cannot be changed by those reading the file. So only use a PDF when you need to send a copy of the file to someone for reading purposes, not editing purposes.

To save a document as a PDF:

1. Click the **File** tab.
2. Click **Export.**
3. Under *Export,* verify *Create PDF/XPS Document* is selected.
4. Under *Create a PDF/XPS Document,* click the **Create PDF/XPS** button.

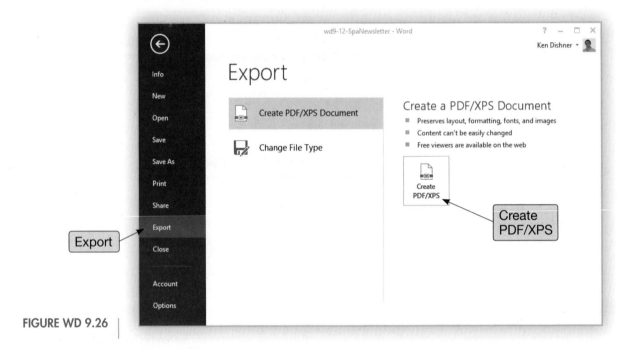

FIGURE WD 9.26

5. In the *Publish as PDF or XPS* dialog, navigate to where you want to save the file.
6. Click in the *File name* box and type a file name.
7. Verify the *Open file after publishing* check box is selected if you want to open the file in Adobe Reader.
8. Click the **Publish** button.
9. Word saves the file and opens it in Adobe Reader.

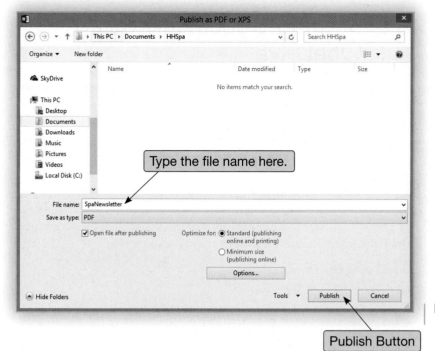

FIGURE WD 9.27

An **XPS (XML Paper Specification)** file is another file format that preserves the formatting of the document and is easily readable but not easily editable. XPS files can be opened with Microsoft's XPS Viewer, which comes installed with Windows Vista, Windows 7, and Windows 8.

tips & tricks

You can also send a document through email as a PDF file:

1. In Backstage view, click **Share.**
2. Select **Email** and click the **Send as PDF** button.
3. Your default email program opens with the subject line filled in and the document in PDF format attached.

tell me **more**

In order to read PDF files, your readers must have the Adobe Reader program installed. This program can be downloaded for free from Adobe's site:

1. Open your browser and navigate to http://get.adobe.com/reader/.
2. Click the **Install Now** button.
3. Follow the instructions for installing the program.

let me try

Open the student data file **wd9-12-SpaNewsletter** and try this skill on your own:

1. Open the **Publish as PDF or XPS** dialog.
2. Name the new file **OnlineSpaNewsletter**.
3. Ensure the file will open after publishing. If you do not have Adobe Reader installed on your computer, skip this step.
4. Save the file as directed by your instructor and close both the PDF and the original Word document.

skill 9.12   Exporting a Document as a PDF

Skill 9.13 Sharing Documents Using OneDrive

One of the benefits of saving files to your **OneDrive** is the ability to share the documents with others. When you share a document through OneDrive, multiple people can work on the document at the same time and all the changes are made to a single document. When people work on a document shared through OneDrive, Word locks any section of the document currently being worked on. This prevents overlapping changes when multiple people are working on the same document.

The first step in sharing a document using OneDrive is to save the document to your OneDrive folder. To learn how to save a document to a OneDrive account, see *Saving Files to OneDrive* in the *Essential Skills for Office 2013* chapter of this book. Once the document is saved to your OneDrive, you can share it with others from Backstage view.

To share a document using OneDrive:

1. Click the **File** tab and select **Share.**
2. Verify the *Invite People* option is selected.
3. If the file has already been saved to your OneDrive you should see a screen similar to Figure WD 9.28.
4. Type the e-mail address of the person you want to share the document with in the *Type name or e-mail addresses* box.
5. Click the drop-down arrow to the left of the box and select whether the recipient(s) can edit or only view the document.
6. Click in the message box below and type a message to the recipient(s).
7. Click the **Share** button.

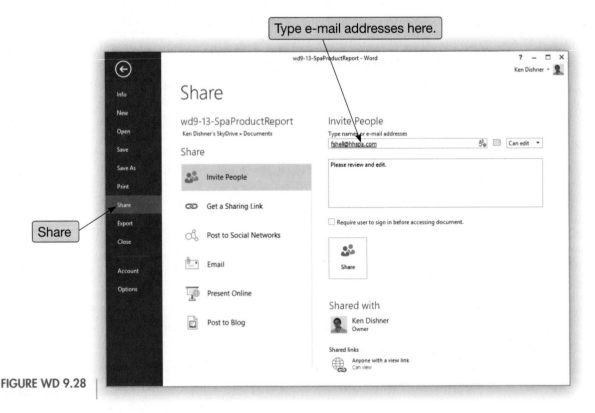

FIGURE WD 9.28

tips & tricks

❱ To share the document with more than one person, enter the e-mail addresses for each recipient separated by a comma.

❱ Click the drop-down menu to the right of the *Type name or e-mail addresses* box to set permissions for the shared document. If you only want others to be able to view the document and not make changes, select **Can View.** If you want others to be able to make changes, select **Can Edit.**

tell me **more**

There are a number of other ways you can share a document from the *Share* page in Backstage view:

Get a Sharing Link—Creates a link on your OneDrive that others can access to either view or edit the document.

Post to Social Networks—Allows you to share documents on social network sites connected through your Microsoft account.

Present Online—Creates a link for you to share with others. The link displays your online presentation as you are giving it. You can also give viewers the ability to download your document.

Publishing to Blog—Allows you to publish a document to a blog site. Word supports the following blog sites: SharePoint Blog, WordPress, Blogger, Windows Live Spaces, Community Server, and TypePad.

let me **try**

Open the student data file **wd9-13-SpaProductReport** and try this skill on your own:

NOTE: You will need a OneDrive account to complete this exercise. In addition, if you are using this in class or in your school's computer lab, check with your instructor before completing this exercise.

1. Save the file to the *Documents* folder on your OneDrive.
2. Open Backstage view and share the document from your OneDrive.
3. Share the document with fshell@hhspa.com and include the message `Please review and edit.`
4. Save the file as directed by your instructor and close it.

Skill 9.14 Creating a Template

A **template** is a document with predefined settings that you can use as a pattern to create a new file of your own. Word comes with a number of built-in templates that you can use to create documents, or you can create your own templates and save them to use to create other documents.

To create a template, create a document with the information for the framework of the template. Your template file should include document property fields and sample content, as well as named styles for formatting parts of the document. Once you have created the template, you will need to save it for future use.

To save a template:

1. Click the **File** tab.
2. Click **Save As.**
3. On the left side of the page, click **Computer** to save the file to a local drive.
4. Word displays a list of recent folders. Since you will be saving the document as a template, click the **Browse** button to open the *Save As* dialog.
5. Click the **Save as type** arrow and select **Word Template.**
6. Notice Word automatically navigates to the *Custom Office Templates* folder.
7. Click in the *File name* box and type a file name for the template.
8. Click the **Save** button.

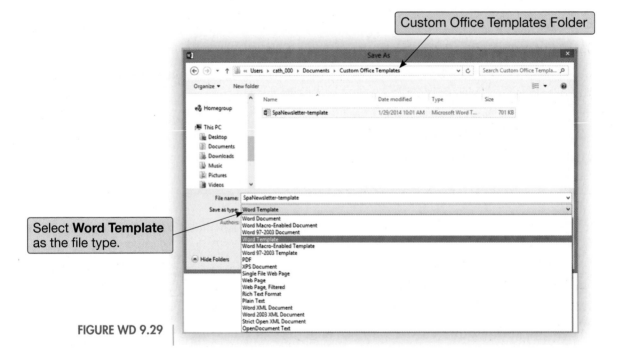

Custom Office Templates Folder

Select **Word Template** as the file type.

FIGURE WD 9.29

To create a new document based on the template you created:

1. Click the **File** tab to open Backstage view.

2. Click **New.** Word displays a page of featured templates. Click **Personal** next to *Featured* to display the templates you have saved to your computer.

3. Click a template thumbnail to create a new document based on the template you saved.

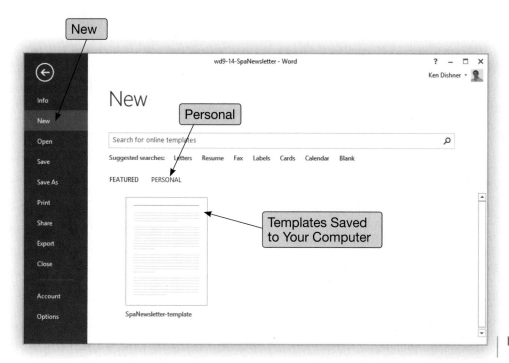

FIGURE WD 9.30

tips & tricks

When you save a template to the default template location, the template will only be available locally on your computer. If you want other people to be able to use the template, you should save the template in a location that is accessible to others, such as your OneDrive.

let me try

Open the student data file **wd14-SpaNewsletter** and try this skill on your own:

1. Open the **Save As** dialog.

2. Save the file as **Word Template** in the *Custom Office Templates* folder. Name the file `SpaNewsletter-template`.

3. Create a new document from the **SpaNewsletter-template** template.

4. Save the file as directed by your instructor and close it.

Skill 9.15 Restricting Editing in a Document

When you share a document with others, they will have the ability to modify your document unless you add editing restrictions to the document. When you add editing restrictions, you limit how others can modify your documents. In the **Restrict Editing task pane,** you can select from four types of editing restrictions:

⟩ **Track Changes**—Forces *Track Changes* on and only allows readers to make changes that are tracked.

⟩ **Comments**—Allows readers to enter comments and not make changes to the document.

⟩ **Filling in forms**—Allows readers to fill in form objects in a document.

⟩ **No changes (read only)**—Restricts readers to viewing the document and not making any changes.

To restrict editing in a document:

1. Click the **File** tab.

2. The *Info* section in Backstage view opens automatically. Click the **Protect Document** button and select **Restrict Editing.**

3. The *Restrict Editing* task pane displays.

FIGURE WD 9.31

4. Under *Formatting Restrictions,* click the **Limit formatting to a select of styles** check box to limit the styles in the document that can be modified and used.

5. Under *Editing Restrictions,* click the **Allow only this type of editing in this document** check box, click the drop-down list, and select an option.

6. Click the **Yes, Start Enforcing Protection** button.

7. The *Restrict Editing* dialog opens.

8. Enter a password that readers will need to enter to remove the editing restrictions in the *Enter new password (optional)* box. Retype the password in the *Reenter password to confirm* box.

9. Click **OK** to begin restricting the editing in the document.

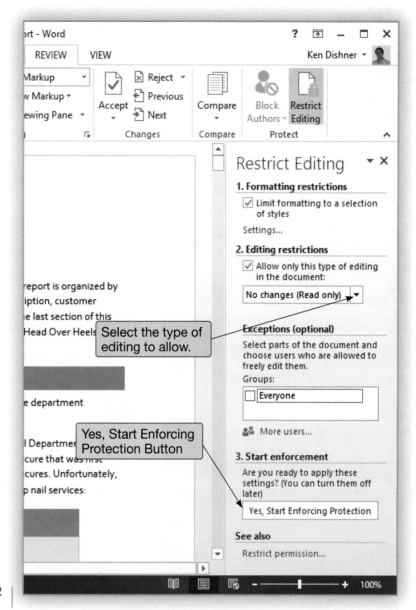

FIGURE WD 9.32

tips & tricks

You can set part of a document to be editable while enforcing editing restrictions in the rest of the document. Select the part of the document you want others to be able to edit. In the *Exceptions* section of the *Restrict Editing* task pane, select the users you want to be able to edit the selected section.

another method

To display the *Restrict Editing* task pane, you can also:
1. Click the **Review** tab.
2. In the *Protect* group, click the **Restrict Editing** button.

let me try

Open the student data file **wd9-15-SpaProductReport** and try this skill on your own:
1. Display the **Restrict Editing** task pane.
2. Limit the formatting in the document to a selection of styles.
3. Restrict the editing so only comments can be added to the document.
4. Start enforcing the protection.
5. Require the password **hhspa135** be entered to turn off editing restrictions and begin protecting the document.
6. Save the file as directed by your instructor and close it.

Skill 9.16 Encrypting a Document with a Password

When you post a document on a network, you make it available to everyone who has access to that network. You may find that you want to distribute a document to a limited group of people. One way to control who can and cannot view your document is to assign a **password** to the document and then share the password with only those people you want to have access to the document.

To add a password to a document:

1. Click the **File** tab.
2. The *Info* section in Backstage view opens automatically. Click the **Protect Document** button and select **Encrypt with Password.**

FIGURE WD 9.33

FIGURE WD 9.34

3. In the *Encrypt Document* dialog, type a password in the **Password** box. Click **OK.**
4. Type the password again in the **Reenter password** box. Click **OK.**

Passwords can contain numbers, symbols, and spaces, as well as letters. Passwords are case-sensitive, so remember to write down the password exactly as you entered it.

tips & tricks

❯ When you create a password, be sure to write it down. If you encrypt your document, you will not be able to open it without first typing in the password.

❯ To remove a password, open the *Encrypt Document* dialog, delete the password, and click **OK.**

tell me **more**

When a password has been assigned to a document, a message appears next to the *Protect Document* button, indicating that a password is required to open the document.

let me try

Open the student data file **wd9-16-SpaProductReport** and try this skill on your own:

1. Encrypt the document with a password.
2. Use **hhspa135** as the password for the document.
3. Save the file as directed by your instructor and close it.

from the perspective of . . .

MARKETING MANAGER

So many times I have sent marketing materials out for review, only to find out people didn't follow my instructions for what I needed. I've heard some people refer to me as a control freak, but I just need things done a certain way to keep track of all the changes and suggestions. To help with that, I restrict the documents I send out to only allow changes that are tracked or comments. That way I know I can find every change made by others. I also share my documents through my OneDrive account so only one person can work on a part of the document at a time. For really sensitive material, I add a password to the document and only share it with the people I trust. And if I only want people to be able to read the document and not edit it, I just publish it as a PDF and send that. Others may view this as constraining, but managing how others interact with the documents I share has saved my sanity on more than one occasion!

Skill 9.17 Inspecting Your Document

When you send a document to business clients or colleagues, you most likely do not want to include any personal information in the document. Other data you may want to remove before sharing a document include comments, revisions, hidden text, and custom XML. The **Inspect Document** command in Word allows you to check your document for hidden data and other personal information before you finish the document and send it to others.

To inspect your document for hidden data or personal information:

1. Click the **File** tab.
2. The *Info* section in Backstage view opens automatically. Click the **Check for Issues** button and select **Inspect Document.**

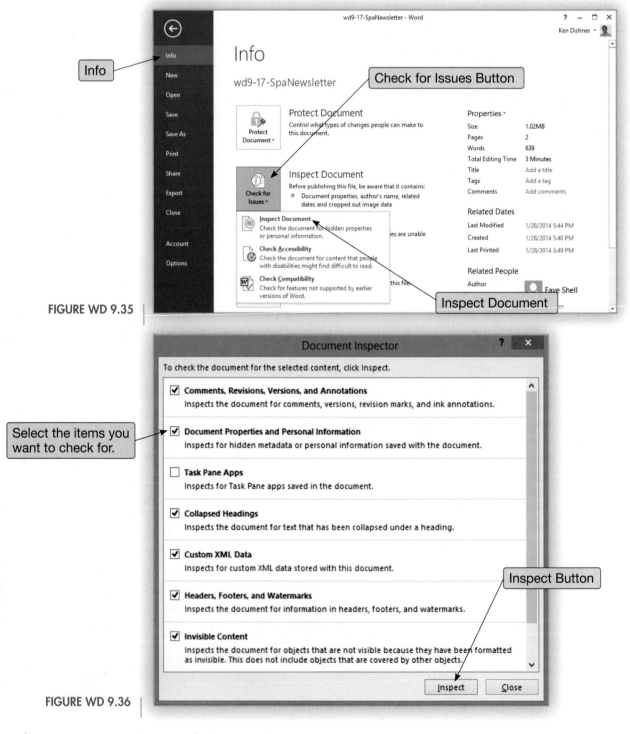

FIGURE WD 9.35

FIGURE WD 9.36

word 2013   chapter 9 Working with Macros and Finalizing the Document

3. In the *Document Inspector* dialog, select the items you want to check.

4. Click the **Inspect** button.

5. Click the **Remove All** button next to the items you want to remove from your document.

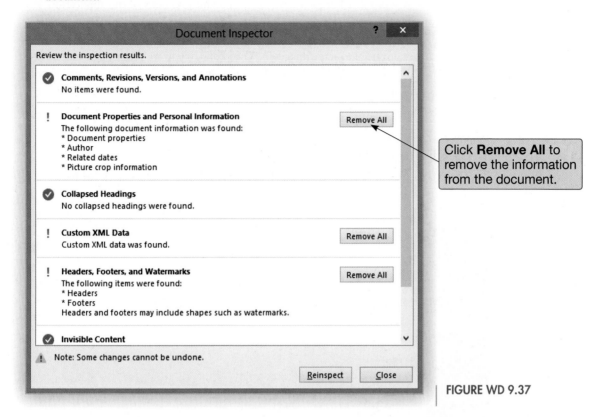

Click **Remove All** to remove the information from the document.

FIGURE WD 9.37

tips & tricks

If you did not choose to inspect all the options in the *Document Inspector* dialog, you can click the **Reinspect** button to return to the list and select additional options.

let me try

Open the student data file **wd9-17-SpaNewsletter** and try this skill on your own:

1. Open the **Document Inspector** dialog.

2. Inspect all content except **Task Pane Apps.**

3. Remove all document properties and personal information.

4. Close the *Document Inspector* dialog.

5. If you will be moving on to the next skill in this chapter, leave the document open to continue working. If not, save the file as directed by your instructor and close it.

Skill 9.18 Checking for Compatibility with Previous Versions of Word

Some features in Word 2013 are not available in previous versions of the application. If a document uses one of the new features, opening it in a previous version of Word may have unintended consequences. For example, if you apply Quick Styles to images in a document, the styles will be converted to static images in Word 2003. If you are sharing a document created in Word 2013 with someone who may be using an earlier version of Word, you should check the document for compatibility issues.

To check your document to see if it contains elements that are not compatible with earlier versions of Word:

1. Click the **File** tab.
2. The *Info* section in Backstage view opens automatically. Click the **Check for Issues** button, and then click **Check Compatibility.**

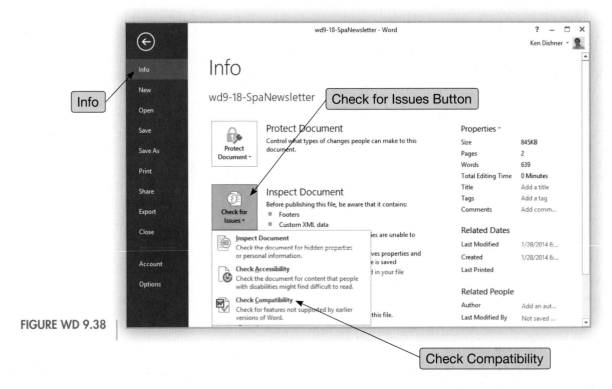

FIGURE WD 9.38

3. The Microsoft Word Compatibility Checker dialog opens. The Compatibility Checker lists the items in your document that may be lost or downgraded if you save the document in an earlier Microsoft Word format. For each item, the dialog lists the number of times the issue occurs in the document (*occurrences*).
4. Review the compatibility issues, and then click **OK** to close the Compatibility Checker.

NOTE: Running the Compatibility Checker does not change your document. It only lists the items that will lose functionality when the document is saved in an earlier Microsoft Word format. It is up to you whether or not you want to make any changes to the document.

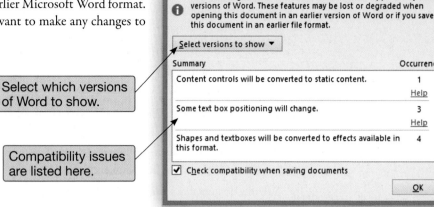

Select which versions of Word to show.

Compatibility issues are listed here.

tips & tricks

If you often share documents with people using an older version of Microsoft Word, you can set the Compatibility Checker to run every time you save the document. Open the *Microsoft Word Compatibility Checker* dialog, and then click the **Check compatibility when saving** check box to add a check mark. Click **OK.**

tell me **more**

In the Compatibility Checker, you can check for compatibility with Word 2010, Word 2007, or Word 97-2003. Click the **Select versions to show** button, and click the option you want. There are few compatibility issues between Word 2013 and Word 2010 and Word 2007, but there may be quite a few between Word 2013 and Word 97-2003.

another **method**

To close the *Compatibility Checker* dialog, you can also click the red **X** in the upper right corner of the dialog.

let me **try**

If you do not have the data file from the previous skill open, open the student data file **wd18-SpaNewsletter** and try this skill on your own:

1. Open the **Microsoft Word Compatibility Checker** dialog.
2. Only show compatibility issues between **Word 2013** and **Word 2007** and **Word 2010.**
3. Close the **Microsoft Word Compatibility Checker** dialog.
4. If you will be moving on to the next skill in this chapter, leave the document open to continue working. If not, close the file.

Skill 9.19 Marking a Document as Final

When you are finished working on a document and are ready to send it out to others, you should mark it as final. Marking a document as final indicates that it will not be edited further. The document is converted to read-only status.

To mark a document as final:

1. Click the **File** tab.

2. The *Info* section in Backstage view opens automatically. Click the **Protect Document** button, and then click **Mark as Final.**

3. A message box appears telling you the document will be marked as final and saved. Click **OK** to mark the document as final.

When a document has been marked as final, the **Marked as Final** icon appears in the status bar, and the *Info* tab displays a message that the document has been marked as final.

FIGURE WD 9.40

tell me **more**

> Marking a document as final does not really prevent another user from editing it. When the document is opened, the Message Bar displays a warning that the document has been marked as final. Any user can click the **Edit Anyway** button to remove the read-only status from the file.

> Files that are marked as final in Microsoft Office 2010 will not be protected with read-only status when opened in Word 2003 or earlier.

let me try

If you do not have the data file from the previous skill open, open the student data file **wd19-SpaNewsletter** and try this skill on your own:

1. Mark the document as final.

2. Close the file.

Track Changes
Reviewing pane
Comment
Lock Tracking
Combine
Compare
View Side by Side
Synchronous Scrolling
Macro
Visual Basic for Applications (VBA)
Macro-enabled documents
Visual Basic Editor (VBE)
Project Explorer

Modules
Objects
Procedures
PDF
XPS (XML Paper Specification)
OneDrive
Template
Restrict Editing task pane
Password
Inspect Document
Microsoft Word Compatibility
    Checker

concepts review

1. When *Track Changes* is active, all insertions, deletions, and formatting changes are marked.

a. True

b. False

2. _____ are notes you add to a document that are not intended to be part of the final document.

a. Tracked Changes

b. Balloons

c. Ink notations

d. Comments

3. If you have two similar documents and want to view the differences between the two, you should use Word's _____.

a. Compare feature

b. Combine feature

c. Compatibility Checker

d. Document Inspector

4. A _____ is a custom set of programming commands written in the Visual Basic for Applications (VBA) language.

a. template

b. comment

c. PDF

d. macro

5. To save a macro in a document you must use the _____ format.

a. .docx

b. .dotx

c. .docm

d. .doc

6. When you share a document through OneDrive, Word creates a new version of the document for each person who works on it.
   a. True
   b. False

7. You can restrict editing in a document to only allow users to enter _____.
   a. comments
   b. insertions
   c. deletions
   d. formatting changes

8. Word's Document Inspector can check for and remove _____.
   a. personal information
   b. comments
   c. custom XML
   d. All of the above

9. If you are sending your Word 2013 document to someone who has Word 2007, you should use Word's _____ to see if there will be any problems between the two versions.
   a. Document Inspector
   b. Compatibility Checker
   c. Accessibility Checker
   d. None of the above

10. When a document is marked as final, users who open the file must click a button on the message bar before being able to edit the file.
    a. True
    b. False

projects

skill review 9.1

In this project, you will be reviewing the document for the Tri-State Book Festival. You will be making changes, accepting and rejecting other changes, and adding comments. You will also prepare the document to send out to others.

Skills needed to complete this project:

- Using Track Changes (Skill 9.1)
- Adding Comments (Skill 9.2)
- Accepting and Rejecting Changes in a Document (Skill 9.3)
- Hiding and Showing Changes in a Document (Skill 9.4)
- Inspecting Your Document (Skill 9.17)
- Checking for Compatibility with Previous Versions of Word (Skill 9.18)
- Locking Track Changes (Skill 9.5)
- Marking a Document as Final (Skill 9.19)

1. Open the start file **WD2013-SkillReview-9-1** and resave the file as: `[your initials]WD-SkillReview-9-1`

2. If the document opens in Protected View, click the **Enable Editing** button in the Message Bar at the top of the document so you can modify the document.

3. Use *Track Changes.*

   a. Click the **Review** tab.

   b. In the *Tracking* group, click the **Track Changes** button.

   c. Select the last sentence in the first paragraph of the document (the sentence beginning with *You don't want to*). Press the `Delete` key to delete the sentence.

4. Accept and reject changes in a document.

   a. Press `Ctrl` + `Home` to navigate to the beginning of the document.

   b. On the *Review* tab, in the *Tracking* group, click the **Next Change** button.

   c. In the *Tracking* group, click the **Accept and Move to Next** button to accept the insertion.

   d. Click the **Accept and Move to Next** button to accept the deletion.

   e. Click the **Reject and Move to Next** button to reject the font size change.

   f. Click the **Accept and Move to Next** button to accept the formatting change.

   g. Click the **Accept and Move to Next** button to accept the insertion.

   h. Click the **Accept and Move to Next** button to accept the deletion.

   i. Click **OK** in the message box.

5. Add a comment to a document.

   a. Place the cursor in the empty line at the end of the document.

   b. On the *Review* tab, in the *Comments* group, click the **New Comment** button.

   c. Type the following comment `Change formatting to fit author list on one page.`

6. Change the markup display of a document.

   a. In the *Tracking* group, click the **Display for Review** arrow.

   b. Select **Simple Markup.**

7. Inspect a document.

   a. Click the **File** tab.

   b. On the *Info* page, click the **Check for Issues** button and select **Inspect Document.**

   c. If you see a message box asking you to save the document, click **Yes.**

   d. In the *Document Inspector* dialog, click the check box next to **Custom XML Data** so a checkmark does not appear in the box.

   e. Click the **Inspect** button.

   f. Click the **Remove All** button next to *Document Properties and Personal Information.*

   g. Click the **Close** button to close the *Document Inspector* dialog.

8. Check for compatibility with previous versions of Word.

   a. Click the **File** tab.

   b. On the *Info* page, click the **Check for Issues** button and select **Check Compatibility.**

   c. In the *Microsoft Word Compatibility Checker* dialog, click the **Select versions to show** arrow and click **Word 97-2003** to deselect it.

   d. Review the issues and click **OK** to close the dialog.

9. Lock *Track Changes* in a document.

   a. On the *Review* tab, in the *Tracking* group, click the **Track Changes** arrow and select **Lock Tracking.**

   b. In the *Enter password (optional)* box, type **3state**

   c. In the *Reenter to confirm* box, type **3state**

   d. Click **OK.**

10. Mark the document as final.

    a. Click the **File** tab.

    b. On the *Info* page, click the **Protect Document** button.

    c. Select **Mark as Final.**

    d. Click **OK** in the message box.

    e. If you see a second message box, click **OK** again.

11. Save and close the document.

skill review 9.2

In this project, you will be reviewing a customer letter from Greenscapes landscaping company. You will also create, edit, and run a macro to format the company name in the letter. Finally, you will inspect and secure the document for distribution to others.

Skills needed to complete this project:

- Accepting and Rejecting Changes in a Document (Skill 9.3)
- Adding Comments (Skill 9.2)
- Using Track Changes (Skill 9.1)
- Exporting a Document as a PDF (Skill 9.12)
- Recording a Macro (Skill 9.9)

- Editing a Macro Using VBA (Skill 9.11)
- Running a Macro (Skill 9.10)
- Inspecting Your Document (Skill 9.17)
- Encrypting a Document with a Password (Skill 9.16)
- Marking a Document as Final (Skill 9.19)

1. Open the start file **WD2013-SkillReview-9-2.**

2. Since this project will require macros, save the file as a macro-enabled document with the following file name: `[your initials]WD-SkillReview-9-2`

3. Accept and reject changes in a document.
   a. If necessary, press `Ctrl` + `Home` to navigate to the beginning of the document.
   b. Click the **Review** tab.
   c. In the *Tracking* group, click the **Next Change** button.
   d. The first change found is a comment. Click the **Next Change** button again.
   e. The next change found is the insertion of the text **99.** In the *Tracking* group, click the **Accept and Move to Next** button to accept the insertion.
   f. The next change found is the deletion of the text **95.** Click the **Accept and Move to Next** button to accept the deletion.
   g. The next change found is the insertion of the text **35.** Click the **Accept and Move to Next** button to accept the insertion.
   h. The next change found is the deletion of the text **22.** Click the **Accept and Move to Next** button to accept the deletion.
   i. The next change found is the insertion of the text **4.** Click the **Accept and Move to Next** button to accept the insertion.
   j. The next change found is the deletion of the text **2.** Click the **Accept and Move to Next** button to accept the deletion.
   k. The final change found is the delete of the text **TBD.** Click the **Reject and Move to Next** button to reject the deletion.

4. Add a comment to a document.
   a. Place the cursor at the end of the sentence above the signature (after *evaluation.*).
   b. On the *Review* tab, in the *Comments* group, click the **New Comment** button.
   c. Type the following comment `Where is our phone number?`

5. Delete a comment.
   a. Click the comment attached to the *Regularly Scheduled Services per Month* text.
   b. On the *Review* tab, in the *Comments* group, click the **Delete Comment** button.

6. On the *Review* tab, in the *Tracking* group, click the **Track Changes** button to turn off the feature.

7. On the *Review* tab, in the *Tracking* group, click the **Display for Review** drop-down menu and select **No Markup.**

8. Export the document as a PDF.
   a. Click the **File** tab.
   b. Click **Export.**
   c. Click the **Create PDF/XPS** button.
   d. Enter `[your initials]WD-SkillReview-9-2.pdf` as the file name. Do not have the file open after publishing.
   e. Click **Publish.**

9. Record a macro.

   a. Select the word **Greenscapes** in the paragraph below the SmartArt diagram (it is the first word in the paragraph).

   b. Click the **View** tab.

   c. In the *Macros* group, click the **Macros** button arrow and select **Record Macro.**

   d. In the *Macro name* box, type **GreenscapesName**

   e. Click the **Store macro in** arrow and select the current document.

   f. In the *Description* box, type **Formatting for Greenscapes name**

   g. Click the **Keyboard** button.

   h. Press Alt + Ctrl + ↑ Shift + G as the shortcut for the macro.

   i. Click the **Assign** button.

   j. Click the **Close** button.

   k. Click the **Home** tab. In the *Font* group, click the dialog launcher.

   l. In the *Font* dialog, make the following changes and then click **OK:**

- Font: **Verdana**
- Font Style: **Bold Italic**
- Size: **14**
- Font Color: **Green** (it is the sixth color under *Standard Colors* in the color palette)
- Underline Style: **Words Only**

   m. Click the **View** tab. In the *Macros* group, click the **Macros** button arrow and select **Stop Recording.**

10. Edit a macro.

   a. In the *Macros* group, click the **Macros** button.

   b. In the *Macros* dialog, verify the *GreenscapesName* macro is selected and click the **Edit** button.

   c. In the *Visual Basic Editor* window, change the font size from **14** to **12.** *Hint:* It is the line beginning with *.Size.*

   d. Click the **Save** button on the toolbar and close the *Visual Basic Editor* window.

11. Run a macro.

   a. Verify the cursor is still in *Greenscapes* in the first paragraph.

   b. In the *Macros* group, click the **Macros** button.

   c. In the *Macros* dialog, verify the *GreenscapesName* macro is selected and click the **Run** button.

12. Inspect a document.

   a. Click the **File** tab.

   b. On the *Info* page, click the **Check for Issues** button and select **Inspect Document.**

   c. If you see a message box asking you to save the document, click **Yes.**

   d. Verify all items are selected, and click the **Inspect** button.

   e. Click the **Remove All** button next to *Comments, Revisions, Versions, and Annotations.*

   f. Click the **Remove All** button next to *Custom XML Data.*

   g. Click the **Close** button to close the *Document Inspector* dialog.

13. Encrypt a document with a password.

   a. Click the **File** tab.

   b. On the *Info* page, click the **Protect Document** button.

   c. Select **Encrypt with Password.**

   d. In the *Password* box, type `greenies468` and click **OK.**

   e. In the *Reenter password* box, type `greenies468` and click **OK.**

14. Mark a document as final.

   a. On the *Info* page, click the **Protect Document** button.

   b. Select **Mark as Final.**

15. Save and close the document.

challenge yourself 9.3

In this project you will be reviewing a paper on acupuncture and lower back pain. You will use *Track Changes* and comments to review the document and then prepare the document to send out to others for further review.

Skills needed to complete this project:

- Accepting and Rejecting Changes in a Document (Skill 9.3)
- Using Track Changes (Skill 9.1)
- Adding Comments (Skill 9.2)
- Hiding and Showing Changes in a Document (Skill 9.4)
- Inspecting Your Document (Skill 9.17)
- Restricting Editing in a Document (Skill 9.15)
- Checking for Compatibility with Previous Versions of Word (Skill 9.18)
- Marking a Document as Final (Skill 9.19)

1. Open the start file **WD2013-ChallengeYourself-9-3** and resave the file as:
   `[your initials]WD-ChallengeYourself-9-3`

2. If the document opens in Protected View, enable editing so you can make changes to the document.

3. Review the document from the beginning make the following changes:

   a. Reject the formatting changes on the word **Acupuncture.**

   b. Accept the formatting on the word **qi.**

   c. Accept the change from **65%** to **80%.**

   d. Reject the deletion of the sentence **Safety and adverse side effects will be discussed throughout.**

   e. Reject the insertion of **hundreds of.**

   f. Accept the formatting change to the **Heading 1** style.

4. Add a comment to the end of the *Treatment on Elderly Patients* section that reads *Check to see if study information has been updated.*

5. Hide the comments in the document.

6. Run the Document Inspector checking all content. Remove all **document properties and personal information** from the document.

7. Restrict the editing in the document to only allow others to add comments and not make other changes. Use the password **pat135** to protect the document.

8. Check for compatibility with all previous versions of Word.

9. Mark the document as final.

10. Save and close the document.

challenge yourself 9.4

In this project, you will be reviewing a paper on behavioral change. You will be accepting and reject changes, changing the markup display, and adding comments. You will also create, edit, and run a macro to add a custom footer to the document. Finally, you will prepare the document to be sent out for review and export it as a PDF.

Skills needed to complete this project:

- Accepting and Rejecting Changes in a Document (Skill 9.3)
- Adding Comments (Skill 9.2)
- Hiding and Showing Changes in a Document (Skill 9.4)
- Using Track Changes (Skill 9.1)
- Recording a Macro (Skill 9.9)
- Running a Macro (Skill 9.10)
- Editing a Macro Using VBA (Skill 9.11)
- Exporting a Document as a PDF (Skill 9.12)
- Inspecting Your Document (Skill 9.17)
- Checking for Compatibility with Previous Versions of Word (Skill 9.18)
- Marking a Document as Final (Skill 9.19)

1. Open the start file **WD2013-ChallengeYourself-9-4.**

2. Since this project will require macros, save the file as a macro-enabled document with the following file name: **[your initials]WD-ChallengeYourself-9-4**

3. If the document opens in Protected View, enable editing so you can make changes to the document.

4. Review the document from the beginning make the following changes:

   a. Reject the insertion of the word **absolutely.**

   b. Reject the formatting of **Language Arts.**

   c. Accept the deletion of **observation** and the insertion of implementation.

   d. Accept all the remaining tracked changes in the document.

5. Add a comment to the *Techniques* heading that reads *Is this section really necessary?*

6. Change the display of the document to show no markup.

7. Save the document.

8. Record a macro.

   a. Open the *Record Macro* dialog. Enter **DisclaimerFooter** for the macro name. Store the macro in the current document and add **Standard Disclaimer Text** for the description.

   b. Assign (Alt) + (Ctrl) + (↑ Shift) + (D) as the keyboard shortcut for the macro.

   c. Record the macro:

      i. Insert a footer using the **Slice** footer format.

      ii. Type the following text **Not for disclosure outside Monroe College Education Department.**

   d. Stop recording the macro.

9. Edit and run a macro.

    a. Edit the **DisclaimerFooter** macro.

    b. Change the word **Monroe** to **Munroe.** Save the macro.

    c. Remove the current footer.

    d. Run the **ConsentFooter** macro.

10. Export the document as a PDF with the file name **[your initials]WD-ChallengeYourself-9-4.pdf.**

11. Run the Document Inspector checking all content. Remove all document properties and personal information from the document.

12. Check for compatibility with Word 2010.

13. Mark the document as final.

14. Close the document.

on your own 9.5

In this project you will be reviewing a memo from the Trade Winds Food company. You will work with *Track Changes* and comments and then prepare the document to be distributed to others. You will also export the memo as a PDF.

Skills needed to complete this project:

- Using Track Changes (Skill 9.1)
- Accepting and Rejecting Changes in a Document (Skill 9.3)
- Adding Comments (Skill 9.2)
- Hiding and Showing Changes in a Document (Skill 9.4)
- Exporting a Document as a PDF (Skill 9.12)
- Encrypting a Document with a Password (Skill 9.16)
- Inspecting Your Document (Skill 9.17)
- Checking for Compatibility with Previous Versions of Word (Skill 9.18)
- Restricting Editing in a Document (Skill 9.15)
- Marking a Document as Final (Skill 9.19)

1. Open the start file **WD2013-OnYourOwn-9-5** and resave the file as: `[your initials]WD-OnYourOwn-9-5`

2. If the document opens in Protected View, click the **Enable Editing** button in the Message Bar at the top of the document so you can modify the document.

3. Review the document and accept and reject the changes as you see fit.

4. Add a comment directing others to review a specific part of the document.

5. Change the display of the document so comments will be hidden.

6. Inspect the document and remove any information you do not want others to see.

7. Check the document for compatibility with previous versions of Word.

8. Export the document as a PDF.

9. Consider who you might have review the document and then restrict the editing others can make to the document.

10. Mark the document as final.

11. Save and close the document.

fix it 9.6

In this project, you will be reviewing and fixing a document for the Spring Hills Community. You will accept and reject changes and add comments. You will also prepare the document for distribution.

Skills needed to complete this project:

- Adding Comments (Skill 9.2)
- Accepting and Rejecting Changes in a Document (Skill 9.3)
- Hiding and Showing Changes in a Document (Skill 9.4)
- Using Track Changes (Skill 9.1)
- Inspecting Your Document (Skill 9.17)
- Checking for Compatibility with Previous Versions of Word (Skill 9.18)
- Restricting Editing in a Document (Skill 9.15)
- Marking a Document as Final (Skill 9.19)

1. Open the start file **WD2013-FixIt-9-6** and resave the file as:
   `[your initials]WD-FixIt-9-6`

2. If the document opens in Protected View, click the **Enable Editing** button in the Message Bar at the top of the document so you can modify the document.

3. Review the document from the beginning make the following changes:

   a. Reject the formatting change on **basic safety strategy.**

   b. Reject the deletion of the word **security.**

   c. Reject the deletion of the bullet point **Don't display your devices.**

   d. Reject the insertion of the text **Pay attention!!!**

   e. Accept the deletion of the text **To get the most up to date information, click here.**

   f. Accept the formatting change on the table.

   g. Reject the text change on **Sabet.**

   h. Accept all other changes in the document.

4. Add a comment to the end of the last paragraph on page 3 (after *surrounding neighborhoods.*) that reads *Too much white space. Fix layout issues.*

5. Turn off **Track Changes.**

6. Inspect the document removing the document property and personal information.

7. Check for any compatibility issues with Word 2007 and Word 2010.

8. Restrict the document so others can only add comments and not change the content. Use the password **spc456** to protect the document.

9. Mark the document as final.

10. Save and close the document.

Office 2013 Shortcuts

Office 2013 Keyboard Shortcuts

ACTION	KEYBOARD SHORTCUT
Display Open page in Backstage view	Ctrl + O
Create a new blank file (bypassing Backstage view)	Ctrl + N
Copy	Ctrl + C
Cut	Ctrl + X
Paste	Ctrl + V
Undo	Ctrl + Z
Redo	Ctrl + Y
Save	Ctrl + S
Select All	Ctrl + A
Help	F1
Bold	Ctrl + B
Italic	Ctrl + I
Underline	Ctrl + U
Close Start page or Backstage view	Esc
Close a file	Ctrl + W
Minimize the Ribbon	Ctrl + F1
Switch windows	Alt + Tab

Word 2013 Keyboard Shortcuts

ACTION	KEYBOARD SHORTCUT
Open a new blank Word document	Ctrl + N
Display Open page in Backstage view	Ctrl + O
Open the *Open* dialog	Ctrl + F12
Select All	Ctrl + A
Open Spelling and Grammar task pane	F7
Undo	Ctrl + Z
Redo	Ctrl + Y
Open Navigation task pane with the search results section displayed	Ctrl + F
Open *Find and Replace* dialog with the *Replace* tab displayed	Ctrl + H
Open *Find and Replace* dialog with the *Go To* tab selected	Ctrl + G or F5
Copy	Ctrl + C
Cut	Ctrl + X
Paste	Ctrl + V
Bold	Ctrl + B
Italic	Ctrl + I
Underline	Ctrl + U
Save	Ctrl + S
Open *Save As* dialog	F12
Open *Font* dialog	Ctrl + D
Increase font size	Ctrl + ↑ Shift + >
Decrease font size	Ctrl + ↑ Shift + <
Left align text	Ctrl + L
Center text	Ctrl + E
Right align text	Ctrl + R
Justify text	Ctrl + J
Single line spacing	Ctrl + 1
Double line spacing	Ctrl + 2

ACTION	KEYBOARD SHORTCUT
Show formatting marks	Ctrl + ↑ Shift + 8
Open *Insert Hyperlink* dialog	Ctrl + K
Open Thesaurus pane	↑ Shift + F7
Open Word Help	F1
Insert line break	↑ Shift + ← Enter
Insert page break	Ctrl + ← Enter
Insert non-breaking space	Ctrl + ↑ Shift + Space
Copy formatting	Ctrl + ↑ Shift + C
Paste formatting	Ctrl + ↑ Shift + V
Insert an endnote	Alt + Ctrl + D
Insert a footnote	Alt + Ctrl + F
Move the insertion point to the beginning of the document	Ctrl + Home
Move the insertion point to the end of the document	Ctrl + End
Display print page	Ctrl + P
Close a document	Ctrl + W
Apply subscript character formatting	Ctrl + = or Ctrl + ↑ Shift + =
Display navigation pane	Ctrl + F
Open the Find and Replace dialog with the Go To tab displayed	Ctrl + G

glossary of key terms

Office 2013 Overview

a

Account page: Page in Backstage view that lists information for the user currently logged in to Office. This account information comes from the Microsoft account you used when installing Office.

b

Backstage: Tab that contains the commands for managing and protecting files, including *Save, Open, Close, New,* and *Print.*

c

Contextual tabs: Contain commands specific to the type of object selected and are visible only when the commands might be useful.

e

Enhanced ScreenTip: A ScreenTip that displays the name of the command, the keyboard shortcut (if there is one), and a short description of what the button does and when it is used.

f

File properties: Information about a file, such as the location of the file, the size of file, when the file was created and when it was last modified, the title, and the author. File properties can be found on the *Info* page in Backstage view.

File tab: Tab located at the far left side of the Ribbon. Opens the Microsoft Office Backstage view.

g

Groups: Subsections of a tab on the Ribbon; organizes commands with similar functions together.

h

Home tab: Contains the most commonly used commands for each Office application.

k

Keyboard shortcuts: Keys or combinations of keys that, when pressed, execute a command.

l

Live Preview: Displays formatting changes in a file before actually committing to the change.

m

Metadata: All the information about a file that is listed under the *Properties* section of the *Info* page in Backstage view.

Microsoft Access: A database program. Database applications allow you to organize and manipulate large amounts of data.

Microsoft Excel: A spreadsheet program. Originally, spreadsheet applications were viewed as electronic versions of an accountant's ledger. Today's spreadsheet applications can do much more than just calculate numbers—they include powerful charting and data analysis features.

Microsoft PowerPoint: A presentation program. Such applications enable you to create robust, multimedia presentations.

Microsoft Word: A word processing program. Word processing software allows you to create text-based documents. Word processing software also offers more powerful formatting and design tools, allowing you to create complex documents, including reports, résumés, brochures, and newsletters.

Mini toolbar: Provides access to common tools for working with text. When text is selected and then the mouse is rested over the text, the Mini toolbar fades in.

n

New command: Creates a new file in an Office application without exiting and reopening the program.

o

Office Help: System for searching topics specifically tailored for working with an application.

OneDrive: Microsoft's free cloud storage where you can save documents, workbooks, presentations, videos, pictures, and other files and access those files from any computer or share the files with others.

p

Protected View: Provides a read-only format that protects your computer from becoming infected by a virus or other malware.

q

Quick Access Toolbar: Toolbar located at the top of the application window above the *File* tab. The Quick Access Toolbar gives quick one-click access to common commands.

r

Ribbon: Located across the top of the application window and organizes common features and commands into tabs.

s

ScreenTip: A small information box that displays the name of the command when the mouse is rested over a button on the Ribbon.

Shortcut menus: Menus of commands that display when an area of the application window is right-clicked.

Start page: Displays when you first launch an application. The *Start* page gives you quick access to recently opened files and templates for creating new files in each of the applications.

t

Tab: Subsection of the Ribbon; organizes commands further into related groups.

Tags: Keywords used for grouping common files together or for searching.

Word 2013

a

Address block: Merge field that pulls in the address from the list of recipients for a mail merge.

Alignment guides: Horizontal and vertical green lines that appear when an object is dragged and the object's edge is aligned with another element on the page.

Artistic Effects: Application of different graphic filters to an image. These filters mimic a wide variety of artistic tools, including paint strokes, pencil strokes, watercolors, mosaics, blurs, and glows.

AutoCorrect: Feature that analyzes each word as it is entered in a document. Each word is compared to a list of common misspellings, symbols, and abbreviations. If a match is found, AutoCorrect automatically replaces the text in the document with the matching replacement entry.

Automatic date stamp: Pulls the current date from the computer's system clock and displays the date in the document.

Automatic hyphenation: Insertion of hyphens to words at the end of a line instead of placing the whole word on the following line.

AutoText: Pieces of reusable content that are stored as building blocks. AutoText entries include not only the text of the entry but any formatting that has been applied.

Axes: The horizontal and vertical grid the data is plotted against. The y axis goes from top to bottom and the x axis goes from left to right.

b

Background: Area of a picture that can be removed.

Bibliography: A compiled list of sources referenced in a document.

Bold: Character formatting that gives the text a heavier, thicker appearance.

Bookmark: An invisible marker that allows you to quickly navigate back to a specific location in a document.

Border Painter: Feature in Word that allows you to quickly apply stylized borders to tables.

Brightness: Control of how dark or light a picture appears.

Building block: A piece of content that is reusable in any document. Building blocks can be text, such as AutoText, or can include graphics, such as a cover page.

Building Blocks Organizer: Lists the building blocks in alphabetical order by the gallery in which they appear; includes Bibliographies, Cover Pages, Equations, Footers, Headers, Page Numbers, Table of Contents, Tables, Text Boxes, and Watermarks.

Bullet: A symbol that is displayed before each item in a list.

c

Caption: A brief description of an illustration, chart, equation, or table.

Cell: The intersection of a row and column in a table.

Cell address: The cell's column and row position in a table.

Cell range: A contiguous group of cells. A cell range is identified by the address of the cell in the upper left corner of the range, followed by a colon, and then the address of the cell in the lower right corner of the range.

Change Case command: Command in Word that manipulates the typed characters, changing how the letters are displayed.

Change Picture: Command that allows you to swap one image for another.

Character effects: Effects applied to text to alter its appearance. Effects include bold, italic, underline, shadow, and strikethrough.

Character spacing: The control of the amount of horizontal space between characters on-screen.

Chart: A graphic that transforms numerical data into a more visual representation.

Chart area: Encompasses the entire chart including the plot area and optional layout elements, such as title and legend.

Chart title: A text box above or overlaying the chart.

Citation: A reference to source material in a document. Citations include information, such as the author, title, publisher, and the publish date.

Clip art: Illustrations and photographs that are made available through Word to use in documents.

Clipboard: Task pane that displays up to 24 copied or cut items for use in any Office application.

Clips: Images, photographs, and scanned material from an external source.

Color theme: A set of colors that complement each other and are designed to work well together.

Column break: Break that marks where one column ends and moves the following text to the top of the next column.

Column (table): A group of cells that display vertically in a table.

Column (text): A vertical arrangement of text on-screen. Text at the bottom of one column continues on to the top of the next column.

Combine: Command that creates a single document from two documents. When you combine two documents, the differences between the two documents are displayed as tracked changes.

Comment: A note you add to a document that is not meant to be a part of the document.

Compare: Takes two documents and creates a single document displaying the differences between the two.

Contrast: Feature that changes the range of color intensity within a picture.

Copy: Command that places a duplicate of the selected text or object on the Clipboard without changing the file.

Cover page: First page in a document that contains brief information about the document, including the title and the date.

Crop: Command that removes part of an image, hiding it from sight.

Cross-reference: A link you add to a document that directs the reader to another part of the document for more or related information.

Cut: Command that removes the selected text or object from the file and places it on the Office Clipboard for later use.

d

Data labels: Display data values for each data marker in a chart.

Drop cap: Effect added to a paragraph where the first letter of the first work is a specified number of lines tall. Drop caps can be in line with the paragraph text or placed in the margin next to the paragraph text.

Dropped style drop cap: Places the drop cap in front of the number of specified lines of text (three by default). In the *Dropped* style, the remaining paragraph text wraps under the drop cap so the drop cap and the text of the paragraph are left-aligned.

e

Embedded objects: Independent objects that are pasted into a document. Double-clicking an embedded object will open the object inside the Word document, using the source program, but not the source file.

Endnotes: References in a document that provide the reader with further information. Endnotes are composed of two parts: a reference mark and the associated text. Endnotes appear at the end of the document.

f

Field: A placeholder for content that might change in a document. Word inserts fields for you when you add certain content to your document, such as building blocks.

Find: Command that locates specific text or formatting in a document.

First line indent: Paragraph indentation where first line of a paragraph is indented and the remainder of the paragraph is left-aligned.

Font: Refers to a set of characters of a certain design. The font is the shape of the character or number as it appears on-screen.

Font theme: A set of fonts that complement each other and are designed to work well together.

Footer: Text that appears at the bottom of every page.

Footnotes: References in a document that provide the reader with further information. Footnotes are composed of two parts: a reference mark and the associated text. Footnotes appear at the bottom of a page.

Form: A document or part of a document that a reader can interact with.

Format Painter: Tool that copies and pastes formatting styles.

Formatting marks: Hidden marks in a document which indicate spaces, paragraphs, tabs, and page breaks.

Formulas: Used to perform calculations on ranges of numbers. A formula begins with an equals sign and contains arguments, operators, and functions.

Functions: Preprogrammed shortcuts for calculating complex equations, such as the sum of a group of numbers.

g

Go To: Command that allows you to quickly jump to a specific page, section, or line number. You can also navigate to a specific bookmark you inserted or comments made by a reviewer.

Graphics: Photographs, clip art, SmartArt, or line drawings that can be added to documents, spreadsheet, presentations, and database forms and reports.

Greeting line: Field in the mail merge for the greeting line of a letter. The greeting line uses a set style and pulls in the name for the letter from the list of recipients in the mail merge.

Gridlines: A series of vertical and horizontal lines that divide the page into small boxes, giving you visual markers for aligning graphics, tables, and other elements on the page.

Group: Command that turns multiple objects into a single object.

h

Hanging indent: Paragraph indentation where first line of a paragraph is left-aligned and the remainder of the paragraph is indented.

Hard page break: Command that forces the text to a new page no matter how much content is on the present page.

Header: Text that appears at the top of every page.

Header row: The first row in a table. The header row contains headings for each column in the table.

Highlighting: Tool in Word that changes the background color of the selected area to make it stand out on the page.

Horizontal line: A decorative element that is used as a visual divider to separate a part of a document without changing the underlying content structure.

Hyperlink: Text or a graphic that, when clicked, opens another file or jumps to another place in the document.

i

Index: A list of topics and associated page numbers that typically appears at the end of a document.

In Margin style drop cap: Places the drop cap in the margin of the paragraph in front of the number of specified lines of text. With the *In Margin* style, the remaining paragraph text is left-aligned with the first lines of the paragraph, not the drop cap.

Insert Control: Used to quickly add rows and columns to tables. Insert Controls appear when you roll your mouse over the left edge of a row or the top edge of a column.

Inspect Document: Command in Word that allows you to check your document for hidden data and other personal information before you finish the document and send it to others.

Italic: Character formatting that makes text slant to the right.

k

Keep lines together: Command that does not allow a paragraph to be split across two pages.

Keep with next: Command that forces a paragraph onto the same page as the following paragraph.

l

Landscape: Page orientation by which the width of the page is greater than the height.

Layout Options: Options for changing how objects appear with text, either in line or with text wrapping.

Legend: A key for a chart defining which data series is represented by each color.

Line spacing: The white space between lines of text.

Linked objects: Dependent objects that are pasted into a document. Double-clicking a linked object will open the source file in the original application for editing.

Lock Tracking: Feature that adds a password to a document that will be required to be entered in order to disable Track Changes.

m

Macro: Custom set of programming commands written in the Visual Basic for Applications (VBA) language. Macros can simplify repetitive tasks.

Macro-enabled documents: Word file format that allows VBA code to be saved with the file. Word will not save macros or other code in documents saved in the regular *.docx* format.

Mail merge: The process of creating several documents based on a main document, merge fields, and a recipients list.

Margins: The blank spaces at the top, bottom, left, and right of a page.

Merge cells: Combines multiple cells in a table into a single cell.

Merge fields: Placeholders that insert specific data from the recipients list you created in a mail merge.

Microsoft Word Compatibility Checker: Dialog that lists the items in your document that may be lost or downgraded if you save the document in an earlier Microsoft Word format.

Modules: Groups of procedures in VBA that are usually available to any open Word document. The code for each macro is stored in its own procedure within a module. A single module may contain the procedures for multiple macros.

Move cursor: Cursor that appears when the mouse is resting over an object that can be moved. When the move cursor displays, click the left mouse button and drag the mouse to move the object to a new location in the document.

Multilevel list: List type that divides the content into several levels of organization.

n

Numbered list: List type used to organize information that must be presented in a certain order.

Navigation pane: Task pane used for working with long documents. The first tab in the *Navigation* pane displays all the headings in your document, like an outline. The second tab displays a thumbnail of each page of a document. The third tab displays the results from searches performed.

o

Objects: Groups of procedures in VBA specific to individual worksheets and the overall workbook. Procedures in objects are intended for use in that object only.

OneDrive: Microsoft's free cloud storage where you can save documents, workbooks, presentations, videos, pictures, and other files and access those files from any computer or share the files with others.

Online video: Videos clips located on the Internet that can be accessed by using the *Bing Video Search* in the *Online Video* dialog.

Orphan: The first line of a paragraph that prints at the bottom of a page.

Outline view: Feature that displays the document grouped by heading levels. Outline view is used to check the structure of a document.

p

Page borders: The decorative graphic element along the top, right, bottom, and left edges of the page. Borders can be simple lines or include 3-D effects and shadows.

Paragraph: Any text separated by a hard return. A hard return refers to pressing the ⎠Enter key to create a new paragraph.

Paragraph alignment: How text is aligned with regard to the left and right margins of a document.

Password: Combination of letters, numbers, and symbols required to be typed before a document can be opened.

Paste: Command that is used to insert text or an object from the Clipboard into a file.

Paste options: Options for pasting text and objects in Word. Paste options allow you to choose to keep the source formatting, merge the formatting of the source and the current document, or paste only the text without any formatting.

PDF (portable document file): Adobe's custom file format that preserves the formatting of the document and is easily readable but not easily editable.

Plot area: Area of the chart where the data series are plotted.

Points: Measurement for the height of a font. Abbreviated "pt."

Portrait: Page layout by which the height of the page is greater than the width (like a portrait hanging on a wall).

Print Layout view: Displays how document elements will appear on a printed page.

Procedure: Group of code that is contained within a module or object in a macro project.

Project Explorer: Area of the Visual Basic Editor that lists open VBA projects.

Property control: An element that is added to a document to save time entering the same information over and over again. Property controls can be used as shortcuts for entering long strings of text that are difficult to type, such as e-mail addresses, phone numbers, and street addresses.

Pull quote: Text from your document that is "pulled" out and displayed as a graphic element on the page.

q

Quick Style: A group of formatting, including character and paragraph formatting, that can easily apply to text, tables, drawings, or other objects.

Quick Table: Preformatted table template that includes sample data that you can replace with your own data.

r

Read Mode: View in Word which is designed for reading documents in electronic format. In Read Mode, documents are displayed as screens rather than pages.

Recipients list: A table of names and address for the people you want to include in a mail merge.

Recolor: Command that removes all colors from a picture and replaces them with shades of one color.

Redo: Reverses the undo command and restores the file to its previous state.

Reference mark: The superscript character placed next to the text for a footnote or endnote.

Reference style: A set of rules used to display references in a bibliography. These rules include the order of information, when and how punctuation is used, and the use of character formatting.

Replace: Used with the *Find* command to replace specified text in a file with new text.

Reset Picture: Command to remove all Word formatting applied to a picture, reverting the picture to its state before any formatting was applied.

Resize handle: One of the six squares that appear when an object is selected. Click and drag a resize handle toward the center of the object to make the object smaller. Click and drag the resize handle away from the center of the object to make the object larger.

Restrict Editing task pane: Task pane where you can set editing permissions on documents.

Reviewing pane: Pane that displays all the changes in a document and shows a summary of the revisions in a document, including the number of insertions, deletions, moves, formatting changes, and comments.

Row: A group of cells that display horizontally in a table.

Ruler: Displays horizontally across the top of the window just below the Ribbon and vertically along the left side of the window. The ruler gives you a quick view of the margins and position of elements in your document.

s

Sans serif fonts: Fonts that do not have an embellishment at the end of each stroke. Includes Calibri and Arial.

Screenshot: Captures the image on the computer screen, such as an application's interface or a Web page, and creates an image that can then be used just as any other drawing or picture.

ScreenTip: A bubble with text that appears when the mouse hovers over a hyperlink. Typically, a ScreenTip provides a description of the hyperlink.

Section: A designated part of a document that can be formatted separately from the rest of the document.

Serif fonts: Fonts that have an embellishment at the end of each stroke. Includes Cambria and Times New Roman.

Shape: A drawing object that can be quickly added to a document.

Shape effects: Graphic effects you can apply to shapes including drop shadows, reflections, glows, and bevels.

Shape fill: The color that fills the object. You can choose a solid color from the color palette or fill the color with a gradient or texture.

Shape outline: The line that surrounds the shape. You can further adjust the outline of shapes by changing the color of the outline, width of the outline, and style of the outline.

Sharpness: Feature that removes any blurriness from a picture, giving it a crisper feel.

Sidebar: A block of information separate from the main document. Sidebars are typically aligned along one side of the page or along the top or bottom of the page. They usually contain information related to the main document but not found in the document.

SmartArt: Visual diagrams containing graphic elements with text boxes to enter information in.

Softness: Feature that removes hard edges from a picture, giving it a smoother feel.

Sorting: Arranges the rows in a table, worksheet, or datasheet in either ascending (A–Z) or descending (Z–A) alphabetical or numeric order.

Special characters: Characters that are not readily available by typing on the keyboard, such as an em dash or en dash.

Split cells: Divides a cell in a table in Word into multiple cells.

Strikethrough: Draws a horizontal line through the text. Strikethrough can be used to show text from a document that is no longer relevant.

Style set: Formatting options for changing the font and paragraph formatting for an entire document based on styles.

Styles: Complex formatting, including font, color, size, and spacing, that can be applied to Office files.

Styles task pane: Task pane that lists all the text styles available in a document.

Subscript: Draws a small character below the bottom of the text. Subscripts are often used in mathematical equations and chemical formulas, such as H_2O.

Superscript: Draws a small character above the top of the text. Superscript are often used for numbers and mathematical equations, such as $E = mc^2$.

Symbol: Command to insert into your document a special text character that isn't available on a keyboard.

Synchronous Scrolling: Feature that allows two documents to be scrolled simultaneously. When the active document is scrolled, the other document will scroll at the same time.

†

Tab leaders: Element that fills in the space between tab stops with solid, dotted, or dashed lines.

Tab stop: The location along the horizontal ruler that indicates how far to indent text when the Tab key is pressed.

Table: Content element that helps to organize information by rows, which display horizontally, and columns, which display vertically.

Table of contents: Lists the topics in a document and the associated page numbers, so readers can easily locate information.

Table of figures: List of all the illustrations, graphs, charts, equations, and pictures in a document, along with their associated page numbers.

Template: A file with predefined settings that can be used as a pattern to create a new file.

Text effects: Predefined graphic styles you can apply to text. These styles include a combination of color, outline, shadow, reflection, and glow effects.

Theme: A group of formatting options that is applied to an entire Office file. Themes include font, color, and effect styles that are applied to specific elements in a file.

Thesaurus: Reference tool that provides a list of synonyms (words with the same meaning) and antonyms (words with the opposite meaning) for a selected word or phrase.

Track Changes: Feature that marks any changes made to a document by reviewers. Such changes include deletions, insertions, or formatting.

U

Underline: Character formatting that draws a single line under the text.

Undo: Reverses the last action performed.

V

View Side by Side: Feature that allows you to view two documents at the same time.

Visual Basic Editor (VBE): Application used for writing and editing VBA code.

Visual Basic for Applications (VBA): Programming language used with Office applications for macros and other procedures.

W

Watermark: A graphic or text that appears as part of the page background. Watermarks appear faded so the text that appears on top of the watermark is legible when the document is viewed or printed.

Web Layout view: Displays all backgrounds, drawing objects, and graphics as they will appear on-screen if the document is saved as a Web page.

Widow: The last line of a paragraph that prints at the top of a page.

Word Count: Feature that provides the current statistics of the document you are working on, including the number of pages, number of words, number of characters (with and without spaces), number of paragraphs, and number of lines.

Word wrap: Automatically places text on the next line when the right margin of the document has been reached.

WordArt: Predefined graphic styles that are applied to text. These styles include a combination of color, fills, outlines, and effects.

X

XPS (XML Paper Specification): Microsoft's file format that preserves the formatting of the document and is easily readable but not easily editable. XPS files can be opened with Microsoft's XPS Viewer.

Z

Zoom slider: Slider bar that controls how large or small the file appears in the application window.

office index

word index

Symbols

a

b

of shapes, WD-317
text, WD-35–WD-45
applying highlights, WD-41
applying text effects,
WD-42–WD-43
bold, italic, and underline effects,
WD-35–WD-36
changing font colors, WD-40
changing font sizes, WD-38
changing fonts, WD-37
changing text case, WD-39
Clear Formatting command, WD-45
Format Painter tool, WD-44
Quick Styles, WD-48–WD-49
revealing formatting marks,
WD-52–WD-53
in shapes, WD-318
Formatting marks, WDG-3
displaying, WD-241
replacing, WD-15
revealing, WD-52–WD-53
XE, WD-177
Formatting styles, copying and pasting,
WD-44
Forms, WD-277–WD-283
defined, WDG-3
designing, WD-277–WD-279
filling in, WD-362
modifying control properties,
WD-280–WD-281
protecting, WD-282–WD-283
restricting editing of, WD-362
Formulas, WD-298–WD-299, WDG-3
Full pages of labels, WD-195
Functions, WD-298–WD-299, WDG-3

g

GB7714 2005 reference style, WD-173
Get a Sharing Link option, WD-359
Glow effects, WD-42
Go To command, WD-257, WDG-3
Go To tab, WD-15, WD-257, WD-259
GOST–Name Sort reference style, WD-173
GOST–Title Sort reference style, WD-173
Graduate students, WD-179
Grammar, checking, WD-7–WD-8,
WD-163
Grammar task pane, WD-163
Graphics, WD-122–WD-127,
WD-306–WD-322
cropping, WD-313
defined, WD-4, WDG-3
images, WD-314, WD-315
online videos, WD-126–WD-127
pictures, WD-113–WD-121
applying artistic effects, WD-307
applying Quick Styles to, WD-121
changing, WD-319–WD-320
changing color of, WD-309
changing layouts of, WD-116

compressing, WD-321
correcting, WD-308
inserting, WD-113–WD-114,
WD-118–WD-119
moving, WD-117
online, WD-113–WD-114
from other programs,
WD-118–WD-119
positioning, WD-120–WD-121
removing background from,
WD-310–WD-311
resetting, WD-312
resizing, WD-115
SmartArt, WD-123
screenshots, WD-322
shapes, WD-316–WD-318
adding text to, WD-318
applying Quick Styles to, WD-124
defined, WDG-5
formatting, WD-316–WD-317
inserting, WD-124
SmartArt, WDG-6
choosing, WD-123
entering text in, WD-123
inserting, WD-122–WD-123
modifying, WD-306
WordArt, WD-125
Greeting lines, WD-188, WD-189,
WDG-3
Gridlines, WD-56, WD-140, WDG-3
Groups of images, WD-315, WDG-3
Grow Font button, WD-38
Gutters, WD-93

h

Hanging indents, WD-55, WD-58,
WD-228, WDG-4
Hard page breaks, WD-94–WD-95,
WDG-4
Hard returns, WD-4
Harvard–Anglia 2008 reference style,
WD-173
Header & Footer Tools Design tab, WD-81,
WD-274
Header font, WD-76
Header Gallery, WD-275
Header rows, WD-295, WDG-4
Headers, WD-274–WD-275
adding, WD-78–WD-79
adding, to Header Gallery, WD-275
adding fields with active, WD-276
alignment of, WD-50
case for, WD-39
defined, WD-78, WDG-4
editing, WD-79
font sizes for, WD-37
inserting different even and odd,
WD-274
and title pages, WD-79
Heading rows, table, WD-130

Headings
expanding and collapsing outline,
WD-266–WD-267
Heading 1, WD-218, WD-234,
WD-256, WD-267, WD-273
Heading 2, WD-218, WD-234,
WD-267, WD-273
Heading 3, WD-218, WD-234,
WD-273
in multilevel lists, WD-234
navigating to, WD-255–WD-256
in tables of contents, WD-273
Headings tab, Navigation pane, WD-234,
WD-255–WD-256
Height
cells, WD-134
pictures, WD-115
tables, WD-134
Help icon, WD-4
Hidden data, inspecting document for,
WD-366–WD-367
Hiding
chart elements, WD-144,
WD-304–WD-305
document changes, WD-340–WD-341
formatting marks, WD-52–WD-53
reviewers' changes and comments,
WD-339
ScreenTips, WD-240
Hierarchy SmartArt, WD-122
Highlighting, WD-41, WD-45, WDG-4
Horizontal alignment, WD-50
Horizontal lines, WD-229, WDG-4
Hyperlinks, WD-90–WD-91, WDG-4
in cross-references, WD-260–WD-261
editing, WD-90–WD-91
removing, WD-90–WD-91
for screenshots of Web pages, WD-322
for sharing documents, WD-359
Hyphenation, WD-236, WDG-2

i

Icons, WD-18
IEEE 2006 reference style, WD-173
Images; see also specific types
aligning, WD-314
Bing Image Search, WD-113, WD-114
groups of, WD-315, WDG-3
In Margin style drop cap, WD-237,
WDG-4
Increase Indent button, WD-55
Indents, WD-55
first line, WD-55, WD-58, WD-228,
WDG-3
hanging, WD-55, WD-58, WD-228,
WDG-4
Index entries, WD-177, WD-179
Indexes, WD-178–WD-179, WDG-4
Info tab, WD-24
Insert Address Block dialog, WD-188

Mathematical equations, adding, WD-221
Mathematical operators, inserting, WD-221
Matrix (SmartArt category), WD-122
MAX function, WD-299
Media assistants, WD-343
Merge Cells command, WD-136, WDG-4
Merge fields, WD-188, WDG-4
Merge Formatting option, WD-19
Merging cells in tables, WD-136
Microsoft Excel, formulas in, WD-298
Microsoft Office, pasting objects from other
    applications, WD-239
Microsoft Office 2010, WD-370
Microsoft Outlook, contacts in, WD-187
Microsoft Word 97-2003, WD-369,
    WD-370
Microsoft Word 2007, WD-369
Microsoft Word 2010, WD-369
Microsoft Word 2013
    administrative assistant on, WD-8,
        WD-227
    college graduate on, WD-49
    community newspaper intern on, WD-119
    compatibility of documents created
        with, WD-368–WD-369
    customizing, WD-240–WD-241
    default font theme, WD-76
    defined, WD-3
    elements of, WD-4
    function of, WD-5
    keyboard shortcuts, A-2–A-3
    librarian on, WD-301
    marketing manager on, WD-97,
        WD-219, WD-365
    master's candidate, WD-259
    media assistant on, WD-343
    parole officer on, WD-185
    physical therapist on, WD-279
Microsoft Word Compatibility Checker,
    WD-368–WD-369, WDG-4
MIN function, WD-299
Mini toolbar
    activating Format Painter with, WD-44
    changing font color with, WD-40
    changing font size with, WD-38
    changing font with, WD-37
    changing Quick Styles of shapes with,
        WD-317
    cropping graphics with, WD-313
    highlighting text with, WD-41
    modifying SmartArt with, WD-306
    opening Define New Bullet dialog with,
        WD-233
    showing, WD-240
MLA Seventh Edition reference style,
    WD-173
Modify Style dialog, WD-219
Modifying; *see also* Changing
    charts, WD-144
    columns, WD-223
    control properties in forms,
        WD-280–WD-281

drop caps, WD-237
pictures, WD-307–WD-312
pull quotes or sidebars, WD-238
SmartArt, WD-306
tables of contents, WD-272–WD-273
text styles, WD-215–WD-217
themes, WD-73
WordArt, WD-125
Modules, WD-354, WDG-4
More >> button, WD-15
More button, WD-48, WD-74
Move cursor, WD-117, WDG-4
Moving
    pictures, WD-117
    tab stops, WD-58
    text to Clipboard, WD-17
Multilevel lists, WD-234–WD-235
    creating, WD-234
    customizing, WD-235
    defined, WDG-4
Multiple copies, printing, WD-100
Multiple option, line spacing, WD-225

n

Navigating
    to bookmarks, WD-258
    between changes in documents,
        WD-339
    between comments, WD-337
    between footnotes, WD-170
    with Go To command, WD-257
    with Navigation pane,
        WD-255–WD-256
Navigation pane
    closing, WD-256
    defined, WDG-4
    searching in, WD-12
    using, WD-255–WD-256, WD-259
New documents
    based on templates, WD-361
    comparing two documents in, WD-346
    renamed styles in, WD-219
New page, forcing paragraphs to,
    WD-264
Next Change button, WD-339
Next Comment button, WD-337
Next Footnote button, WD-170
Next Page option, WD-268
No changes, restricting editing to, WD-362
Nonbreaking space (°), WD-52, WD-53,
    WD-263
None (page color option), WD-181
Normal style, WD-218
Normal template, WD-211, WD-218
Numbered lists, WD-47, WDG-4
Numbering
    of endnotes, WD-270
    of figures, WD-171
    of footnotes, WD-170, WD-270
    in multilevel lists, WD-234

O

Objects
    defined, WDG-4
    drawing, WD-121, WD-314, WD-315
    embedded, WD-239, WDG-3
    linked, WD-239, WDG-4
    in Visual Basic Editor, WD-354
Odd Page section breaks, WD-268
Odd pages, inserting different headers/
        footers on, WD-274
Office.com, WD-113–WD-114
One-off labels, WD-195
OneDrive, WDG-4
    saving templates to, WD-361
    sharing documents with,
        WD-358–WD-359
Online pictures, WD-113–WD-114
Online Video button, WD-126
Online videos, WD-126–WD-127,
    WDG-5
Orientation, page, WD-269, WDG-4,
    WDG-5
Orphans, WD-265, WDG-5
Outline, shape, WD-316, WD-317,
    WDG-6
Outline effects, WD-36, WD-42, WD-210
Outline topics, WD-266
Outline view
    defined, WDG-5
    for long documents, WD-266–WD-267
    uses of, WD-180

p

Page, numbering footnotes and endnotes by,
    WD-270
Page borders, WD-96–WD-97, WDG-5
Page breaks, WD-94–WD-95, WDG-4
Page color, changing, WD-181
Page Layout tab, WD-120
Page Number gallery, WD-84
Page numbers, WD-84–WD-85
Page orientation, WD-269, WDG-4,
    WDG-5
Page ranges, printing, WD-101
Page Setup dialog
    adjusting margins in, WD-93
    changing page orientation with,
        WD-269
    margin specifications in,
        WD-92–WD-93
    opening, WD-56, WD-93, WD-269
Page width, WD-23
Paragraph alignment, WD-50, WDG-5
Paragraph breaks, WD-264–WD-265
Paragraph dialog
    adjusting spacing before and after para-
        graphs with, WD-227
    changing line spacing with, WD-225
    opening, WD-225, WD-228, WD-264

photo credits